MICHAEL R. T. MACNAIR

The Law of Proof in Early Modern Equity

Comparative Studies
in Continental and Anglo-American Legal History

Vergleichende Untersuchungen zur kontinentaleuropäischen
und anglo-amerikanischen Rechtsgeschichte

Herausgegeben von

Helmut Coing, Richard Helmholz, Knut Wolfgang Nörr
und Reinhard Zimmermann

Band 20

The Law of Proof in Early Modern Equity

By

Michael R. T. Macnair

Duncker & Humblot · Berlin

Gedruckt mit Unterstützung der Gerda Henkel Stiftung, Düsseldorf

Die Deutsche Bibliothek – CIP-Einheitsaufnahme

Macnair, Michael R. T.:
The law of proof in early modern equity / by Michael R. T.
Macnair. – Berlin : Duncker und Humblot, 1999
(Comparative studies in continental and Anglo-American
legal history ; Bd. 20)
ISBN 3-428-09198-1

Fremddatenübernahme und Druck:
Berliner Buchdruckerei Union GmbH, Berlin
Printed in Germany

ISSN 0935-1167
ISBN 3-428-09198-1

Gedruckt auf alterungsbeständigem (säurefreiem) Papier
entsprechend ISO 9706 ♾

Preface

This book is a substantially revised version of my D.Phil dissertation of the same title (Oxford University, 1991). In the course of writing both the thesis and the book I have incurred numerous debts of gratitude, both intellectual and practical. Many will be apparent in the text. My thanks are due in particular to Dr. David Ibbetson, who supervised the thesis, and Professor Colin Tapper and Mr David Yale, who examined it; to Professors John Langbein and Charles Donahue, Jr., and their colleagues, who made helpful critical comments on a paper which tried to summarise my argument; to Professor Nörr, who pointed out the basic flaw in the construction of the dissertation and gave me the fundamental direction for this revision, and more recently for editorial comment; and to Professors Richard Helmholz and Alain Wijffels, who have helped me with civilian sources. Leeds University, Southampton Institute and my present employers, Lancaster University, have all in various ways supported the research, and I am also indebted to the helpfulness of library staff in the Brotherton Library and its Law Library at Leeds, in Duke Humfrey and St Cross in the Bodleian Library, Oxford, and at Cambridge University Library. Last but not least, Sue Owen has put up with the somewhat glacial progress of this project while writing her own thesis and revising it for publication, and has given me helpful literary references and advice on style. For all errors and infelicities in the end product I am, of course, solely responsible.

Michael R. T. Macnair

Contents

Abbreviations used in the footnotes

Citations to the English nominate law reporters follow the conventional abbreviations used in the *English Reports* reprint. The text used is the *English Reports* text unless otherwise indicated. Abbreviated citations to other printed books and manuscripts are listed in the first section of the Bibliography, below. In the dates, letters before dates indicate the law term: M - Michaelmas, H - Hilary, P - Easter, T - Trinity. Dates in Hilary Term are given as e.g. (H1573/4) reflecting varied treatment of the beginning of the year in the sources; other multiple dates indicate prolonged proceedings or uncertainty as to date.

aff'd	affirmed	JP	Justice of the Peace
arg.	arguendo (in argument)	KB	King's Bench
Ass.	Assizes	LK	Lord Keeper
B	Baron (of the Exchequer)	MR	Master of the Rolls
C	Lord Chancellor	NP	nisi prius
CB	Chief Baron	P	Plaintiff
CJ	Chief Justice	QB	Queen's Bench
CP	Common Pleas	rvsd.	reversed
D	Defendant	SC	Same case
Ex	Exchequer	Sjt.	Serjeant
Ex. Ch.	Exchequer Chamber	SP	Same point
Ex (E)	Exchequer, equity side	SR	Same report
Ex (L)	Exchequer, common law side	SS	Selden Society
HL	House of Lords	UB	Upper Bench

Chapter One

Introductory

This book is a contribution to our understanding of two problems in the relationship between the common law and civil law traditions. The first relates to the proof of facts. In modern common law systems, the proof of facts is to a considerable extent governed by legal rules affecting the evidence which can be led to prove a fact; while in modern civil law systems, the trier of fact is generally free from such rules. Why? The explanation is necessarily partly historical, but the traditional view established at the turn of the nineteenth and twentieth centuries and still repeated in modern textbooks[1] is that it is partly functional: the rules of evidence are necessary to control the vagaries of the lay trier of fact, the jury. More recent work has offered historical critiques of this explanation, which move in two different directions: the common law of evidence is to be explained either by the intellectual culture of early modern England and Europe and the place of the proof concepts of the contemporary civil and canon laws within it, or by the dynamics of the common law trial in the later eighteenth century. Missing from both the traditional story, and these more modern approaches, is the role of the english courts of equity and *their* doctrine and procedure in relation to proof.

The second problem is more purely historical: the relationship between common law and civil law in early modern England and the role in this relationship of the equity (here including conciliar) jurisdictions. This is an aspect of the much disputed question raised by F.W. Maitland in his *English Law and the Renaissance*: how far were contemporaries in the early modern period justified in seeing a possibility that the distinctive features of the common law tradition would disappear and English law become merely a variant of the civil law tradition? How far, on the other hand, was common law thought governed by a purely insular *'mentalité'*, as J. G. A. Pocock and D.R. Kelley have argued? The courts of equity, where common lawyers and civilians worked together, are important to this question; but discussions of their relationship to common law and civilian ideas have generally focussed on substantive rather than procedural doctrine.

---

1 E.g. *Cross on Evidence* (7th ed by Colin Tapper, London, 1990), 1-4; P. B. Carter, *Cases and Statutes on Evidence* (2nd ed., London, 1990), 4; M. N. Howard, P. Crane & D. A. Hochberg, *Phipson on Evidence* (14th ed., London, 1990) § 1-02; J. D. Heydon & C. M. G. Ockelton, *Evidence Cases & Materials* (3rd ed., London, 1991), 3; P. Murphy, *Murphy on Evidence* (5th ed., London, 1995), 3.

This book, then, contributes to these discussions a systematic study of the conceptual structure of the doctrine and procedure of proof of facts in the courts of equity, and the relationship of this doctrine to the proof concepts of contemporary civilians (lawyers trained in the civil law tradition, working both in the civil and canon laws). My argument is that contemporaries were right to see the courts of equity as fundamentally civilian in their proof procedure and concepts; and that the earliest phase of the development at common law of rules governing the evidence to be led to a jury was also influenced by civilian proof concepts.

The structure of the study follows contemporary discussions of proof and evidence by both civilians[2] and common lawyers[3] in using the instruments of proof as its organising principle: confessions (Chapter 2), documents (Chapters 3-4), witnesses (Chapters 5-8) and burden and standard of proof and presumptions (Chapter 9). In this chapter I propose to set the scene by identifying in more detail the nature of the two problems identified above and the relevance of equity proof to them; and the nature of the present study and the sources used for it.

---

2 For the civilians, the starting point is the *Corpus Iuris*: D. 22.3, *De Probationibus et Praesumptionibus*, 22.4, *De Fide Instrumentorum* ..., 22.5, *De Testibus*, 42.2, *De Confessis*; C.4.19, *De Probationibus*, 4.20, *De Testibus*, 4.21, *De Fide Instrumentorum* ...; 'Alciatus' 199r ff, confessions, 207r ff, witnesses, 220v ff, documents, 226r ff, presumptions; Maranta 551ff, confessions, 558 ff, witnesses, 583 ff, documents (though the editor Petrus Polleriumas inserts a substantial body of material on documents as an *Additio* to the section on witnesses); Covarruvias *QP* Ch 18, witnesses, Chs 19-22, documents; *Reformatio* 232 ff, documents, 243ff, witnesses, 266ff, presumptions; Vulteius 368r-370r, presumptions & oaths, 370v-371r, confessions, 371v-372v, witnesses, 372v-373v, documents; Wood 310-2, confessions, 312-4, presumptions, 314-9, witnesses, 319-325, documents. This separate treatment of the distinct instruments of proof is also shared by Cotta, Gaill, Clerke, Conset and Ayliffe, but the inference of a conceptual separation is weaker because these works are not organised by proof concepts; Gaill, and Clerke (and hence Conset), may be to some extent structured by the time order of the steps in litigation, while Cotta and Ayliffe are alphabetical.

3 Common lawyers mainly distinguished "evidence", meaning documents, from witnesses: Co.Lit. f 6b (nothing can be made of organisation in Coke upon Littleton, but the distinction is here made explicit, citing Bracton; cf also f 283: "evidence" does not only cover writings but also, in a wider sense, testimony); Rolle (written c.1638-40, though not published till 1668) has sub-sub-titles *Evidence* (writings) and *Testimonies* under the title Trial, sub-title *Trial per Pais*; William Shepherd's *Epitome* (1656) has subtitles *Evidence* and *Witnesses* under title Trial, as does his *Abridgement* (1675); Hughes' *Abridgement* (1660-3) and that of William Nelson (1725) and Comyns' *Digest* (written before 1741, when Comyns died, but not published until 1762-7) have separate titles *Evidence* and *Witnesses*. The first single title *Evidence* covering both witnesses and documents is in the *New Abridgement* (Vol 2, 1736) usually attributed to Matthew Bacon but thought to be based on some MS by Gilbert; by this time Nelson's *The Law of Evidence* (1717), covering both topics, though in separate chapters, was in its second edition.

I. Equity proof and the origins of the common law of evidence

Given the absence of evidence rules from modern civil law systems, an obvious explanation of their existence at common law is that the law of evidence is necessary because of the existence of the jury, which is apt to be misled by certain types of evidence, unlike a judge sitting alone. This was the explanation favoured by the older historians of the law of evidence, J.B. Thayer and J.H. Wigmore: the law of evidence arose, they argued, to allow the judiciary to control the eccentricities of the lay judges of fact[4].

This hypothesis had two historical implications which could provide an empirical test of it. The first is that the law of evidence would have had a more or less prolonged "pre-legal" period of gestation in which a regular course of practice was built up by individual discretionary rulings by judges, beginning in the late mediæval period as juries ceased to be composed of witnesses or self-informing, and becoming gradually visible in the scattered trial reports of the early modern period; Wigmore found these especially in the *State Trials*, the pamphlet reports of sensational political and criminal trials which began to be published in collected form in the 1690s. This body of discretionary rulings then flowered fully into a *law* of evidence with the development of regular *nisi prius* reporting in the late eighteenth century. The second was that the rules of evidence would "belong to" jury trial, and only be imported into the equity jurisdiction, where the judges sat alone, by a process of equity (inappropriately) following the law[5].

More recently the traditional account has been challenged in two ways, both of which deploy history and the relations of the common and civil law traditions to criticise the theory of evidence law as a necessary jury control mechanism.

The first line of objection is that while modern civil law systems generally follow a régime of "free proof", this was not true of the early modern period when the law of evidence appeared at common law. Rather, there was an elaborate body of proof law, the roman-canon law of proof or system of legal proofs, in use in the church courts and in most of continental europe from the later middle ages until it was swept away by the French Revolution. The law of proof required the (professional) judge of facts to decide on the basis of an objectively fixed quantum of proof - two concurring independent witnesses of good character, or an equivalent combination of proofs. Around this principle was built up a highly elaborate body of law concerning confessions, the competence and credibility of witnesses, their compulsion and its limits and their examination, the different types of admissible

---

4 J. B. Thayer. *A Preliminary treatise on evidence at the common law* (Boston, 1898; reprint, 1969) Introduction 1-2, and *passim;* J. H. Wigmore, *Treatise on Evidence at Common Law* (3rd edn, Boston, 1940) § 8 and *passim.*

5 On the first point, Thayer 1-2, Wigmore § 8; on the second, Wigmore §§ 4 (general), 575 (competence of witnesses), 2250, 2256 (self-incrimination), 2426 (parol evidence rule), 3426 (Statute of Frauds).

documents, circumstantial evidence and presumptions. Fact-finding by professional judges did not, therefore, automatically imply a régime of "free proof". Moreover, there is some reason to suppose that the roman-canon law of proof influenced the english common law of evidence. Thayer and Wigmore recognised as much in relation to the parol evidence rule[6] and presumptions[7]. More recently, such influence has been argued or suggested in a number of areas, by Prof. Barbara J. Shapiro on standard of proof doctrine, Prof. R.H. Helmholz and myself on the privilege against self-incrimination, and Prof Mirjan Damaska on hearsay in the roman-canon law[8].

Shapiro's work in particular suggests a mechanism for the knowledge by common lawyers of roman-canon proof concepts. This is that these concepts were absorbed into the general concepts of proof current in the seventeenth century in history, theology and the natural sciences, and were thus part of the common stock of knowledge of the educated man, just as elementary scientific ideas are today. This view may find some corroboration in the fact that an M.A. was thought to be sufficient qualification to be professional judge in an Archdeacon's court, the lowest in the ecclesiastical hierarchy, and a B.A. to act as a proctor (attorney) in the church courts[9].

Wigmore considered the possibility of influence of the roman-canon law of proof in the origins of the common law of evidence, but he rejected it in general. In part this rejection depends on technical evidence of divergences between the two laws and issues as to dating, which are discussed below in the relevant chapters of this book. In discussing the rules as to the competence of witnesses he also offered a general principled argument[10]. This was that general influence of the learned laws was antecedently improbable because of the state of jurisdictional conflict, and also conflict over procedure, between the common law courts and the church and civilian courts at the decisive period (towards the end of the reign of Elizabeth and during that of James). This argument is *prima facie* unconvincing, because jurisdictional conflict is not inconsistent with doctrinal influence. For example, Helmholz has argued that the common lawyers imitated the principal doctrinal characteristics of ecclesiastical defamation within decades of using prohibition to restrict its availability[11], and Wigmore himself recognised that the common lawyers borrowed the maxim *nemo tenetur seipsum prodere* from the canonists to

---

6 Discussed below ch 4 § 1 (2).

7 Discussed below ch 9 § 2.

8 Shapiro, *Beyond Reasonable Doubt and Probable Cause* (Berkeley, 1991); Helmholz, 'Origins of the Privilege Against Self-Incrimination: The Role of the European *Ius Commune*' (1990) 65 *NYU LR* 962-990, Macnair, 'The Early Development of the Privilege Against Self-Incrimination' (1990) 10 *OJLS* 66-84; Damaska, 'Hearsay in Cinquecento Italy' in *Studi in onore di Vittorio Denti* (Padova, 1994) 59-89.

9 Levack, *The Civil Lawyers* 22-24.

10 § 575.

11 101 SS *Introduction* pp xli-xlv, lxxv-vi.

use as a weapon against these selfsame canonists (though he argued that they misunderstood its significance)[12].

In fact, there is a significant body of instances of citation of civilian or canonist authority or reception of argument from civilians in court in the common law reports of the later sixteenth and early seventeenth centuries[13], summed up by Bacon in the *Case of the Union of the Realms* (1606), as proceeding on the basis that the learned laws are citable in matters of matrimony, deprivation and legitimacy[14]. In effect, by refusing to give the church courts an exclusive jurisdiction over these matters, the common lawyers required themselves to consider the substantive law affecting them, and therefore received argument from the learned laws. I am not arguing that this was the mechanism by which the proof concepts came to be parallel with the learned laws, merely that this mechanism shows the falsity of Wigmore's assumption that jurisdictional conflict rules out doctrinal influence.

If Wigmore's arguments against influence of the roman-canon law of proof are not *prima facie* satisfactory, they do draw attention to two problems with Shapiro's mechanism for influence and other specific arguments of this type. In the first place, the fact that something is common knowledge among intellectuals does not automatically mean that it will be absorbed into legal doctrine: other considerations, like the existing doctrinal framework and materials, or (for example) inter-jurisdictional competition and politics, are also relevant[15]. The second is that studies of *particular areas* of proof or evidence doctrine can never establish more than occasional borrowings, which may even be no more than borrowings of language into an alien environment where it immediately becomes meaningless - as Thayer argued was the case in relation to late eighteenth and nineteenth century Anglo-American use of presumption concepts from the civil law tradition[16]. In this book I hope to escape this trap by surveying the whole field of proof doctrine to

---

12 Below Ch 2 § 2 (2).

13 *Trial of Treasons* (M1556) Bro NC 50, (Bro Corone 219), all JJ, distinction between witness and party; *Lane v Cowper* (P1575) Moo KB 103.248 (*Humfreston's Case* (T1574) 3 Dy 337a, SC breve), QB, meaning of "seniori puero" in an instrument; *Bunting's Case* (P1581) Moo KB 169.303, QB, validity of marriage; *Anon* (M1584) 4 Leo 211, QB, multiple administrations; *Viscountess Bindon's Case* (M1585) Moo KB 211.354 (2 Leo 166 *breve*), Ex (L), paraphernalia; *Morris v Webber* (1585-7) Moo KB 225.366, 2 Leo 169, CP, legitimacy; *Bewacorne v Palmer* (H1588/9) Moo KB 272.426, CP, rejection of executorship; *Stephens v Tot* (P1602) Moo KB 665.910, effect of judicial separation; *Countess of Rutland's Case* (M1605) Moo KB 765.1063, 6 Co Rep 52b, Star Ch, whether the widow of a peer has the privileges of peerage; *Fryer v Gilding* (T1614) Moo KB 855.1174, whether making debtor executor discharges debt; *Powell v Harman* (P1616) Moo KB 849.1155, KB, effects of absolution of excommunication.

14 Moo KB 790.1091, in Parliament, at 791; civilian arguments as to naturalization are then received, at 791-4. *Calvin's Case, Case of the Post-Nati* (1608) 7 Co Rep 1a, 2 St Tr 559, is not SC, but it is apparent from the report of Ellesmere's speech in the State Trials that Coke's claim, 7 Rep at 4a, that civilian arguments were not used in that case, is false.

15 Cf. the discussion of explanatory problems approached from another angle in Baker, 'English Law and the Renaissance' (1985) 44 *CLJ* 46-61, esp. at 45-51.

see how far this fitted with, and how far diverged from, roman-canon proof doctrine.

The second approach to the critique of the traditional theory, however, is more clearly counterposed to the idea of roman-canon influence at the roots of the law of evidence. This starts with the work of J. H. Langbein. Langbein's work started with a critique of the view taken by Holdsworth[17] that the introduction in the 1550s of new pretrial mechanisms for the preparation of criminal prosecutions was a product of the influence of continental practice through the legislature. To refute this view Langbein compared the new legislation with French and German institutions of the same period, and concluded that the English mechanisms were radically distinct from those on the Continent, precisely in their *separation from* the learned law of proof on which the French and German institutions were founded[18]. Langbein went on to argue that the absence of the law of proof also explains the absence of routine judicial torture from early modern English criminal procedure[19].

If, then, the absence of rules of evidence was a key to understanding early modern english criminal procedure, the origin of the law of evidence must be sought later than Thayer and Wigmore had placed it. Langbein rules out the indications of evidence rules in the *State Trials* on which Wigmore relied, on the ground partly of the unreliability of the reports and more crucially because of the unrepresentative nature of the trials in question. This led him to other sources: newspaper reports of 'ordinary' criminal trials, the *Old Bailey Sessions Papers,* and judges notes of trials, especially those of Dudley Ryder, Chief Justice of King's Bench 1754-6. These sources showed that leading aspects of the modern law of evidence - the rule against hearsay, the right to silence, controls on cross-examination, etc - do not have a prehistory beyond the mid eighteenth century. Thus the early eighteenth century - and earlier - felony trial was substantially unregulated, governed by *discretionary* judicial control of jury fact-finding; and, as far as the *modern* law of evidence goes, much the same appears to be true for the civil trial and the misdemeanour trial[20]. This account of a mid to late eighteenth century transition has been corroborated, using similar sources, by J.M. Beattie, Stephan Lansdmann and James Oldham[21].

---

16 Below ch 9 nn 73-4 and text there.

17 *HEL* iv 528-9.

18 *Prosecuting Crime in the Renaissance* (Chicago, 1974).

19 *Torture and the Law of Proof* (Chicago, 1977).

20 'The Criminal Trial Before the Lawyers' (1978) 45 *U Chic LR* 263-316; 'Shaping the Eighteenth Century Criminal Trial, (1983) 50 *U Chic LR* 1-136; 'The Historical Origins of the Privilege Against Self-Incrimination at Common Law' (1994) 92 *Mich. LR* 1047-1085; 'Historical Foundations of the Law of Evidence: A View from the Ryder Sources' (1996) 96 *Col. LR* 1167-1201.

21 J. M. Beattie, *Crime and the Courts 1660-1800* (Oxford, 1986), 341-378; Stephan Landsmann, 'The Rise of the Contentious Spirit' 75 *Cornell LR* 497-609; J. Oldham, *The Mansfield Manuscripts* (Chapel Hill, 1992), i, 118-160.

This creates a large gap between the late mediæval decline of the 'witness' or self- informing jury postulated by Thayer and Wigmore, and a mid to late eighteenth century emergence of rules of evidence. In fact, this gap can probably be substantially lengthened, since it is by no means clear how far the fourteenth or even later thirteenth century trial jury was actually self-informing[22]. This requires a re-theorisation of why the rules of evidence arose, and one has been offered by Langbein in terms of the eighteenth century introduction of lawyers into the felony trial, and by Landsmann in terms of a political battle between the judges and counsel over the control of the trial[23].

This work, then, identifies an important mutation in the character of jury trials in the later eighteenth century. This mutation is associated with changes in the roles of counsel and judge in trials, with an increased prominence of *nisi prius* reporting and evidence law, and with changes in the character of evidence law – specifically, a new focus on what witnesses can say and what they can be asked. At this period, then, the common law of evidence begins to assume its modern form.

However, these scholars have identified important *changes* in trial practice and evidence doctrine; they have not identified (or explained) the *origin* of the law of evidence. This is partly a matter of the choices they have made about sources. If one wishes to date the origin of a body of legal doctrine, the *prima facie* starting point must be in citable doctrinal sources: statutes, case-law and treatises. Langbein, however, largely rules out these sources at the outset. He rules out the *State Trials* on the ground of the exceptional character of the trials reported; but this misses the circumstance that the *State Trials* were citable for evidence propositions as if they were ordinary law reports; as early as the fourth edition of the widely used trial lawyers' manual *Tryals per Pais* in 1702, and extensively in Hawkins' *Pleas of the Crown* (1721) (on which Langbein himself relies)[24]. Conversely, Langbein tells us that *nisi prius* (trial) reporting, which is our primary source of knowledge for common law evidence doctrine, begins in the late eighteenth century[25]. But this is merely an inference from the *English Reports* reprint of the printed reports. There is a series of circuit reports in print, though not included in

---

22 For the criminal trial jury see the essays by McLane, Post and Powell in Cockburn and Green ed., *Twelve Good Men and True* (Princeton, 1988). As far as the civil trial jury is concerned, the extension of jury trial from its origin in matters which were locally notorious such as seisin, disseisin, feoffment and boundaries into transitory matters of trespass, and the extension of the limitation dates of the real actions, together make self-informing in the sense of juror knowledge *a priori* unlikely. Some positive indication is given by instances of party case-preparation in the work of Sutherland, *Novel Disseisin*; the provisions of the Statute of Westminster II (1285) on assises (c 25) and nisi prius/ juries (c 34) indicate that already at this stage the use of the general issue was producing issues to which juries could not give an unassisted answer, while class considerations were beginning to outweigh vicinage in jury composition.

23 Langbein, above n 20; Landsmann, above n 21.

24 At e.g. 92 *Mich. LR* 1053.

25 At e.g. 96 *Col. LR* 1170-71.

the *English Reports,* Clayton, covering cases from the 1630s and 40s; various other series exist in manuscript, going back into the middle ages; and trial reports, both of trials at bar in the central courts, and trials at *nisi prius* at Guildhall, are commonly included in the main series of printed nominate reports from their inception in the sixteenth century[26]. The citable doctrinal sources are not, therefore, so poor as to require us to rely on non-doctrinal sources like newspapers and judges' notebooks to date the origin of evidence doctrine.

When we start from these sources, a clear *terminus ante quem* for common law evidence doctrine is provided by the appearance of books and parts of books on the law of evidence. Without getting too far into jurisprudential issues, it would be odd to say that there was no law on a subject when lawyers were writing books on it which discuss the relevant cases and statutes. The first free-standing book on evidence is William Nelson's *The Law of Evidence,* published 1717[27]. Slightly earlier is Sir Jeffrey Gilbert's "Treatise" on *Evidence;* this was originally written in the reign of Queen Anne as part of a larger general work on English law, but was published as a free-standing book in 1754[28]. There are earlier instances of the general usage. The trial lawyers' manual *Tryalls per Pais,* first published in 1665, had a short chapter on *Evidence* in this sense, elaborated in subsequent editions[29]; and

---

26 For MS collections of circuit cases see e.g. J. H. Baker, *English Legal Manuscripts in the U.S.A* (London, 1990) Nos. 746, 828, 1194e, 1520n. For early criminal trial reporting, id., 'Criminal Justice at Newgate 1616-27' (1973) 8 *Ir. Jur.* 307-322, and 'Some Early Newgate Reports' in C. Stebbings ed., *Law Reporting in Britain* (London, 1995) ch 3 and literature referred to there. Trial cases in the main series of nominate reports can be found by casual reading.

27 The book is anonymous, and the *National Union Catalogue* offers an attribution to Gilbert. The traditional attribution in England is to Nelson, and the style is most unlike Gilbert's style.

28 I have discussed the dating and character of Gilbert's 'treatises' in my article, 'Sir Jeffrey Gilbert and his Treatises' (1994) *15 JLH* 252-268; esp. 266-7 n. 107 on the detailed evidence on the dating of the *Evidence.* Further to this, I have now been able to consult Columbia Law School MSS Singleton 65 and 66 (J.H. Baker, *English Legal Manuscripts in the USA Part II* (London, Selden Soc., 1990) Nos 328, 329) and Harvard Law School MS No 2107 (Baker No 726). Col LS MS Singleton 65 is an amalgamation of a version of Gilbert's *Evidence* derived from HLS 2017 with Nelson's *Law of Evidence* and cases on evidence from Strange's Reports cited from the printed text, which dates the MS to the 1750s. HLS 2017 is very close to the printed text, but not derivative from it. Col LS MS Singleton 66, on the other hand, is dated on the fly-leaf "Robert Linsay September 12 1710", and there is nothing in the text inconsistent with this date; the MS is a fairly poor copy. It covers the context of the printed text up to p. 99, the remainder of the material before the section *ISSUES* (with some slight overlap) being contained in Col LS MS Singleton 26, (Gilbert on *Actions*) item (2). Variations between this MS and HLS 2017 on the one hand, and the MS traditions represented by Add 36090 and LI MS Hill 79 on the other, indicate that the *Evidence* was probably in MS circulation before 1710.

29 The first edition is by S.E. of the Inner Temple; chapter 11 on evidence occupies 18 pages. The second edition by G.D. of the Inner Temple is attributed to Giles Duncombe. Duncombe added a preface which *inter alia* laments the lack of common law writing on trial and proof by comparison with the roman-canon writers Mascardus and Farinaccius, and expanded

Coke upon Littleton (1628) f 283 asserts that in a "larger sense" the word evidence contains not only documents, but also testimony and other proofs presented to a jury. The "larger sense" is not the most common one at this period, however. The early modern Abridgments treat "Evidence" as meaning documents, and have a separate title or sub-title for "Testmoignes" or "Witnesses"; in Brooke's Abridgment (1573), the first to refer at all to "Evidence", the topics referred to are remedies for the recovery of title deeds, and what matters can be raised on the general issue rather than pleaded[30].

When we go behind the contemporary treatises to the reports and statutes of the period, the existence in the seventeenth century of legal rules governing, at least, the competence of witnesses and the admissibility of documents presented in evidence to a jury is confirmed: there are very numerous cases on these subjects in the mid to later seventeenth century, a few in the early seventeenth century and even some in the reign of Elizabeth I[31].

However, on the other hand, as we go back from the Restoration we find, increasingly, positive evidence for the proposition that there are no rules governing the evidence presented to a jury. The clearest form of this evidence is the argument that the jurors, being on oath to deliver a true verdict, are witnesses, not judges,

---

the chapter on evidence to 67 pages, in a somewhat (but not much) more organised form. The third edition of 1695 added more material (up to 84 pages); the fourth, of 1702, which is otherwise identical, adds to the book a treatise on "Tryals per pais in capital matters" based on the State Trials, and the book is advertised as "with a treatise upon evidence". In the fifth edition of 1718 the treatment of evidence is considerably more organised, probably stimulated by the competition of Nelson's *Evidence.* Further editions in this form were produced in 1725, 1739 and 1766. Thereafter the book, which had evidently been the leading work in the field, was superseded by Buller's *Nisi Prius,* in which the treatment of evidence was based on Gilbert.

30 For bibliographical and other information on the Abridgements see J.D. Cowley, *A Bibliography of Abridgements* (London, 1932). Fitzherbert (printed 1514) has titles for neither evidence nor witnesses. Brooke (1573) has neither title, but in the Table refers from "Evidence de terres" to "Chartres de terres", i.e. title deeds, and from "Evidence al jurie" to "General Issue", i.e. pleading/ relevance issues. Rolle (written 1638-40, though not published till 1668) has sub-sub- titles "Evidence" and "Testimonies" under title "Trial", sub-title "Trial per Pais". Shepherd's *Epitome* (1656) and his *Abridgement* (1675) both have sub-titles "Evidence" and "Witnesses" under title "Trial". Hughes (1663), Nelson (1725) and Comyns *Digest* (not published till 1762-7, but probably written a good deal earlier, certainly before Comyns' death in 1741) all have "Evidence" and "Witnesses" as separate full titles. "Evidence" first appears as an Abridgment title covering both documents and witnesses in the *New Abridgment* of Matthew Bacon (1736) (though the *New Abridgment* makes considerable use of material by Gilbert, in the case of the title *Evidence* this is true only of the section on evidence in equity, which is drawn from Gilbert's *Forum Romanum*). Viner (1742-57) has a full volume on evidence, one of the last volumes to appear.

31 The authorities cited by Gilbert and Nelson are mostly pre-1700; but they by no means cite all the pre- 1700 cases in the printed reports. Around 1,000 cases are cited in this book; these are predominantly, but not exclusively, in equity, and conversely do not include numerous cases at common law from the second half of the seventeenth century. Several of the small but significant group of the earliest cases are cited below in the appropriate chapters.

and hence can find a verdict without or against evidence[32]. A late instance of the use of this argument is the controversial decision in *Bushell's Case* (1670), as a ground to reject the practice of punishing the jury for a verdict against the evidence. It was also used, however, as an argument against the existence of legal rules controlling the admissibility of documentary evidence, in *Newis v Lark* (1571) and *Olive v Gwin* (1658), or its weight, in *Goddard's Case* (1583) and *James' Case* (1584); against the use of defence witnesses in criminal trials and (on the other side of the same debate) against legal rules disqualifying witnesses, in parliamentary debates in 1606; and against the idea that two concurring witnesses were required at law, in *Reniger v Fogossa* (1550)[33].

If this evidence indicates that there were theoretical reasons to suppose that there were not rules, in the earlier period there are also other indications that rules did not exist which later did. Before the mid sixteenth century the printed reports are largely silent, and early cases in the second half of the sixteenth century and around 1600 show some indications that new law is being made, a matter which will be further explored in relation to the particular topics, below.

We can, therefore, be fairly confident that (a) there were no legal rules governing the evidence presented to a jury before about 1550; (b) some judges at least thought that there were rules, but their existence was uncertain and controversial, in the reigns of Elizabeth and James I; and (c) there were definitely legal rules, a "law of evidence", by the 1660s, though it was still a matter of argument whether these rules were binding on the jury.

It is true that the 'law of evidence' as it appears before the late eighteenth century is most unlike the modern law of evidence. The modern law of evidence consists largely of a body of general rules governing what witnesses can be asked, and can say, at trial: the hearsay rule, the opinion rule, the rules relating to use of character, and so on. The law of evidence stated in Gilbert and Nelson, and in earlier treatments, and which appears in the cases (which I will call for convenience the 'old law of evidence') had two fundamental elements.

The first, though usually treated second in the sources, is a body of rules about what evidence will maintain an issue; that is, the substantive relevance of evidence. These are rules which we would now regard as rules of pleading, or of substantive law. To give a couple of examples from the first edition of *Tryalls per Pais:*

> But if a feoffment be pleaded in fee, upon issue non feoffavit modo et forma, a feoffment upon condition is no evidence, because it does not answer the issue: and wheresoever Evi-

32 T. Jon. 13, 1 Mod. 119, 1 Freem. 1, Vaughan 135, 6 St. Tr. 1199. The controversial character of the decision is evident from the comment of Francis North, Chief Justice of Common Pleas 1675-82 and Lord Keeper 1682-5 that the decision was "sans reason ag[ains]t [th]e whole cours of p[re]sidents", BL Add MS 32518 f 6v; cf also Langbein, 'Criminal Trial Before the Lawyers' at 297-300.

33 These cases are discussed below in their more specific contexts.

dence is contrary to the issue, and does not maintain it, the evidence is not good. 11 Hen 3 Feoffments 41;

Upon an assumpsit to the husband, an assumpsit to the wife, and his agreement, is good evidence. 7 Hen 8, 29[34].

The first of these two points is one of pleading; the second concerns the law of contract and that of marriage. The procedural context for such points being described as "evidence" is that it was possible to "demur to the evidence" as a way of raising points of law at trial, the predecessor of moving no case to answer on legal grounds. If this was all, or even most, of the old law of evidence, we could still say that the early modern trial was unregulated.

However, the second branch of the old law of evidence was a body of rules about the admissibility of documents, the competence of witnesses, the relative weight of documents and witnesses, and presumptions. The separation of 'witnesses' and 'evidence' meaning, mostly, documents, as we have seen, antedates 'evidence' as a single topic: it continues down through the eighteenth century treatments of evidence. The most elaborate version of this approach is that of Gilbert. In his *Evidence* he organises the instruments of evidence in a "Scale of Probability" ranging from statutes as the highest form of evidence to hearsay (i.e. oral hearsay) as the lowest.[35]

Besides this divergence of organisation, the old law of evidence is alien to modern lawyers for three reasons. The first is that most of the concrete rules discussed are obsolete. Almost all the law relating to the competence of witnesses was swept away by statute in the nineteenth century, and the rules relating to the admissibility of documents diminished into exceptions to the hearsay rule, while those relating to the proof of documents by production of the original and when 'secondary evidence' could be used have largely withered away in the face of mechanical reproduction. The old law of evidence, on the other hand, did not contain the modern rule against hearsay, the opinion rule in its modern form, etc.

The second alien feature of the old law of evidence is that the distinction between the admissibility of evidence (for the judge) and its weight (for the jury), which is a foundational element of the modern law, is so attenuated as hardly to exist at all[36]. For example, Gilbert's treatment is entirely in terms of the relative

34 Page 141.

35 The subsequent reorganisation of the treatment of the topic can be seen from treatises. The Hardwicke MS of Gilbert BL Add MS 36090, probably dating from 1743-4, adds to Gilbert's treatment a list of six maxims of general rules of evidence. Bathurst's *Theory of Evidence,* which is largely a re-edition of Gilbert dating from slightly later, expands these maxims to nine general rules of evidence. In Phillips' treatise the general rules were much enlarged; in Greenleaf, Taylor and Best the general rules form the larger part of the book, the analysis of the instruments of evidence the smaller part; in modern textbooks distinctions between types of evidence are likely to be confined to a single chapter.

36 There is some evidence for the distinction: Gilbert 75, for the proposition that the judges cannot supply the defects of an incomplete verdict; *Olive v Gwin,* on documents; *Langham v*

weight of differing items of evidence, and where particular items are excluded it is because they lack weight[37]. The procedural context of this characteristic is the legal significance of a verdict which was "against the evidence", i.e. against the judge's direction as to the weight of the evidence. Such a verdict was in theory a ground for the jury to be attainted, i.e. convicted of perjury by a jury of 24, a principle which found expression in the mid sixteenth century in the rule that the plaintiff in attaint could lead no more evidence than the evidence he had led at the original trial[38]. The jury could also be punished for a verdict against the evidence and direction until 1641 by the Star Chamber[39], and until *Bushell's Case* in 1670 by the presiding judge at trial. Even after *Bushell's Case* had made this practice questionable, it was in the 1690s and 1700s a standard ground for a new trial in civil causes that the trial judge certified that the verdict was against the evidence and his direction[40]. In other words, the judges were *telling the jury what verdict to find;* their direction had legal effect; and it was this direction on the weight of the evidence which was governed by legal rules affecting the weight of evidence. Hence the weakness of the distinction between the roles of judge and jury in relation to admissibility and weight.

The third radical difference between the old law of evidence and the modern law is that the old law of evidence generally preferred documents to witnesses; a preference which is, as it were, the negation of the preference for *viva voce* testimony enshrined in the modern rule against hearsay. This preference is very striking in Gilbert, but it was not Gilbert's invention: it was embodied in the seventeenth century law in the conclusive effect of pleadable documents (estoppel by record and by deed), the parol evidence rule, and the Statute of Frauds.

Laurence (1661) Hardres 180, distinguishing evidence at law from proof in equity; and in relation to the distinction between the competence and credibility of witnesses, Hale *HPC* ii 276-7, North in 'A Fragment' at 143.

37 Gilbert, 3-4 (best evidence rule), 7 (copy of a copy), 19-20 (irregular office copies), 103 (infidel witnesses), 107-8 (hearsay); or where a contrary presumption deprives the evidence of weight: 41 (comparison of hands in criminal cases), 74 (ancient deeds *ex facie* questionable), 101 (infamous witnesses).

38 For the attaint procedure in general cf Baker, *Introduction to English Legal History* ((3rd edn, London, 1990) 156. For this rule, *Heydon v Ibgrave* (P1557) 2 Dy 129b, *Paramor's Case* (P1562) 2 Dy 212a. For the availability of attaint on a verdict contrary to the judge's direction, *Lee v Boothby* (M1639) W Jones 449. Though there seems to have been some attempt to revive the attaint in the mid-sixteenth century, the use of the procedure seems rarely to have been successful: in *Stephens v Westbrooke & al'* (M1564) 2 Dyer 235b, an instance of a successful attaint, Dyer thought it worth while to make a special note of the forms to be followed. No doubt attaint juries were unwilling to reverse verdicts, given the penal consequences for the trial jury.

39 The Lawson essay in Cockburn & Green ed., *Twelve Good Men*, at 138 n 95 collects several authorities.

40 Mitnick, 'From Neighbour-Witness to Judge of Proofs' 32 *Am Jnl LH* 201 at 212f; & cf below Ch 10 §§ 1 (1) and (2).

No doubt the nature of trials, and the rules governing evidence to a jury, did mutate in the mid to later eighteenth century; though it should be remembered on the one hand that the older law of documents and witness competence continued to be relevant into the nineteenth century, and, on the other hand, that some aspects of the rules affecting the examination of witnesses (self-incrimination, legal privilege and a rule of uncertain shape about oral hearsay) had substantial antecedents before the mid-eighteenth century watershed. This mutation was clearly connected, as Langbein and Landsmann have argued, with the introduction of lawyers into the ordinary felony trial and the development of 'adversarialism'; though which was cause and which effect remains uncertain. But the underlying idea that there are legal rules governing the evidence which can be led to a jury appeared in the late sixteenth and early seventeenth century. Wigmore's dating was not wildly out.

This point being once accepted, the question of the relationship between common law evidence and equity proof, which ceased to be important in the theory of eighteenth-century origins, becomes important again. At the time of the first appearance of law governing evidence to a jury, the courts of equity were at their height. Contemporaries, both civilians and common lawyers, thought that these courts used civilian procedure, and in them civilians and common lawyers worked together. If the Thayer / Wigmore argument that the rules of evidence appeared through *ad hoc* discretionary jury control decisions was right, the rules of the 'old' law of evidence should have appeared first at common law, and only afterwards in equity. If, on the other hand, the rules appear first in equity, the question of their relationship to the roman-canon law of proof is more strongly posed.

II. Common law, civil law and equity procedure

During the sixteenth and seventeenth centuries there were episodically surfacing complaints about a perceived threat to the common law. In the reign of Henry VIII the issue was raised in 1522-3 in relation to the decisions of Stokesley, a Master of Requests[41]; in 1529-30 it found its way into House of Lords' articles against Wolsey[42]; in 1546 common lawyers petitioned on this basis against Wriothesley C's use of civilian Masters as judges delegate[43]. In the reign of James I, the question was successively focussed by controversies over prohibitions (1605-10), the proposal for a 'perfect union' of England and Scotland and the question of the *post-nati*

41 Guy, *Cardinal's Court* 45; P. Gwyn, *The King's Cardinal* (London, 1990) 128.

42 The articles are printed in Cobbett, *The Parliamentary History of England* i (London, 1806), 491-501; relevant are arts 20 (equity relief after judgment at law), 21 (general citation and *ex parte* injunctions), 26 (injunctions at a late stage of common law proceedings) and 44 (general subversion of the common law). Their origins and status are discussed by A. F. Pollard, *Wolsey* (London, 1929), 260-1.

43 Holdsworth *HEL* v 253; Jenkins, 'Eighty Years On', 124-5.

(1606-9), Cowell's *Interpreter* (1610) and the conflict between Coke and Ellesmere over the limits of the Chancery jurisdiction (1615-6). The issues were still alive in the debate over martial law in 1628, and an aspect of the controversy, the question of the immemoriality of the common law, resurfaced in 1679-83 in the Brady controversy[44]. The argument that equity procedure was subversive of the common law also resurfaced in 1665, 1676, and the early 1690s[45].

This episodic controversy raises two issues. The first is: was there in the early modern period a real likelihood of a 'Reception' of roman law along the lines of developments in contemporary Germany, the Low Countries or Scotland, resulting in an english legal development more along the lines of developments on the continent? The second is: even if there was no strong likelihood of a 'Reception', was the belief, which certainly existed in certain quarters, in a threat to the common law, wholly baseless? If so, was it perhaps a result of the common law "*mentalité*" identified by Pocock[46], which saw the common lawyers as believing that their law was immemorial custom and entirely separate from all other laws?

Maitland at the turn of the century suggested that there had been a threat of 'Reception' in the early Tudor period; which, however, did not materialise because the common law was itself a national law and a 'learned law' and as such less vulnerable to displacement by civilian doctrine than the miscellanous collections of local customs found in the Holy Roman Empire or in Scotland[47]. Subsequent work tended to play down this threat. In particular Holdsworth argued that Maitland had overestimated the decline of the common law at this period and the civilian character of the conciliar and equity jurisdictions; the expressions of concern about Wolsey and Wriothesley were mere political manouvrings[48]. J. H. Baker has argued that this period was in reality one of modernisation and expansion of the common law, and that in a certain sense the question is falsely posed, since the changes which occurred in the common law were parallel to those occurring on the Continent at the same time[49]. As far as the late sixteenth and early seventeenth century was concerned, W. J. Jones explained the Chancery controversy in terms of a combination of the partially competitive relationship between Chancery and the common law courts with a personal antagonism between Coke CJ and Ellesmere LC, a

44 This brief account is drawn synthetically from R. Lockyer, *The Early Stuarts: A Political History of England 1603-1642* (London, 1989), chs 3 and 9, Levack, *The Civil Lawyers* chs 3 and 4, and Pocock, *The Ancient Constitution and the Feudal Law.*

45 For this see my essay 'Common Law and Statutory Imitations of Equitable Relief under the later Stuarts', in C. W. Brooks & M. Lobban ed., *Communities and Courts* (London, 1997).

46 *The Ancient Constitution and the Feudal Law.*

47 *English Law and the Renaissance* (Cambridge, 1901).

48 *HEL* v 252-292.

49 Baker, 94 Selden Society *Introduction* at *24-46* (and *passim*); 'English Law and the Renaissance' [1985] *CLJ* 46-61.

view which has largely become orthodox[50]. Brian Levack has pointed to the very limited scope of civilian jurisdiction and business in the Admiralty, the Court of Chivalry and the church courts; if anything, the period was one in which the common lawyers extended their business at the expense of the civilians.[51]

In 1981, however, Dafydd Jenkins argued that the criticisms which had been made of Maitland's thesis had been overstated[52]. If the criticisms of Wolsey and Wriothesley were political gambits, the fact that such political gambits could be used indicated that there must be *some* basis for them; "Even if one has personal or political motives for attacking somebody, one does not base a case against him on grounds which have no colour of truth"[53]. In particular, the *possibility* existed of 'romanisation' through a civilian development of the conciliar (equity procedure) courts. G.R Elton's riposte, in his *F. W. Maitland* (1985)[54] relies heavily on Holdsworth for the proposition that "equity owed far more to the common law than to any other system; in the new courts the law administered was greatly affected by the fact that the common lawyers ran those courts", and on Jones for the view that in the quarrels between law and equity "what was at issue was rivalry for business, not disputes over the fundamentals of the law"[55].

It is probably common ground that, whether for Maitland's reason or some other, there was no great likelihood of a complete displacement of the common law tradition. But there is a real issue about whether contemporaries were unreasonable to think that this was a possibility; and this depends in part on the character of the courts of equity, and in part on the receptivity of common lawyers to arguments drawn from the civilian tradition. If we leave out these possibilities we are left only with the church courts, which were never likely to be the centre of a civilianizing trend in secular law, and the relatively marginal spaces allowed to the civilians in the Admiralty and the Court of Chivalry.

If the civil law really was marginal, then we are left with a legal system in which common law thought was absolutely dominant; and this dominance can itself be used to explain the perception of 'threats' to the common law. The argument here is that the common lawyers were, because of their dominance, incapable of thinking in terms of a single political order containing several legal orders, or, indeed, of legal change: they saw their own law as *the* national and immemorial law, and the mere existence of other laws as a challenge to it. This was the thesis of J. G. A. Pocock's *The Ancient Constitution and the Feudal Law*, and similar arguments

50 Jones, *Chancery* 462-473; Baker, *IELH* 125-6. For some qualifications cf Baker, 'The Common Lawyers and the Chancery: 1616' (1969) 4 *Ir. Jur.* 368-392, C.M. Gray, 'The Boundaries of the Equitable Function' (1976) 20 *Am. J. LH* 192-226.

51 *The Civil Lawyers* 124-6.

52 'Eighty Years On: In Defence of Maitland' 2 *JLH* 107-142.

53 Id. 124.

54 London, 1985, 79-88.

55 Id. 84, 85.

have been made by D. R. Kelley[56]. The idea of the dominance of common law thought and the marginality of civil law thought in England, and their separation, has also been used by Glenn Burgess as a way of explaining an early Stuart political 'consensus' which balanced different political-theoretical languages, that of the civil law belonging only to the sphere of foreign relations[57]; and by J. C. D. Clark to argue that the idea of the absolute sovereignty of the King-in-Parliament defended against the Americans in the later eighteenth century was deeply rooted in sixteenth and early seventeenth century legal thought[58].

However, the *mentalité* thesis has itself been questioned both by Hans Pawlisch[59], who argues that Pocock overestimated the extent to which Coke's attitude was representative, and by C. W. Brooks and Kevin Sharpe[60], who argue that the common lawyers were far from being blinkeredly unable to draw on civilian ideas, and instead see the idea of the 'immemorial common law' as a legal-rhetorical move in a political argument; and some part of this argument has been accepted by Pocock[61]. The *mentalité* thesis is also inconsistent with Baker's arguments for the existence of common features of the development of early modern English and European law.

In this context, the question of the character of the equity and prerogative courts and in particular of their proof procedure, and of their relationship to the common and civil laws, is of considerable importance. Procedure is central for two reasons[62]. The first is that, apart from the rather special question of sovereignty and *princeps legibus solutus*, most of the evidence for serious controversy between common lawyers and civilians, and between common law and equity courts, concerns questions of procedure, like general citation, compulsion to confess and the secret examination of witnesses, and matters which (like the conclusive effect of documents) are on the borders of substantive and procedural law[63]. The second is that there is a good deal of contemporary evidence for the view, held both by common lawyers and by civilians, that the procedure of the courts of equity was civilian in character. Among civilians, Sir Julius Caesar's book on the Court of Re-

---

56 'History, English Law and the Renaissance' (1974) 65 *Past & Present* 24-51; rejoinder to Brooks and Sharpe, (1981) 72 *Past & Present* 143.

57 *The Politics of the Ancient Constitution* (London, 1992); *Absolute Monarchy in Early Stuart England* (New Haven, 1996).

58 *The Language of Liberty* (Cambridge, 1994) ch 1.

59 'Sir John Davies, the Ancient Constitution, and the Civil Law' (1980) 23 *Hist. J.* 689-702.

60 'History, English Law and the Renaissance' 72 *Past & Present* 137-142.

61 'The Ancient Constitution Revisited' in *The Ancient Constitution and the Feudal Law* 253f, at 280f. Kelley has also to some extent 'toned down' his argument on this point: see *The Human Measure* (Cambridge, Mass., 1990) ch 10.

62 Jenkins, 127, makes the point that "for the lawyer, the contrast between different systems of law is more often a matter of differences in procedure than in substance".

63 For evidence on these points see below in the relevant chapters.

quests, dating from the 1590s, says that the procedure in that court was entirely according to the summary form in the civil law[64]; and the Chancery was characterised as using civilian procedure in in Sir Thomas Smith's *De Republica Anglorum* written in the 1560s, by Cosin in the 1590s, Ridley in the 1600s, Duck in the 1640s and Wood in the 1700s[65]. Among the evidence from common law sources is a petition in Parliament in as early as 1415 and Sir Robert Atkyns' tract on Chancery in the 1690s[66]; and Gilbert's *Forum Romanum,* written between the early 1700s and 1721-3, which is entirely founded on the idea of Chancery procedure as derived from the civil law[67]. This evidence was discounted by Dawson for reasons which, as will appear in the main body of the book, do not seem to me to be satisfactory.

If the courts of equity were broadly civilian in their procedure, it will be apparent that civilian thought was by no means marginal in the legal thought of the period. What was in question was not the 'threat' of a small number of professional civilians. Rather, what was in question was the intersection of the civilians' political influence with the existence of a complete parallel system of jurisdiction and procedure and some tendency for civilian procedural ideas to infiltrate the common law system. The common lawyers themselves, as a profession, were by no means unequivocally trustworthy defenders of the ancient common law. Thus, while the real likelihood of a 'Reception' was probably not very great, this was as much be-

64 Caesar *Ancient State* p. 8.

65 Sir Thomas Smith, *De Republica Anglorum* (written 1562-5, first published 1583; ed Mary Dewar, Cambridge: CUP, 1982) p. 94; Cosin iii 51-3; 51-3; Ridley 393-5; Duck, *De Usu et Auctoritate Iuris Civilis* (London, 1679) 328-331; Wood, x.

66 *Rotuli Parliamentorum: ut et petitiones, et placita in Parliamento* (London, 1765, 6vv) Vol IV p 84a; Sir Robert Atkyns, *An Enquiry into the Jurisdiction of the Court of Chancery* (London, 1695) 26, 31.

67 Sir Jeffrey Gilbert, *Forum Romanum* (London, 1758) *passim.* The book originated as part of a larger work written in the reign of Queen Anne (Macnair, 'Gilbert and his Treatises'), dividing the law into *Persons* (probably; none of this survives), *Property, Personal* and *Real,* and *Actions.* The outline of *Actions* is extant in Columbia Law School Singleton MS 26 ff 35-6 and 57 ff 1-2. The topic is divided into a general part and treatment of particular actions; the general part contains discussion of the jurisdiction of courts, and the general features of process. The Chancery is discussed in outline notes at ff 37-40 of this. The next stage was a fuller text called *The Originall of the Chancery* which appears in Col LS MS Singleton 34 (1), item (ii); this contains no material later than 1714, and was still not intended as an independent book, since it is without chapter divisions. In the 17-teens someone, presumably Gilbert, extracted the disorganised procedural material from this text and reorganised it on the basis of civilian procedural sources under the title *Forum Romanum.* Early versions of this, containing no material later than 1720, are in Harvard Law School MSS 1064 item (iii) and 5141 item (ii). In around 1722-3, both texts were updated using the writer's MS reports and personal memory. Versions in this form are (*The Originall*) Col LS MSS Singleton 28 and 27 (a fair copy from 28); (*Forum Romanum*) Col LS MSS 33 and 34(1) item (i). Finally, the *Forum Romanum* version of procedure was substituted for the procedural material in *The Originall*; the work takes this form in HLS MS 1163. In this form the work was printed in 1758.

cause of the political relation of forces as for reasons internal to the common law system; and, given the continental context, it was not unreasonable to fear that the distinctive features of the common law, particularly in the sphere of procedure, might disappear.

To make this point clear demands some brief consideration of the extent of the operation of courts following equity procedure, and of their staffing. In the first place, at around 1600 there was a complete parallel system of jurisdictions. The property and contract 'core' jurisdiction of the Common Pleas was shadowed by the Chancery and, for small claims, the Requests. The crime and tort 'core' jurisdiction of the King's Bench was shadowed by the Star Chamber and, in the regions, the Councils in the North and in Wales. The revenue jurisdiction of the common law Exchequer was shadowed by its equity side, by the Court of Wards, and by the Duchy Chamber of the Duchy of Lancaster. Below these courts were a range of local equity courts; while the Privy Council and Star Chamber exercised a direct disciplinary jurisdiction over Justices of the Peace[68].

As far as the staffing of these courts is concerned, there is some variation. The simplest case is the regional councils and the Star Chamber. The regional councils were executive and policy-making bodies as well as courts, and though some of their personnel were legally qualified this was by no means a requirement of office[69]. The Star Chamber's personnel were in principle simply the members of the King or Queen's Privy Council, i.e. the central government[70]. In practice the lawyers and in particular the Lord Chancellor or Keeper tended to take a leading role, and common-law judges were from time to time commissioned to sit[71]. In both

68 The largely proprietary and contractual focus of the Chancery jurisdiction is indicated in F. Metzger, 'Das Englische Kanzleigericht unter Kardinal Wolsey' (unpublished Ph.D. dissertation, Erlangen, 1977) Ch 3 and Table 2B, p 333, and Jones, *The Elizabethan Court of Chancery* (Oxford, Clarendon, 1967) pp 420-2; elements of a wider jurisdiction were certainly present but by no means as important, and the view of the Chancery as a property court tended to become dominant; what was certainly clear was that the Chancery was *not* a court which had a primary criminal jurisdiction. For the Requests cf Sir Julius Caesar, *The Ancient State, Authority and Proceedings of the Court of Requests* ed LM Hill (Cambridge, CUP, 1975) p 8, and Lambarde, *Archeion* (1591; ed CH McIlwain & PL Ward, Cambridge, Mass., Ames Foundation/ Harvard UP, 1957). For the Star Chamber cf Lambarde, *Archeion* 52-5, 97ff; JA Guy, *The Cardinal's Court* (Hassocks, Harvester, 1977); Hudson, *A Treatise of the Star Chamber* (in F. Hargrave ed, *Collectanea Juridica* (London, 1971-2) Vol II p 1. For the equity side of the Exchequer cf Bryson, *The Equity side of the Exchequer* (Cambridge, CUP, 1975); on the jurisdiction esp Ch 2. For the Court of Wards cf Bell, *The Court of Wards and Liveries* (Cambridge, CUP, 1953) Ch 5, and Crompton, *LAucthoritie & Jurisdiction des courts de la Maiestie de la Roigne* (London, 1594) f. 112f, cited by Bell p. 109; for the Duchy Chamber, Somerville, *Transactions of the Royal Historical Society* 4th Series Vol 23 p 159. On the local equity jurisdictions see Jones, *Elizabethan Chancery* Ch 9 and (on London) pp 387- 9.

69 P. Williams, *The Council in the Marches of Wales under Elizabeth I* (Cardiff: University of Wales Press, 1958) Ch 7; R.R. Reid, *The King's Council in the North* (London: Green, 1921) 245-54.

70 Hudson 22-36.

these cases the result was a collegiate court which was a mix of common lawyers, civilians, and political figures without legal training.

The equity jurisdiction of the Exchequer appears from Bryson's study to have been mainly though not exclusively the creation of Sir Walter Mildmay, Chancellor of the Exchequer 1559-1589[72], and the Lord Treasurer and Chancellor of the Exchequer sat as judges in equity causes at least down to the civil war[73]. The Treasurers were primarily political figures, the Chancellors financial administrators. Both common lawyers and civilians could be appointed; thus the Treasurers included Montagu (1620-1) and Ley (1624-8), formerly Lord Chief Justices, and Bishop Juxon (1636-41) who held a B. C. L., while the Chancellors included Julius Caesar as well as several who had attended the Inns of Court but not become barristers[74]; the Barons, the common law judges of the court, also sat in equity cases[75]. In the Wards the Masters of the Wards, technically the sole judge of the Court, were financial administrators; the surveyor-general of the Liveries and the Attorney of the Wards were regularly common lawyers, and the court made regular use of common law judges in the later sixteenth and early seventeenth centuries[76].

The Requests was in theory, like the Star Chamber, an arm of the Privy Council, and the court was nominally composed of councillors[77]. However, its effective judiciary was specialists, the Masters of Requests. The Masters were traditionally two, one civilian and one common lawyer; Elizabeth I appointed a majority of civilians, but James I appointed exclusively common lawyers[78].

The Chancery presents the most complicated picture. N. Pronay has shown that down to the later fifteenth century Chancery staffing seems to have been governed primarily by the bureaucratic character of the institution: the Chancellors were primarily great officers of state, and the lesser officials started at the bottom and worked up. The Yorkist kings and Henry VII, however, seem to have adopted a policy of appointing persons qualified in civil or canon law both to the Chancellorship and the Mastership of the Rolls[79]. The continuity of this policy was

---

71 Hudson 20 for the practice of referring cases to the judges; 25-35 for the pre-eminence of the Chancellor in the Court.

72 Bryson 20.

73 Bryson 39 (Lord Treasurer, occasionally), 44 (Chancellor of the Exchequer, regularly till the Civil war, occasionally between 1660 and 1735).

74 From the list of the personnel in Bryson, 173-4, compared with D.N.B. s.nn.

75 Bryson, 46.

76 Bell Chs 1 & 2 pp 16-19, for the Masters, 21-4 for the Surveyor-General and Attorney, 98-100 for the use of common law judges by reference or as judges assistant.

77 Leadam, *Introduction* to *Select Cases in the Court of Requests*, Selden Soc Vol 12, pp. l-li.

78 Levack, *Civil Lawyers* p. 61.

79 N. Pronay, 'The Chancellor, the Chancery, and the Council at the End of the Fifteenth Century' in H. Hearder and H. R. Loyn ed., *British Government and Administration* (London, 1974) 87-103, at 90-92.

broken by Henry VIII's appointment of Wolsey, who was chief minister rather than a lawyer[80], and after his fall of More, a common lawyer[81]. From then on the chancellors were normally common lawyers[82], and the three exceptions, Hatton under Elizabeth I, Williams under James I, and Shaftesbury under Charles II, were not trained civilians either[83]. The Masters of the Rolls began to be common lawyers from the reign of Henry VIII, but two civilians, Sir Julius Caesar and his son Sir Charles, held the post in the early seventeenth century[84]. The Masters of the court were still mainly civilians down to the early seventeenth century. Though common lawyers began to be appointed in 1584, around 1600 it was still possible to characterise reference to a Master as "reference to the Doctors". In 1633, after a period of mainly common law appointments, the Council ordered that at least eight of the eleven Masters should be civilians, and thereafter only civilians were appointed until the regime collapsed in 1640-41[85]. On the other hand, common law judges were episodically commissioned to hear Chancery causes throughout the period[86].

---

80 Gwyn, *King's Cardinal* ch 4, esp. 142-3 on the break in law enforcement policy associated with the fall of Empson and Dudley of Henry VII's death and the disappearance of the 'KIng's Council Learned in Law'.

81 For this appointment cf Guy, *The Public Career of Sir Thomas More* (Brighton, 1980) Chs 1 and 2.

82 Holdsworth *HEL* ii 557-8, v 218-9.

83 For their judicial careers cf Foss, *The Judges of England* (London, 1857) Vols V 497-510 (Hatton), VI 379-89 (Williams) and VII 70-84 (Shaftesbury). All three had, in fact, some common law legal education at the Inns of Court, and both Hatton and Shaftesbury had prior experience as judges in english bill courts, Hatton as a Master of Wards and Shaftesbury as Chancellor of the Exchequer. The reason for Hatton's appointment is obscure. Williams is said to have been appointed precisely because James I did not want a common lawyer in the post (Holdsworth *HEL* V 226-7), though Hacket, his near-contemporary biographer, attributes the appointment to James accidentally discovering that Williams had as chaplain to Ellesmere acquired extensive knowledge of the Chancery (*Scrinia Reserata*, London, 1693, p 52). Shaftesbury's biographer attributes his appointment to political considerations; in addition the former Lord Keeper, the common lawyer Bridgman, had made difficulties about the legality of some of Charles II's proposed uses of the prerogative (K.H.D. Haley, *The First Earl of Shaftesbury*, Oxford, Clarendon, 1968, pp 304-6).

84 For the emergence of the Master of the Rolls as a second regular judge of the court, subject to appeal to the Chancellor or Keeper, at an early stage in this period, see Spence, *Equitable Jurisdiction of the Court of Chancery* (London, 1846-9) i 358 (cited Holdsworth *HEL* i 419-420); Jones, *Elizabethan Chancery* 53-8. Cf Sainty, *The Judges of England* (London, Selden Society, 1993) 150; Holdsworth, *HEL* vi, 260-1.

85 For civilian dominance to the early seventeenth century, the complaints of the civilians under James I that they were being displaced, and the order of 1633, see Levack, *Civil Lawyers* 60-66, the 1633 order at 62-3. The detailed chronology of appointments can be seen from E. Heward, *The Masters in Ordinary* (Chichester: Barry Rose, 1990), p 5 and *passim* in the lists of Masters: the earliest common law appointment was in 1584, the latest civilian appointment in 1699. Between these dates the percentage of civilian appointments fluctuated, falling to low levels in the 1620s, 1650s, 1670s and 1690s. For reference "to the Doctors" see *Observations* f 439r No 21: "If a bill be demurred upon & therefore be referred to the Doctors {illegible} if the Doctor shall think the Bill insufficient for the pl[ainti]ff to offer to pay the

If the judicial officers of the courts thus had a mixed character, the bar was certainly dominated by common lawyers from an early stage[87], and in 1546 a proclamation restricted admittance of pleaders in the central courts, including the Chancery, Star Chamber, Exchequer and Wards, by requiring admission by the Chancellor and Chief Justices on the advice of Benchers of the Inns of Court[88].

The idea that "in the new courts the law administered was greatly affected by the fact that the common lawyers ran those courts" (Elton, quoted above) is therefore seriously overstated. On the other hand, except for the case of the Chancery in the later fifteenth century, it would be an overstatement in the other direction to characterise these courts as dominated by the civilians. They were, rather, a site of co-operation between the practitioners of the two laws, as well as a subject of conflict between them. The financial courts were probably closest to 'common law dominance', and the Chancery, with a period of exclusively civilian staffing in its past, furthest from it. Even in the Chancery the relative strength of the common lawyers clearly tended to increase over the period, but the process was uneven, and we cannot really speak of common law 'dominance' until the crisis of the 1640s destroyed the Star Chamber, regional councils, Requests and Wards and ended Charles I's policy of appointing civilians in Chancery.

This understanding is reflected in the approach taken in this book to the question of the relationship between equity proof and the common law on the one hand and the civil law on the other. In the first place, I am *not* arguing that equity proof was simply civilian in the same sense as, for instance, proof in the Admiralty. A quick comparison of the early seventeenth century materials on proof in equity, discussed in the main body of this book, with the arguments of Gentili on matters of proof in the Admiralty collected in the second book of his *Hispanicae Advocationes,* shows radically different levels of sophistication and of use of civilian authorities; there is some direct evidence that the rules were different in relation to exceptions to witnesses[89], and it is fairly clear that the core concepts of documentary proof in equity were those established in the medieval common law, which varied from those of the medieval *jus commune*[90].

What I *am* arguing is that the overall conceptual framework of proof and proof procedure in equity, the basic principles, were closer to civilian concepts than to medieval, or to nineteenth century, common law concepts; that in a number of areas there are similarities in detail which cannot plausibly be attributed to parallel

---

Def[endan]t his costs soe as he will answer to the bill the same being amended in the matter defective w[i]thout new p[ro]cess to be sued forth ag[ains]t him".

86 E.G. Jones, *Chancery* 55; cases appear frequently in the Chancery reports of the later seventeenth century, 3 Chan Rep, Chan Cas, 2 Freeman and Vernon.

87 Metzger, *Kanzleigericht* 355-7, cited Jenkins 'Eighty Years On', 133.

88 Jenkins, 'Eighty Years On', 133.

89 *Prawnce v Hodilow* (1581-2), below ch 6 n 14.

90 Below chs 3-4.

evolution; and that there is some direct evidence of citation of civilian sources. The most extensive instance of citation is the chapter on proof in a manuscript treatise on Chancery, dating from the 1600s: in a treatise the majority of whose chapters are drawn out of the Year Books and the medieval records, we find a chapter on proof which cites two cases from the reports published as 'Keilwey' and otherwise draws eclectically on the Bible, the Visigothic Laws, and (mainly) various civilian and canonist sources[91]. But there are also other instances in treatises and the case-law.

The other side of the coin is that instances of citation to the learned laws, and parallelism of rules both in general and in some specific details, are not restricted to equity jurisdictions, but appear also in common law cases and authors: for example, Hale, discussing witnesses in common law criminal trials, cites the Spanish canonist Covarruvias on the evidence of non-Christians[92].

Moreover, as will be seen in the main part of the book, though there are a few reported cases which indicate that civilian rules may have been applied in Chancery in the later fifteenth and early sixteenth century, the bulk of the evidence for proof rules in equity starts in the reign of Elizabeth I, and though in some areas this is earlier than the evidence for rules at law, the gap is not great and in some cases rules appear first at law. This may be a trick of the evidence: it was common lawyers, not civilians, who made reports of equity cases[93]. On the other hand, Gentili's arguments make clear that in a fully civilian system there was almost no rule of proof law without extensive exceptions and almost no argument which could not be run on the basis of some authority, so that simple reliance by civilian judges on civilian authorities might have had much the same effect in the equity jurisdiction, in terms of results observable in the records, as a complete absence of rules; and certainly, the law of proof in equity *as it existed in the seventeenth century* was primarily the result of developments in Chancery and Star Chamber at around the turn of the sixteenth and seventeenth centuries, and particularly under Thomas Egerton, Lord Ellesmere, Lord Keeper 1596-1603 and Chancellor 1603-1617.

---

91 *Forme et Certenty*, CUL MS Gg 2.31 ff 520r-551v, this chapter (*Testes et Probaciones et Iurando*) at ff 544r – 546v. The same mixture is found in the chapters *Testaments et Volunts*, *Suerties et charger de eux*, *Grants Commissions etc.*, *Limitation etc*, *Bankrupts*, *Fraus Dolus Fallatia Calliditas* and *Usurie;* the other thirteen chapters are wholly based on medieval common law authorities.

92 *HPC* ii 279. For other instances see below in the relevant chapters and ch 10 § 2.

93 Though case-law was used to some extent in continental systems at this period (see J. H. Baker ed. *Judicial Records, Law Reports, and the Growth of Case-Law* (Berlin, 1989)) the english civilians made reports only of ecclesiastical cases, which were not printed (Helmholz, *Roman Canon Law in Reformation England* (Cambridge, 1990) ch 3. The nearest approach in print is Gentili's *Hispanicae Advocationes* and in MS Caesar's annotations, discussed by A. Wijffels, 'Sir Julius Caesar's Notes on Admiralty Cases: An Alternative to Law Reporting' in C. Stebbings ed., *Law Reporting in Britain* (London, 1995). For the early equity reports see Macnair 'The Nature and Function of the Early Chancery Reports' also in Stebbings.

The problem of theorizing the relationship between equity proof (and common law evidence) and the learned laws cannot therefore be resolved simply on the basis that (as Langdell argued) canonists in the early Chancery brought their law with them from the church courts[94]. The relationship of the equity courts to the civilian jurisdictions was more complex; and even if undiluted civilian or canonist doctrine was applied at an early date, the law of proof as it appeared from the late sixteenth century looks more like a new departure, and one which went hand in hand with similar developments affecting the law of evidence to a jury. We are, in short, looking for borrowing of roman-canon proof principles which did not involve high-level civilian advocacy; and to which at least some common lawyers were party. Why and how could this happen?

Alan Watson has written extensively on problems both of the "Reception" of Roman law in continental Europe and of other instances both of complete and partial "transplants" of or "borrowing" from existing legal systems[95]. He argues, *inter alia,* that the practice of transplantation or borrowing is extremely common[96]; that it is commonly a response to perceived gaps or uncertainties in the existing law[97]; that it works to a considerable extent through the role of authority in law[98]; and that Roman law has been very much borrowed because of its division into more or less self-contained "blocks" which can, therefore, be received without unnecessarily disturbing the rest of the law[99].

The frequency of borrowing makes it easier to believe that the roman-canon proof concepts were borrowed, and what seems to be borrowed can be regarded as (though not part of the classical law) a self- contained block, i.e. the proof system developed in the mediæval canon law on the basis of the disorganised authorities on proofs in the *Corpus Iuris Civilis*. The difficulty is that the English common law was in this period itself a developed and structured body of thought[100], which also possessed its own proof concepts, viz. requiring the confession of the defendant on the pleadings, records or deeds pleaded, or the verdict of a jury. Both an

94 'The Development of Equity Pleading from Canon Law Procedure' in *Select Essays in Anglo-American Legal History* ii (Boston, 1908), 753. Cf also H. Coing, 'English Equity and the Denunciatio Evangelica of the Canon Law' (1955) 71 *LQR* 223-241, which similarly proceeds from the starting point of the clerical Chancellors.

95 *Legal Transplants* (Edinburgh, Scottish Academic Press, 1974); *The Making of the Civil Law* (Cambridge, Harvard UP, 1981), esp Chs 1-7; *Sources of Law, Legal Change and Ambiguity* (Edinburgh, Clark, 1984), esp Chs 2 & 3; *The Evolution of Law* (Oxford, Blackwell, 1985) esp Ch 3.

96 *Legal Transplants,* p 95; *Evolution,* Ch 3.

97 *Sources,* Chs 2 & 3; *Evolution,* Ch 3.

98 *Legal Transplants,* Ch 15; *Sources,* Ch 3; *Evolution,* pp 71ff.

99 *Making of the Civil Law,* Ch 2.

100 This point is taken as an explanation for the absence of a general reception of roman law in early modern England by Maitland, *English Law and the Renaissance,* Baker, *Introduction* to Spelman's Reports, Vol II, 94 SS at *24-28,* and Jenkins, 'Eighty Years On'.

argument for gaps or uncertainty in the law in this area, and one for regarding the learned laws as authoritative, therefore seem at first sight to be weak.

However, the picture changes if we abandon the modern legal-positivist idea of the common law as a fully autonomous system of law which took its authority solely from custom or the power of the king, and place the common law instead, as local positive law, within the general hierarchy of laws accepted in later medieval and early modern thought (divine law, natural law, law of nations, positive law); the framework certainly accepted by Fortescue[101], and arguably still accepted by Selden and Hale[102]. Within this framework, the basic ideas of the law of proof were considered to be of *divine law*, since they could be supported from the Bible, and as such binding on all tribunals whatever. Thus among european sources used by equity writers, Catellanius Cotta and Andreas Gaill both discuss the validity of customs and statutes varying proof rules, on the basis that some proof rules are of divine or natural law[103], and Robert Maranta says that in summary causes the judge cannot omit *probationes necessarias*: "*quia illae sunt de jure divino*", though on a fair number of points of detail he allows summary causes to be exceptions to proof rules[104]; in England in the 1590s Lancelot Andrewes justified the whole course of canon law procedure, including *ex officio* procedure, compulsion to confess, the use and required number of witnesses, and of presumptions, on the basis of divine law as found in the Bible, and Cosin developed a more limited argument along the same lines for the defence of *ex officio* procedure in parts of his *Apologie for Certain Proceedings Ecclesiasticall*[105]; and in the 1600s Ridley, and in the 1700s Wood, tell us that the rule requiring two witnesses followed divine law[106].

As "divine law" began to be replaced by a more general natural law concept drawn from the universal usages of nations, basic proof ideas found a place here, too. Thus the English civilian Robert Wiseman, writing in the 1650s, attributes to natural law the rejection of the evidence of children against their parents, the right to put the adverse party to his oath, the use of presumptions as well as proofs, commissions to examine witnesses not able to attend court, exceptions to witnesses and the requirement of two witnesses; Willem Groot's *De Principiis Juris Naturalis Enchiridion*, published in England in 1673, incorporates discussion of the basis of documentary evidence and the distinction between public and private documents; and Samuel Pufendorf's *De Jure Naturae et Gentium* discusses the oath,

---

101 N. Doe, *Fundamental Authority in Late Medieval English Law* (Cambridge, 1990).

102 Cromartie, *Sir Matthew Hale 1609-1676* (Cambridge, 1995), chs 1-3, 6-7.

103 Cotta 635 (private and public documents), 867 (witness' grounds of knowledge); Gaill ii Obs. 101 Nos 11-14 (testimony without oath).

104 217 No 10; exceptions to specific rules are found *passim* in this section.

105 Andrewes is printed in E. Lake, *Memoranda Touching the Oath Ex Officio* (London 1662) 67-89; Cosin, ii ch 15, iii 38-9, 48; & cf the argument of Dr. Davenant (undated) printed in Lake 60-66.

106 Ridley 191, "agreeably to the Law of God, and the Law of Nations"; Wood 316, "in initation of Divine law".

preference for documents over witnesses, exceptions to witnesses, the number required and hearsay[107].

This approach has two implications for the relationship of equity proof and common law evidence to the learned laws. The first concerns the justification of the equity jurisdictions themselves, and their interference with the common law; the second the availability of civilian proof concepts to common lawyers. A widely accepted theoretical basis for these new courts was the prerogative right and duty of the Crown to do justice: when justice was unobtainable through the ordinary courts and law, an appeal could be made to the sovereign or 'absolute' power of the king[108]. This meant that these courts were closely analogous to the summary procedure of the civil and canon laws, which also depended on an appeal to the 'absolute' power of the prince from his 'regulated' power[109]. This theory did not mean that the court was entitled to act wholly arbitrarily; in an early statement of the theory in 1469 Stillington C said that (as Maranta also says of summary procedure) natural law rules would apply[110]. To quote:

> "Sont 2 maners poyars et processes, *s. potentia ordinata & absoluta; ordinata* est lou un certain order est observe, come en ley positive, mes ley de nature *non habet certum ordinem,* mes per quecunque meane le verity poit estre conus, &c. *& ideo dicitur processus absolutus, &c. In lege naturae requiritur* ques les parties soient presentes, &c, ou que ils soient absentes per contumacie, cestascavoir, lou ils soient garnies & font defaut, &c, *& examinatio veritatis*".

This view of the equity jurisdiction has two corollaries. The first, as already indicated, is that the proof rules applied would be likely to be a simplified version of civilian proof doctrine, those elements of it which could be maintained to be of "natural" or "divine" law.

The second is more complex and concerns the interrelationship of the jurisdictions. In the first place, it tells us that these jurisdictions would be in principle supplementary to the existing common law jurisdictions. They would only intervene where the common law involved a denial of justice; and if the common law corrected itself, so that justice was available through regular means, the equity juris-

---

107 Wiseman, *Law of Laws: or, the Excellency of the Civil Law Above all Humane Laws whatsoever* (London, 1657) 11, 14, 15, 73; Groot, (Cambridge, 1673) Ch 19; Pufendorf, 1688 edition, cited here from facsimile reprint in the *Classics of International Law* series, Bk. v ch. 13 §§ 8-9.

108 The earliest explanation of this type is probably Fortescue's in *De Natura Legibus Naturae* c 24. More direct is Stillington C's statement in YB T 9 Ed 4 f 14 pl 9, below; cited in the core of the period Crompton 42v, *F&C* f 521v, and *Earl of Oxford's Case* (1615) 1 Ch Rep 1 at 15, BL Stowe MS 415 f 55v at f 59r.

109 K. Pennington, *The Prince and the Law 1200-1600* (Berkeley, 1993) Ch 5. The development of summary procedure in statutory criminal jurisdictions is discussed by J.G. Bellamy, *Criminal Law and Society in the Late Medieval and Tudor England* (Gloucester, 1984) ch 1.

110 YB T 9 Ed IV f 14 pl 9.

dictions would begin to follow the law in this point; the point made by More to the judges in the 1530s[111].

Secondly, a good deal of 'denial of justice' in the later medieval common law related to proof rules. If we look at the later medieval common law from the standpoint of a conception of a simplified version of roman-canon proof doctrine as natural law, the common law could appear to be consistent with this system in its broad outlines: judgment for a party required either a confession (on the pleadings), documents (records or deeds pleaded and produced in court), or a verdict (conceived as 12 unexceptionable witnesses). But this system, if it worked as it claimed to in theory, would be an extraordinarily rigid version of the old plenary procedure of the civil and canon laws: it required exact certainty in pleadings; there was no procedure for compulsion to confess; extrajudicial confessions had no value at all; there was no scope whatever for the cumulation of half proofs, and hence for the use of private documents or lesser presumptions; documents were in many cases conclusive; nothing less than local notoriety would produce a verdict.

Conversely, in practice Fortescue's (and later St German's)[112] theoretical claim that the jury were witnesses would not hold water: at best they were witnesses *de credere*, a critique made by civilians against the Norman *verité de pays* (jury) in the fourteenth century[113]; in reality, they were judges of fact completely unregulated by any rules of proof and notoriously liable to bias and corruption, a critique made by More (himself a common lawyer) in defending canon law procedure in 1533[114].

Equity courts relieved against these defects of the common law. But if the common lawyers could reform their own procedure and proof rules, they would remove the denial of justice which was the justification for equitable intervention. The instruments for change lay ready to hand: all that was necessary was to displace more matters onto trial by jury on the general issue, to reconceptualise the jury as a trier of facts, and on that basis to apply to it the requirement that a judge must act *secundum allegata et probata* and some 'natural law' version of proof concepts. There is no need, on this account, to suppose that the common lawyers took proof rules *from* the equity jurisdictions; they were perfectly capable of citing civilian or theological sources for themselves at this level. For example, when Fortescue in the 1460s defended jury trial he argued that it was not inconsistent with natural

111 Roper, *Life of More*, quoted by T.F.T. Plucknett, *A Concise History of the Common Law* (5th ed., London, 1956) 687; Guy, *More* 87-9.

112 Fortescue, *De Laudibus*, 74; St German, *Salem & Bizance*, in J.A. Guy et al. ed., *The Complete Works of Saint Thomas More* x (New Haven, 1987), 360-361.

113 R. Besnier, 'La Dégénérescence des caractères Normands des preuves dans la procédure civile après la Rédaction du Grand Coutumier' (1959) 37 *Rev. Hist. de droit francais et étranger* 48-61 at 52-57.

114 *The Debellacyon of Salem & Bizance* in *Complete Works* x, at 134-5 (judges more trustworthy than juries), 149 (jury are not witnesses).

law to require a higher number of witnesses, i.e. the twelve "witnesses" who were the jurors[115]; in the early 1630s St German and More carried on an intelligent polemic on the canon law in relation to proof of heresy[116]; in *Reniger v Fogossa* (1551) Bradshaw AG argues from divine law for the application of the requirement of two witnesses, and hence the rule that their depositions must agree[117]; Coke in the Fourth Institute cites to civil law sources, either without attribution or *via* Bracton[118]; in *AG v Mico* (1659) Hardres argues from divine and natural law for *nemo tenetur seipsum prodere*[119].

If, however, a development of this type was carried to its logical conclusion, the result would be that the jury was simply a fully regulated trier of fact: and then it would make sense to turn jurors into professionals. Thus the civilian Sir Edward Lake argued in 1662 that "The meaning of *Legalis homo,* to qualifie him to be of a Jury, is not, nor formerly was, meant to be onely a man of 40s *per annum,* but to be at least in some good measure *in legibus peritis*, as some are of opinion, and so as it were a kind of assistant to the Judge"[120]. This did not, in fact, happen; but the story of why it did not is not a simple one of the intellectual strength of the common law tradition, as the absence of a general 'Reception' of substantive civilian doctrine and methods may be.

To tie all this together: the nature of the equity courts shows that civilians and their ideas were not an alien marginal element of english legal thought in the early modern period. Questions of proof and procedure were critical to relations between the common law, the learned laws and equity; but this does not mean that the equity procedure was 'simply' civilian, like that of the Admiralty or the church courts. Rather, the originally summary character of the equity procedure meant that basic roman-canon proof concepts could be applied there on the justification that they were of divine or natural law. The same reasoning could justify equitable interference with or departure from common law proof procedure. This concept, present in the early equity courts, tended to die out as common lawyers gained the upper hand; leaving behind a residual concept of the equity procedure as 'civilian' in a general sense, but in practice governed by rules and authorities specific to the equity courts. However, reasoning from divine or natural law could be equally applied by common lawyers to introduce proof concepts into the operation of trial by jury; and they could be motivated to do so in order to eliminate the need for parties to go to equity.

115 *De Laudibus Legum Angliae* c 32.

116 The complete exchange is printed in *The Complete Works of Saint Thomas More* vols ix (ed. J.B. Trapp (New Haven, 1979)) x (above).

117 (M1551) 1 Plowd 1 at 8.

118 At p 279; e.g. D. 22.5.12, cited from Bracton Book 5 f 359.

119 Below Ch 2 § 2 (2) n 152 and text there.

120 *Notes Touching Alteration of Some Laws* (London, 1662; appended to *Memoranda Touching the Oath ex Officio*) 117.

This theoretical approach provides, I hope, a context for the discussion of the development of the rules in the following chapters; and the discussion a test of the theoretical approach. In places the discussion is necessarily technical and detailed: the proof of the theoretical pudding is in the technical eating.

III. A note on the scope and sources of the study

I argued earlier that the starting point for an enquiry into the origins of the law of evidence has to be citable sources: cases, statutes and treatises. This does not imply that the study of other evidence for judicial practice has no place; it is merely that we need first to have some idea what lawyers thought was law, before the evidence for judicial practice really begins to make sense. The same methodological point holds for the relationship between equity proof and civilian proof doctrine.

The core materials used in this study are therefore reported cases and treatise literature relating to the courts of equity between the accession of Elizabeth I in 1558 and the death of Queen Anne in 1714. The reason for beginning with the reign of Elizabeth is simply the availability of the sources used. Systematic reporting of cases in Chancery began in the 1590s; though one of the earliest collections of reports, Lambarde's printed in *Cary* and *Choyce Cases in Chancery*, looks backwards to the 1550s, and there are occasional cases in equity courts in the later Year Books and earlier nominate reports, and some equity treatise literature (particularly Caesar's *Ancient State* for the Requests, Hudson's *Star Chamber* for that court, and the manuscript treatise *Forme et Certenty* for the Chancery) refer to earlier decisions in the records of the equity courts. Systematic reporting of Star Chamber cases begins at the same period, but less of this material is in print[121]. My research has been primarily focussed on the printed reports, with only limited use of manuscript materials (chiefly early MS Chancery reports). It may well be possible in the future to correct the chronology proposed in this book and some details by a more extensive use of manuscript sources; but, as with non-doctrinal evidence for judicial practice, the first step is to establish a framework from the printed materials.

The same consideration applies to the unpublished records of the courts[122]. In Chancery, these formed the basis of some varieties of early Chancery reports[123],

---

121 I have used J. Hawarde, *Les Reportes del Cases in Camera Stellata* ed. & trans. W.P. Baildon (privately printed, 1894), and cases encountered in the general printed series. For MS Star Chamber series see e.g. Baker, *English Legal Manuscripts in the USA* ii Nos 380, 457, 458, 538c, 615, 938, 1006g, 1108, 1248, 1249, 1520m.

122 For discussion of these see Bryson, *Exchequer* for that court; Bell for the Wards; Guy, *The Court of Star Camber and its records to the Reign of Elizabeth I* (London, 1985) for Star Chamber; H. Horwitz, *Chancery Equity Records and Proceedings 1600-1800* (London, 1995) for the Chancery.

123 See Macnair, 'The Nature and Function of the Early Chancery Reports' in Stebbings ed. *Law Reporting in Britain* ch 8.

and these and other published extracts from the records[124] make it clear that they contain valuable information about procedural doctrine in Chancery. However, the sheer volume of the material in the records precludes their use for my present purpose[125].

I have chosen the end of the reign of Anne as a convenient stopping point for the survey of case-law because by this time the law of evidence at common law clearly had a definite existence, reflected in the fact that Gilbert's *Evidence* was probably written during this reign and Nelson's *Law of Evidence* was published shortly after it. In using treatise literature I have gone a little further forward, using materials published later, but which deal in the main with later seventeenth and early eighteenth century authority, and I have occasionally discussed cases from the 1730s which are referred to by Wigmore.

I have referred to common law authority where it is relevant to the argument, but I have not usually treated this material in as much detail as the equity material. The dominance of the Chancery materials means that I have been primarily concerned with civil, rather than criminal matters. For both these reasons I have made only very limited use of the *State Trials* and of the statutes, both of which offer considerable amounts of material on evidence at common law in the later seventeenth century.

The second substantial source for equity procedure and proof doctrine is treatises and practice books[126]. Here, as with reporting, there is a marked watershed in the time of Egerton. "Before Egerton" treatments of the equity jurisdiction fall into two classes. The first class are discussions in the tradition derived from the books *Diversity de Courtz et lour Jurisdictions* (printed 1526): Richard Crompton's *LAucthoritie & Jurisdiction des Courts de la Maiestie la Roigne* (1594), William West's introductions to the court forms and precedents in *The Second Part of Symboleography* (1594), William Lambarde's *Archeion* (c. 1600; printed 1635), and, rather later, Sir Edward Coke's *Fourth Institute* (written in the 1630s; published 1644). These treatments relied basically on authority in the Year Books, with in Coke's case some additional use of records. The second class are contributions to the controversial literature about the proper scope of the equity jurisdiction, starting with Christopher St German's *Doctor and Student,* the *Replication* to this of the anonymous 'Serjeant at law', and St German's *Little Treatise*. *Doctor and Student* was incorporated into later common lawyers' treatments of equity, and Ed-

---

124 E.g. Monro.

125 The records of the equity courts have been used to generate valuable broadly *statistical* information bearing on features of the jurisdiction, e.g. by Metzger, *Kanzleigericht*, Guy, *Chancellor's Court* and *More,* and most recently on the Chancery by a team led by Henry Horwitz, for which see *Chancery Equity Records and Proceedings* (above). However, to add *doctrinal* information to that provided by the reports and treatises would require a different type of search, precluding e.g. sampling techniques.

126 Bibliographical details for the texts used in this book will be found in the Bibliography.

mund Hake's *Epieikeia* (c. 1600[127]) is in the same tradition. Committed to a wider view of the jurisdiction were Sir Julius Caesar's *Ancient State* (1597) for the Requests and the anonymous treatise *Forme et Certenty* (1600s) for the Chancery, both of which used the records of the equity courts to defend claims based on prescription to areas of jurisdiction contested by 'pro-common law' writers. Apart from *Forme et Certenty,* none of these books have more than occasional points to make about equity procedure and proof.

'After Egerton' there appeared a new genre, the practice book or treatise founded on Egerton's decisions (with later decisions and Orders of Court added to a greater or lesser extent). The classic instances are *The Proceedings of the High Court of Chancery* (1649) which was bound with the subject index to precedents attributed to Tothill, and *The Practice of the High Court of Chancery Unfolded* (1651). Within the same framework are the treatments of Chancery in Powell's *Attorney's Academy* (1623) and Sheppard's *Faithful Counsellor* (1651). The same heavy dependence on Egerton is found in Hudson's *Star Chamber* (1621) and Norburie's *Abuses and Remedies of the Chancery* from the same period; as late as 1694 the *Praxis Almae Curiae Cancellariae* attributed to W. Brown is founded on Egerton's decisions, and Lord Nottingham's *Practice* and *Prolegomena,* dating to the early 1670s, share the same conceptual framework, though they are more systematic and make extensive use of contemporary cases.

The latest works I have used represent another shift. Gilbert's *Forum Romanum,* from the 1720s, uses civilian treatments of procedure as an explanatory framework for Chancery procedure; and the *Treatise of Equity* attributed to Henry Ballow (1737)[128] uses a natural law theory of contract as the basis for the description of substantive equity doctrine and to some extent of proof doctrine.

The character of the equity sources means that our direct evidence for what the english civilians thought about equity proof is largely limited to the fact that they thought that equity procedure was civilian in character, and that Caesar thought it was summary. To compare equity proof concepts with civilian ones, I have therefore used two groups of sources. The first is english civilian literature; the second is continental civilian authors who we can show to have been used by writers on equity procedure or evidence at common law.

The first of these groups, the english civilian literature, is markedly patchy in its treatment of proof questions. The fifteenth century english canonist William Lyndwood's *Provinciale,* a collection of Canterbury provincial constitutions with glosses, makes brief reference to some points on proof; it was printed in 1679. The *Reformatio Legum Ecclesiasticarum,* a draft for a Reformed code of canon law dating from the 1550s, published in 1571, contains outline sections on proof. Probably

127 Ed. D.E.C. Yale, New Haven, 1953.

128 Simpson, "The Rise and Fall of the Treatise" (1981) 48 U Chic LR 632 suggests that Gilbert may have written this book, which is usually attributed to Ballow, but it seems to me to be stylistically very different to most of the work attributed to Gilbert.

the major English work on civilian procedure was Francis Clerke's *Praxis*, dating from the 1590s, widely circulated in MS, and the sections on the Court of Arches printed in 1666 and that on the Admiralty in 1667[129]; but the book is essentially a collection of court forms for proctors with only limited doctrinal explanation. Some further explanatory material is added in Henry Conset's *Practice of the Spiritual, or Ecclesiastical Courts* (1685), which is basically an English version of Clerke[130]. Thomas Wood's *New Institute of the Imperial or Civil Law* (1704) has chapters on proof and procedure, and John Ayliffe's alphabetically arranged *Parergon Iuris Canonici Anglicani* (1727) covers various matters of proof and procedure under distinct titles.

There are also some more detailed discussions of specific points. Henry Swinburne's *Brief Treatise of Testaments and Last Wills* (1590) contains a discussion of witnesses and exceptions to them. Richard Cosin's *Apologie of Certain Proceedings Ecclesiasticall* (1593), Sir Edward Lake's *Considerations touching the Oath Ex Officio* (1663) and the arguments by Lancelot Andrewes and Dr Davenant printed by Lake, are contributions to the debate on *ex officio* prosecution and self-incrimination which also touch on some other matters of proof. The second book of Alberico Gentili's *Hispanicae Advocationes* (1613) concerns mainly questions of proof, but which are covered is dictated by the needs of advocacy in the particular cases.

Beyond these sources are very outline references to basic points in *Principia Quaedam et Axiomata ex Iure Civile Sparsim Collecta*, an anonymous alphabetical collection of maxims published in 1581, and in Sir Thomas Ridley's *A View of the Civil and Ecclesiasticall Law* (1607), William Fulbecke's *A Parallele or Conference of the Civill Law, the Canon Law and the Common Law...* (1618) and Robert Wiseman's *Law of Laws* (1657), which were propagandist accounts of the law for lay consumption[131], and Richard Zouch's *Elementa Iurisprudentiae* and *Descriptio Iuris & Iudicii Ecclesastici* (1631) and *Specimen Quaestionum Iuris Civilis* (1653), which were teaching books of a fairly basic character.

The continental sources used by equity and common lawyers were not much more detailed in character. I have used mainly six books. Three were used by the author of *Forme et Certenty:* Catellanius Cotta's *Memoralia*, first printed 1511, an alphabetical collection of particular points[132]; the *Iudiciarii Processus Compen-*

129 Discussed in R.H. Helmholz, *Canon Law in Reformation England* (Cambridge, 1990) 128-132.

130 Oughton's *Ordo Judiciorum* (1738) is a Latin edition of Clerke, revised by one of the MSS and rearranged according to Oughton's conceptions.

131 This is also true of Wood and probably of Ayliffe; but these books go into rather more detail on proof.

132 *Dizionario Biographico Degli Italiani* xxx (Rome, 1984) 464-5, gives the date of 1545, which seems more consistent with the other biographical information given there. However, Lipenius, *Bibliotheca Realis Iuridica* (Leipzig, 1757) gives an edition of 1511, and this is corroborated by the British Library Catalogue and the union catalogues of Oxford and Cambridge college libraries.

dium attributed (probably falsely) to Andreas Alciati (1536)[133]; and the *Speculum Aureum* of Robert Maranta (d. c. 1540). Of the other three, Hermann Vulteius' *Jurisprudentia Romana* (1590) was used by West in the introductory part of his *Symboleographia*[134]. The section *de Iuramenti forma* in Diego Covarruvias y Leyva's *In Constitutionis Secundae ex Rubrica de Pactis* lib. vi was used by Hale in his *Pleas of the Crown;* I have also used the same author's discussions of witnesses in his *Variarum resolutionum* and chapters on documents and witnesses in his *Quaestiones Practicae* (1568) (which english civilians used to annotate MSS of Clerke[135]). Andreas Gaill's *Practicarum Observationum* was used by Gilbert in his *Forum Romanum* (another significant source was Maranta).

I have made limited use of three books of the 'natural law' approach, more relevant to the latter end of the period. An edition of Willem Groot's *De Principiis Iuris Naturalis Enchiridion* was printed at Cambridge in 1673. Samuel Pufendorf's *De Jure Naturae et Gentium* was translated into english in the early eighteenth century and heavily used by eighteenth century english lawyers. Jean Domat's *Les Lois Civiles en Leur Ordre Naturel* (1689-97) was published in an english translation by William Strahan in 1722 and can thereafter be found cited by english lawyers (including, in one instance at least, on proof in equity).

Beyond these sources I have contented myself with following up direct citations as far as I can. *Forme et Certenty* refers to the *Summa Angelica de Casibus Conscientiae* of Angelus de Clavasio, to Phillipus Decius *De Regulis Iuris*, (probably) to D. Antonius Corsetus' *De iureiurando et iuramenti privilegiis*, and to one of the numerous books of *Singularia* (alphabetical collections); and among wider sources, to John of Salisbury's *Policraticus,* the Visigothic laws, the Constitutions of the German emperors, and to the Bible. Gilbert refers in the proof section of the *Forum Romanum* to Amator Rodriquez' *Modus et forma examinandi processum in causis civilibus* (1615); to Dionysus Gothofredus' edition of the *Corpus Iuris*; to Johannes Arnold Corvinus' *Digesta per aphorismos strictim explicata*; to Daniel Venatorius' *Analysis Methodica Iuris Pontifici* (1579); to the *Institutiones Iuris Canonici* of Joannes Paulus Lancelottus[136] and references I have not been able to "trace to 'Peers' and 'Nevius in Nov. 189' ". In his *Evidence* he uses direct references to the *Digest,* Corvinus, and "Vinnius 32.21 in Justinian"[137].

---

133 *Dizionario Biographico Degli Italiani* ii (Rome, 1960) s.n. at 73 says that the attribution is probably false.

134 This point is made by Wood, ix-x.

135 Helmholz, above n 37.

136 I am indebted to Prof. Nörr for the explication of this reference, which appears in Gilbert as "Lanul Justif of Canon Law".

137 The last of these references does not appear to be either to Arnoldus Vinnius' *Justiniani Institutionum* (Amsterdam, 1669), or to his *In quattuor libros Institutionum imperialium commentarius* (Amsterdam, 1692).

These references are pretty eclectic. What they probably indicate most notably is an orientation towards collections, summaries and practitioners' books rather than major academic discussions. Some bias towards practitioners' books has been found by Alain Wijffels in his study of law books in Cambridge libraries[138]; but the range of references here is far less than in english civilian literature. It may therefore represent the view of the civil law of fairly open-minded common lawyers who would have said of themselves what Egerton said in *Calvin's Case*, that

> Whatsoever I have spoken or shall happen to speake of the civile lawe; or whatsoever I shall cite out of any writer of that law, I pray favour of my masters that professe it. I acknowledge that law to be ancient and generall in many parts of the world; and I reverence the professors of it, as men of great learning, wisedome, and iudgement. I professe it not; I have learned little of it; but in that little I have found that in the reall and essentiall partes of iustice, the civile and the common lawe doe in many things concurre, though they differ much in the forme and manner of proceeding ...[139]

The fact that this knowledge may have been superficial does not mean that it did not leave a profound mark on equity proof and on the common law of evidence.

---

138 'Law Books at Cambridge 1500-1640' in P. Birks ed., *The Life of the Law* (London, 1993) ch 5 at 64-5.

139 *Case of the Post-Nati* (1608) 2 St. Tr. 559 at 673. Holdsworth, *HEL* v, 277, quotes this passage selectively to increase the distance between Egerton and the civilians.

Chapter Two

Allegations and Confessions

In modern work it is conventional to separate out the law of evidence from its procedural context – except insofar as trial by jury is said to allow the existence of the rules[1]. This separation is, however, in large part dependent on the assumption of trial by jury, and can be quite misleading outside the context of the criminal trial. In modern english civil procedure, pleadings define what must and what can be proved and who must prove it; discovery and interrogatories furnish means of settling disputes of fact which are as important as the evidence ultimately led at trial[2]. The same considerations apply to proof in the early modern period. Pleadings defined the scope of proofs, in ways which differed fundamentally between the common and the civil law; and the compulsion of parties to plead on oath, found in civilian doctrine and in equity, furnished a means of settling disputes of fact by compelling a confession. In these matters equity was not identical to civilian doctrine, but it was closer to civilian doctrine than to the common law. Some rules about confessions, moreover, appear in equity well before they appear at law. In this chapter I will explore these two areas.

I. *Secundum allegata et probata:* Variance from the bill

Civilian doctrine held that the judge must decide *secundum allegata et probata.*[3] This tag could be used in three senses, one of which is peculiar to England. The first sense (*secundum probata*) is that the judge is bound by the law of proof: he is not to give judgement except upon proved facts. The second sense (*secundum alle-*

---

1 Thayer, 4, explicitly argues that this separation is necessary; Carter, *Cases and Statutes on Evidence*, 3-4, sees it as problematic.

2 Even in modern English criminal procedure, in practice a very large proportion of the caseload of the criminal courts is dealt with by police interrogation leading to a confession which is then either repeated as a plea of guilty or led as a critical item of evidence. See Ian Bryan, *Interrogation and Confession: A Study of Progress, Process and Practice* (Aldershot, 1997).

3 Cotta 443-4, *Principia Quaedam* 20, and Zouch *SQ* cl. 9 No. 8 (Sig D2v). The medieval origin and history of this maxim is discussed by K.W. Nörr, *Zur Stellung des Richters im Gelehrten Prozess der Frühzeit: Iudex secundum allegata non secundum conscientiam iudicat* (Munich, 1967).

gata) is that the parties' proofs are limited by their allegations, i.e. the judge is to give judgment only on matters alleged in the pleadings, disregarding proofs which varied from those allegations. The local English sense is that the system is, unlike the common law, not a formulary one: the plaintiff alleges facts and seeks relief on them, rather than, as at common law, selecting a particular form of action[4].

The practical conclusion from the first sense of *secundum allegata et probata* is the law of proof itself. The practical conclusion from the second is limitations on the ability of parties to introduce new matter at a late stage of the proceedings[5]. The principle involved was shared with the common law: St German says that the common law judges *secundum allegata et probata,* that is *secundum placitata et triata,* but this is questionable in conscience (equity)[6]. In fact, the late medieval and early modern common law was more rigorous in this respect than the civilians. The common law procedure was begun by a writ of summons (citation in civilian terms) which, unlike the civilian citation, specified the cause of action.[7] Variance of subsequent pleadings or evidence from the writ was fatal to the plaintiff' action. The plaintiff's count or declaration (comparable to the civilians' libel) and subsequent pleadings on both sides, once enrolled, all had the same preclusive effect and were non-amendable, subject to very limited exceptions. They were required to conform to very high levels of certainty and formality. In the pleadings, anything not explicitly denied was taken to be confessed, and if the parties pleaded specially, they were required to dispute only a single issue of fact or law.[8] As to proof, in the absence of a default judgment at law could not be given except on the basis of a confession on the pleadings, a document tendered to the court, a jury verdict or some other special mode of proof.[9]

4 Cf. Baker *IELH* Ch 4.

5 There is a comparative discussion of these issues, under the heading "Sequence, Preclusion and Contingent Cumulation" in Millar's "Prolegomena", Engelmann 27-39.

6 *D&S* 116-7.

7 This difference was regarded as a matter of principle in the period. Parliament legislated against general citation in the church courts in 1414 (Stat. 2 Hen 5 Stat. 1 c 3, requiring a copy of the libel to be delivered with the citation); the issue of a *subpoena* without a previously submitted bill was regarded as an abuse in Star Chamber under Henry VIII (Guy, *Cardinal's Court* 82) and in the Elizabethan Chancery (Jones, 191-2) and in the seventeenth century objections were made to the bill of Middlesex procedure in King's Bench on this ground (13 Car 2 Stat 2 c 2; there is some discussion in Nottingham, *Practice* Title 18 and the Appendix by North, Nottingham *TT* 169-174 at 172, where the argument is characterised as a "specious pretence"). The civilian sources, on the other hand, say that citation ought to come *before* the submission of the libel. (below n. 12).

8 Holdsworth *HEL* ix, 274-5.

9 This point is obscured in the secondary literature by the authors' focus on trial by jury as a quasi-judicial process. It is also an absolutely elementary point of the type of which direct evidence is unlikely. But it seems to be taken for granted, e.g. in arguments in error as to the sufficiency of special verdicts: *Hitchins d Nosworthy v Basset* (1688-92) Comb. 90, 2 Show. KB 537, 3 Mod. 203, 2 Salk. 592, error in HL (1694) Show PC 146, 2 Show. KB 555; and compare also Ellis, counsel for the prisoners', argument in *Bushell's Case* (1670) 1 Freem 1

The civilians recognised two forms of procedure, plenary or *solennis ordo,* and summary; neither involved the same rigorous application of *secundum allegata* as the common law[10]. Though Caesar tells us that the equity procedure in the Requests conformed to the civilian summary procedure,[11] 'summary procedure' itself could have several meanings, and some issues are clarified by consideration of the plenary procedure.

The plenary procedure in theory opened with a general citation of the defendant, which committed the plaintiff to nothing.[12] The plaintiff then submitted a libel, which stated the cause of action; like a common law declaration, this was required to be clear and certain[13]. The next step in the procedure was *litis contestatio*, in which the parties appeared and the defendant formally contested the litigation. Down to *litis contestatio* the libel was generally amendable, subject to payment of costs. After *litis contestatio* it was only amendable in special cases.[14] After *litis contestatio* the parties would submit *positions* which stated the essential points of fact in their case. The adverse party was required to answer the positions on oath, subject to certain exceptions (discussed below section II.1.(a)).[15] An admission in these answers would be a judicial confession and as such conclusive against the party confessing, though there were exceptions to this rule.[16] Conversely, the allegations of fact in the positions themselves were (again subject to exceptions) to be treated as confessions by the party proponent: *qui ponit fatetur.*[17] Once the answers

at 4 (not in other reports): "the judge is to go *secundum allegata et probata*, notwithstanding his own private knowledge, Plow. 83; but if the jury know the falsity of their evidence, they are not bound by it; & for that reason they come *de vicineto*. The judge is bound by estoppels, but the jury is not"); and Roger North's annotation to his brother's commonplace on witnesses, printed Macnair 'A Fragment' at 144, (argument that the House of Lords as judges must decide *secundum allegata et probata*).

10 There are convenient general discussions of mediaeval church court procedure in R.H. Helmholz, *Marriage Litigation in Medieval England* (Cambridge, 1974), ch 4, N. Adams and C. Donahue Jr., *Select Cases from Ecclesiastical courts in the Province of Canterbury c 1200-1301* (Selden Soc vol 95) *Introduction, 37-59*, Jane E. Sayers, 'The Procedure of the courts of the Judges Delegate' in id., *Law and Records in Medieval England* (London, 1988) and James A. Brundage, *Medieval Canon Law* (London, 1995) at 129-136, 139-150; some of the controversies around summary procedure are discussed by Pennington, *The Prince and the Law* chs 4-7.

11 Above Ch 1 n 63.

12 Wood 329; Ayliffe 351. Maranta 478.26 says that in theory citation precedes the libel, but in (Neapolitan) practice the libel is usually submitted to the judge at the time of the request for citation.

13 Maranta 477 *Additio* Nos 22-3; Cotta 538-542; Vulteius 473r; Wood 329.

14 Cotta 541-2; Gaill ii Obs. 74 Nos. 4, 8; Vulteius 474v, 492v-493r; Clerke 276; Conset 77, 82; Ayliffe 350, 351.

15 'Alciatus' *De Positionibus*; Maranta 547-551; Vulteius 479v; Clerke 36, 70-71; Conset 87, 99; Wood 330; Ayliffe 65. On inadequate answers, Clerke 277-281, Conset 101ff.

16 Below § 2 (*2*) n 178.

17 Below § 2 (*3*) (a) nn 196-7.

had been received, the parties produced *articles* containing the allegations of fact which had not been confessed, and these defined the scope of the proof.[18] The positions and the answers to them thus *prima facie* closed the issues of fact. However, new positions and articles could be added even after witnesses had been examined and their depositions published, down to the *conclusion in the cause* which was a formal act closing the issues before judgment.[19]

In this system, the parties' allegations did limit their subsequent pleading and proofs to some extent: thus, for example, Clerke says that it was possible to object to irrelevant articles and to obtain costs for the wasted costs of proof they entailed, and Gaill that a deposition irrelevant to the articles was to be rejected[20]. But there was much more flexibility than in the common law procedure. The requirements of certainty in pleading were less firm, there was no rule against multiple issues, and the availability of amendments to libels and of new positions and articles meant that, though matters proved must be alleged somehow, errors at an early stage of pleading were less likely to be fatal to a good case than at common law.

The summary procedure required neither a libel nor a formal *litis contestatio,* and all that was required, in terms of certainty of the plaintiff's allegations, was that the defendant should be given enough information to decide whether or not to confess the action.[21] Maranta in one place, and Ayliffe, say that a *petition* is required for this purpose,[22] but Maranta elsewhere says that the positions and articles stand in the place of the libel, and that the current practice in Naples is simply to use articles; if the defendant confesses an article, it is then deemed to be a position.[23] He also tells us that in summary procedure the sentence is not required to conform to the original libel or petition[24].

Clerke (and following him Conset) offer an account of the practice of the Court of Arches and of the Admiralty which makes this sharp distinction between plenary and summary procedure less clear. The libel, positions and articles were rolled up into a single document called a *libellus articulatus.*[25] There was, however, a formal *litis contestatio* and following this the plaintiff would petition that the libel be treated as articles. In summary causes the the formal *litis contestatio* was replaced by offering the libel with a petition for summary procedure against which the defendant's proctor would enter formal dissent.[26] The rolled-up *libellus articu-*

18 'Alciatus' 205v; Andrewes 79; Clerke 109.

19 'Alciatus' 192r; *Reformatio* 228 c 12; Clerke 208-9.

20 Clerke 109; Gaill ii Obs. 105 No. 4.

21 Cotta 34, 540; Maranta 218.12; Gaill i Obs. 6 pr.; Ayliffe 351.

22 Maranta 218.12, Ayliffe 351.

23 549 Nos 4 & 5.

24 222-3 No. 33.

25 Clerke 36. The *libellus articulatus* is also discussed by Gaill ii Obs. 79 Nos. 1-3 and Vulteius 471v, so this aspect of the practice was not unique to the English civilian courts.

26 Clerke 40; Conset 178-9.

latus makes the plenary procedure more 'summary'; but it is retained in the summary procedure, making this more 'plenary' than the summary procedure described by Maranta. There was also, however, a really summary version of criminal procedure *per inquisitionem* employed by Archdeacons' Officials in minor criminal cases. Here the defendant would be cited on the basis of *fama* (public suspicion), interrogated, and if he did not confess put to compurgation.[27] This is so summary that issues of variance from pleadings and of sufficiency of proof have effectively disappeared.

How far did *secundum allegata et probata* apply in the English equity procedure? Though the tag is applied to the Chancery in the sources, in some cases the application has the "local" meaning that the equity procedure is not formulary[28].

As far as the first application of the tag, *secundum probata*, is concerned, the burden of the argument of this book as a whole is that in the early modern period proof was generally thought to be required and a version of the rules of proof generally thought to apply. The point is, moreover, the sort of point which is so basic that there is unlikely to be clear direct evidence for it. However, there is some evidence that in the later mediaeval period and down to the 1530s the tag was thought not to apply to Chancery. In 1469 Stillington C is reported as saying that

> home ne serra prejudice, per mispleder ou per defaut de forme, mes solonque la verity de son matter, & nous avomus adjudger *secundum conscientiam, & non secundum allegata,* car si home suppose per bill que un ad fait tort a luy, & le defendant ne dit rien, si nous avomus conusans que il n'ad fait tort al plaintif, il ne recovera rien.[29]

This statement seems to contain the claim that the Chancellor is entitled to act on personal knowledge ("si... le defendant ne dit rien... & nous avomus conusans que il n'ad fait tort...", and St German suggested that the Chancellor could make a decree on the basis of personal knowledge[30]. Some continuance of this view of the Chancellor as "judge in conscience" is suggested by the practice of examining parties and witnesses *ad informandam conscientiam judicis*[31] used in the later six-

27 Ingram, *Church Courts, Sex and Marriage 1570-1640,* (Cambridge, 1987) 51-2; compare the secular statutory procedure 'by examination' discussed by Bellamy, *Criminal Law and Society* ch 1.

28 Crompton 42b; West B2; *Earl of Oxford's Case* (M1615) 1 Ch R 1 at 15, Stowe 415 f 55b at 59.

29 YB T 9 Ed 4 14, pl 9. The remainder of the passage is quoted above Ch 1 n 109 and text there. This statement was frequently quoted in the late sixteenth and early seventeenth century: Crompton 42b, West B2; F&C f 521v; *Earl of Oxford's Case* (cited previous note).

30 SGCS 120. At 121, however, St German explains the point in terms of the limits of *secundum allegata,* i.e. the possibility of changing the allegations to fit the proofs, and it is possible that this is also what is meant by Stillington C's statement: i.e., "nous avomus conusans" because in spite of the defendant's failure to plead, the plaintiff's case is disproved on the proofs.

31 Jones pp 250-2. Egerton characterised the practice as corresponding to the suppletory oath, and said it was only to be used on special points of doubt: *Downes(?) v Cooper* (T1598)

teenth and early seventeenth centuries[32]. However, St German also says that proof is required[33], and that it is safest for the judge to decide according to the proofs[34]; and Metzger says that in Wolsey's time decrees were invariably said to be founded on evidence and witnesses[35]. Hudson tells us that the Star Chamber "ought to punish nothing but what is *allegatum et probatum* by testimony"[36]; and in the seventeenth century authorities in general, as will appear below, proof or presumption seems to be required.

The second sense of the tag, *secundum allegata,* is a more specific problem. How far could the parties depart from their initial pleadings, or could decrees be made on matter proved but not alleged on the pleadings? As already indicated, the common law approach was rigorous: departures in pleading and variance of the evidence from the issue were fatal[37]. The civilians, as already indicated, maintained the principle that decision must be *secundum allegata* but allowed amendment of the libel and the introduction of new positions and articles, subject in the summary procedure to judicial discretion.

The position in equity seems to have differed as between the bill and the answer, the answer having much greater force as a confession and on oath: this is discussed later in this chapter, section 2.2. As to variance from the bill, the position seems closer to the civilians' approach. There is evidence that the *secundum allegata* principle was accepted, but amendments were allowed and there was a substantial degree of judicial discretion in the application of the rules. There is some evidence

---

Observations f 438r No. 16, and fuller discussion of the point *Observations* ff 444v-445r No. 59. In *Seed(?) v Pike(?)* (T1598) *Observations* f 438v No 16 Gawdy J seems to have been prepared to read to himself an affidavit to a material fact omitted from the depositions, and Coventry *arg* is reported as calling this testimony *ad informandam conscientiam Iudicis. Observations* f 464v Egerton is reported as saying that where a cause is referred to a Master to hear and determine, the Master also has the power to examine witnesses *ad informandam conscientiam* provided that they are not to be published if examined after publication in the original cause.

32 Cf also *Mynn v Cobb* (H1603/4) Cary 25, *full* proof necessary to make a precedent; *Lady Bodmin v Vandenbendy* (H1685) 1 Vern 356, Jeffreys C, reference to a Master to take examinations as to matters of equity suggested but not proved; but the bill was eventually dismissed by Somers C ((T1683) 1 Vern 179, Lord Guilford, (H1685) 2 Ch Cas 172, (M1696) Pre Ch 65, 2 Freem 211, Somers C, (1697) Show PC 69, HL, (M1709) 1 Comyns 185, CP, all not SP).

33 D&S pp 108-9.

34 SGCS 120

35 'The Last Phase of the Mediaeval Chancery' in A. Harding ed., *Law Making and Law Makers in British History* (London, 1980). "Evidence" at this period, as conjugated with witnesses, probably means documents: above Ch 1 n. 3. The *secundum allegata et probata* formula is to be found in the entry of a decree from 1545: Monro 328.

36 79, "unless the party will voluntarily confess it"; & cf *Parsons v Herne* (H1593/4) Hawarde 5, Star Ch., "pregnant and sufficient proof" required in this court, *per* reporter; proofs *luce clariores* & witnesses *omni exceptione maiores,* per Lord Buckhurst.

37 On departures in pleading, Holdsworth HEL IX 294-5; on variance, ib. 304-5.

of evolution in the period. In 1469 the bill is said not to be demurrable for uncertainty because "il nest forsque petition"[38], which assumes that english bill procedure is a variant of the summary procedure, as was suggested in Chapter 1; but the amendment rules, discussed below, are close to the rules for amendment of the libel in the plenary procedure, and the later seventeenth century sees the disappearance of various forms of judicial discretion.

The first point made in Stillington C's 1469 dictum quoted above seems to be that the Chancery is not tied to the strict common law rules of pleading, a point which is also made by St German: the Chancellor is in general to decide *secundum allegata et probata,* but (in an exceptional feature of the jurisdiction) the strict rules of pleading do not apply and new matter may be pleaded with leave of the court[39].

The practical implications in terms of conclusiveness of pleadings which were derived from the idea of the "judge in conscience" were that pleadings were not demurrable for uncertainty[40], that the bill was amendable[41] and that in certain cases the court would allow either plaintiff or defendant to introduce new matter after proof[42]; and not all of these disappeared in later equity. Chancery bills never became demurrable for uncertainty[43], and they continued to be amendable, and, indeed, the use of amendments became by the later eighteenth and early nineteenth century the dominant form of pleading[44].

However, Lord Nottingham in his *Prolegomena* says that proof which varied from the bill was to be disregarded, and gives *secundum allegata et probata* as a reason for this[45], and there is other authority for the rule, if not for the explanation[46]. In addition Lord Nottingham gave as a reason that the defendant had to

---

38 Fitz *Subp.* 12? cited F&C f 521r as YB P 9 Ed 4 41, ground to allow bill for discovery of documents not identifiable by P.

39 SGCS 121.

40 YB P 9 Ed 4 41, No 36, cited above; *F&C* f 521v, Crompton 42b, West B2.

41 *Doctor & Student,* 91 SS pp 121-2; this continued up to the nineteenth century: Holdsworth HEL IX 404-5.

42 St German, *Little Treatise* 121 explaining that "the very trouthe yn conscience is to be serchede"; new matter as ground for new bill on same cause of action, YB 27 Hen VIII f 16b, cit Stowe 415 f 24b, *Stanley v Young* (H1590) Toth 19, *Cosset v Crowther* (H1604) Cary 24, Stowe 415 f 97b, *Maynard v Moseley* (P1674) Nott CC No 78, (M1679) Nott CC No 967, *Warman v Seaman* (T1675) Nott CC No 290, (M1675) Nott CC Nos 313, 370, *Taylor v Wood* (1691) Nels 193

43 Though they could be referred to a Master: Holdsworth HEL IX pp 386-7; Horwitz 14, 25.

44 Holdsworth HEL IX pp 387, 404-5.

45 24.2, TT p 299.

46 *Rewse v Tuthill* (P1566) Monro 360, no interrogatories on matters not contained in the pleadings, & cf 1635 Orders No 3, i Sanders 177. *Observations* f 442r No 45 and f 458v No 176 say that a replication varying from the bill is acceptable if the defendant joins issue on it and proceeds to proof, but that if the defendant demurs to it the plaintiff's proofs of points in the replication will be disregarded. Bacon's Orders No 66, i Sanders 118, repeated Nott. Prac.

know what case he was expected to meet in order to plead and to examine and cross-examine witnesses[47].

In exceptional circumstances proof of matter not alleged could be used[48]. In the main, however, procedural means seem to have been used to solve problems of variance, of a type which imply that the basic rule was generally accepted.

The obvious course was to amend the bill; this was certainly possible until joinder of issue, and seems in Lord Nottingham's time to have been possible by motion of course if a new answer was not required[49]. Joinder of issue normally took place when the plaintiff replied generally to the defendant's answer, and for the purpose of examining witnesses this step corresponded to *litis contestatio* in the civilian procedure. The amendment rules therefore corresponded to the civilian rules for the amendment of libels, which similarly allowed amendment routinely before l.c. but only exceptionally thereafter. By the 1730s, however, the discretion to allow amendment after joinder of issue seems to have been in decay. The regular course was, according to the editor of 1 *Equity Cases Abridged* (1732), to obtain leave upon motion and affidavit of new matter to file a supplemental bill[50] – which implies that at this date the bill could not regularly be amended after joinder of issue, as was the case later[51].

If the cause reached hearing without the matter being included in the allegations by amendment of the pleadings, the early practice seems to have been to dismiss the bill without prejudice to a new bill being brought[52]. The disadvantage to this

3. 44, are on the face of it slightly stricter: replication not to contain new matter unless to avoid new matter in answer; *Fleetwood v Pool* (T1660) Hardr 171, Ex(E); *Style v Martin & Bosvile* (M1669) 1 Ch Cas 150, replication & proofs not to depart from bill; *Whaley v Norton* (M1687) 1 Vern 483, 1 Eq Ca Ab 87.5 (Trevor MR); *Rolfe v Harding* (M1713) 8 Viner 591.31, 2 Eq Ca Ab 732.4. Possibly analogously, a plaintiff who fails in proof will be barred from then arguing at the hearing the the matter is at common law: (1505) YB M 21 Hen 7 f 34b pl 40, & cf Jones pp 456, 484-5.

47 *Warman v Seaman* (1675) Nott CC No 313 at 73 SS 217, No 370 at 73 SS 248, in the context of an answer ((T1672) Nott Proleg 16.22, TT 230, (T1675) Nott CC No 290, Rep t Finch 279, (M1675) Pollex 112, Rep t Finch 279, 2 Ch Cas 209, all not SP)

48 *Strode v Strode* (P1674) 2 Ch Cas 196, (M1674) Nott CC No 137, bill of review, (1672) Nott Proleg 13.13, (P1675) Nott CC 211, *semble* not SC), answer alleging a lease; production at hearing of a conveyance in fee; *Hoxton v Withbridge* (H1674/5) Nott CC No 206, variance from bill as to the value of land, D having denied a trust which was then proved.

49 *Trip v Rands* (P1677) Nott CC No 656 ((T1677) Nott CC No 682, & SC at law 2 Lev 198, 3 Keb 769, 800, not SP).

50 29.

51 Holdsworth HEL IX 387, 404-5. Yale, *Introduction* to Nott. *TT* at p 55 states this rule as applying to this period, but this seems inconsistent with the fairly clear statement in *Trip v Rands*.

52 YB 27 Hen 8 f 15b, cit Stowe 415 f 24b, *Clifford v Adams* (1569) Toth 19; *Stanley v Young* (H1590) Toth 19, *Cosset v Crowther* (H1604) above n 22, *Samuel v Samuel* (1633) Toth 22, *Seymour v Nosworthy* (1664) Hardr 374 (Ex(E)) and *Maynard v Moseley* above n 22

practice, by the later seventeenth century, was that it was uncertain whether the depositions in the first cause would be admissible in the second[53] or whether re-examination of the witnesses examined in the first cause would be permitted in the second[54]. Another solution seems to have been, at the hearing, to order a trial at law on the issue which had not been alleged in the bill[55]; this overcame the cross-examination problem, but was open to objection on the basis that it was a departure from deciding *secundum allegata et probata*[56]. The nature and limits of these expedients for dealing with matter proved but not alleged in the original bill indicate that the *secundum allegata* principle was generally accepted.

The overall picture, therefore, seems to be as follows. (1) There is some evidence that the *secundum allegata et probata* tag was considered to apply to the equity jurisdiction during this period. (2) In particular the *secundum allegata* aspect seems to have been applied in much the same way as by the civilians: i.e. that matters proved were generally only of use if they were somehow alleged, but there was a fairly wide judicial discretion as to how this was applied – unlike the rigidity of the common law system of pleading. (3) The evidence seems to indicate an early view of the equity procedure as summary and hence not much subject to these rules, but a tendency as time went on towards greater rigidity, with the earliest sources suggesting a certain flexibility as to both allegation and proof, but an increasing tendency over time to require regular allegations and proofs as the foundation of the decree, and to treat the bill as a libel, rather than a petition.

II. The confession of the adverse party

In the civil and canon laws in general the confession of the adverse party makes a full and conclusive proof, on the basis of the statement in the Digest that *Confessus pro judicato est*[57]. Indeed, in some versions of the learned laws confession is

---

may be examples of this; cf also *Wakelin v Walthal* (M1679) 2 Ch Cas 8 (Nott CC 904, Dick 15, not SP), new original bill on new matter *arising* after decree.

53 Since the matter had not been alleged, the issues might be different. Cf below Ch 5 §§ 2 (*1*) (b) and 2 (2) (b) and (c).

54 Probably not: *Basset v Nosworthy* (P1674) Nott CC No 76, 73 SS 37, Rep t Finch 102. Cf below Ch 5 pp 203-4.

55 *Stutville v Russell* (P1674) Nott CC No 86, rejected on grounds of *laches; Bevan v Dike* (M1679) 2 Chan Cas 3 (not in Nott CC), Lord Nottingham; *Balch v Tucker* (H1682-3) 2 Chan Cas 40 (not in Nott CC), applied to matter proved but not pleaded by the defendant.

56 *Balch v Tucker* per counsel (possibly the reporter) arg; also objecting that since the matter was not in issue the witness could not be punished for perjury. The response of the court was that the plaintiff, who was arguing for a rehearing after a motion for a new trial had failed, "came too late".

57 D 42.2.1; 'Alciatus' 199v, Maranta 556.21, *Reformatio* 225 c2, Andrewes 78, Clerke 72, Ridley 107, Zouch *EI* 89, Conset 93, Wood 310. Judicial confession is said to be the

capable of overriding a prior judgement in favour of the party confessing[58], or an 'irrebuttable' presumption of law[59]. Civilian doctrine provided a procedure for the compulsory interrogation of the adverse party on oath with a view to the extraction of confessions[60]. The probative effect of confessions out of court is less clear and seems to have varied in the different municipal jurisdictions, perhaps because it was inextricably connected with the rules for the formation of contracts[61]. Confessions, whether extracted in judicial procedure or out of court, were generally only proof against the party confessing, not against others; exculpatory elements were not normally proof in his favour, though there were exceptions to this rule[62].

To consider how close the English equity procedure was to these conceptions it is convenient to consider in turn compulsion to answer and its exceptions; the conclusive effect of the answer as against the defendant; the effect of other admissions; and the use of the answer for purposes other than to convict the defendant.

1. Compulsion to answer on oath, and its exceptions

a) Compulsion

The equity courts were distinguished from the civil procedure of the civil and canon laws in requiring the defendant's first pleading, the answer, to be a detailed

strongest form of evidence by Vulteius 370v ("probationem probatam, nec ullam esse probationem illa majorem"); Cosin Part 3, p 49 ("liquidissima probatio, & plusquam probatio"); Gentili 144 ("creditur magis confessioni principalis, quam testibus mille, contrarium adferentibus"); Wiseman 16; and Ayliffe 443, 447. For a common lawyer's view to the same effect, Doderidge, *The English Lawyer* (London, 1631; reprint, Abingdon, Professional Books, 1980) 254.

58 *Reformatio* tit. *De Probationibus* c 20, p 229.

59 Cotta 156-7; Maranta 556 No 22.

60 'Alciatus' 191r *De Positionibus* 2.1, explained as avoiding unnecessary proofs. Andrewes 79, Cosin Part 2 Ch 15, Part 3 38-9 and 48, Davenant 60-66, Wiseman 14, all justify the procedure as founded on divine or natural law.

61 Cotta 161, a confession in the absence of the adverse party "licet non valeat in vim pacti obligatori, tamen valeat in vim merae probationis"; 'Alciatus' 201v-202v distinguishes criminal from civil matters, types of contract one from another, and title from possession. Maranta 551-8 offers an extensive discussion similarly largely concerned with contract and conveyance; he says that an exrajudicial confession generally is a half proof. Vulteius 371r says that an extrajudicial confession is easily revoked, nec habet vim, quantum illa, quae est judicialis; Wood 311-2 says that it is a half proof, except in the case of a dying declaration (and even that is not conclusive as between heir and creditors).

62 Vulteius 370v, "quae ipsi quidem confitenti ita praeiudicat, non etiam alii"; not against another party, 'Alciatus' 201r No 14 (proctors and guardians); not in one's own favour, 'Alciatus' 200r No. 4; Maranta 556-7 No. 27, same, subject to qualifications; Zouch *SQ* cl 9 Nos 35, 36 puts as disputable questions issues about qualified confessions in criminal proceedings, and Wood 311-12 discusses related issues in civil proceedings.

response on oath to the plaintiff's allegations. In the absence of a cross-bill or special circumstances the plaintiff would not be put to answer the defendant's case on oath. In contrast, the use of interrogation on oath in civilian doctrine was after *litis contestatio,* was at the election of the party (subject to judicial discretion) and was available to defendants as well as plaintiffs[63]. An additional difference was that in the ecclesiastical practice positions were normally answered *per verbum credit* by the party's proctor; a separate petition was required for the party's personal answer[64]. Langdell suggested that the answer on oath in Chancery came from an antecedent peculiarity of procedure in the English church courts (as distinct from the canon law generally)[65]. However, the evidence does not seem to support this view. Though the English church courts and Admiralty did amalgamate the libel, positions and articles into a single document, the earliest clear evidence for this amalgamation is after the development of the Chancery[66]; and in any event, the procedure described by Clerke entails a general citation of the defendant, followed by the plaintiff, on the appearance of the defendant's proctor, asking (a) for the libel to be treated as positions, and (b) after the defendant's proctor had answered *non credit,* that the defendant be cited to answer personally[67]. In contrast the first process served on the defendant in equity was a *subpoena ad respondendum* requiring an answer in person and on oath[68]. These differences in concept and practice, as well as the problems of dating, mean that migration of the english ecclesiastical practice is not a sufficient explanation of the answer on oath in the english bill procedure.

If migration of the church court practice probably won't hold, there are three other possible explanations. The first, Dawson's suggestion, is that the *subpoena ad respondendum* was originally merely a pragmatic conciliar administrative de-

---

63 'Alciatus' 191r, Clerke 36-7, 70-72, Conset 87, Ayliffe 65. Maranta distinguishes interrogations before l.c., which are founded on and correspond roughly to Roman *interrogationes in iure* (D. 11.1), which he discusses 488-92, from answers to positions, discussed 547-51. Vulteius makes a similar distinction, discussing *interrogationes* at 492r-v and positions and responses to them at 497v-499v.

64 Clerke 36-7, Conset 87-8; both immediately follow this petition with dissent by the defendant's proctor, followed by the judge assigning a term for proof. The defendant's oath was clearly, therefore, not a pre-requisite to further steps, as it was in equity.

65 Langdell 764, 776.

66 Helmholz, *Marriage Litigation in Mediæval England,* 16, 17, gives some fifteenth century instances of the combination of libel or articles with positions.

67 Clerke above n 64, i.e. after *litis contestatio* in the plenary procedure; Clerke, Prax. Adm. pp 24/5, in the request for summary procedure.

68 Jones pp 177-181. Although the Exchequer is mentioned as issuing subpoenas in the same breath as the Council and Chancery in the Commons' petition of 1415, (Rot. Parl IV 84a), Bryson, 13-15 considers that there is no firm evidence for the equity jurisdiction of the Exchequer before the reign of Edward VI, and the answer in the Exchequer was not upon oath until 1580 (Bryson, 117). Answers in the Star Chamber and Requests were on oath, and Star Chamber added the refinement of regularly examining the defendant on oath after answer (Guy pp 86-7).

vice[69], but this is difficult to reconcile with the view expressed in the 1415 petition that

> les queux plees ne purront prendre fyn, sinon per examination et serement des parties, solonc la forme de ley cyvyle & ley de Sainte Eglise, en subvercion de vostre commune ley[70]

as this view comes at a relatively early date in the development of the equity jurisdiction.

The second alternative is that the original equity procedure may have derived from a more summary version of the summary procedure than that described by Clerke. As already indicated, the summary procedure in minor crime consisted of nothing but citation and examination of the defendant, and Helmholz has made the point that the summary procedure in marriage cases in the late-medieval ecclesiastical courts was extremely variable.[71] There is some reason to suppose that the early fifteenth century Chancery english procedure consisted of nothing but a petition and the examination of the defendant and possibly the plaintiff;[72] and it is therefore arguable that early Chancery procedure is simply summary procedure of a very summary kind.

It is less clear, however, why a very summary kind of summary procedure should be thought appropriate to the kind of matters handled in equity. H. Coing suggested in 1956 that the Chancery equity jurisdiction might be derived from the canon law *denunciatio evangelica*[73]. This would explain the both the supplementary character of the jurisdiction, and its summary character, as he tells us that the procedure applied in the *denunciatio* is summary procedure with an inquisitorial element[74]. This may, however, be an over-precise analogy; though in equity, as in the *denunciatio*, plaintiffs appeal from the denial of justice in the ordinary procedure, the same is true of the general appeal to summary procedure based on the absolute power of the prince; and equity procedure, though summary, is not inquisitorial. The author of *Forme et Certenty*, writing in the early seventeenth century, thought it appropriate to quote Maranta to the effect that merely possessory causes are summary,[75]

69 *Lay Judges* 148.

70 Rot Parl IV 84a. Dawson loc cit cites the petition but attributes its expression to a confusion with the church court procedure. Claiming that contemporaries were "confused" about the character of legal procedures, about which modern historians are forced to speculate because of lack of clear direct evidence, is manifestly an artificial device for dealing with inconvenient evidence.

71 *Marriage Litigation* Ch IV.

72 This is given as a point in support of his argument by Dawson loc cit; & cf also Avery 86 LQR 84 at 90 and sources cited there.

73 'English Equity and the Denunciatio Evangelica of the Canon Law' 71 LQR 223-241.

74 Id., 229, 237-8.

75 *F&C* f546v citing Maranta 141 no. 143; in the edition I have used 224 No 43; "1"43 in the MS is presumably a scribal error. CF also Gaill i Obs. 6 for the proposition that possessory causes are (highly) summary.

and it could perhaps be argued that Chancery dealt only in possession, leaving title to the common law; but there is nothing to corroborate this interpretation[76].

My third point, therefore, is that the answer on oath itself, rather than the more generally summary form of the procedure, may be the key to the jurisdiction. The common law made no provision for the interrogation of adverse parties on oath as a means of proof[77], and this might be regarded as a defect in the system by canonist and contemporary European standards[78]. The preponderant element in early Chancery proceedings seems to be relief against defects or abuses of common-law procedure by taking the defendant's oath[79], and there is some reason to suppose that Chancery did not at first involve itself in any regular way in the business of examining witnesses[80]. It may be, then, that the sworn answer is itself the initial core of the english bill jurisdiction, and that it is for this reason that the proceedings start with the *subpoena ad respondendum.*

If this was the case it would go some way to explaining the shape of the substantive equity jurisdiction. The primacy of the confession as proof overriding other rules of proof, might be being used to get around the estoppels by feoffment and deed, which might have been seen as blocking common-law enforcement of the use of land and certainly caused hardship in relation to contracts. But if this was what was going on, it might be argued that to justify interrogation the nature of the matter must be such as to lie in the peculiar knowledge of the defendant[81]; such an argument would fit with the direction of the equity jurisdiction to fraud, and accident, and confidence.

The answer is not only the principal mode of proof in the early Chancery; that the matter lies in the knowledge of the defendant continues to be a major reason to give the Chancery jurisdiction up to the early seventeenth century[82]. From the late sixteenth century onward there is evidence that counsel were carrying the use of

76 It was certainly prohibited by statute for conciliar courts to determine title finally: Stat. 25 Edw. 3 sess. v c 4, cited Baker *IELH* 136 n 6. However, by the Jacobean period the standard explanation was that equity acts on the person of the defendant, not *in rem (Earl of Oxford's Case* at 1 Ch Rep 1-16). There does not seem to be any other evidence that the argument that equity acted merely on possession was used, and it is possible that the author of *F&C* was thinking of interlocutory injunctions, which did not require full proof.

77 Compurgation is a different matter since it is decisory in effect, and so is the examination of contemnors etc (below n 87) which was primarily criminal.

78 The point is argued explicitly by Wiseman at 14, though this is a too late to be direct evidence.

79 See the analysis of early Chancery proceedings in Avery, 42 BIHR 129. The criticisms of this analysis which have been made by Guy and others (summarised in Guy, "The Development of Equitable Jurisdictions, 1450-1550", in *Law, Litigants and Legal Profession, Papers Presented to the Fourth British Legal History Conference*) in fact concern the later rather than the earlier period of Avery's study and do not affect this particular point.

80 Below Ch 7 § 1 n 7.

81 Wiseman at 14, 16; cf Domat 3.6.5 introduction, para 2.

82 Jones pp 194-6.

the answer as a major mode of proof to a point which the Chancellors and Keepers thought was an abuse; thus Egerton around 1600 rejected "pressing and urginge of the def[endan]t to certainties and particularities", Lord Nottingham in the 1670s deplored "torturing the defendant with nice exceptions to his answer", and Norburie in the 1620s and Lord Guilford in the 1680s had similar concerns[83]. The practice continued down to the nineteenth century[84]. If the answer was used in this way throughout the existence of the jurisdiction, this may explain the somewhat underdeveloped appearance[85] of other aspects of the law of proof.

In addition to the general requirement of answer on oath, parties could be examined on oath with a view to the extraction of confessions in a number of other cases. After four insufficient answers a defendant would be committed and examined on interrogatories[86]. Defendants were examined in relation to contempts allegedly committed by them[87], and where an account was ordered the parties accounting would be examined on oath[88]. It was also possible, at least in the early seventeenth century, for plaintiffs to opt to have the defendant examined on interrogatories as an alternative to proceeding to proof. If this course was adopted, Bacon C ruled that the defendant's answers should be conclusive[89].

83 Egerton in *Observations* f 464r No 204; & cf also f 437r No 1, answer good if good "to common intent", No2, simple denial of the whole content of the bill acceptable provided it is not a negative pregnant, f 463v, no new exceptions after second answer, Nottingham, *Practice* 8.5, *TT* pp 128-9. Norburie, 423 at 441f; Guilford, reference in Roger North, *Lives of the Norths* (ed Jessop, London, Bohn, 1890) Vol I p 263, to his limiting interlocutory injunctions where exception was taken to the answer; Roger North's notes from Guilford's MSS, BM Add MS 32518, also contain the comment (f15) "Bills in Chanc[ery] sont narrations a q[ue] Councell difficultm[en]t poyent traher suffic[ient] answer. P[ro]pose si soyent interrogatorys annex all bill, q[ue] def[endan]t soit responder, ou en nature del allegations" (square brackets expansions of the contractions in the MS).

84 Holdsworth HEL IX pp 357-8. Cf also Horwitz *CER* 24: in his samples, in 1627 221 cases (77.5%), in 1685 110 cases (75.3%), and in 1785 92 cases (65.7%) proceeded no further than pleadings. Witness evidence was taken in 16 of 30 decreed cases in 1627 (5.6% of total sample), 12 of 26 in 1685 (4.8%), and 21 of 36 in 1785 (15%).

85 By comparison with the roman-canon system and with the later common law. As will be seen, rules later adopted at common law in some cases appear first in equity, but they get their elaboration in most cases at common law. Ballow's *Treatise of Equity* (1737) discusses proof as a distinct topic, but in this it is unusual; in general neither books nor Abridgement titles on evidence, or on Equity, treat proof in equity in any detail.

86 Bacon C's Orders, Sanders 117; 1649 Orders, Sanders 226; Clarendon's Orders, Sanders 301; Nott Prac 3.28, TT p 99. Lord Nottingham loc cit proposed to reduce the number of insufficient answers to three where a plea had been overruled; Wright LK in 1701 reduced it to three in general (Sanders 421). Egerton seems to have been willing to decree *pro confesso* if the defendant simply refused to answer: *Observations* f 437r No 4.

87 Jones p 245 cites *Utley ex p* C24/293 No 86; *York v Haidon* (1569) Toth 85 and *Bowser v Savage* (P1596) Toth 85, Stowe 415 f 204b, may be examples of this; for other examples cf Monro pp 42, 106, 130, 174, 226, 264, 334, 508, 511, 594, 616, 640, 670. This also applied at common law, for which see Macnair "The Early Development" 81-2.

88 Jones 280-1, 404, and cf below § 2 *(4)* (a) (ii).

It is important to grasp that the oath to the answer was a serious matter and not just a point of form. This can be seen in a number of ways, the simplest of which is the peers' argument that they should answer on honour, not on oath[90], and later and at the opposite end of the social scale the refusal of the Quakers to swear[91]. The force of the oath may be related to the existence of a number of exceptions to the general compulsion to swear (below); it certainly added weight to the possibility of the answer concluding the defendant or being used as evidence in subsequent proceedings[92], and may have suggested the possibility of the answer being evidence generally, rather than merely usable against the individual defendant as a confession[93].

b) Exceptions

In a number of cases the court would not compel the defendant to answer, or would not compel an answer on oath. The two major areas were the protection of purchasers, and the rules which subsequently became part of the privilege against self-incrimination. The protection of purchasers in equity was a substantive rule, the plea of purchase a substantive defence, rather than one based on principles of the law of proof; though it was used to bar the obligation to answer, it could also

---

89 Cf below Ch 6 § 4 *(1)* (c), where I refer to the instances from the late sixteenth and early seventeenth century of the examination of parties *ad informandam conscientiam iudicis* at or after the hearing, as it is not clear that the aim was the extraction of confessions; rather, the party may have been being given an opportunity to swear in his own favour.

90 According to Jones 322, peers could not in general be subjected to compulsory process (& cf *Dacres v Lord Dacre* (1564) Monro 353, Chancery, *Countess of Rutland's Case* (M1605) Moo KB 765.1063, (6 Co 52b not SP), Star Ch, *per cur* peer to give evidence on honour. But Crompton 33b makes it a *Quære* whether peers are to answer on honour or on oath, and Egerton took the view that peers were to be sworn: *Willoughby v Lord Wharton* (1597) Toth 10, Stowe 415 f 206b, Harg 281 f 110b), *Observations* f 475v No 268; and this view seems to have been followed; *Countess of Shrewsbury's Case* (T1612) 12 Co Rep 94 at 95 *per* Phellips MR, *Rivell v Earl of Shropshire* (M1612) Toth 11; Hudson 167-8, reporting the controversy and arguing that Egerton's view was not an innovation; *Mayor of Salisbury v Bishop of Salisbury* (1627) Toth 12 (bishop to answer on oath); *Earl of Lincoln's Case* (H1626-7) (Star Chamber; peer to answer on oath, *per cur.*) The Lords raised this as an issue of privilege in Parliament: *Earl of Lincoln's Case*, and HL order 31 Dec 1640, Sanders i.207, but a new order had to be made in 1685 to stop the Masters tendering the Bible to peers, Sanders i.364-5; by 1699 peers were entitled to answer on their honour: *Duke of Hamilton v Lady Gerrard* (P1699) Pre Ch 92, 2 Eq Ca Ab 13, though as witnesses they must still be on oath: *Meers v Lord Stourton* (1711) Dick. 20, 1 P Wms 146. If the right to answer on honour is seen as an attenuated version of an original exemption from compulsory process, there is some analogy with the statements in 'Alciatus' 220r (citing Durantis) *Reformatio* 247 c.15, Gaill ii Obs 100 No 22, Gentili 129-130 (citing Gaill), Domat 3.6.3.21 that certain persons are too important to be compelled to appear as witnesses.

91 Below Ch 6 § 3 *(2)*.

92 Below § (2).

93 Below § (4).

be used to bar examination of witnesses *in perpetuam memoriam* and substantive relief, unlike the self-incrimination rule. Detailed discussion is therefore not appropriate here[94]. It is worth noticing, however, the existence both of this and of some other limitations on the obligation to answer[95]. The "self-incrimination" limitation is of some importance because it may be[96] connected to the evolution of witness privilege and of the common-law right to silence.

'Alciatus' tells us that a party is not obliged to answer positions which are superfluous, unnecessary, irrelevant, obscure, to the act of another, prejudicial, negative, over-general, captious (tricky), to points of law, calumnious (defamatory), impossible, or incriminating[97]. Maranta goes slightly further into the rule prohibiting incriminating positions. He makes exceptions for frauds which leave the defendant in possession of the plaintiff's property, and for offences which disqualify the defendant from a benefit; of these latter the example is an invalidly procured tacit *fideicommissium* (in modern english terms secret trust)[98]. The general proposition that incriminating positions do not require an answer is stated by Clerke, Conset and Ayliffe; Clerke and following him Conset draw the conclusion that in defamation cases the defendant's answer is deferred till after proof[99].

---

94 There is a discussion of the plea of purchase, in general, in DEC Yale *Introduction* to Selden Soc Vol 79, at pp 160-175. For purchase as a bar to examination *in perpetuam memoriam* cf *Tufton v Norton* (M1673) Nott CC No 28, *Pitt v Hill* (H1673/4) Rep t Finch 70, *Botham v Townsend* (M1674) Nott CC No 150, *Ramon v Stacy* (M1675) Nott CC No 320, *Jefferson v Dawson* (M1675) Nott CC No 324 (1 Ch Cas 267 not SP), *Evenden v Vanacre* (T1675) Nott CC No 545, Rep t Finch 255 (1 Ch Cas 303 not SP), *Bechinall v Arnold* (H1685-6) 1 Vern 334, 1 Eq Ca Ab 234.6, 333.2; *contra Seabourn v Chilston* (1668) Nels 125 exceptionally available to remainderman. For the contrary position in relation to self-incrimination cf below p

95 The area of "self-incrimination" was certainly wider than the modern law (see below) and the plea of purchase could be a bar to discovery to support an action at law (Yale loc cit pp 161-3). Notice also the rule that discovery of a tenant to the *præcipe* to enable a real action to be brought was generally not available (*Bishop Jewel's Case* Cromp J. Cts 48, Bacon LK, *AG v Mico* (H1658-9) Hardr 137 *per* Shaftoe *arg.*, *Stapleton v Sherrard* (H1684-5) 1 Vern 212, *Sherborne v Clerk* (M1684) 1 Vern 273) and the restrictive attitude of the court to discovery in aid of execution (*Monteage v Grocers' Co* (M1675) Nott CC No 354, *Angell v Draper* (P1686) 1 Vern 399, 1 Eq Ca Ab 77.14, *Taylor v Hill* (M1705) 1 Eq Ca Ab 132.15

96 For this point see below and also Macnair 'The Early Development of the Privilege against Self-Incrimination' (1990) 10 OJLS 66 ("The Early Development"); Helmholz, 'Origins of the Privilege Against Self-Incrimination: the Role of the European *Ius Commune*' (1990) 65 *NYU LR* 962-980; Langbein, 'The Historical Origins of the Privilege Against Self-Incrimination at Common Law' (1994) 92 *Mich LR* 1047-1085; Eben Moglen, 'Taking the Fifth: Reconsidering the Origins of the Constitutional Privilege Against Self-Incrimination', id, 1086-1130.

97 195r-197r.

98 490 Nos 6-7.

99 Clerke 74, Conset 10, Ayliffe 65; on defamation, Clerke 36-7, Conset 88. Gaill and Vultieus offer variant views. Gaill ii Obs. 82 No 11 says that the *Reichskammergericht* does not recognise this or other *jus commune* limits on the obligation to answer, because parties use

The self-incrimination rule was thus well-established in civilian doctrine, and Helmholz has found instances of its application in the practice of the late sixteenth and seventeenth century church courts[100]. It was not, however, by any means indentical to the modern common law privilege. The fullest discussion of the issue, albeit one which was certainly slanted for polemeical effect, is offered in Richard Cosin's *Apologie of Certaine Proceedings Eclesiasticall* (1593)[101]. Cosin says that

> If the suite be but civilly mooved, the criminous position or interrogatorie, may concerne such a crime; as being concealed, brings benefit, & commoditie to him, with another mans losse. And in this case (albeit there be no fame, or no detection precedent) the partie is bound to answere it upon his oath.
>
> But if the concealing of it, cannot procure his gaine, with another mans losse; then is not the partie himselfe (in such case) bound to answere a position criminous mooved by his oath, yet even in this case, if such crime bee notorious, or be otherwise sufficiently discovered by fame &c, then is he bound to answere it, upon his oath.
>
> Now if it bee mooved criminally, to the intent of publike punishment; it is either touching a crime altogether hidden, or a crime which (in some sorte) is bruted abroad and manifested. if it be simply hidden, and secrete, the rule is; that a man is not bound to answere such crime, upon his oath: *quia nemo tenetur, propriam turpitudinem revelare.*[102]
>
> ...
>
> "And yet there be also certaine cases, which are excepted out of this rule ..."[103]
>
> ...
>
> "Hitherto of offences meerely secrete. But when they are by signes or otherwise (in some lawful sort) manifested abroad, they are then of a farre different consideration. And yet if they be but blowen abroad, by reason of an Accusation co[m]menced, or by one, who voluntarily maketh himselfe a partie, and so is presumed to do it of malice, or for some other sinister respect: in this case, the defendant is not to be urged, upon his oath to answere the truth of the crime; nor yet any thing, which very neerely & presumptively inferreth it, for no man is bound (simply) to furnish up his adversaries intention, who (at his owne perill) ought to come (otherwise) sufficiently prepared. Nevertheles, if the Accuser, or partie, do

---

them to cause delay, but the judge is to exercise discretion to protect parties for captious positions. Vulteius 492r says that on interrogation before l.c. the defendant is not obliged to answer *de crimine vel turpitudine sua*.

100 65 *NYU LR* at 969-974.

101 London, 1593 (This is the second edition and much enlarged; only 40 copies of the first edition were printed) Part III Ch 9. Theological discussions to the same effect were offered by Lancelot Andrewes (1591) and Dr Davenant (no date) both printed as appendixes to Lake, *Memoranda Touching the Oath Ex Officio* (London, 1662) which itself summarises Cosin's argument.

102 Cosin Part III p 113. Square brackets indicate expanded contractions. Side-note references in the original have been omitted. The ellipses between this and following quotations cover passages in the argument which are either merely elaboration or not pertinent (in the degree of detail given) to the present point.

103 Ib. p 114. The exceptions are (1) offences which give rise to a disqualification from office (eg simony) and (2) heresy and dilapidations / waste of livings.

make an halfe proofe, as by one upright, and untouched witnesse, or by any thing equivalent thereunto in law: then may the Judge tender to the defendant an oath (which he cannot refuse) *de veritate ipsius criminis* ...

But when the proceeding is to be of meere office, & where the crime is manifested, and discovered abroade, by some wayes and meanes (sufficient to ground an Enquirie upo[n]) yet those meanes not prooved before an Ordinarie Judge; the Judge is not thereupon to urge the parties oath, upon the very crime it selfe: albeit he may require him to sweare, whether he beleeve such an infamie do runne of him; or whether he have bene adjudged by sentence to be convicted of it: whether he have at any time confessed it, or whether he beleeve it, to be notorious. If he shall deny to take oath to answere but unto these, upon his credulitie: he doth thereby incurre contumacie ...

Now if the partie defendant shall denie upon his oathe, all these aforesaide matters, whereof he is interrogated, and none other sufficient detectio[n] besides, being against him, the[n] cannot the Ordinarie Judge proceed; to give him an oath touching the trueth of the very crime it selfe objected: untill he shall have made proofe by witnesses, that the partie is (in deede) thereof infamed, hath else-where confessed it, is convicted thereof, or some such like. For when all these, or any of them, is either prooved, or by the partie himselfe confessed judiciallie: then may the Judge lawfully give unto the partie defendant, an oath; touching the trueth of the very crime it selfe: ...[104]

This account may be summarised as follows. In civil proceedings answer on oath may be compelled to charges of crimes which benefit the party interrogated (respondent) at the expense of someone else. This may be translated as matters which form the burden of the interrogating party (questioner)'s allegations but are incidentally criminal, since other crimes would generally be irrelevant. It appears by implication that answer may not be compelled where the offence merely causes loss without benefit to the respondent unless *fama*/ notoriety is shown[105].

In criminal proceedings pure "fishing expeditions" are prohibited except in the cases of disqualifications, heresy and dilapidations of livings[106]. If there is *fama*, in private prosecutions a half proof of the offence must be made before the oath is administered. In *ex officio* proceedings, however, it is sufficient to establish the *fama*, and this may be done not only by the usual methods of proof but also by interrogating the accused on oath, since (by an appalling piece of logic-chopping) to ask whether you are suspected is said not to be an incriminating question[107].

---

104 Ib. pp 116-7.

105 The concepts of notoriety and *fama*, as they developed in the medieval law, are discussed by Levy, *Hierarchie des Preuves* Ch 2 and pp 113-7. Cosin's usage here is not entirely clear, but appears to be looser than the developed medieval concepts in Levy's discussion, amounting merely to widespread public suspicion. It may be, in the light of the treatment of *fama* in *ex officio* proceedings (final paragraph quoted, above n 59) that an extrajudicial confession would suffice.

106 These are, of course, ecclesiastical offences. Civil, i.e. state, parallels would be treason and proceedings against public officers; the analogy between heresy and treason is made by Cosin, iii, 342-3.

107 Cosin loc cit pp 116-7, at first ellipses in quotation above.

This put the suspect back in the position from which the original *nemo tenetur* rule had sought to free him, i.e. Catch-22[108].

Obviously, if these principles are relevant at all to English equity proof, the rules on civil cases are most directly relevant. The rules on criminal cases are also relevant, however, since the Star Chamber was primarily (in theory) a criminal court; the Chancery preserved the residue of its early quasi-criminal function in the shape of the fictitious allegations of confederacy and abuse of process in bills[109]; the Exchequer had a "live" criminal jurisdiction in Revenue matters; and both courts exercised criminal jurisdiction over contempts, and Chancery at least also over perjury and abuse of process, in their own proceedings.

It is fairly obvious that the equity courts did not follow the detail of the rules stated by Cosin[110]. It does seem, however, that something quite like the conceptual framework of the roman-canon approach to incriminatory positions can be found reflected in equity limitations on the obligation to answer. Wigmore's explanation of these cases in the later seventeenth century was as applications of the privilege against self-incrimination which he saw as developed at common law in the mid-seventeenth century by an "association" or confusion of ideas with the rejected practice of the Star Chamber and High Commission[111]. There are a number of reasons for rejecting this view[112], but the one relevant here is that Wigmore's view required him to offer unsatisfactory explanations of the early equity cases, and to see decisions in the Exchequer in 1657-61 as the starting point of the "extension" of the privilege from common-law criminal proceedings into civil cases and equity.

Equity authorities refusing to compel defendants to answer to charges carrying criminal liability start in the reign of Elizabeth I. In *Fenton v Blomer* (1580)[113] Chancery refused to make a defendant answer so as to expose himself to (criminal) liability for usury; in *Anon* (T1588)[114] the Exchequer refused to entertain an English bill on a penal statute; in *Viscountess Montague's Case*[115] Chancery refused to

108 Cosin's account has a polemical purpose, i.e. to defend the use of the *ex officio* oath by the High Commission (cf his introduction). The resulting account is a good deal more liberal than the contemporary criminal procedure in France and Germany, for which see Langbein, *Prosecuting Crime in the Renaissance* and *Torture and the Law of Proof*, *passim.*

109 For the quasi-criminal function of the early Chancery cf Avery article cited above n 79. For the persistence of the fictitious allegation of confederacy in bills, Holdsworth HEL IX 379-381.

110 In particular, the use of the concept of *fama* or notoriety would only be really practical to a local court disposing of executive power.

111 § 2250.

112 Macnair "The Early Development" 68-9

113 Toth 72; Jones p 209 n 3 refers to the records; the bill had been exhibited to obtain a collateral advantage for the plaintiff in pending litigation in the Exchequer.

114 3 Leo 204.

115 (1595-6) Cary 9, Stowe 415 f 93r, Harg 281 f 14v, HLS 1090 f 7v. (This date (38 Eliz) is given in Stowe 415, but not in the printed report or Harg 281; Wigmore dates the case

order defendants to answer to a charge of abducting a ward on the basis of liability to a criminal penalty; and in *Loveday v Skarming* (1595)[116] the same rule was applied to liability for maintenance. If these cases show a rule, it extended to forfeitures. West (1594) says that penalties are not recoverable in equity until established at law[117]; in *Wolgrave v Coe* (1595)[118] the court expressed the opinion that the defendant need not answer so as to expose himself to forfeiture of the penalty of a bond; in *Cary v Cottington & Mildmay* (1600)[119] the defendant was "not enforced to answer ... to discover a forfeiture to his own hurt". Similarly in *Hubberd v Hubberd* (c1600) a bill "against one to fish out from the def some matter to discover a forfeiture" was said by Egerton to be demurrable[120]. In the Star Chamber, too, Hudson tells us that the defendant can demur to a bill which alleges a capital crime or a penal law which involves a forfeiture[121]. In this the early equity authorities fit the civilian rule[122], which prohibited calumnious as well as incriminating positions, better than the view of the rule as growing out of common-law criminal procedure.

On the other hand, Chancery could certainly examine parties allegedly in contempt on their oaths[123], and this principle seems to have extended to cases of perjury in Chancery proceedings and other abuses of process[124]. In cases of contempt

---

to 1599, but this neither appears in the printed report nor the MSS, nor is deducible from them; though the case does not appear under this name in the Chancery indexes in the PRO for either year, the Viscountess need not have been plaintiff).

116 Harl 1576 f 163b

117 Sig B5v No V.

118 Toth 18, Stowe 415 f 202v, Harl 1576 f 159r.

119 Toth 7. Harl 1576 f 159, *Carey v Codrington* and Mildmay (M1591), "a forfeiture of his own estate". Cf also *Roe v Waforer* (M1594) Toth 80, Stowe 415 f 203r, Harl 1576 f 159 (bill by heir against purchaser to prove breach of condition dismissed) ((M1596) Moo KB 300 not SP) and *Cromer v Peniston* (1597) Cary 9, Stowe 415 f 93r, Harg 281 f 15r, an obscure report: "The Lord Keeper overruled, that the defendant should not answer". Toth 10, Stowe 415 f 206v, Harg 281 f 111r has "Whether a surviving joint tenant should be enforced to answer to disclose a partition, in the life of his fellow, *Best v Cage* two orders (M32&3) *Crowner v Peniston* (M39&40) doubted. I take it that the question is whether the principle of not discovering forfeitures applied to the severance of a joint tenancy.

120 *Observations* f 442v No. 47; & cf *Observations* f 437r No. 5.

121 164.

122 cf the formulation in Cosin quoted above p 39, *quia nemo tenetur, propriam turpitudinem* revelare (my emphasis). Chancery also tried to stop the inclusion of "scandalous", i.e. defamatory, matter in its proceedings. Bills were demurrable if they were scandalous (Jones pp 196, 209); and bills, answers and other pleadings, interrogatories and depositions could all be struck out and parties or counsel punished if they were scandalous (For examples cf Monro pp 36, 212, 253, 258, 310, 627, 632, 644, 732 (bill); 72, 193, 261, 284, 311, 314, 319, 508, 511 (answer); 263, 284, 639 (replication); 253 (depositions)). In *Ognell v Trussell* (M30 Eliz) 3 Leo 219 (Owen 69 other procs) Hatton C refers to *nemo tenetur* as a bar to a Star Chamber bill alleging the defendant had fraudulently procured his own conviction of felony, but this seems to be a confusion on his part.

123 Above n 87.

prosecuted by the party injured, an affidavit of the contempt seems to have been required before the court would proceed to examine the defendant[125]; but a single affidavit, i.e a half proof, was a sufficient basis to require examination, though not for proof of the contempt if the defendant denied it[126].

In some cases defendants were ordered to answer to criminal matters. In *Cotton v Foster* (1595)[127] the bill was "to have the defendant answer whether the contract was to receive more money for interest than warranted"; a demurrer was overruled, "and if it was found the defendant lent it without consideration, then to take the forfeiture in". This report is rather obscure, but it looks as if the bill was for relief against forfeiture of the penalty securing the debt, with the usurious level of interest used as a ground for relief[128]. The explanation may be the statement reported in *Wakeman v Smith* (1585)[129] that "though criminal causes are not here to be tried directly for the punishing of them, yet incidently for so much as concerneth the equity of the cause, they are to be answered"; this makes the primary rule seem to prohibit collateral allegations of crime, i.e. those outside the jurisdiction of Chancery or not directly in issue. Again, in *Hubberd v Hubberd* Egerton says that if a bill demurrable as fishing for forfeitures also charges "fraud, trust, or practice", these aspects are to be answered[130]. This has a limited resemblance to Cosin's rule for civil cases, but none at all to a general privilege derived from the common law.

Wigmore suggested three possible explanations of those cases from this period he cited[131]. The first was that the cases declining to enforce discovery of a forfeiture were based on general equitable hostility to forfeitures – the point to which he returned in saying that the extension of the privilege to cover civil forfeitures was

124 *Anon* (1570) 3 Dy 288a (*per* CP); *Phillips v Benson* (1577-8) Toth 11, Cary 68 (bill of perjury, the defendant to be examined on interrogatories); Jones p 253, viva voce examination to "track down" abuses of process; *Winn v Swayne* (1630) Toth 12, "a commissioner [not "commission", as per Wigmore s 2250 n 95] to answer bribery and corruption"

125 For examples of affidavits see the instances in Monro cited above.

126 Bacon C's Orders (Sanders i.119) provide for the imprisonment of the contemnor before examination on the basis of one affidavit in cases of violence against process servers and scandalous words against the Court; the Parliamentary Commissioners (Sanders i.240), Clarendon (Sanders i.307,8) and Nottingham (Prac tit. XI, nos 16, 17., TT p 142) distinguish force and words, requiring two affidavits for proof in the latter case.

127 Toth 25.

128 Compare *Bridges v Bromwich* (P1605) Monro 43.

129 Toth 12. Tothill cites the Carew MS reports, but the case does not seem to be in the MS versions of Carew I have so far seen. In *Sir Arthur Gorges' Case* (M1599) Moo KB 737.1021 an english information in the Wards for detaining the body of a ward of the Crown was answered, but the circumstances suggest that the defendant chose not to demur. *Eland v Cottington* (T/M4 Car) Toth 12, "ordered to answer, though it be to his prejudice by statute laws" is too brief a report to make anything of.

130 *Observations* f 442v No 47 (above n 120).

131 § 2250, VIII Wigmore at p 288, citing *Cromer v Peniston, Wolgrave v Coe, Cary & Cottington v Mildmay,* Toth 10, *Wakeman v Smith,* and *Viscountess Montague's Case.*

attributable to confusion with this rule[132]. The difficulty with this view is that by 1630 while discovery of a forfeiture was not available, it was possible to examine witnesses *in perpetuam memoriam* to establish a forfeiture[133], and once the plaintiff has established the forfeiture at common law, he has made a title which is perfectly good in equity and is entitled, therefore, to equitable remedies including discovery[134]. If the defendant wants the court to relieve against the forfeiture, he will have to show some positive equity against it – whether by tender of the performance it is intended to secure[135], or by showing that the condition on breach of which the forfeiture arises is one of which equity disapproves[136]. The rule against discovery of forfeitures is, therefore, a rule about discovery, not an aspect of the wider rules about forfeitures. In addition it could not explain the case of incriminating bills, since Chancery never claimed a jurisdiction to relieve against criminal penalties.

Wigmore's second argument, therefore, was that in reality refusal to order an answer was merely a way of Chancery declining jurisdiction, given that it had a very limited criminal jurisdiction (essentially in contempt of court and in perjury and abuse of its own process). This point is pertinent, since a bill which sought only to establish a breach of a penal law by discovery might well be regarded, on the interpretation of *nemo tenetur* offered above, as unlawful "fishing"[137]. It is unsatisfactory as an alternative explanation, for three reasons. In the first place, bills for discovery of contractual liability intended merely to make subsequent enforcement at law possible were commonplace; so why should the same principle not be applied to penal laws? Secondly, a bill of discovery was available in tithe cases if the penalty was waived[138]; this does not fit very well with an objection to the jurisdiction. Thirdly, there was nothing to stop the defendant pleading or demurring directly to the jurisdiction, and it was, in fact, quite common. If the objection was to the jurisdiction, the natural course would have been to say so. On the contrary, *The Practice of the High Court of Chancery* says directly that

---

132 VIII Wigmore p 288 and s 2256.

133 *Egerton v Egerton* (1629) cit Nott Proleg 29.14 (W Jon 265 not SP). In this case the answer, which was necessary as a matter of form for issue to be joined and the witnesses examined (below Ch 7) would not be on oath.

134 Cromp. J. Cts. 45, Cary 15 (Harg. 281 f 20, Harv. 1090 f 12v), and *The Practice* 145, cite YB 36 Hen 6.26; *Protector v Lord Lumley* (M1655) Hardr 22, 1 Eq Ca Ab 75, Ex (E).

135 As in the common case of redemption of mortgages.

136 As eg in conditions in restraint of marriage.

137 Stat. 18 Eliz. I c 5 s 1 (1576) prohibits *qui tam* proceedings except by original writ or information, i.e. common law procedure; *Anon* (T1588) 3 Leon 204, Ex (E), no equity proceedings on a penal statute; *Coward v West* (T1597) Toth 18, Stowe 415 f 203r, Harl 1576 f 159 bill *qui tam* disallowed.

138 *Fenner & Robinson's Case* (1603) Ex (E), cited by Sjt Archer arg in *AG v Mico* at Hardr 137 seems to be the earliest authority; but cf also 2 & 3 Edw VI c 13 s 9, excluding the defendant's oath in ecclesiastical proceedings for the recovery of personal tithes, and *Anon* (T1588) 3 Leo 204, no English bill in Ex. for the treble value on this statute.

"... he must answer things plainly and directly to his knowledge, as also of his own Act, unless it be a means to make him subject to a forfeiture or action at Law"[139].

Wigmore's third explanation was that "the chancery practice is to be interpreted by the rules of the ecclesiastical courts"[140]. This served Wigmore's purpose because he had previously argued that the canonist rule was purely procedural[141], so that these decisions could be argued to have nothing to do with the later development of the privilege against self-incrimination (except by way of the "association of ideas". This latter argument is an extremely artificial use of the distinction between procedure and proof (which is in any case by no means straightforward) whose only purpose is to support Wigmore's general argument about the privilege at common law. The primary point offers by far the simplest explanation of the Chancery rules: what was being applied may not have been the detailed canonist rules, but it was a version of the general principles of the roman-canon system.

In the latter part of the seventeenth century the basic rule that a bill containing collateral allegations of crime or other misconduct, or which would expose the defendant to a forfeiture, was demurrable, is supported by a wide range of authority[142]. Two sorts of changes do, however, seem to have occurred.

The first was that the rule against compelling the defendant to answer where he would be exposed to a penalty became firmly established in the revenue jurisdiction of the equity side of the Exchequer, where it doesn't seem to belong on the

139 8. In spite of the later date of publication, this book is mostly derived from Ellesmere's decisions, and this in particular seems to qualify a dictum of Ellesmere's: "The defendant's answer was held good and sufficient by the Lord Ellesmere, if it be good to a common intent. But he must answer..." then as text quoted.

140 § 250 at VIII Wigmore 288.

141 Ib. pp 271-7.

142 W. Brown (attr), *Praxis Almæ Curiæ Cancellariæ* (London, 1694) p 3: "not criminal or scandalous against the defendant, or any other... and the defendant may refuse to answer such a bill, ..."; *Fry v Porter* (1669) Nott. Proleg. 29.14 (1 Ch Rep 26, 1 Ch Cas 138, 1 Mod 300, etc, not SP); *Monnins v Monnins* (1672) 2 Ch Rep 68, Nott Proleg c 30.47; *Churchill v Isaack* (M1673) Nott CC No 27; *Williams v Countess of Arundel* (M1673) Nott CC No 39; *Pensax v Litten* (H1673-4) Nott CC No 46; *Penrice v Parker* (T1674) Nott CC No 110, Rep t Finch 75; *Duke v Duke* (M1675) Nott CC No 357, 2 Ch Cas 209; *Fisher v Michel* (M1675) Nott CC No 362; *Deacon v Lucas* (P1676) Nott CC No 463; *Wynn v Wynn* (T1676) Nott CC No 517; *East India Co [E.I.Co] v Maniston* (T1676) Nott CC No 521, 2 Ch Cas 218; *Cook v Arnold* (M1676) Nott CC No 599; *Harrison v Houblon* (P1680) Nott CC No 1024; *Micklethwayt v Merrett* (P1681) Nott CC No 1097; *E.I.Co v Fortescue & al'* (H1681-2) Nott CC No 1147; *Anon* (1682) 1 Vern 60; *Bird v Hardwicke* (M1682) 1 Vern 109, 1 Eq Ca Ab 76.4; *Hinks v Nelthorp* (M1683) 1 Vern 204, 1 Eq Ca Ab 77.11; *E.I.Co v Evans* (H1684-5) 1 Vern 305; *Smithier v Lewis* (P1686) 1 Vern 398, 1 Eq Ca Ab 77.13; *Hungerford v Goreing* (H1687-8) 2 Vern 38; *African Co. v Parish* (M1691) 2 Vern 244; *Fane v Atlee* (H1700-1) 1 Eq Ca Ab 77.15; *Heathcote v Fleete* (M1702) 2 Vern 442, 1 Eq Ca Ab 76.6; *Morse v Buckworth* (M1702) 2 Vern 443, 1 Eq Ca Ab 76.7; *AG v Reynolds* (M1705) 1 Eq Ca Ab 131.10; *AG v Hesketh & al'*, (P1706) 2 Vern 549, Pre Ch 214, 1 Eq Ca Ab 131.11, 2 Eq Ca Ab 377.1; *Anon* (M1709) 2 Eq Ca Ab 70.7; *AG v Cresner* (M1710) Parker 277.

basis of the roman-canon conceptions or the earlier Chancery authority. Though there are some earlier cases which may be relevant[143], the starting point for the change seems to be *AG v Mico* (H1658-9)[144]. The bill in *Mico* charged the concealed importation of customable goods and bribery of customs officers and sought discovery and relief; the defendant demurred on the ground that the bill and charge concerned misdemeanours for which the defendant could be subjected to penalties and forfeitures. Serjeant Archer for the defendant argued that it was against law to compel a man to answer to accuse himself, and that it was common practice in the Exchequer that the defendant was not compellable to answer a bill for tithes unless the plaintiff waived the penalty of treble damages[145].

The arguments for the plaintiff responded to this argument not by denying it but by distinguishing it. The Attorney-General argued that discovery in such cases was necessary to the revenue function of the Exchequer, and that customs and excise duties, being "given to defend and guard the seas for the benefit of merchants" were *pro bono publico.* Atkins argued that the defendant ought to answer, because the plaintiff was not demanding the penalty or forfeiture by the bill, but merely discovery; that it was usual to prefer a bill to discover the quantity of wine imported in a ship to make prisage exigible; and cited four cases of the punishment of royal officers by english bill procedure[146]. Stevens argued that the equity side of the Exchequer had a statutory criminal jurisdiction[147] and that the point at issue had been decided in favour of the Crown in 1634[148]. All of these arguments are designed not to deny the rule against self-incrimination in general but to take the present jurisdiction of the Exchequer out of the rule, essentially by saying that bills of discovery in such cases are within the specific jurisdiction of the Exchequer.

The defendant's counsel's arguments, in contrast, assert the generality of the rule. Shaftoe cites a case of 1635 in which a demurrer on the present ground was upheld[149]; Coke upon Magna Carta; and a general rule in Chancery that the defendant will not be compelled to discover a tenant to the præcipe to make a real action possible except in dower and partition[150]; and argues that "though the party do not directly accuse himself, yet *oblique* he would be forced to do it, if he were put to answer, as in this case"[151]. Hardres reports his own argument very fully. The

---

143 Cited in *Mico* and referred to below.

144 Hardres 137.

145 Citing *Fenner & Robinson's Case* (1603), unreported (Ex). Cf above n 138.

146 *Atkinson v Hewet* (T1579) Lib Dec f 262; – v Fisher (P1602) Lib Dec f 144; *Dudley* (H1625/6) and *Rooks* (M1635).

147 Under 33 Hen 8 c 39.

148 *Blackford and Guyer's Case* (10 Car) Lib. Dec. f 185.

149 *Huntley's Case* (11 Car).

150 Cf above n 95.

151 I think this is a response to the point made by Atkins that the bill did not directly demand the penalty.

burden of it is that *nemo tenetur* is natural law and as such superior to any statute; that in any event the self-incriminating oath is prohibited by Magna Carta; that Star Chamber was abolished because of its use or abuse of the oath and in any case was not to use the oath to subvert the common-law jurisdiction; that the precedents on the other side are too few to amount to a course of the court; that the availability of the oath in these circumstances would tend to subvert procedure by information and indictment, would imply that the whole apparatus of customs enforcement was unnecessary, and is hard to reconcile with the rule in cases of tithe; and that the balance of authorities is on the side of the defendant[152].

He responds to the Attorney-General's argument from public policy by saying that it proves too much and would apply to all crimes; that once the forfeiture is properly established, a bill of discovery is proper; and that the revenue ought to be collected according to law. He responds to Atkins' argument from prisage of wines by saying that prisage is a common-law, i.e. private, title of the Crown which can be alienated by charter – unlike statutory customs – and so discovery is as much available as in any case where the plaintiff claims a title against a defendant. He responds to a point raised by Widdrington CB, that it was usual to compel discovery of tenure in capite in the Court of Wards by saying that in the first place this is again not penal, but a private right of the Crown, and secondly that this discovery was a grievance which led to the abolition of tenures. He responds to Stevens' argument from the statutory criminal jurisdiction of the court and discretion as to procedure by saying that nonetheless in exercising statutory jurisdiction the court is to proceed *secundum lege terrae*. He distinguishes the precedents offered for the plaintiff by saying that most of them are cases of ministers and officers of the Crown, who are excepted from the relevant provision of Magna Carta[153].

The arguments for the defendant are obviously strongly influenced by Coke, as Wigmore pointed out[154]. It is notable, however, that they concede the cases of officers of the Crown and of the incidental discovery of criminal conduct where a title – as in the case of prisage – is properly to be discovered. Although a very wide right against self-incrimination is claimed, it is not absolute. Moreover, even conceding the general rule against discovery of forfeitures and penalties, the Attorney-General's case was a substantial one: the Exchequer undoubtedly had a criminal jurisdiction and the specific function of recovering the revenue, so that the bill could not really be said to involve abuse of process or pure fishing for evidence to obtain penalties[155].

---

152 Citing *Vavasor v Radcliffe & al'* (T1591), *Bowes v Bore & Peacocke* (P1592) and *AG v Lewkner* (T1595).

153 Hardr 137 at 139 – 147. Cf *AG v Henton, Searcher of Hull* (M1608) Add 25207 f 4, Ex (E), customs officers compellable to answer English information charging various misdemeanours in office, overruling a demurrer that "null est bound d'accuse luy mesme" on the ground *inter alia* that such a bill will lie against a royal officer.

154 § 2250 n 104.

Though no order in *Mico* is reported or recorded[156], it seems that professional opinion preferred the defendant's argument.

AG v – (T1661)[157] is another case with no decision reported. On a bill for discovery of breaches of the Navigation Act, the Attorney-General waived the penalties involved, but the defendant argued that the Crown would not be bound by this waiver. The Court "inclined" to the opinion that the waiver would be effective, "*sed adjornatur*". This argument proceeds on the assumption that Mico would have been decided for the defendant. Roger North's copy of Lord Guilford's commonplace book contains the comment "Roy ne p[oe]t aver single duty p[er] discovery del p[ar]ty's oath, q[u]a penalty. Mes se[mbl]e q[ue] sil renounce le penalty, e[st] reason q[ue] s[er]roit law p[u]r enabler recovery"[158]; this suggests that at the time when it was written[159] the waiver was seen as ineffective. By the time of the reign of Anne the rule, as stated in *AG v Cresner* (1710)[160] was that the waiver was effective so far as the Crown was concerned, but did not bind a common informer, so that the bill was demurrable unless the common informer was barred by lapse of time.

Wigmore[161] saw the Exchequer cases of *Protector v Lord Lumley*[162], *AG v Mico* and *AG v –* as representing the first acceptance of the privilege in civil cases "though not without ambiguity and hesitation". This view, as with his explanation of the early equity cases (above) was required by the structure of his argument, i.e.

---

155 There is a hint of a somewhat similar argument to the Attorney-General's of *pro bono publico* in Cowper LK's decision in *AG ex rel Hindley v Hesketh, Scarisbrick and Sudell* (P1706) above n , a simony case, where he said that "... though this be called a penal law, yet this Court will aid remedial laws, not by making them more penal, but to let them have their course, ... and this Court will take care that its own notions shall not be made use of to evade so good and beneficial a law" as a ground to force the defendants to answer to disclose a trust and thereby prevent a mortgagee's title being set up as a bar to a *Quare impedit* brought by the purchaser of the Queen's title under the forfeiture. On the facts, however, this is analogous to the rule that after establishment of a forfeiture equity will aid recovery (above).

156 The only record references seem to be adjournments for the parties to deliver precedents: 29 January 1658/9, PRO E 125/39 f 35v, for a week, also noting that arguments had been heard from the AG, Atkins and Stephens for the Protector and from Archer, Shaftoe and Webb for Mico; 7 Feb, PRO E 125/38 f 268r, until the second Saturday of the next term. It seems likely that the proceedings were overtaken by the political crisis of 1659, as Protector Richard's regime fell in the vacation. It also seems from these entries that Hardres' own argument was probably never delivered.

157 Hardres 201. Wigmore §2250 n 104 identified this case as further argument in *AG v Mico*, but the misconduct charged in the two cases is different.

158 Add 32518 f 14. Square brackets indicate hypothesised expansions of contractions.

159 It is preceded (f 6b) by adverse comments on the conduct of Hale CJ *inter alia* in *Seymour v Nosworthy* (1664) Hardr 374, identified as *Nosworthy v Basset* which is a reference to subsequent proceedings in the 1670s.

160 Parker 277.

161 §2250 at pp 289-90, n 104.

162 Hardres 22, cited above n 134.

that the privilege against self-incrimination started with the right to silence in criminal proceedings. I have argued more extensively elsewhere[163] that this general view is wrong. For present purposes the point is that it gets *Mico* and following cases almost exactly upside down. Rather than representing hesitant movement from the right to silence in criminal causes to privilege in civil cases, they represent movement towards the general right to silence from more limited rules already applied in equity civil proceedings.

The other change was an apparent narrowing of the rule in the direction of the modern approach in which it is largely confined to allegations of crime. Up to the time of Lord Nottingham the rule was certainly wide enough to cover all sorts of "scandalous" allegations[164], and there are instances which require the wider interpretation in his time[165] and that of Lord Guilford[166]. The beginnings of the limitation of the rule appear to be in cases involving the chartered trading companies. In *Fisher v Michel* (M1675)[167] Lord Nottingham refused a discovery of interloping trade to a private individual on the basis that it would subject the defendant to penalties under the East India Co's laws operating in India. However, in *East India Co. v Maniston* (T1676)[168], a bill against a factor to discover *inter alia* unlawful trading in breach of covenant, he said that the rule did not apply, because

> "covenants against unlawful trading are not properly penalties but contracts such as a man may forfeit and yet be a gainer too, and if the defendant were plaintiff to be relieved against those penalties he should be dismissed ..."[169]

In *African Co. v Parish* (M1691)[170] the Lords Commissioners said that this principle had been "several times" applied, and ordered discovery of unlawful trading by a shipowner who had agreed in a charterparty with the company that he would

---

163 Macnair "The Early Development".

164 Nott. Prac. Title 3 Nos 7, 8. Cf at common law *Onbie's Case* (1642) March NC 83 "you are not to question the whole life of a witness, as that he is a whoremaster &c", *Anon* (M1647) Style Prac Reg 355 (witness not compellable on the voir dire to expose himself to an action), and the general rule (below ch 5 § 2 *(4)*, ch 6 § 3 *(1)*) that infamy must be proved by record, i.e. cannot be proved by cross-examination.

165 *Williams v Countess of Arundel* (M1673) Nott CC No 39, "not to discover against themselves matter tending to the dishonour of the Court"; *Duke v Duke* (M1675) Nott CC No 357, not to bastardise the defendant's children; *Harrison v Houblon* (P1680) Nott CC No 1024, not to expose the defendants' trading associates to criminal penalties under Spanish law (contrast Wigmore §2258).

166 *Hinks v Nelthorp* (M1683) 1 Vern 204, 1 Eq Ca Ab 77.11 (marital misconduct).

167 Nott CC No 362.

168 Nott CC No 521, 2 Ch C 218, Nott CC No 651 not SP.

169 73 SS 385. *E.I.Co v Fortescue & al'* (H1681-2) Nott CC No 1147 (discovery against interlopers of what goods shipped with them by a factor were the goods of the company) is not a case of the present principle but rather of the older principle conceded in *AG v Mico* that a plaintiff can obtain discovery to establish his own title even if this involves incidental discovery of criminal conduct of the defendant.

170 2 Vern 244.

pay liquidated damages for such trading. In *Fane v Atlee* (H1700-1)[171] the plaintiff tried to use this argument to obtain a discovery of an assignment of a lease in breach of covenant, but failed; but this seems to set the limits of the new principle rather than to reject it altogether.

The other aspect of limitation of the principle is the development of discovery of torts. In *East India Co. v Evans* (H1684-5)[172] the company sought a discovery of unlawful trading and to charge the defendants with a proportional part of the costs of their diplomatic and military operations. The defendants inter alia demurred to the bill on the ground that it would subject them to penalties and forfeitures under the Company's charter, and objected in argument that the charge of the bill sounded in tort only. The plaintiffs responded that it was common to bring bills to enable the plaintiff to bring trover; to which Serjeant Pemberton for the defendants replied that trover was founded on a right, i.e. a property interest[173]. Lord Guilford said that "it is a mistake" to say that discovery was not available for matters sounding only in tort[174].

This was essentially a political case and may have involved some stretching of a point by Lord Guilford; nonetheless it is clear that discovery was available in some cases of torts. In *Heathcote v Fleete, Morse v Buckworth* (M1702)[175] plaintiffs were allowed to obtain discovery of persons who would be vicariously liable in tort, in the first case for the negligence of a lighterman, in the second for that of the captain of a ship. The defendants compared the cases to that of liability for fire, said to be not to be assisted in equity, but the court said that the liability for negligence in the instant cases, unlike liability for fire, arose out of a "contract or undertaking" of the party so that discovery was available.

The law at the end of the period seems unsettled. The cases do not seem to me to suggest a rule growing out of the problems of criminal procedure, but rather an old-established rule whose scope is nonetheless (like many rules in equity) uncertain and at least potentially fairly wide; and a tendency in the later part of the century to restrict the operation of this rule to some narrower scope. At this period, however, this is only a tendency; the modern limitations or exceptions to the rule have not acquired a hard and fast character, and the older limitations and exceptions to the older rule have not altogether disappeared.

---

171 1 Eq Ca Ab 77.15.

172 1 Vern 305.

173 The penalties point was argued on the questions whether the penalties were avoided by the Statute of Monopolies, and whether the plaintiffs' waiver of the penalties would bind them if they abandoned the bill after answer; Lord Guilford decided on the basis that the penalties were void.

174 Citing one case of trespass by mining and another of theft of a casket of jewels.

175 2 Vern 442, 443, 1 Eq Ca Ab 76.6, 76.7. It appears from the report in Vernon that both cases were argued together, though this is slightly confused by the dating.

2. Answer conclusive against the defendant

It seems that in general the defendant was bound by his answer, so that proof varying from the answer would be discarded. Thus *Observations* says "If a Defend[an]t or pl[ain]t[iff] confesse any thing in his answer or bill w[hi]ch is against himselfe though he prove the contrary to that he confesseth by the oath of 20 witnesses yet it matters not att all but his confession will lye in his way still"[176]. While amendment of bills was freely available[177], amendment of an answer at the instance of the defendant seems to have been much more difficult. The same rule held in civilian doctrine: Clerke, Zouch and Conset all limit revocation of answers to proved specific errors[178]. In *Chute v Lady Dacre* (M1663)[179] the defendant was allowed to amend before replication, on an affidavit that errors had been added in the margin of the draft answer after she had read it, and in the absence of opposition from the plaintiff the motion was still heard by both Chancellor and Master of the Rolls sitting together. In *Hitchcock v Buckeridge* (T1676)[180] Lord Nottingham

176 *Observations* f 461r No. 190 (c. 1600). This is unusual in treating a confession in the bill as equivalent; see below § 3 (a). Cf also *Robinson v Robinson* (1589) 2 Leo 32, Ex(E), bound by plea in equity though at law not till joinder of issue; *Ward v Colmer* (1597) Toth 9, Stowe 415 f 206, bar to new answer adding part of title; *Dacres v Stanhop* Toth 9, Stowe 415 f 206, SP; *Carew, Raleigh, Thinne* (c. 1600) *Observations* f 469v No 234, inaccurate recital of a deed in the answer bars D from using the true terms; *Button v Honey* (M1658) Hardr 130, Ex(E) admission of title in answer bar to objection that title not shown in bill; *Crispe v Nevil* (M1664) 1 Ch Cas 60, 1 Eq Ca Ab 35, Clarendon C, answer to exceptions varying from bill bar to raising variance; *Norcliff v Worsley* (M1674) 1 Ch Cas 234 at 236, generally conceded ((M1669) 3 Ch Rep 29, Nott Proleg 21.20, (M1674) Nott CC No 130, not SP); *Lingen v Foley* (H1674/5) Nott CC No 183, Lord Nottingham, allegations in bill not denied in answer to be presumed true; *Warman v Seaman* (1675), above n 27 (Lord Nottingham); *Porey v Hampson* (M1677) Nott CC No 709, Lord Nottingham, defendant not to disprove his own answer because "an answer to a matter of fact which must needs be in his own knowledge is above a thousand witnesses" (79 SS 532, citing a case which appears to be *Walker v Sydenham* (below); for the idea of preference to a thousand witnesses cf Gentili 144); *Harvey v Montague* (H1682-3) 1 Vern 122 at 125 *per* counsel *arg* (for earlier proceedings before Lord Nottingham, (T1682) 1 Vern 57, Nott CC No 1156; for the litigation between widow and son to which these proceedings were ancillary, *Harvey v Harvey* (M1680) Nott CC No 1066, (H1681-2) 2 Ch Cas 82; n.d., 3 Ch Rep 87; (M1686) 2 Chan Cas 180 (application for rehearing before Jeffreys C)).

177 Above § 1.

178 Clerke 277-8, Zouch *EI* 89, Conset 104-5; at 82 Conset says that revocation is generally prohibited. Maranta 549.6 takes the same line. Cotta 157-9 says that a confession can be revoked on the ground of specific error up to the conclusion in the cause, but not if it has been accepted by the adverse party. 'Alciatus' 200r-203r gives a longer list. He says that a confession is ineffective by a minor, under duress, or under a specific error of fact, and that an erroneous confession can be revoked before *litis contestatio* for good cause; for the errors of advocates if the correction is immediate, and those of proctors if they are proved before sentence; and that a guardian's confession is revocable by the ward.

179 1 Ch Cas 29, 2 Freem 173, 1 Eq Ca Ab 29. North i 61-3 discusses this case from the standpoint of Guilford, who acted at one stage in it, & seems to suggest that obtaining leave to amend was straightforward; but this may reflect his bias.

allowed an executrix to amend her answer where she had formerly relied on an account stated in a note acknowledged by her testator, but had since found the detailed account and other evidence which falsified the account stated – again special circumstances.

There is one case which is difficult to fit with this view, and some others which appear to show exceptions to it. *Hodgson v Thornton* (H1702)[181] is a very brief report; P sued D for relief against a resignation bond taken on D's presentation of P to a living[182]; D did not allege any misbehaviour in his answer, but Wright LK allowed him to read depositions alleging misbehaviour, and founded the decree on these depositions. The basis of this decision is completely unclear, but it is possible that the point is that the allegations of misbehaviour were not inconsistent with the answer but merely absent from it[183].

Other cases on the point seem to decide that in the particular circumstances the defendant is not bound, which suggests that in general he is bound. The cases in general concern the use of the answer as a bar to a later bill brought by the original defendant. It seems to have been a commonplace that an infant's answer by guardian did not bind the infant, against whom any decree was to be *nisi* giving him an opportunity to show cause when of age[184]. Other cases turn on specific facts. In *Walker v Sydenham* (1666,7)[185] the defendants argued that the plaintiff's testatrix "could not have been relieved" against her former answer, so that the plaintiff, her executor, could not be in a better position; Lord Clarendon "conceived that the plaintiff ought not to be concluded" apparently because the issues were different, but his decision was reversed by Bridgman LK (for reasons that do not appear in the report). In *Jones v Lenthall* (M1669)[186] Grimstone MR excluded a former answer of the plaintiff's from being read in evidence for the defendant on the basis that it was merely made to avoid Parliamentary sequestration. In *Smith v Palmer* (M1669)[187] Bridgman LK rejected a plea of the plaintiff's former answer as a bar

---

180 Nott CC No 559, 73 SS 420.

181 1 Eq Ca Ab 228.5.

182 A penal bond to resign the living at request. In general such bonds could be relieved against on the basis that they were simoniacal, but this was not true in the case of a bond to resign in case of misbehaviour.

183 Compare *Observations* f 448v (un-numbered), may prove what can be "materially asserted" out of the answer, though not expressly stated.

184 *Ecclestone v Speke* (M1689) Carth 79, Comb 156, *per* counsel *arg* (as a reason why the answer should not be admitted as evidence at law); *Levinge v Calverley* (P1704) Pre Ch 229, *per cur.* (the point being that this rule did not apply to the answer of a "superannuated defendant"); *Grice v Goodwin* (T1706) Pre Ch 260, 1 Eq Ca Ab 165.5, 2 Eq Ca Ab 281, per counsel arg, (the point rejected by Lord Cowper on other grounds, viz. that in a bill of review for error of law the facts were to be taken to be as stated in the decree); *Lord Guernsey v Rodbridges* (1708) Gilb Rep 3, 2 Eq Ca Ab 518, per cur. (the point recognised but distinguished as here the infant had acquiesced 21 years when of age). Cf 'Alciatus' 203r.

185 1 Ch Rep 270.

186 1 Ch Cas 154.

on the basis that the plaintiff was alleging that he had been induced to answer in this way by the fraud of Brown, his solicitor and co-defendant in the former proceedings, against whom the present bill was brought. In *Wiseman v Beake & Tyson* (1690)[188] the Lords Commissioners overruled an argument that the plaintiff "ought not to be relieved against his own election and oath" in a former answer on the basis that the former proceedings were collusive, Lord Commissioner Keck saying that "as the fortifications of fraud do increase, so the Courts of equity must invent new batteries against them"[189].

This evidence is, I think, sufficient to support the conclusion that the answer was, at least in principle, conclusive against the defendant. This conclusive character seems unlikely to be based on an analogy with the conclusiveness of pleadings at common law. The common-law rules applied as much to plaintiffs as to defendants[190], while in equity the bill is not conclusive in the same sense[191]. And at common law what was not denied was taken to be admitted[192], while in equity it was necessary to force the defendant to perfect his answer if he failed to affirm or deny the matters alleged in the bill[193]. Rather, it seems to me, the explanation of the binding character of the answer has two elements. One is a direct application of the maxim *confessus pro judicato accepitur*, which may form the basis of the compulsory answer procedure in the first place. The second is the magic of the oath, which gives the sworn answer a special weight.

3. Other admissions

A number of statements could be used as admissions, i.e. read in proof against the person who made them (or someone privy to that person) though they were not admissible in his favour. These admissions did not have the conclusive force of the answer when it was taken in the instant proceedings or pleaded in bar. We have already seen the use of answers in previous proceedings in this way[194], and there was a fairly substantial body of law concerning the use of equity answers in com-

---

187 1 Ch Cas 133.

188 2 Vern 122, 2 Freem 111, 1 Eq Ca Ab 91.14.

189 2 Freem 111 at 112.

190 Holdsworth HEL IX 274-5.

191 Above § 1 on amendments; below § 2 (3) (a).

192 Langdell 756.

193 Jones 217-8, and above n 86.

194 Previous section; and cf *Winchcomb v Winchcomb* (1674) 2 Ch Rep 101, father's answer admissible against son, and *Jones v Purefoy* (P1682) 1 Vern 45, same and *per* Lord Nottingham, the son "would have a difficult defence, when he went about to perjure his own father". (NB that the earlier proceedings in *Purefoy v Jones* (T1679) 2 Freem 44, Nott CC No 947, are reported by Lord Nottingham as decided purely on the basis of *tabula in naufragium* and not on this point).

mon law proceedings[195]. It also seems to have been possible in principle to use the bill in this way, or statements out of court either in documents or orally. Out of court documentary admissions are best dealt with as an aspect of proof by documents (below Ch 3). The bill, and out of court oral admissions, posed specific problems.

a) The bill

In civilian doctrine, *qui ponit fatetur,* i.e. factual allegations in the plaintiff's positions which were favourable to the defendant could be used as confessions against the plaintiff[196]. The rule applied specifically to positions, not to articles; hence, not to libels or petitions in summary procedure[197]. It *might* therefore have applied to the rolled-up *libellus articulatus,* but it is not mentioned by Clerke; it is very hard to see how it could have applied to the bill in Chancery, which may well have originated as a petition, but by the seventeenth century was being treated for the purposes of amendment rules as analogous to a libel. A document which was readily amendable could hardly be a conclusive confession, and apart from the statement in *Observations* quoted above in relation to answers, there are only a couple of cases which suggest, weakly, that the bill might conclude the plaintiff[198]. In the later seventeenth and early eighteenth century, however, bills do seem to have been readable in subsequent litigation against the original plaintiff[199], though,

195 Gilbert pp 38-41, and cf *Anon* (P1623) Godb. 326, KB; *Greenwood's Case* (1634) Clayt 28, NP, *Ecclestone v Speke* (M1689) Carth 79, Comb 156, KB; *Wright v Carew* (H1689/90) Nels 175, *per cur* in Chancery; *Mathew d Earl of Sussex v Tompson* (H1699-1700) 5 Mod 384, 1 Ld Raym 311; *Ford v Lord Grey* (H1703/4) 1 Salk 285, 6 Mod 44, KB.

196 Cotta 159-160 (unless the adverse party denies the position in question); 'Alciatus' 198 v. Langdell 771 cites Maranta, tit. *De Positione* No 6 (in the edition I have used, *De Interrogatione* No. 6, p 490; *De Positione* Nos 6-9, 13, pp 549-50); Gaill Obs. 79 No 6; Burn, *Ecclesiastical Law* (ed. Phillimore, 1842) 264; Oughton, *Ordo Judiciorum* (1738) tit 54 n (c) 4.

197 Sources cited at last note and Gaill ii Obs 79 No 7.

198 In *Chichly v* – (T1658) Hardr 117 on a bill to bind tenants to a former decree for enclosure of a common, the defendants put a title by prescription in their answer. P's replication denied this title. The court after saying that the defendants were not bound by the former decree, to which they had not been parties, ordered a trial at law of the defendants' title to the common, saying that as laid in the answer it was void at law. Hardres comments that this seemed hard on the defendants, because the bill by seeking to bind them to the improvements admitted their title to the common; but besides being a reporter's criticism rather than authority, this seems to me to betray common-law thinking; the title was effectively put in issue by the answer and replication. In *Ives v Medcalfe, Medcalfe v Ives* (1737) 1 Atk 63, West t Hard 82, Cas t Hard 382 a defendant's cross-bill was dismissed at the Rolls, and the defendant did not appeal this decision; Lord Hardwicke allowed the abandoned cross-bill to be read to bar the defendant taking the same point of law on an appeal from the principal decision at the Rolls. Wigmore, §1065, cites the brief report of the point in Atkyns for the use of the bill as an admission of fact, but this does not seem to be the real issue.

not being on oath, the bill was regarded as weak evidence[200]. This development may betray a diluted influence of the common law principles which made pleadings on both sides judicial confessions.

b) Oral admissions out of court

There is some evidence to suppose that oral admissions out of court were regarded with suspicion by the courts at this period. The objection seems not to be connected with the modern rule about confessions in criminal cases, but rather to be analogous to or connected with the view that oral hearsay was "the weakest sort" of evidence (below, Ch 8 § 5)[201].

---

199 In equity, *Woollet v Roberts* (1664) 1 Ch Cas 64, , Nels 102, 1 Eq Ca Ab 227.1, Chancery, readable provided shown to have been exhibited with the privity of the party; at law, *Snow d Crawley v Phillips* (1664) 1 Sid 220, 1 Keb 780, KB, privity of the party to be presumed, but *per* Siderfin, provided there are subsequent proceedings on it; Gilbert, *Evidence* at BM Add MS 36090 f 24b.

"But it is said that in this Case there must be proceedings upon it, for if there were not proceedings upon it it sho{ul}d rather be supposed to be ffyled by a Stranger to bar the party of his evidence and therefore a Bill ffiled meerly without any Proceedings upon it has not the force of any Evidence, for no man can suppose that the party did himself fyle the Bill without any Proceedings to bring his adversary to answer; such a bill is of no use to the party and therefore must rather be supposed to be ffyled by a stranger to do him injury"

and

"But where a bill is exhibited and there are no Proceedings upon it there it cannot be given in Evidence unless they prove a privity in the party for any man may ffile a Bill in another's name to Robb him of his Evidence by a sham confession"

(printed text is garbled); *Despard v Ormsby* (1713) Colles 459, HL(I), said by counsel that the "constant practice in equity" is not to admit bills unless they were prosecuted and an answer put in.

200 *Snow v Phillips,* said to be "not as valid" as a letter from the party, and *Mews v Mews* (1670) 1 Vent 66 (trial of an issue out of Chancery), "of slight moment". It could also be objected that the bill contained allegations known to everybody to be fictitious (eg confederacy) and could therefore not be taken as a statement of fact, just as the declaration at common law would generally not on its own create an estoppel (Co Lit 352). This may be the point made by counsel objecting to reading the bill in *Snow v Phillips* at 1 Sid 221; a bill was rejected as evidence, on unclear grounds, in *Lord Ferrers v Shirley* (1730) Fitzg. 195, and according to Wigmore §1065 by the end of the eighteenth century bills were excluded at common law.

201 Cotta 161, 'Alciatus' 201v-202r, and Maranta 553-5 Nos. 2-20, are heavily dominated by questions related to contracts and dispositions. At 553, however, Maranta says that in criminal matters an extrajudicial confession is not generally full proof, but can be an *indicium* to support torture (No. 3), and that in civil matters an extrajudicial confession proved by two witnesses to the same confession is a half proof; it only becomes a full proof if made in the presence of the adverse party (No. 2) and by dispositive words (No. 4) – i.e. if it is in fact a contract. Vulteius 371r says that an extrajudicial confession is easily revoked and does not have the force of a judicial one; and Wood 311-312 that "extrajudicial discourse" is merely a half proof unless made at the point of death. This does to some extent suggest a view of extra-

Such oral admissions were admissible[202], but seem to have been regarded as weak evidence: in *Gascoigne v Thwing* (H1685-6)[203] the reporter comments that the proofs amounted "only to what had passed in discourses, and been owned by the defendant, and the proofs beings doubtful" Trevor MR dismissed the bill for insufficiency of proof[204]. In *Anon* (M1702) Holt CJ is reported as saying that "confession is the worst sort of evidence, that is, if there be no proof of a transaction or dealing, or at least a probability of dealing between them."[205]. And in *Gilbert v Emerton* (T1705) counsel "insisted, that little regard ought to be given to witnesses, who only swore a confession, when the defendant had denied it upon his oath";[206] Wright LK directed a trial of a feigned issue on the point in question. This again brings us back to the specific weight of the oath, here making the defendant's denial on oath in court stronger than his alleged confession out of court.

4. Use of the answer otherwise than against the defendant

In the roman-canon system the party's answers when interrogated are generally evidence against him and not in his favour[207]; nor are they evidence against any other party[208]. On balance it seems that this was also the general rule in equity in this period. There are two difficulties with this, however. The first is that the point that the defendant's answer is (in general) merely a confession is the sort of "obvious" point which is likely to be taken for granted and not made explicit. The second is that there are a substantial number of cases in which the answer does seem to be used for other purposes.

---

judicial confessions as generally weak evidence. On the other hand, Gentili 146 argues that a confession can be proved by a single witness and is strong evidence.

202 As well as the cases cited below cf *Gould's Case* (n.d.) Hob 93, Jenk. 300.63 at common law, *Curtess v Smallridge* (H1663/4) 1 Ch Cas 43, 2 Freem 178, 1 Eq Ca Ab 81.4, 377.1, 2 Eq Ca Ab 173 (Chancery, *per cur.*, admissible both at common law and in equity). Also possibly relevant is *Osborne v Greaves & al'* (1641) Harg 174 f 8 (dated in MS 6 Car, but this is inconsistent with the judge named in the report, so probably 16 Car), Littleton LK, oral admissions that a conveyance was a mortgage "merely voluntary"; compare Maranta 554 No. 6, requiring *causa* for an effective confession.

203 1 Vern 366, 1 Eq Ca Ab 232.7. The case is mainly on the application of the Statute of Frauds to presumed resulting trusts; the reporter comments that in fact the purpose of the transaction was the (illegal) establishment of a nunnery, which had fallen through.

204 1 Vern 366 at 366-7.

205 7 Mod 49, KB.

206 2 Vern 503.

207 'Alciatus' 200r No. 4; Maranta 557.27, the first point.

208 'Alciatus' 200r No. 21, citing D. 42.2.6.4; Zouch *El* 98, citing D. 42.2.6 and D. 11.1.11.

However, I would argue that these cases do not force an inference that the answer was generally a proof in the cause. First, a number are instances of clear exceptions; these therefore actually tend to support the view that the answer was in general merely a confession. Second, there are several instances of the use of the answer against co- defendants. But these, too, seem to involve exceptions to a general rule. Third, in a number of cases the answer seems to be given a specific weight because it is on oath. This is plausible in view of the "exceptional" character of the requirement to answer on oath (above § 2 *(1)*). On investigation, however, they seem mostly to be later seventeenth century rationalisations of independently existing rules.

a) Exceptions

There are two areas in which the defendant's answer serves for proof in his favour which seem to be exceptions to a general principle that it cannot be so used. The first is what the civilians called a "qualified" confession[209]; the second concerns small sums of money.

(1) *QUALIFIED CONFESSIONS:* In several cases it is said that when the answer or other admission is the only proof to charge the defendant, in an account, there it is also proof to discharge him. The first reported application of this principle is *Digs v Digs* (1595):

> The plaintiff would have charged the defendant with a receipt by the defendant's own accompt whereupon hee must also allow his owne discharge made by the said accompt for if hee beleeve him in one hee shall doe the like in all[210].

In Lord Nottingham's *Prolegomena* the rule appears as a settled one with exceptions of its own. Thus in *Holstcomb v Rivers* (1669)[211] the the defendant and C were factors for the plaintiff in Spain, and in 1654 sent the plaintiff an account charging themselves with various goods. In 1656 the Spanish government seized all the goods of English merchants in Spain, including the defendant's and C's books. The plaintiff, having previously sued C's executrix, brought a bill to compel the defendant to account. The defendant swearing in his answer to the seizure of the books, Bridgman LK, assisted by Wilde and Rainsford JJ, ordered that he was not to be charged in the account for more than he could remember on his own oath was made by sale of the goods before the seizure. But in *Acourt v Chambers & Gifford* (H1669)[212] the defendant executor Chambers had burned the testator's books; it was ruled:

---

209 Wood 311; Maranta (quoted below), "confessio qualificata".

210 Harl 1576 f 150.

211 1 Ch Cas 127, Nels 139, 1 Eq Ca Ab 5.1, Nott. Proleg c19 pl 1.

212 Nott. Proleg. 19. 3, 9.

1. That generally where the plaintiff cannot charge but by his own proper oath, there the defendant's oath shall likewise be a discharge. 2. But not so here, because the burning of the books by the defendant hath disabled the plaintiff...

but

because Gifford was not privy to the burning of the books and could not otherwise be charged but by his own account, his own oath was accepted in discharge.

The principle was accepted in *Darston v Earl of Orford* (1701)[213] and *Bayly v Hill* (1702)[214]; and the general argument was also used in the 1690s by Holt CJ in relation to admissions and confessions at common law both in civil[215] and criminal[216] proceedings. A restriction seems to be placed on it by Lord Cowper in an anonymous case of 1707 reported in Gilbert, *Evidence,* where it is said that

... when an answer was put in issue, what was confessed and admitted need not be proved, but it behoved the defendant to make out by proofs what was insisted on by way of avoidance, but this was held under this distinction; where the defendant admitted a fact and insisted on a distinct fact by way of avoidance, there he ought to prove the matter of his defence, because it may be probable that he admitted it out of apprehension that it might be proved, and therefore such admittance ought not to profit him so far as to pass for truth whatever he says in avoidance, but if it had been one fact, as if the defendant had said that the testator had given him 100l. it ought to have been allowed unless disproved, because nothing of the fact charged is admitted, and the plaintiff may disprove the whole fact as sworn, if he can do it ...[217]

This account corresponds roughly to that given by Maranta of the issue:

... & tunc sit distinctio, an sit unum capitulum in confessione vel plura. ... aut confessio qualificata continet unum capitulum, & debet tota acceptari, vel tota repudiari, & non potest dividi, ut si reus confitetur se promississe sub conditione, vel si dicat, verum est quod recepi a te centum, quae mihi debebas ex causa mutui, istud est unicum c. & confessio in isto casu non praeiudicat confitenti ... Aut continet plura capitula, si dicit, verum est, quod mutuasti mihi centum, sed fecissi mihi pactum, de non petendo, & tunc potest acceptari pro parte, & tenetur reus probare pactum de non petendo alias condemnatur[218].

Similarly, Wood says that

... when the Confession is regular, and admitted by the other party, he ought to admit the whole as it is qualified ... unless there is a presumption against that part.

---

213 1 Eq Ca Ab 10 (Wright LK); 1 P Wms 401n, Pre Ch 188, 2 Eq Ca Ab 460 (Wright LK), Colles 233 (HL), not SP.

214 1 Eq Ca Ab 10.10 (Trevor MR).

215 eg *Worrall v Holder* (1696) Skin 572; & cf *Brockman's Case* (Trin Ass 1701) Gilbert *Evidence* p 39 *per* Gould J, answer or affidavit given in evidence at law.

216 eg *Paine* (1696) Comb 358, 5 Mod 163, 1 Ld Raym 729.

217 Gilbert Evidence 39, sidenoted as *Anon* Hill Vacat 1707 per Cowper, at 40.

218 Maranta *de Confessione* No 27, p 557. Ellipses within the quotation replace authorities cited in the original.

... The Libel charges that you receiv'd 100 *l.* of me. You answer, that you did receive 100 *l.* of me which I ow'd you, and no other sum; This is but one Sentence, and cannot be divided; for with one breath I do as it were absolutely deny the charge. But where the Sentences are divided, there the Confession shall be divided, and part accepted and part rejected ...[219]

The rule in *Digs v Digs* and following cases is cruder than this version, but recognisably follows the same principles. These may also be involved in the rules under which the defendant's answer was conclusive if the plaintiff asserted that he had no other evidence[220], went to hearing on bill and answer[221], or had the defendant examined on interrogatories after perfect answer[222].

(2) *SMALL SUMS:* The second exceptional area is that parties examined before Masters on accounts were permitted to discharge themselves by their own oath of small sums paid out. This rule appears to have existed in the practice of the ecclesiastical courts in the 1590s[223], with a limit of 40s. In first appears in the 1630s as a rule that "a man may dispose [?depose] for small disbursements which he cannot make proof of"[224]. However, the 40s limit is reported in the time of Lord Nottingham[225], and there are other signs of a hardened approach in the later period: Lord Guilford requires the accountant to state who he paid the sums to, what for and when[226]; in Jeffreys' time the total of such sums must be less than £100, and Jeffreys characterises the rule as "unreasonable"[227]; Trevor MR, in 1702, states the rule as limited to servants[228].

---

219 311.

220 *Madox v Jacks* (1596) Harl 1576 f 151; *Observations* f 443v No. 54, also saying that this dismissal is a bar to a new bill on the same facts.

221 *Observations* f446r No 91 (follows No. 70) (c. 1600); Bacon's Orders 1618 No 64, i Sanders 117.

222 *Juramentum delatum a parte* Cary 11, Stowe 415 f 93b, Harg 281 f 15, *Fyfield v Vimore* (1559-60) Cary 45 (*Ffyfoile v Vinonde*) Stowe 415 f 106 (*Anfield v Vinor*) Lansd 599 f 26; and for all these points cf above n 89 and below Ch 6 § 4 *(1)* (c).

223 Clerke, *Prax. Ecc.* Tit 66, pp 82-3; Swinburne Part 6 § 20 n 1; Conset 289, citing Lyndwood *De testamentis, c. statutum,* § *inventar vero,* v. *reddere rationem* (p 177), where it is said that proof of small payments is difficult, and that therefore an executor who is of good character may prove them by oath (without specifying any specific figure). Zouch *DIE* 43 says that in canon law proof by party oath is accepted in minor causes, but this seems to simplify the rules for the *suppletory* oath, which required a half proof to have been made ('Alciatus' 228r-229r, Maranta 598-9) and mix them with canonical purgation (Maranta 601 Nos 28-9).

224 *Weldon v James* (1634) Toth 136; cf *Peyton v Green* (1640) 1 Ch Rep 146 (old account).

225 *Elvard v Warren* (1679) 2 Ch Cas 249, 1 Eq Ca Ab 11.13, Nott CC No 841. The 40s limit does not appear in *Tredcroft v White* (1671) 3 Ch Rep 72 (Bridgman LK) ((1673) Rep t Finch 36 not SP), (and Lord Nottingham allowed £40 stolen on the party's own oath in *Morley v Morley* (H1679) 2 Ch Cas 2, but this appears to be an exception), but does in the subsequent cases except *Holstcomb v Rivers* and *Bayly v Hill.*

226 *Anon* (1684) 1 Vern 283, 1 Eq Ca Ab 11.13.

There is one example of an application of this rule to an answer. In *Bayly v Hill* (1702) the defendant received money for her aunt, who lived with her, and on the aunt's dying intestate, the plaintiff, who was one of the next of kin, sought an account. The defendant's answer set out sums received, some of them put out at interest to named persons, and some paid to the aunt. The cause being heard without proof, an account was decreed; on which the master referred to the court whether the defendant was to be discharged as well as charged by the answer. Trevor MR

"said that, though he looked on the defendant in this case to have acted only in the nature of a servant, who by the justice of this court may, on a bill brought against him by his master's executors, discharge as well as charge himself by his answer; yet as the defendant might in this case have proved her answer, as appears by the answer itself, and had not done so, he referred it back to the master, and each side to make what proofs they could; and if the answer was disproved, as to the sums put out at interest, he should give no credit to it as to other particulars, else inclined it should be a discharge as well as a charge"[229].

Given the prior and identical rule in the church courts and the statement in *Brudnell v Buxnell* (1596-7)[230] that equity follows the civil law as to whether it will order executors or administrators to account on oath, it seems likely that the rule in Chancery is derived from the canon law.

b) Co-defendants

In a case of 1597 "a defendant by answer accuseth himself and his fellow and is beleeved against himself but not his fellow"[231]. In *Eyre v Northey* (1627)[232] it is said that one defendant's answer is not to prejudice another defendant; *The Practice* (1651) says that a confession in the answer does not bind a co-defendant[233]; and in his *Practice* Lord Nottingham said that "The confession of one defendant cannot be made use of at the hearing to bind another."[234].

In some cases, however, answers do seem to have been used against co-defendants. In *Observations* it is said that if one of the defendants appears to have been

227 *Whicherley v Whicherley* (1687) 1 Vern 471, 1 Eq Ca Ab 11.13. Neither the £100 limit, nor criticisms like Jeffreys', appear in *Marshfield v Weston* (1690) 2 Vern 176, 1 Eq Ca Ab 11.14, and Equity Cases Abridged describes the rule after this case as "the estáblished practice in Chancery".

228 *Bayly v Hill* (T1702) 1 Eq Ca Ab 10.10.

229 1 Eq Ca Ab 10.10.

230 (Undated, but among cases of H1596-7) Harl 1576 f 152.

231 *MIchel v Webb* (1 Nov 40 Eliz) Harl 1576 f 164r, Stowe 415 f 206v, Harg 281 f 110v. *Mitchell v Webb* Toth 10 dates to 4 Eliz (1561), but given the surrounding cases the later date, given in all the MSS, seems preferable.

232 (c 3 Car) Toth 13.

233 P. 19.

234 Title VI No 15, *TT* p 118.

put in the bill merely to take away his testimony by making him a party, then that defendant's answer may be read[235]. In *Thorold v Saville & al'* (1637)[236] the bill was for legacies chargeable on Saville's estate under a will. Saville by answer said he did not know of any such will or legacies; his co-defendants, who were alleged to be trustees to raise the legacies under the will said by answer that they believed Saville to have suppressed the will. Lord Coventry decreed for the plaintiff, though there was only one witness to the existence of the will. In *Collingwood v Basset* (H1681)[237] the principal defendant's wife answered separately and admitted the trust alleged by the plaintiff. The plaintiff was only able to produce one witness, and Lord Nottingham dismissed the bill:

> "This will not serve, for the answer of a feme covert executrix cannot charge her husband in Chancery, any more than her assent to a legacy without assets shall charge her husband at common law."[238]

This exclusion on the basis of the rights of the husband suggests that otherwise the answer might have been used against the co-defendant. In *Cookes & Ux' v Mascall & Cookes* (1687,1690)[239] a husband and wife sued their fathers for specific performance of an agreement to make a settlement on their marriage; the wife's father pleaded the Statute of Frauds. Jeffreys C inclined to dismiss the bill but gave the plaintiffs 12 months to try at law whether there was any actionable agreement; but the Lords Commissioners on a rehearing in 1690 decreed specific performance on the basis that the couple were married from the wife's father's house and with his approval – which appears to have been proved only by the husband's father's answer. In *Pring v Pring* (1689)[240] a testator made his will, but in it did no more than to appoint three executors in trust and give them 20s each for costs and charges. The bill charged that this was a trust for the plaintiff, the testator's wife. Two of the executors admitted the trust; the third denied it. The two executors who admitted the trust were read against the third and the trust decreed[241].

In *Eyton v Eyton* (1700)[242] on a bill for discovery of a settlement under which the plaintiff claimed, the plaintiff produced what he claimed was a counterpart of the settlement. In previous litigation one of the present defendants had answered admitting the terms of the settlement, but his present answer said that he might

---

235 f 457v No 168.

236 Harg 174 f 3.

237 2 Ch Cas 39, 1 Eq Ca Ab 65.9, Nott. CC No 1070.

238 79 SS p 854.

239 (H 1687) 2 Vern 34 (Jeffreys C); (H 1690) 2 Vern 200, 1 Eq Ca Ab 22.18 (Lords Commissioners).

240 2 Vern 98; *cit per* Hutchins Ld Cssr 2 Vern 254.

241 Hutchins at 2 Vern 254 says that the two executors were *examined and* read against the defendant, ie as witnesses, which may mean their answer itself was not usable.

242 (1699,1700) Pre Ch 116, 2 Vern 380, 1 Eq Ca Ab 169; (1706) 4 Bro PC 149 (HL) not SP.

then have been mistaken and the co-defendants denied all knowledge. Counsel for the defendants insisted that (i) the counterpart was not admissible unless it could be supported by the answer, and (ii) the answer wasn't evidence against the co-defendants. Trevor MR rejected this argument and made a decree for the plaintiff, which was affirmed by Somers C[243].

In *Tidcombe v Cholmley, Boddington & al'* (1700)[244] the plaintiff sought relief against personal liability at law on a contract for regimental uniforms, alleging fraud by M, one of the defendants who was an agent for both sides. M by answer admitted a parol agreement limiting the plaintiff's personal liability. Wright LK accepted the defendants' argument that this was parol evidence which should not be admitted to vary the written contract; and on the plaintiff's appeal to the House of Lords, Attwood for the defendants argued *inter alia* that M's answer should not be credited because he was alleging himself guilty of a fraud on both sides[245]. Both these arguments assume that the answer could be used against the other defendants; and the Lords "seemed disposed to reverse the decree"[246], with the result that the matter was compromised.

It is not easy to extract general rules from these cases, since the case for using the answer does not seem to be clearly reported. There seem to be two possibilities. The first is that the defendant who confesses the whole charge of the bill is no longer interested; so that he or she could in principle be examined as a witness, and the answer is used as a substitute for this examination[247]. Most of the cases so far discussed could fit this approach, and a clearer instance is *Pitt v Willis* (1715), briefly reported by Dickens[248]: "the answer of a defendant, not brought to hearing, read as evidence against another defendant at the hearing".

Another possibility is that if the defendants have a common interest, they may be regarded as privies, so that the answer of one may be usable against the others. The evidence for this is of the converse, viz. arguments by defendants that since there is no common interest, they should not be obliged to answer because the aim of the bill can only be to take their evidence away from the other defendants. Thus in *Harvey v Baker* (P1678)[249] a defendant pleaded that he was merely an agent to

243 Wright LK on a rehearing in 1701 ordered the defendants to bring an ejectment against the plaintiff, in which they succeeded by setting up a recovery of part of the settled property in 1648; there was then an appeal to the HL on other points on the equity reserved.

244 Pre Ch 143 (Wright LK); (1701) Colles 166 (HL).

245 Colles 166 at 170; cf below Ch 6 pp 224-5.

246 Ib. 171. There may have been non-legal reasons for the Lords' "disposition" to relieve the plaintiff: corrupt practices in army clothing and supply were particularly notorious problems at this time. For an account of this and other cases cf Childs, *The British Army of William III 1689-1702* (Manchester UP, 1987) Chs 6, 7, esp pp 167-171.

247 Cf the modern rule as to criminal defendants, Cross 194f, *R v Lord Desmond & al'* (P1621) Noy 154, Star Ch, a criminal defendant who confesses may be used as a witness against co-defendants, and below Ch 6 §§ 4 *(1)*, *(2)*.

248 Dick. 24 (Cowper C).

the trustees, the principal defendants, so that his answer could not be used against them. Lord Nottingham rejected the argument on the basis that the plaintiff had a direct cause of action, since he might be able to trace assets into this defendant's hands. In *Steward v East India Company* (1700)[250] a similar argument was successful, a group of individual defendants who had been brought in as assisting the principal defendant in a fraud successfully demurring on the ground that "the plaintiff could have no decree against them and their answers would be no evidence against the company, and the plaintiff might examine them as witnesses". It is possible that unity of interest / privity is the basis of the argument for use of the defendant's answers in *Eyton v Eyton,* where the only interest of the defendant who made the admissions was as one of the co- defendants' husband[251]. Gilbert[252] says that answers are evidence as admissions which also have the force of an oath; he does not discuss the question of evidential value as against co-defendants in the same proceedings.

c) The weight of the oath

Arguments and dicta in a number of cases seem to imply that the answer has some weight in favour of the defendant because it is on oath. But the rules to which the argument is applied seem to have an existence independent of any positive weight being given to the answer. Thus, in *Gilbert v Emerton*[253] counsel's argument rests in part on the alleged conflict between the alleged confession and the defendant's positive denial on oath; but, as I have already argued, out of court admissions are independently seen as weak[254]. Similarly, in *Langton v Tracy & Astrey* (1669)[255] denial in the defendant's answer is part of the grounds argued by counsel for the exclusion of a (trustee) plaintiff's deposition; but the exclusion of parties as witnesses is not based on conflict with the defendant's oath[256].

---

249 Nott. CC No 817, 79 SS 631. Cf also *Atterbury V Hawkins* (P1678) Nott. CC No. 814, 2 Ch. Cas. 242, *per* counsel *arg* (rejected, but probably because irrelevant in the circumstances) ((P1677) Nott. CC No. 663 not SP).

250 (T 1700) 2 Vern 380, 1 Eq Ca Ab 40.8, 73.14.

251 Though the relationships in question, except for the agency relation in *Tidcombe v Cholmley,* would not serve to make admissions admissible in the modern law: see Wigmore §§ 1076-1087. In *Eyton v Eyton* the admissibility of the counterpart may have been reinforced by the presumptions arising from length of time and spoliation, from non-production by Jane & Anne as successors to BE; for these see below, Chs 3 & 8.

252 *Evidence* pp 38-9.

253 Above n 206 and text there.

254 Cf above § 2 (3) (b); though obviously if the defendant admitted the matter in his answer the question would not arise.

255 2 Ch Rep 30.

256 Cf below Ch 6 § 4.

The clearest instance of this sort of use of the defendant's oath as rationalisation is in explanations of the two-witness rule as grounded on "oath against oath". "Oath against oath" initially appears as a prohibition of affidavit against affidavit in the context of service of process and contempt[257]. In *Hobbs v Norton* (1683)[258] an item of evidence proved only by one witness, denied by the defendant's answer, and inherently improbable, is rejected. *Alam v Jourdan* (1683)[259] is reported purely on the point that there can be no decree on one witness against the defendant's answer. In *Lady Montague v Earl of Bath* (1692)[260], the plaintiffs alleged inter alia concealment from the settlor of the conditions for revocation of a settlement. The defendant said in his answer that the deed was delivered to and kept by the settlor. At a hearing before Somers LK assisted by Holt and Treby CJJ and Powell B, counsel for the plaintiff argued that since the plaintiff had replied generally to the answer, it was not evidence. Treby CJ responded to this by saying that the onus of proof is still with the plaintiff;[261] Somers LK said that

> "as to their Answer, I take it no Decree can be made against a man's Answer upon the proof of one witness; then why should a Decree be expected against a man's Answer when there is no proof to the contrary at all?"[262]

In *Ibbotson v Rhodes* (1706)[263] the plaintiff was seeking to gain priority for his mortgage by setting up an estoppel by representation. One witness deposed that he had at the plaintiff's direction asked the defendant whether he had any mortgage on the estate, which the defendant denied. The defendant's answer had confessed that he had met the witness in a public market and said that the witness had asked him how much Shipley owed him, but that the witness hadn't told him the plaintiff was proposing to lend Shipley money. On appeal from Trevor MR's decree for the plaintiff, the defendant argued that

> "The plaintiff proved it by one witness, which by the usage of this Court is not sufficient to found a decree for the plaintiff, being oath against oath; but the course has been to direct a trial at law;"[264]

Lord Cowper's response is interesting:

> "he did not see the Difference between doing it *per Plura* and *per Pauciora;* for to send it to law to be tried, where the jury will certainly find it on the testimony of one witness, and

---

257 *Observations* (c 1600) ff 472r-v No. 248; Bacon's Orders of 1619 No 76, Sanders 119, repeated Nott Prac 7.7, *TT* 119 with the note that the rule has been omitted in subsequent orders. Compare Clerke 81: because contempts are summary, a defence is rarely admitted.

258 1 Vern 136, 2 Ch Cas 128.

259 1 Vern 161, 1 Eq Ca Ab 229.12.

260 2 Ch Rep 421, Nels 196, 2 Freem 121, 193, 3 Ch Cas 55, 2 Eq Ca Ab 671. The fullest report is in Ch Cas.

261 3 Ch Cas at 84.

262 Ib. at 123.

263 2 Vern 554, 1 Eq Ca Ab 229.13.

264 1 Eq Ca Ab 229.

then decreeing it on that verdict, is the same thing as decreeing on one witness, without trying it at all; and so directed it to be tried; but that the plaintiff should admit the defendant's answer to be read at the trial, not as evidence, for that he said it could not be, nor should they admit it to be true; but to be sworn, so that the defendant might have the benefit of his oath at law, as in this Court, if it would weigh anything with the jury."[265]

In fact it appears from Vernon's report that the reason the defendant wanted a trial may have been that the witness had proved shifty under cross-examination[266], so that the more vigorous cross-examination possible at law might break him down completely. What Lord Cowper seems to be saying here is that (1) the defendant's answer is not "evidence", that is, probably, not an admissible document[267], at law (and therefore not in a feigned issue); but (2) the defendant in Chancery "has the benefit of" a positive denial on oath – that is, the two-witness rule, assuming the "oath against oath" explanation of this rule offered by counsel; and therefore (3) he will direct the plaintiff at trial to allow the jury to be told that the defendant has in his answer, on oath, contradicted the witness' claim, in case it would "weigh anything with the jury".

This suggests that the "oath against oath" argument is beginning to have some substantive effect; and Gilbert says that the course of the Chancery is to direct a trial at law where there is only one witness, on the basis that "there the credibility is equal"[268]. However, this does not fit very well with the restrictive view taken at this period of the "charge/discharge"[269] and "small sums"[270] rules, and it later became the clear orthodoxy that the answer was only evidence in so far as it contained admissions[271].

There is one instance of what appears to be a decree "against" a plaintiff on the basis of the defendant's answer[272]. In *Hampton v Spencer* (1693)[273] P conveyed a house and surrendered a copyhold estate to D, expressedly in consideration of £80 paid. P's bill alleged that this was in reality a mortgage and sought redemption; D's answer denied it was a mortgage, but said it was a trust for the

---

265 Ib.

266 2 Vern 554: "Nor did Gargrave on cross-examination take upon him to swear it, but slides in the fact".

267 For this usage, above ch 1 n 3.

268 *Evidence* p 109. The cases sidenoted in the printed text are not in the MSS.

269 *Anon* (1707) Gilbert Evidence 39, above n 217 & text there.

270 *Bayly v Hill* (1702) above nn 228-9 and text there.

271 Wigmore §1065.

272 *Observations* ff 462v-463r No 199 tells us that it is exceptionally possible to make a decree against a plaintiff where it falls out on proof that the plaintiff has law on his side but the defendant has equity on his, though the more regular procedure is to obtain leave to bring a cross-bill after publication using only the existing proofs. But this concerns matter set out in the answer but proved by witnesses; the answer is not being used as a proof in the defendant's favour.

273 2 Vern 287.

maintenance of P's wife and children. Trevor MR decreed the trust over the objection, from P's counsel, that D had not proved the trust. This decision is also apparently anomalous in view of Lord Nottingham's statement that there can be no decree against a plaintiff[274]. On both points, however, the anomaly is merely apparent. P failed to prove his allegation that the transaction was a mortgage and was therefore not entitled to a decree. Decreeing the trust was therefore not detrimental to P, so not a decree against P; nor was it beneficial to D, who was subjected to the duties of a trustee. So the decision is in fact consistent with the view of the answer as a confession.

On balance, therefore, it seems probable that the general rule was, as in the roman-canon systems, that the defendant's answer was only evidence against and not for him. On this analysis, the authorities which give the answer some larger effect fall to be explained as exceptions. It may be that these exceptions were more readily acceptable because of the special weight of the oath.

III. Conclusion

The picture that emerges is of a body of rules very largely consistent with the principles of the roman-canon system. The bill, not tied to rigid forms and readily amendable, is in this respect similar to the canonist libel, and unlike the plaintiff's pleadings at common law; but it remains in principle true, as in civilian doctrine, that judicial decision must be *secundum allegata et probata.*

As in the roman-canon system, and unlike the common law, the defendant was required to answer the plaintiff's allegations on oath. The requirement of an answer on oath varied from the roman-canon systems in being immediate and automatic, rather than at the election of the plaintiff. I suggest, however, that this peculiarity is attributable to the auxiliary character of the equity jurisdiction. Defendants were not required to answer certain bills, particularly those which were incriminating or "scandalous". Maguire and Levy argued that this rule was a basic feature of the distinctness of the common law procedure; Wigmore, though attributing early cases in part to canonist influence, saw the general rule as emerging in the mid seventeenth century as a result of political developments and confusion. Neither of these views seems acceptable; rather, the equity rules are earlier in date than those at common law and seem closer to roman-canon doctrine about incriminating or defamatory positions.

The law as to the effect of the answer and other admissions seems similarly broadly consistent with the civilian doctrine of confession as the highest form of proof. The answer appears in general to have been conclusive against the defendant (subject, as always in equity, to exceptions); other admissions could be used

274 Prac 9.22, Proleg. 24.1.

but had lesser weight; in general (again subject to exceptions) the answer seems to be used as a confession, rather than as an item of proof generally usable.

In most of these areas there are some indications in the later seventeenth and early eighteenth century of some shift towards what might be called a "common law" approach: a greater rigidity in relation to decision *secundum allegata,* signs of a reconceptualisation of "self-incrimination", an emphasis on the weight of the oath in relation to the effect of the answer (but also a restrictive approach to those cases in which the earlier law had given the answer a decisory effect). The conceptual foundations of the basic rules, however, were much closer to those of the roman-canon system than to the common law.

Chapter Three

Proof by Documents – Concepts, Contexts and Conditions of Use

In the modern law of evidence documentary evidence and its effects are governed by a number of branches of the law which are seen as essentially separate. The admissibility of documents is largely governed by the rule against hearsay and its exceptions; the rule requiring the production of the original of a document introduced in evidence, and its exceptions, is analysed by Wigmore as a species of rule of preference[1] and is in any event only rarely discussed in modern English law; the parol evidence rule, requirements of writing where they operate, and the requirement of proof of execution of certain documents, are all seen as matters of the relevant area of substantive law, not of evidence/ proof. Gilbert's treatment of evidence, however, begins by distinguishing written and oral evidence[2] and treats admissibility, the requirement of the original, and the relative weight of documents together, separately from topics of witness evidence[3]. As already indicated, this feature is shared by most civilian and common law treatments of proof/ evidence[4]. The distinctions drawn between the different instruments of proof (confession, writings, witnesses, presumptions) are, in fact, the primary organising principle of general discussions of proof[5].

The rational basis of this primacy in civilian and canonist writing is that the character of the law of proof as a system for the objective evaluation of the weight of evidence, binding the trier of fact, requires the instruments of proof to be ranked[6].

---

1 173 ff.

2 P 4.

3 Pp 5 ff.

4 Above Ch 1 nn 2 & 3.

5 As opposed to the modern common-law approach first adumbrated in the lists of general rules annexed to the English tradition MSS of Gilbert, and incorporated in Bathurst's *Theory of Evidence* and thence in Buller's *Nisi Prius*. The analysis of the instruments of evidence continues to be a major organising feature of books on evidence for some time, but by the time of Phillips the general rules were much enlarged; by that of Greenleaf, Taylor and Best the general rules formed the larger part of the book, the analysis the smaller part; and in modern books the drawing of distinctions between the instruments of evidence tends to be confined to one chapter.

6 In contrast modern systems, including the common law of evidence, rest in the last analysis on the subjective persuasion of the trier of fact.

Are witnesses to be preferred to documents, or vice versa? The mediæval canonist view seems to have been that proof by witnesses was to be preferred; this period saw the emergence of the view that writings were to be preferred[7]. Gilbert[8] takes the view that writings are preferred; Ballow is ambivalent[9].

In other words, common lawyers, equity lawyers, civilians and canonists in the seventeenth century all regarded proof by documents as a separate and coherent topic in discussing proof, and to understand their arguments it is necessary to follow their approach.

In relation to documents, unlike confessions, we are not primarily concerned with equity diverging from the common law and following the lines of an established body of civilian doctrine. In the first place, though there was a fairly clear body of medieval academic roman-canon doctrine, the practice relating to the use of documents varied from country to country: *consuetudo loci facit instrumentum authenticum*[10]. Moreover, as already indicated, the early modern period was one of transition in this matter in European legal thought.

Secondly, english law already possessed an established body of doctrine relating to proof by documents: the medieval common law rules governing the use of *records* and *deeds*. This body of doctrine, too, was in transition in the early modern period. In the first place, the common law practice first moved away from the strong preference for documents found in the later medieval law (through changes in the forms of action); then, through the development of the parol evidence rule in the seventeenth century and the passing of the Statute of Frauds in 1677, preference for documents returned. On the other hand, the old body of law of documents tendered to the court as proof came to be paralleled by a new body of law of documents tendered to the jury as evidence: a body of law whose rules as to the nature of admissible documents and the requirements for their use were wider and more flexible than the medieval rules.

Prima facie there are good reasons to anticipate that equity would follow the common law in relation to documents. Besides the general weight of the maxim *Æquitas sequitur legem*, the area is one which is inevitably heavily affected by considerations of certainty of title to property and of commercial expectations, both considerations arguing against innovation in the law of documents. Moreover, the variety of civilian doctrine on the topic and its dependence on the practices of particular jurisdictions must have reduced the persuasive authority of civilian ideas. However, a closer examination will show that equity consciously diverged

---

7 For the medieval view, Lévy 86-105; for the transition, Gilissen 17 Soc. J. B. 757 at 820-7.

8 Pp 4-5.

9 At 124-5 he says that writings are preferred, and at 128 that in natural law witnesses are necessary *where instruments cannot be produced.* At 125-6, however, he says that in natural justice deeds and writings are merely "memorials" and any other proof will do as well. For this topic in general see below Chapter 4.

10 For the doctrine, Lévy 72-9; for this tag, Cheney, *Notaries* 11.

from the law at some points, particularly those related to the weight of documents, but also in relation to what counted as public documents and to the use of secondary evidence of unavailable originals; and, in addition, that the new law of documentary evidence to a jury shows some signs of borrowing from civilian ideas.

It is convenient to consider separately two issues: first, in this Chapter, the general requirements for the use of documents as evidence; and second, in Chapter 4, the relative weight of documents and witnesses. At the outset, however, some outline indication is needed of the general principles found in the civilian literature, in the common law, and in the one clear discussion of documents in equity, that of Ballow.

I. General conceptions of proof by documents

1. Roman-canon principles

In the roman-canon system *instrumenta,* documents usable as proofs, were divided into two classes, public and private documents[11]. On the face of it this distinction is self-explanatory: a public document was one made by a public authority, a private document one made by a private person[12]. But in practice the distinction is heavily obscured. In the first place, civilian systems made extensive use of notarised instruments, which were "public" since made by a notary who was a public person, but in practice included ordinary contracts and conveyances made by notaries in private practice[13]. Indeed, the notarised instrument was the central case of a public document, and judicial acts were required to be notarised[14]. Secondly, instruments subscribed by the party and three attesting witnesses are said by Conset to "have the effect of" public documents, and 'Alciatus', indeed, says that such instruments are public and that instruments can generally be described as public if they are acceptable either by law or special custom[15]; in contrast, other writers

11 'Alciatus' 221r, 224r; Maranta 585 pr., 593 32-4; Covarruvias QP Chs 19-21, 22; *Reformatio* 232 *De Fide* cc 2, 3; Vulteius 372v-373v; Ridley 107; Conset 147 ("174"); Wood 321; Ayliffe 305-8. Groot, ch 19 treats the distinction as an element of his account of natural law, but does not make it do any work, as he explains the use of documents entirely in terms of confession and express or implied contract. Domat distinguishes four types of documents: private writings, notarised documents, acts in the course of justice and other registered acts (3.6.2.2), but as he says in the introduction to the section that notarised transactions "have the force of public documents" it is clear that the public-private distinction underlies his thought.

12 'Alciatus' 224r; Vulteius 373r; Wood 321.

13 'Alciatus' 224r; Maranta 593.22; Covarruvias QP Ch 19 Nos 5-9; *Reformatio De Fide* c 2; Conset 147 ("174"); Ayliffe 305, 382-6.

14 Maranta 607.1; Ayliffe 27-8.

15 Conset 147 ("174"); 'Alciatus' 224v: "Et generaliter hic nota omnem scripturam dici. publica. seu de iure vel speciali consuetudine credatur. extra de fide inst. c. cum dilectus, vide latius Specul.".

treat attested documents are private but acceptable if supported by the attesting witnesses[16].

The boundaries of the distinction were thus less than clearly principled; its consequences were also quite varied in the work of different authors. Three threads can be discerned running through the literature. First, there was in principle a difference between the weight of public and private documents. Second, there was a difference between the persons for and against whom the two types could be used. And third, there was a difference in the proof required of the existence, making and content of the document.

The first two of these points are more or less inextricably mixed in some of the sources. A public document was clearly a full proof, good for and against both parties to it[17]. A private writing, in contrast, presented a more complex picture. 'Alciatus' distinguishes documents *tibi tantum* (made for the maker's own purposes) which were valueless, *alii tantum* (made for others) such as a receipt, which were to be believed, and *tibi et alii*, such as books of accounts, which might have some weight in some circumstances. This was mediæval doctrine, which also saw a private writing as a half proof, a formula found in one or another form in 'Alciatus', Covarruvias, Vulteius and Conset[18]. Maranta, on the other hand, does not make these distinctions[19]; and his editor allows the use of a wide range of private writings, chiefly merchants' accounts and various forms of commercial paper[20].

Among the english authors, the *Reformatio* requires private documents to have three attesting witnesses, as does Fulbecke[21]. Cosin appears to say that *only* public documents are acceptable[22]. This apparently extreme position may be corroborated by the fact that Cosin's contemporary Clerke offers as a common form objection to documents that they are "scripturas privatas & inauthenticas ac tales quibus nulla

16 Maranta 593.34; Covarruvias QP Ch 22 §§ 1-4; *Reformatio, De Fide* c 4, p. 232; Fulbecke, *Parallele* Part 2 p 28; Ayliffe 305, 307-8.

17 'Alciatus' 224r; *Reformatio, De Fide* c 1, p 232; Vulteius 373v; Cosin Part I, 69-70; Zouch *EI* 90; Conset 108 ("most evident" or "evident"); Ayliffe 306, "probationem probatam". Though Covarruvias does not make the point explicitly, it can be inferred from the distinctions he draws at Ch 20 § 6 (can witnesses *dis*prove a public document), § 9 (third party can use a public document to prove the transaction took place) and Ch 22 §§ 2,6,7,8 on the weight of private documents.

18 'Alciatus' 206r, "scripturam domesticam"; Covarruvias QP Ch 22 §§6-8; Vulteius 373v, "nisi alia adsistant adminicula sive probationes"; Conset 108, "less evident". Levy 78 says that this rule applied in the mediæval law where the document was either proved only by comparison of hands (which was a half proof independently), or used for a third party rather than against its maker. Covarruvias applies it to private writings proved by comparison of hands or by witnesses other than attesting witnesses.

19 *De Instrumentorum Productione*, 585 pr, §1; 593 §§ 32-4.

20 *De Testibus, Additio* §§ 23-72.

21 *Reformatio, De Fide* c 4 p 232; Fulbecke *Parallele* Part 2, 28.

22 Part I pp 69-70: "there be but two wayes ... to proove any thing: that is by *witnesses*, or by a *publicke instrument*, called by the *common Lawe, matter of Record*."

fides est adhibenda"[23]. However, the *Reformatio* accepts comparison of hands as a half proof[24], and Clerke accepts it in the context of disputed and holograph wills, though Ridley limits this to disputes between children and gifts to charity[25]. Ridley allows private documents more generally[26]; Wood and Ayliffe say that they are good against the maker, but not in his favour[27].

The remaining area was proof of the document. It seems clear that a document which was on its face a public document was *prima facie* good, so that the question of proof would only arise if its genuineness was disputed[28]. If so, the mode of proof would depend on the nature of the document's public character. A notarised instrument depended on the public authority of the notary, which would have to be proved (but might in the case of old documents be presumed)[29]. The attesting witnesses should also be produced, if available[30]. A document under public seal depended on the public character of the seal[31]. A document from a public archive depended on proof or presumption that the archive had been diligently kept[32]. A private document, in contrast, was not *prima facie* good. It was only usable if proved by the confession of the party, witnesses, or comparison of hands[33].

Whatever the type of document, the original document was supposed to be produced in court[34]. However, a copy made under judicial authority was acceptable[35], and in the case of public archives Clerke describes a procedure for scrutiny and copying by commissioners[36]. It seems that public documents could more or less routinely be proved by public copy[37]. Private documents might also be proved by

---

23 P. 229.

24 *De Fide* c 7 p 223.

25 Clerke 231-5; Ridley 192. For the general development of the position on comparison of hands and holograph wills see R.H. Helmholz, 'The origin of Holographic Wills in English Law' (1994) 15 *JLH* 97-108.

26 P. 107; but he is here summarising Book 2 of the Decretals, so may not be stating current law.

27 Wood 321-2; Ayliffe 307. Cf Vulteius 373r.

28 Covarruvias QP ch 19 No 9; Ayliffe 306.

29 Covarruvias QP ch 21 No 7 contains an extensive discussion.

30 Their unavailability does not destroy the authority of the document: *Reformatio* 234 c 11; Wood 322.

31 'Alciatus' 224r; Covarruvias QP ch 22 No 9; *Reformatio* 237 c 19; Conset 147 ("174"); Ayliffe 482-3.

32 *Reformatio* 232 c 3; Vulteius 373v; Clerke 228; Conset 147 ("174"), 148.

33 Maranta 593.34, by witnesses, 614 *Additio* 28, confession; Covarruvias QP ch 22 Nos 1-4; Wood 323; Ayliffe 307-8.

34 Maranta 593.33; Covarruvias QP ch 19 Nos 1-4, 20 Nos 6 (final para),7; *Reformatio* 233-4 c 8; Vulteius 373v, 505v; Clerke 228; Zouch *EI* 90; Conset 149.

35 Cotta 296; Covarruvias QP ch 21 Nos 3-5; *Reformatio* 233-4 c 8; Clerke 228; Conset 147 ("174").

36 222-226. Cf also Gaill ii Obs 104 Nos 2-3, Vulteius 505v-506v, Zouch *EI* 99.

public copy; but private copies were only acceptable in special cases where loss of the original was proved, and the witnesses must be to the original transaction[38].

Both these sets of rules, and those restricting the use of private documents, were subject to exceptions for old documents: *ex diuturnitate temporis omnia præsumuntur rite et solemniter esse acta,* and in any case the passage of time might make e.g. the production of attesting witnesses impractical[39]. In addition, the detention of documents by the adverse party could be relieved by an order to produce them, provided the applicant had some interest in the documents;[40] and spoliation or destruction of documents by the adverse party would let in other evidence of their contents, including the proponent's own oath[41].

This summary account tries merely to draw out general principles and issues posed. I would reiterate the point made at the outset, that this was an area of considerable diversity both of academic opinion and of national practice. The mediaeval common law was comparatively simple and certain.

2. The common law

a) Estoppels, pleading and profert

The mediaeval common law contained a body of rules – the doctrines of estoppel by record and by deed, and the rules for pleading such estoppels, as distinct from trial by jury – which were, in substance, an approach to proof by documents similar in its basic structure to civilian conceptions. This has been obscured by two features of these rules. In the first place, the common law rules appear *ex facie* as rules of pleading, rather than as rules of proof, and it is now normal to regard estoppels and pleading rules as limiting what can or has to be proved rather than as rules of proof. However, the substantial effect of the rules was to regulate the proofs which could be put forward to support a claim or plea[42]. To impose on them the modern view of pleadings and estoppels is to project back on the mediaevals the modern conception of the jury as the only trier of facts in issue, and to forget the extent to which all aspects of law tended in the mediaeval common law to appear as rules of pleading.

---

37 Maranta 615.30 (judicial *acta*), 619-20 No 66; Covarruvias QP ch 21 No 5; Wood 323.

38 For the general point, Maranta 619-20 No 66, Cotta 296, Covarruvias QP ch 21 Nos 1-3, Wood 322, Ayliffe 307-8; for the point that the witnesses must be to the original transaction, Covarruvias QP ch 22 No 1; *Reformatio* 234 c 12.

39 Covarruvias QP ch 21 No 7; *Reformatio* 236 cc 17, 18; Wood 323.

40 Maranta 610 Nos 8-11; Covarruvias QP ch 19 No 3; *Reformatio* 237 c 20; Zouch *EI* 99

41 Ayliffe 309 ("305"). Gentili ii 114 says merely that spoliation of documents "indicet mala causa".

42 Cf Glanvill (ed Hall) 126-7, Bracton f 400b, ed Thorne IV 248.

Secondly, these rules were radically simpler than the developed roman-canon system. The common law only recognised two limited categories of documents as pleadable, records and deeds, and it did not recognise degrees of proof at all: a record or deed was either conclusive as to its contents, or valueless for this purpose[43]. For this reason Thayer, Wigmore and Holdsworth tended to assimilate these mediaeval rules to the "Germanic" tender of an "irrational" or magical proof (ordeal, battle)[44]; and this obviously cut across recognising any parallelism with the roman-canon system. This is not to say that the simplicity of the common law rules is not a "Germanic" effect of the recent history of trial by ordeal and by battle at the time when these rules were developed[45]. I am concerned only to point out that there are structural parallels between the common law rules and the roman-canon system, and that views of "Germanic" origin of the common law rules have led to these parallels being overlooked; the point being that these parallels may have a bearing on seventeenth-century thought about proof and evidence.

The rules about documentary estoppels and the pleading rules appear relatively early in the common law: Holdsworth cites authority for the principal propositions from the 1290s and 1300s[46]. The probative effect of documents as creating an es-

---

43 Though an unpleadable document might be of use in persuading a jury: below § 1 *(2)* (b).

44 Thayer pp 13, 504; Wigmore § 1177; Holdsworth HEL IX pp 144-5.

45 For this point see the authorities just cited, and (in the context of the development of the jury) Hyams, "Trial by Ordeal" in Arnold et al, *On the Laws & Customs of England: Essays for SE Thorne* p 91, pp 118ff, Bartlett, *Trial by Fire & Water* (Oxford, Clarendon, 1986) 137 f. In contrast Dawson, *Lay Judges* 122-9 argues that the jury could have developed into a French-style *inquisitio* but did not because of a shortage of trained lawyers; Cf Sutherland, *The Assize of Novel Disseisin* (Oxford, Clarendon, 1973) p 73, and Arnold, *Select Cases of Trespass 1307-99* (Selden Soc Vol 100) pp xx – xxvi, for thirteenth and fourteenth century methods of inducing juries to find facts specifically. M.T. Clanchy, *From Memory to Written Record* (London, Edward Arnold, 1979) pp 241-248 argues that the failure of English law to receive the use of notarised instruments is attributable primarily to the greater convenience of the seal; C.R. Cheney, *Notaries Public in England in the Thirteenth and Fourteenth Centuries* (Oxford, Clarendon, 1972) Chs 1 & 5 suggests that a clash of interests between the notaries and the previously developed non- contentious business of the royal courts may have been involved. W. Prynne, *Brief Animadversions on, Amendments of, and additional explanatory Records to, the Fourth Part of the Institutes of the Lawes of England* (London, 1669), at the epistle *To the King's Majesty* sig A1r – A2r, cites decisions of 13 Edward II (1319) and 3 Edward III (1329) excluding imperial and papal notaries, for the view that this was connected with the autonomy of the common law.

46 HEL IX pp 148ff: 148 n2, record conclusive, cites Glanvill viii.5 and YB 21&22 Ed I (RS) 146; n5, record to be proved by rolls, not by country, YB 20&21 Ed I 406, YB 6 Ed II (SS) 20-26, and n6 YB 33-5 Ed I (RS) 528 *per* Toudeby *arg;* 148-9 n1, fine & record pleadable in bar, YB 1&2 Ed II (SS) 139-141, YB 6 Ed II (SS) 52-3 (& on this point cf Bracton f 435b, *exceptio rei judicatæ,* Thorne ed IV 353-4); 150 n6, only parties bound, YB 1&2 Ed II (SS) 113 *per* Passeley *arg;* 154 n2, deed as estoppel, YB 21&2 Ed I (RS) 436, 1&2 Ed II (SS) 68-9, 3 Ed II (SS) 171 *per* Herle *arg;* 156 n11, only parties bound, YB 3 Ed II (SS) 173 *per* Friskeney *arg;* & cf the discussion of proof of charters in Bracton f 396, Thorne ed IV 235 f.

toppel would, in general, be determined by the court, not by jury. Estoppel and the pleading of documents which would create an estoppel was, therefore, the subject of a good deal of law. The large bulk of this concerned questions of privity – how far a party, A would be affected by an estoppel affecting a non-party, B – and to this extent concerns real property law rather than proof.

The underlying rule was the rule of pleading which took these matters out of the cognisance of the jury. If a claim or plea was dependent on the terms of a deed or record, it would be necessary to plead this deed or record, setting out the contents[47], and in the case of a deed at least conclude with a proffer of the original deed[48].

The category *records* corresponds broadly to the roman-canon category of public documents. It differs, however, in a fundamental feature. The central case of the roman-canon public document is a notarised instrument, which rests on the *personal* official status of the notary and on archives (the protocols) dispersed in the hands of individual notaries. The central case of the record is the rolls of the central common law courts. The personal status of the clerk who made the roll is irrelevant; the authority of the document rests on its presence in the required form in the central archive. Starting with the records of the judgments of the King's court, the category came to cover all matters recorded by the King's courts, thus including matters contained in the Parliament Rolls, Exchequer records, and records of the Latin side of Chancery[49]. The obvious sort of record is a prior judgment, but in practice by far the largest groups of records were probably conveyances in the forms of fines and recoveries, and securities for money in the forms of recognizances and statutes (statutory recognizances under the Statutes of Merchants and Staple)[50]. Other matters which we would now regard as public records, and which would probably have been regarded as public documents in the roman-canon system, (Church registers, records of decisions of local courts) were not records for the purpose of creating an estoppel[51].

---

47 This is a summary statement of the rule. The "standard case" where a deed is required to be pleaded is that given in Littleton 365 f, of showing a feoffment to be conditional; to this might be added showing a cause of action in covenant or debt *sur obligation*. In the case of records, the party would usually be seeking not only to show the terms of a transaction but also to rely on the specific advantages of a record, e.g. to bar prior estates or to gain priority for a security.

48 For profert of deeds, Holdsworth HEL IX pp 155, 167 f. The position in relation to records is not entirely clear. It is clear that in the sixteenth century profert was required of letters patent, since statutory provision was made for exemplifications from the patent rolls to be pleadable (3 & 4 Ed VI c 4; 13 Eliz c 6). Co Lit 128a-b says that outlawry if pleaded as a dilatory plea must be accompanied by profert of an exemplification, secus if pleaded in bar; this seems to imply that the records of the central courts were pleadable without profert.

49 Holdsworth HEL IX 148 cites Glanvill viii c 5; cf Co Lit 117b, 220a.

50 Cf Simpson, *Contract* 126-135. For continental parallels see K.W. Nörr, 'Procedure in Mercantile Matters: Some Comparative Aspects' in V. Pergiovanni ed., *The Courts and the Development of Commercial Law* (Berlin, 1987) 195 at 200.

Once a record had been pleaded, the opponent party would then have the option of (1) demurring on matter of law in the declaration or plea; (2) confessing and avoiding the matter contained in the record; or (3) pleading *nul tiel record*. This plea would bring the parties to issue on the existence of the record, which would then be tried by examination of the record[52].

Deeds correspond roughly to the strongest roman-canon class of private documents, the contractual instrument with attesting witnesses, which as we have already seen, was on the border between public and private documents. There were, however, additional formal requirements: the seal, and execution and delivery as a deed. Like private documents in the roman-canon system, deeds were required to be proved by witnesses. But like roman-canon notarised instruments, this question would only arise if the opponent party denied the genuineness of the deed by pleading *non est factum*, i.e. that the deed was never delivered, or was forged, or the maker incompetent for some reason[53]. This plea would be tried by a jury, to which, originally, the witnesses named in the deed would be added[54]; or, according to Bracton, comparison of seals and of hands could be used[55].

Alternatively, the opponent could ask to inspect the deed in court and could then raise any objections to its formal validity (seals torn off, apparent alterations to the deed, etc)[56]. This issue would be decided by the court, not by jury. In the case of deeds evidencing the terms of feoffments of real property the estoppel was the feoffment, not the deed, so he could plead *riens passa per le fet*, i.e. that there was no feoffment, or the grantor had no seisin, so that no estate passed, or a feoffment on different terms. This would lead to an issue tried by jury[57]. If none of these options were likely to succeed, he would be forced to admit the deed and either demur on matter of law, or confess and avoid.

While some records would bind the world, many would only bind parties and privies[58]. Deeds would only bind parties and privies, and, in addition, for a deed to work an estoppel the estoppel must be mutual; i.e. the deed must be capable, if it had contained obligations on the proponent, of binding the proponent as well as the person sought to be estopped[59]. Who exactly was affected by reason of privity

---

51 For church registers, *Worley's Case* (M1565) Moo KB 75; for local courts, Co Lit 117b-118a.

52 Co Lit 260a; also saying that *nul tiel record* could not be pleaded against an exemplification under the Great Seal.

53 The result is probably not attributable to *prima facie* validity but to the fact that in common law pleading everything not expressly denied was admitted.

54 Thayer 97-102, 503-5; cited Holdsworth HEL IX pp 167f: the witnesses continued to be summoned with the jury, rather than produced by the party, down to the fifteenth century (ib).

55 f 398b, Thorne ed IV 242.

56 *Dr Leyfield's Case* (1611) 10 Co Rep 88 at 92b.

57 *Trials per Pais* 1682 ed p 234 for the name given here to this plea.

58 Holdsworth HEL IX pp 150-2.

became involved with doctrines which were associated with the mediæval doctine of warranty and were in substance a part of land law[60].

Records and deeds were thus capable at common law of supplying a full, and conclusive, proof of the allegations in the pleadings – though, as in the roman-canon system, there were exceptions to the possible conclusiveness of these instruments. Records and deeds were *prima facie* to be judged by the court, in contrast to matters lying *in pais,* in the province of the jury (i.e., by the seventeenth century, witness evidence). Records and deeds themselves were treated differently, with records "proving themselves" while deeds could be put to proof by their witnesses, and records having fewer exceptions to their potential conclusive effect. And like "party & party" instruments in the roman-canon system, only parties and privies were affected. In all these respects, whatever the origin of the rules, there was a fairly clear structural similarity between the roman-canon system and the common law pleading rules.

b) Evidence to a jury

If the instruments were not introduced at the pleading stage, none of these rules would apply. At first, therefore, the parties had merely to try to persuade the jury of their case using any means they could, and there were probably no rules about what documents could be used, how, and their effect[61]. Obviously in these circumstances the document would not be conclusive, but on the other hand the proponent would escape from the controls of the system of profert, and from the possibility of being put to prove deeds by their witnesses, who might be unavailable.

The rules requiring certain documents to be pleaded, discussed above, sought to restrict the extent to which the rules could be evaded in this way. In practice, however, these rules became to a large extent superseded (among others) in the changes in the forms of action in the early modern period (rise of ejectment in real property matters and of *assumpsit* and *indebitatus assumpsit* in relation to contracts).

In the same general period (though it is not clear that there is any connection) the common-law courts began to concern themselves with the question of what documents could be produced as evidence to a jury and how. This development was evidently not wholly uncontroversial. For example, in relation to the rule requiring production of original documents to the jury, which first appears in the early seventeenth century[62], some courts continued as late as the 1650s to assert

---

59 Co Lit 352a, Holdsworth HEL IX 156.

60 Holdsworth, above n 59.

61 Thayer, Ch 3 and Wigmore (§ 8), though Thayer does cite authorities suggesting an early development of controls on the use of documents. Cf Dawson, Sutherland & Arnold cited above n 45.

62 *Dr Leyfield's Case* (1611) 10 Co Rep at f 92b.

the older rule that as long at it was only evidence and not to work an estoppel any evidence of the terms of a document could be introduced[63].

The effect was that by the later seventeenth century two separate bodies of rules, which had distinct results, existed in parallel: rules about estoppel and rules about the use of documents as evidence to juries. This was by no means simply a matter of the application of the estoppel rules to juries. There were significant differences in content between the two sets of rules: for instance, public documents other than records, and private documents other than deeds, could be presented to juries, though they would not work an estoppel[64]; and the rule requiring the production of an original document which was to be used in evidence to a jury was more flexible in its exceptions than the requirement of profert.[65]

However, contemporaries often did not think it necessary to distinguish clearly between the two sets of rules; for example, Gilbert's account of documentary evidence mixes them together[66]. This is important, because it indicates that though the rules about the use of documents as evidence to juries appear, at first sight, as a mere "historic congeries",[67] they could easily be rationalised by contemporaries in terms either of the rules of estoppel[68], or of the roman-canon principles. The same overall approach, of distinguishing public and private documents, requiring production of originals, rules of privity, requiring documents for some purposes, and making documents conclusive for some, could be taken to explain the rules.

3. Proof by documents in equity, according to Ballow

The only convenient general summary of the rules of proof by documents in equity is rather late: Ballow's *Treatise of Equity,* published in 1737. Ballow deals with proof in his Book 6, divided into three Chapters. Ch 1 deals with witnesses (§ 1) and evidence, i.e. writings[69] (§ 2 covering depositions from previous causes, which is treated as a species of documentary evidence by common law writers[70],

---

63 Eg *Olive v Gwin* (T1658) Hardr 118, 2 Sid 145, at 2 Sid 145 *per* Widdrington CB.

64 Gilbert, pp 36ff, summarises some of the authorities up to that date.

65 Below § 2 *(3)* (a).

66 Pp 58 ff.

67 Cf Harris, *Law & Legal Science,* (Oxford, Clarendon Press, 1979) pp 11-12.

68 Thus the first clear statement, possibly the introduction, of the rule requiring the production of original documents, by Coke in *Dr Leyfield's Case* (above n 56) was by way of an *obiter dictum* in a case actually concerned with *profert.*

69 Above § 1 *(2)* (a).

70 Gilbert pp 44f sees depositions as "public matters not of record"; Nelson pp 88f deals with them in his chapter on documentary evidence; the Abridgements deal with them as documentary evidence. In this book, unlike the sources, I have treated the admissibility of depositions in subsequent causes as an aspect of the examination of witnesses. This is simply for

and § 3 requirements of proof of documents). Ch 2 deals with the weight of documents, i.e. estoppel by record (§§ 1 and 2) and deed (§ 3) and the parol evidence rule (§§ 4-7).[71]

There are three noteworthy features of this brief treatment. The first is that 'evidence', i.e. documents, and witnesses are treated separately, as in contemporary common law and civilian treatments. The second is that the distinction between public and private documents is present in its common law form, i.e. as a distinction between records and deeds[72]. In this respect it seems that equity follows the common law, as was anticipated. However, the third feature, which becomes clear in the discussion of estoppels, is that this was also an area in which equity consciously diverged from the law, by giving relief against the effects of the common law rules in some cases. Ballow gives two justifications for this divergence. The first (§ 2) is the traditional explanation that the equitable decree "... only meddles with the corrupt Conscience of the Party."[73] The second (§ 3) is jusnaturalistic:

> "So in natural Justice, Deeds and Writings are consider'd only as Memorials of the Contract, not as a substantial Part of them; and therefore any other Proof is as well, and the Estoppel will not in Equity be regarded against the Truth."[74]

This argument is clearly influenced by the generally jusnaturalistic character of Ballow's account of equity. But the jurisdiction to relieve against estoppels itself is one of the older elements of equity, and St German also used (slightly different) jusnaturalistic arguments to support it.[75]

In addition, as already indicated, a number of specific common law rules about the use of documents as evidence to juries appeared in the course of the late sixteenth and seventeenth centuries. Of these Ballow only discusses the requirement of production of the original document (Ch 1 § 3) and the parol evidence rule in its application to wills (Ch 2 §§ 4-7). However, identical or similar rules make their first appearance in reported equitable authorities in the same period. In relation to these rules, as will appear below, the picture does not seem to correspond to Wigmore's account of rules developed pragmatically to control the jury and subsequently transplanted into equity.

---

convenience, as some of the rules in relation to their admissibility depend on the procedure for taking witness evidence.

71 Ch 3 deals with discovery and feigned issues.

72 Cf the discussion of enrolments, p 124; and estoppel by record and by deed treated separately, Ch 2 §§ 1-2, 3.

73 P 125.

74 P 125.

75 91 SS 116-7 (in general), 289-90 (collateral warranty).

II. Conditions for the use of documents

In this context it is necessary to consider four topics: public documents; the question whether private documents are admitted as admissions, or for some other reason; the requirements of proof of documents to be used as proofs, i.e. of production of the original document and of proof of execution; and the requirements of privity and mutuality.

1. Public documents

That records, in the common law sense, could be used as proofs in equity throughout the period is obvious[76], and is apparent from the discussions of estoppel in St German[77], West[78] and Ballow[79]. In addition it is also obvious and apparent that previous equity proceedings (bills, answers, depositions and decrees), which the common lawyers did not recognise as records[80], could be used in equity courts[81]. In relation to these, questions would arise as to privity/ mutuality. Moreover, the court in which the original proceedings took place would have to have had jurisdiction; this would rarely be a problem with Chancery proceedings, but there are a few cases in which the point is taken in relation to inferior courts of equity[82]. This indicates that previous proceedings are being used as public documents, not merely in an unregulated way as a convenient source of information.

A number of other types of document could be used which seem to have been, or to have been seen as in the nature of, public documents[83]: church registers[84], episcopal certificates[85] and church court proceedings, especially probate of wills[86], and old surveys of manors by lords of the manor[87].

---

76 Cf also the use of inquisitions *post mortem*, as in *Floyer v Strachley* (1631) Nels 13.

77 D&S at eg pp 54-5, 285, 292-3.

78 At sig B4v ff (mostly cited from *Doctor & Student*).

79 Bk VI c 2 §§ 1-2.

80 Gilbert pp 36-7.

81 See cases cited below *passim*.

82 E.g. *R v Arundel & Howard* (T1616) Hob 109, Moo KB 832 (Egerton C, Coke, Hobart CJJ, Caesar MR), depositions before the Council of the North excluded for want of jurisdiction.

83 This rather clumsy expression is necessary because some of these items would not, to the modern eye, seem to be "public" documents.

84 *Wood v Wageman* (1586) Toth 12. Cf at law *Worley's Case* (M1565) Moo KB 75, *Vickery v Farthing* (M1594) Cro El 411, Moo KB 451.

85 *Bloomer's Case* (H1603-4) Cary 26 (to be considered as a judicial proceeding). At common law this was a mode of trial in certain cases (matrimony, bastardy, etc) and was conclusive (Holdsworth HEL IX p 151) and *semble* this was so also in Chancery: *Doctor & Student* Second Dialogue c 5 and West § 37 para kk.

In the later seventeenth century this area appears rather more developed in the common law authorities. These permitted the use of the "records" (i.e. in a modern, not a contemporary sense) of manorial[88] and other inferior courts[89], and the use of history books to prove matters of general history[90] and of the College of Heralds' records to prove pedigrees[91]. An order, apparently in the nature of *mandamus,* could be made to require the production of certain other public or quasi-public documents[92]. The question of jurisdiction, referred to above in connection

---

86 The bulk of the authority is at common law and concerns the rule that a probate of a will containing lands is *not* usable, because the church court lacks jurisdiction to verify the will: *Netter v Brett* (H1634-5) W Jon 355 (KB), probate "nest dascun force al common lay pur les terres"; *Preston v Hall* (1638) Clayt 66 (NP, Vernon, Henden JJ), probate admissible to prove death testate to bar an action brought by an administrator; *Beamsley's Case* (1640) Clayt 90 (NP, Whitfield J); *Brooks v Foxcroft* (1649) Clayt 137 (NP, Sjt Thorpe); *Garrett v Lister* (P1661) 1 Lev 25, 1 Keb 15 (KB), book of the church court admissible to prove administration; *Lord Gorges v Foster* (1661) Nels 82 (Chy), special order for D to admit the probate at common law, the original having been lost; *Anon* (P1684) Skin 174 (KB, *per* Jeffreys CJ); *Hoe v Nathorpe (?Nelthrope)* (H1696) 1 Ld Raym 154, 3 Salk 154 (KB, *per* Holt CJ), other church proceedings good; *Smartle d Newport v Williams* (P1694) Skin 423, 431, Comb 247, 3 Lev 387, 2 Salk 245, 280, Holt KB 478, at Skin 431 (KB), probate of a will of chattels good to show an executor; *Haines* (T1696) Skin 583, Comb 337 (KB, *per* Holt CJ); *Selby v Harris* (P1698) 1 Ld Raym 745 (NP, Treby CJ), books of the office of faculties; *Dike v Polhill* (1701) 1 Ld Raym 744 (NP), copy of probate to prove a pedigree, excluded by Holt CJ but later admitted by Tracy B at trial of a feigned issue.

87 *Hutchings v Strode* (1634) Nels 26; *Lord Wharton v Squire* (1702) Colles 270; *Pilley v Madden* (1706) Colles 366. At common law cf *Bridgman v Jennings* (1699) 1 Ld Raym 734 (NP, Holt CJ).

88 *Duncalfe's Case* (1639) Clayt 75 (NP, Henden B), recovery in court baron admitted; *Greene v Proude* (P1674) 3 Keb 310, 1 Vent 257, 1 Mod 117, KB; *Anon* (1693) 1 Ld Raym 735, NP, Holt CJ, also posing the question of jurisdiction (admittance of devisee to a copyhold, reciting the will, is good between devisee and a stranger, not between devisee and heir).

89 *Anon* (1640) Clayt 85 pl 142 (NP, Foster J), proceedings of corporation court rejected; *Olive v Gwin* (T1658) Hardr 118, 2 Sid 145, exemplification of recovery in Great Sessions of Wales accepted; *Fuller v Fotch* (1695) Carth 346 (NP, Holt CJ), judgments of commissioners of excise admissible and "prove themselves"; *Haines* (T1695) Comb 337, Skin 583 (KB), proceedings of corporation court admitted, *semble* where the maker of the entries is under a duty to do so, on the ground, *per* Holt CJ, that they are public documents.

90 *Lord Brounker v Atkins* (M1681) Skin 2, 15 (KB), historical question arising in legal argument; *Steyner v Droitwich* (M1695) 1 Salk 281, Skin 623, 12 Mod 85 (KB), admissible to prove matters of general history, but not pedigree (citing the rejection of Dugdale's *Baronage* in *Percy's Case* (M1681) T Jon 164), status of an Abbey (citing an unreported case of the same term in the Exchequer) or local custom (the point at issue). It is said in *Steyner v Droitwich* that in *Lady Ivy v Neal* (*Lady Ivy's Trial, Mossam d Neal v Ivy* (1684) 10 St Tr 555) chronicles were given in evidence to prove the style used by Philip in the early part of the reign of Philip and Mary and so establish that an instrument was a forgery, but this does not appear in the State Trials report.

91 *Plumpton v Robinson* (P1610,P1614) 2 Rolle Ab 686-7, pedigree drawn by herald rejected as evidence, so not to be taken away by jury; *King d Earl of Thanet v Foster* (M1682) T Jon 224 (KB), heralds' records, but not a pedigree drawn by them, admitted; *per cur* in *Steyner v Droitwich; Pitton v Walter* (H1719) 1 Stra 162 (NP, Pratt CJ).

with equity proceedings, was also significant in connection with the use of church court proceedings[93] and of enrolments and *inspeximus*'s of deeds[94].

Though the class of public documents was wider than records, notarised documents did not become public documents[95], in spite of Egerton's comment in 1603 that "here appeareth what want we have of notaries and their protocols"[96]. They were, however, receivable at law in connection with some ecclesiastical matters, by mercantile custom in connection with bills of exchange, and in connection with matters overseas[97]. The most plausible explanation of the failure to accept notarised documents as public documents in this period is Helmholz'[98]: a document was defined as public by its relation to a public authority. A notary did not under English municipal law (common law or statute) have any public authority to record contracts, etc. This view may draw added support from the significance of issues of jurisdiction in relation to those public documents that were accepted.

---

92 *Bracy's Case* (H1696-7) 1 Ld Raym 153 ((M1696) Comb 390, 1 Ld Raym 98, Holt KB 94, Salk 358 not SP) (KB) depositions before commissioners of bankrupts; refused, on the ground that they are "not of a public nature"; *Cox v Copping* (P1698) 5 Mod 395, 1 Ld Raym 337 (KB) parish books; refused, on the ground that P had no proprietary interest in the books; *R v Worsenham* (M1701) 1 Ld Raym 705 (KB) Custom House books; refused, on the ground that they "are a private concern, in which the prosecutor has no interest"; *Geery v Hopkins* (1702) 2 Ld Raym 851, 7 Mod 129 (KB) East India Co cash and transfer book; ordered, on the ground (Modern) that they are "books of a public company, and kept for public transactions, in which the public are concerned"; *Ward v Apprice* (M1704) 6 Mod 264 (KB) partnership books; refused, on the ground that D entrusted the books to P and must therefore sue in Chancery to get them back; *R v Mead* (1704) 2 Ld Raym 927 (KB) books of surveyors of highways; refused, on the ground that this would be to "compel the defendant to produce evidence against himself in a criminal cause"; *Anon* (P1707) 11 Mod 111 (KB) court rolls of manors and corporations, *per* Holt CJ allowed; *Love v Dr Bentley* (T1707) 11 Mod 134 parish books; allowed, on the ground that every parishioner has a right to the books.

93 Above n 86.

94 The early rule was that only exemplifications or copies of matters of record were admissible: *Read v Hide* (M1612) 3 Co Inst 173, CP; in consequence the rule developed that only where the enrolment was required by law could it be used: *Eden v Chalkhill* (M1661) 1 Keb 117, T Raym 25, KB; *Boteler v Massey* (M1675) R t Finch 241, *semble*, from the need for Chancery proceedings, deed enrolled at Chester in 1517 not usable at law; *Woodward v Aston* (T1676) 1 Vent 296, KB. But *semble contra Greenwood's Case* (1634) Clayt 28, NP, where an enrolment of a release by a joint tenant (which would not have been required by law) was admitted to show the remaining joint tenants were sufficient parties. This rule was still being applied in Chancery in the 1700s: *Lady Holcroft v Smith* (T1702) 2 Freem 259, 261, Harv 1105 pp 233, 235, 1 Eq Ca Ab 224. By this time, however, the common law courts had started to allow the use of enrollments as secondary evidence of deeds lost or in the hands of the opponent even where they were not required by law (below n 172 and text there).

95 Brooks et al, *Notaries Public in England since the Reformation* (Norwich, Erskine, 1991) 40-41.

96 *Anon* (M1603) Cary 31, Harv 1090 f25b, Stowe 415 f99b, Lansd 599 f10, quoted in full below text at n 162; "protocols" is in the Harvard and BL Stowe MSS, where printed text has "deputies"; protocols seems more apt.

97 Brooks et al, *Notaries* 41-3.

98 In Brooks et al, *Notaries* at 41.

In the discussions of public documents at common law in the 1690s and 1700s the admission of the documents is in some cases attributed to their being the best evidence, i.e. the best available evidence of the type of fact asserted[99]. The predominant type of argument, however, is from the public character of the documents. For example, in *Haines* Holt CJ is reported by Skinner as saying that probate of a will where the court has jurisdiction is good because "the probate in such case is an original act of the court"[100], and by Comberbach as saying of the "records" of inferior courts that

> "We know it is not usual for inferior courts not to draw up their records, but only short notes, and copies of these short notes being publick things are good evidence; otherwise of private things ..."[101]

Similarly, counsel arguing for the admission of Camden's Britannia in *Steyner v Droitwich* argues that "Camden was a public person, being historiographer Royal, &c., and that a grave-stone had been allowed in evidence"[102]; the court rejects this on the ground that there would be no certainty as to which historians would be usable and when, but says that heralds' books are admissible in part because "this is their proper business about which they are employed, and therefore there is some credit given to them"[103]. These are very explicit examples; the public character of the documents and the issue of jurisdiction runs like a thread through the cases on church court and equity proceedings (above) and is evident in Gilbert's treatment of public documents[104]. It is also noteworthy, however, that 'public documents' remain by and large, as in the mediæval rules, official and analogous archives and copies from them. Notarised instruments are not generally accepted; the argument that "Camden was a public person" is reminiscent of the civilian basis of the distinction, but it, too, is not accepted.

---

99 Eg the reports of *Steyner v Droitwich* in Skinner at 623, to justify the use of heralds' books, and 12 Modern at 85, 86.

100 Skin 584.

101 *Haines* at Comb 337; one of the "not"s in this passage is superfluous.

102 Skin 623. On the gravestone, cf 'Alciatus' 206r, citing D.22.3.10; this fell into the category of 'sculptum' in the mediæval law (Lévy 75 n 48); it is treated as a type of public document by van Espen (1700), 3.7.7.38, citing Damhoud c 174 and Gloss ad x *De Probationibus* c 13.

103 Ib. "but they do not deserve much, because they are negligently kept".

104 Pp 5-58 *passim*. As instances of public documents other than those already discussed, Gilbert (pp57- 8) gives Papal licences and bulls from before the Reformation to prove matters of church jurisdiction (citing [*Cope v Bedford* (P1626)] Palmer [426 at] 427); Domesday Book, to prove whether land is ancient demesne (citing [*Anon* (?1617)] Hob 188); a survey of the Cinque Ports, to prove their extent (citing *Anon* (P1701) (unreported) (Ex)); and an old map of lands found with title deeds (citing *Yates v Harris* (H1702) (unreported) (NP)).

2. Private documents, as admissions?

In the civil and canon laws it is fairly clear that in general private documents were primarily usable on the basis that they contained admissions by their maker[105]. was rather less clear in common law, or in equity at this period. The cases permit the possible interpretations that (1) private documents were generally used as admissions, subject to exceptions; or (2) private documents could be read either as admissions, or as testimony of unavailable witnesses, or as raising presumptions / conjectures (circumstantial evidence). The significance of this question is twofold. The first is that it raises a specific issue of parallelism with the roman-canon system, or the absence of such parallelism. The second is in terms of the general approach of this system, i.e. of the place of documentary evidence in the hierarchy of proofs or "scale of probability". If private documents were used as admissions they might be expected to have a high place in this hierarchy; if they were considered as a variant of testimony, or as circumstantial evidence, their place would be considerably lower. Strictly speaking this more general issue belongs to Chapter 4 rather than this Chapter. How it is relevant to this Chapter is: how far were documents used whose use could not be explained within the roman-canon framework?

The obvious example of a private document was a deed, and West's *Symboleography* (1590)[106] in its introductory part treats deeds as made to serve as evidence as admissions by the maker in favour of the party in whose favour they were made. That this was the primary view of documents is to some extent confirmed by the existence of the requirement of privity[107], and the commonest use of deeds and other private documents does seem to have been against the maker or someone claiming under him[108].

---

105 Above nn 18-20 and text there. Note, however, that Zouch *SQ* cl 9 No. 15 makes it a disputable question "an instrumento pro parte quis uti possit".

106 London, 1590; Lib I 1, sig q1v. § 9, sig qqq2 attributes the effect of instruments to the confession of the maker.

107 Below § 2 *(4)*; though this point is somewhat weakened by the existence of privity requirements in relation to public documents.

108 In relation to deeds this is too obvious and commonplace to justify citation of authority, which would merely amount to examples drawn from the numberless cases in which title to land, or a formal contract, was in issue. For equity cases on other private documents used as admissions cf, for example, *Lady Hatton v Jay* (1637) 1 Ch Rep 117 (letters from obligor, to rebut the presumption of payment); *Cropley v Marquess of Newcastle* (1662) 1 Ch Rep 225 (letters from D); *Bright v Frampton* (M1675) Nott CC No 341 (No 303 not SP) (letters from D disproving his answer); *Ray v Stanhope* (1679) 2 Ch Rep 159 (letter from D); *Darston v Earl of Orford* (1701) 1 Eq Ca Ab 10 (Pre Ch 188, 1 P Wms 401n, 2 Eq Ca Ab 460, (1702) Colles 233, not SP) (Ds' testator's account book); *Worts v Pern* (1707) 3 Bro PC 548 (draft articles, accounts and letters from Ds' testator, to prove partnership with P); *Fowler v Ayliffe* (H1708) 2 Eq Ca Ab 184.4 (receipt, contradicted by letters explaining why false receipt given). I have not found any direct common law authority, but cf the cases *temp* Holt on merchants' books below, which seem to assert that the books are to be used primarily as admissions.

However, private documents were used for some purposes which are not easy to reconcile with the view that they were used as admissions. I have put the cases in two "categories", though it is less clear that these groupings reflect contemporary approaches. The first is the use of third party documents. In modern (pre-1968) "hearsay" terms these would mostly either be *res gestae,* or fall into the hearsay exceptions for proof of the state of mind of the maker, statements against interest and regular entries; but this analysis is anachronistic, as the word "hearsay" was not applied to documents, nor a unified set of rules thought to apply to out of court statements, at this period[109]. The uses in question clearly do not comply with privity rules, though in some cases they may be admitted on the basis of mutuality. In 'Alciatus'' terms it is possible that some of them could have been *alii tantum* or *tibi et alii,* and as such could have been used as a half proof by anyone except the maker[110].

The second category is the use of documents apparently made by the proponent himself as proof in his favour, particularly shopbooks. The admissibility of "shopbooks" is on the face of it difficult to reconcile with the view that private documents were used as admissions.

a) Third party documents

The cases here cover three sub-types: receipts and notes from third parties, to prove payments and deliveries; counsel's opinions and abstracts; and old documents and documents produced by people since dead.

(1) *Third party receipts and similar documents*: The authority for the use of third party documents to prove payments, etc, is almost entirely at common law[111]. The one equity authority is *AG v Crofts* (1708), an Exchequer equity appeal to the House of Lords. In this case receipts endorsed on a deed seem to have been allowed, to prove that the consideration expressed was paid, at least in a feigned issue directed out of the Exchequer as to whether the deed was fraudulent[112]. In

109 Below Ch 8 § 5.

110 Above n 18 & text there, & cf *Reformatio, De Fide* cap 5 (p 233).

111 *Arden & Goad's Case* (P1610) 4 Leo 243, CP, upholsterers' inventory to prove goods taken in execution in trover; *Barraclough's Case* (1638) Clayt 65 (NP, Henden and Vernon JJ), an acquittance from a creditor admissible to show the amount paid on *plene administravit; Sot's Case* (1648) Clayt 112 (NP, Turner Sjt) the same point *contra; Thurle v Madison* (M1655) Style 462 (UB), recital of consideration paid in a deed is not evidence of payment; *Dockwra v Dickenson* (P1696) Skin 640, Comb 366 (NP, Holt CJ), bill of lading admissible, where the signatory, the master of the ship, is dead, to show the contents of the ship in trover; *Pyke v Crouch* (M1696) 1 Ld Raym 370 (KB), letter from a third party acknowledging receipt of a copy of a will admissible "as circumstantial evidence" to prove that the will was sent to the third party.

112 4 Bro PC 136. This was part of the same proceedings as *Allibon v AG* (1707) Colles 393 (HL). The question arose on a forfeiture for treason committed in 1690, so that political

'Alciatus' terms receipts are *alii tantum* and therefore should be usable. At common law in *Dockwra v Dickenson* (1696)[113] the admissibility of a bill of lading is explained, over an objection from Shower that it can only be evidence as an admission[114], in terms of mercantile custom ("the bill of lading is always read in case of a policy to prove goods on board"[115]) and by analogy with the case of attesting witnesses who are dead, saying that the signatory would have been a competent witness if alive[116]. These arguments at common law indicate an assumption that private documents should in general be admissions.

(2) *Abstracts and opinions*: Legal opinions and abstracts were used as evidence in three reported cases in equity in the later seventeenth and early eighteenth century. In *Master v Cook* (1712)[117], an Exchequer equity appeal to the House of Lords, a note by one Webb, a conveyancer, was read in the Exchequer to show that the title offered by the plaintiff (respondent) vendor of land was satisfactory to Webb. The only objection taken by the defendant (appellant) was that Webb's hand was not proved. The contract was conditional on the vendor's showing a title satisfactory to Webb, so it is blindingly obvious that this must be usable somehow. How is less clear, and does not appear from the arguments. In modern terms this would be admissible as non-hearsay (the point not being to prove that the title was good) or as evidence of Webb's opinion at the date of the note, which was directly in issue. In 'Alciatus'' terms Webb's opinion is *alii tantum*, so usable. In contemporary common law terms it might be usable either as the best evidence (assuming that Webb was unavailable)[118] or by virtue of the contract, since it was a commonplace that rules of proof/ evidence could be varied *inter partes* by contract[119].

In *Cropley v Marquess of Newcastle* (1661)[120] the defendant's counsel's advice was read to show that the defendant intended at the time of sale to consent to a sale of his whole, and not merely of his reversionary, interest in property. This is together with letters from the defendant, and I take it, though the report does not mention more than that these items were read, that this is a sort of indirect admission or circumstantial evidence of an admission. That is, that counsel advised on

---

considerations entered into the decision. The Exchequer directed a trial as to *inter alia* whether the money was really paid; the ultimate decision of the HL, reversing the Exchequer, was that the Crown should be let in to redeem, i.e. that the deed was really a mortgage, which is consistent with the consideration recited actually having been paid and the receipt therefore being acceptable.

113 Above n 111.

114 Comb at 367.

115 Skin 640.

116 Skin 640; Comb 367.

117 Colles 433.

118 Cf *Pitman v Maddox* and *Price v Torrington*, below nn 142-3 and text there.

119 Wigmore § 575 and cases cited there.

120 1 Ch Rep 225.

the basis of a sale of the whole interest, and therefore it is to be inferred that the defendant asked for advice on this basis.

In *Lady Montague v Earl of Bath* (1692)[121] counsel's drafts and abstracts of a settlement deed were read to show that the deed was not fraudulent or a surprise against the client, and that the client had notice of the existence and terms of the deed. The question was whether the deed or a later will, which attempted to revoke the deed but did not comply with the terms of a power of revocation contained in the deed, should prevail. This, again, could be regarded as a species of admission, since the plaintiffs derived title under the will, or as circumstantial evidence of the state of mind of the client (here knowledge / notice).

In contrast at common law in *Lady Scroop v Lady Carr* (M1684)[122] counsel's abstract of a deed and opinion on it were rejected as evidence that the deed (at some unknown date cancelled and cut up) had not been revoked at the date of the settlor's death.

The difficulty with the equity cases is the absence of explanation or argument for or against the use of the documents in question. It is possible, therefore, that they merely passed *sub silentio* or by consent. It is unlikely that they are evidence of a complete absence of rules, at least towards the end of the period, in view of the arguments that did arise on other types of document.

(3) *Old documents*: The use of old documents and statements by people dead at the time of the litigation may reflect either an initial absence of rules, or an exception. The earliest reported instance is *Clench v Tomley* (1603)[123], where old account books and other writings were used to prove a party's predecessor in title illegitimate. If what was involved was originally merely an absence of rules, it must later have been seen as an exception, as in *Newburgh v Newburgh* (1712)[124] old rent-rolls and papers were said to be admissible to support a title on the ground that considering their age they could not have been made with a view to the present litigation.

It may be on the same basis, the absence of the danger of fabrication, that testators' memoranda, notes and letters were allowed to be used by their executors in *Tilsley v Wright* (1698)[125], *Despard v Ormsby* (1713)[126] and *Jacobsen v Hennekius*

121 2 Ch Rep 421, Nels 196, 2 Freem 121, 193, 2 Eq Ca Ab 671, 3 Ch Cas 55; at 3 Ch Cas 58, 80, 85.

122 Skin 205 (KB).

123 Cary 23; Stowe 415 f 90, *Townley & Clench*: per Egerton C, "being a thing so long past, it rested not properly in notice de Pais, but to be discerned by [Stowe MS: writings] books and deeds..." Contrast *Anon* (1603?) (undated, but among cases from 1603) Cary 24, old deeds not to "pare or defalk" a manor, but the contents of the manor to be proved by reputation.

124 3 Bro PC 553 (HL(I)). 12 Viner 221.1 dates this case to 1729, but Brown's dating is clearly preferable *inter alia* in view of the counsel engaged.

125 Colles 33 (HL) *per* counsel. The appellant's case was that in the instant case the memorandum-book was *not* admissible, at trial of a feigned issue, because the testator's handwrit-

(1714)[127]. These, however, are again without argument directed to the point; it is also possible that there is a connection with the use of the oral statements of the testator[128].

Again, the fact that there is argument in *Newburgh v Newburgh* indicates that at least at the later period this is not merely an absence of rules but an exception.

b) Documents used for their maker

Shopbooks are the most striking case of the use of documents as evidence by their makers. An Act of 1609 provided that traders and craftsmen were not to be allowed to give their shopbooks in evidence in actions for customers' debts unless the action was brought within one year from the date of the transaction[129]. The creation of this rule obviously implies that such books were previously admissible, and the Act makes the point absolutely explicit by explaining in its preamble that delay had hitherto prevented customers from adducing sufficient evidence to controvert the books. *Ceteris paribus* this is strong evidence that there were either no rules at all, or at least no rule against using your own documents in your own favour, at common law at this period. However, in view of the contemporary arguments over public documents in *Vickery v Farthing* (1594)[130] and *Plumpton v Robinson* (1610-14)[131] this would imply that there were rules about the admissibility of public, but not of private documents, which would be an odd conclusion.

There are two possible explanations. First, it is possible that shopkeepers' accounts were usable by way of exception. Ibbetson shows that this was the case in several continental jurisdictions[132], and it may be that there is a connection with

---

ing had not been proved; which implies that had the writing been proved it would have been admissible.

126 Colles 459 (HL(I)), testator's draft answer, in fact incorporated into the defendants' answer.

127 5 Bro PC 482 (HL), letters to the testator's nephew, under whom the respondents claimed, to show that a partnership between them was nominal, allowed as new matter to support a bill of review. Though lay peers sat in judicial appeals in the House of Lords at this period, the instances in these last three cases are drawn from the arguments of counsel which evidently had been accepted by the courts below.

128 Below, ch 4 § 1 *(2)*, ch 8 § 5. In this context both oral and written statements may fall into Maranta's instance of an extrajudicial confession usable by its maker or his successors, where the matter in question depends wholly on the intention of the maker: Maranta 555.18.

129 7 Jac 1 c 12. The legislative history and context of the Act is discussed by Ibbetson, "Sixteenth Century Contract Law: *Slade's Case* in context", 4 *OJLS* 295 at 313-4 & n 103. The discussions in Parliament which he cites do not, however, assist with the question why the shopbook was initially admissible.

130 Above n 84.

131 Above n 91.

the statement in the *Reformatio* that, notwithstanding that no-one can prove a debt due to him by his own writings,

> "Mercatorum tamen et aliorum artem exercentium libris et rationibus, cum aliis adminiculis, plenam fidem adhiberi volumus"[133].

The second possibility is that "shopbooks" at the time of the Act were not simply shopkeepers' journals, but books in which the customer signs for credit purchases. In this case they would be merely admissions by the customer, and the customer's problem would be the standard one of paying without taking an acquittance[134]. The difficulty about testing this hypothesis is that it is not apparent what a "shopbook" was[135], and a brief examination of some private account books in the British Library which might be "shopbooks" was inconclusive[136].

Shopbooks were "read as evidence at the hearing" in two cases in Tothill in 1639, in the second case "concerning the Statute of Limitation and by great advice"[137]. The second case is not traceable from the indexes[138]. In the first, *Bourn v De Best,* what was read was an entry of payment to the defendant's servant in the plaintiff's shopbook, *made by the servant.* This tends to corroborate the view that at this time the way the entries were made allowed their use by the shopkeeper as admissions by the customer[139].

At common law, in 1661 in *Crouch v Drury* Twisden cited an unreported (and undated) case, *Lee v Lee,* as deciding that

---

132 Loc. cit. above n 129; & cf also 'Alciatus' 207r, citing Panormitatus; Maranta 564-8 *Additio* §§ 23-37; Covarruvias *QP* Ch 22 § 8; Gaill i Obs. 36 No 8, ii Obs. 20; Clerke 89, acceptable to prove standing to sue; Gentili ii 114, 162; Ayliffe 446.

133 *De Fide* c 5.

134 This is suggested by the objection to the 1601 bill made by Mr Hackwell of Lincoln's Inn that it merely assisted buyers who had not taken care to protect themselves (Simonds D'Ewes' *Journals of the Parliaments of Elizabeth I,* p 667).

135 In the materials collected in Yamey, Edey & Thompson, *Accounting in England and Scotland: 1543- 1800* (London, 1963) (YET) there is no direct indication, though Monteage (1675) at YET 12 says a shopkeeper should keep a "book of goods bought, another of goods sold, a third of men's accounts upon trust, a fourth a cash-book", and Mellis (1588) at YET 76 "Beware that ye never enter any person in your book, either for debtor or for creditor, for your said shoppe, without the consent of the said person".

136 Harl 70, "Mr Leonard's book of debtor & creditor 1581", memoranda of debts & credits cross- referenced to other documents; Harl 1454, apothecaries' accounts, organised by customer name; early seventeenth century, ff1-62, in one hand throughout, mid century, ff 62-158, hand varied between customers, but notations seem to be apothecaries'; Sloane 1808, W. Aston's day-book 1673- 4, a very rough notebook, hand varies considerably and some entries are signed.

137 *Bourn v Debest* (M1639) Toth 90, *Harrison v Bludder* (M1639) Toth 91

138 It does not appear either in the MS index for this term, or in the printed *Index to Chancery Proceedings* for the reign of Charles I.

139 23 Oct 1639, PRO C 33/177 f 93v. The entry does not suggest that the usability of the book was argued; the 1609 Act is not applicable on the facts.

> "the book of any merchant is no good proof, nor may be allowed to be read touching any debt due to him; but of any debt against himself it may be good enough, which was agreed per Curiam"[140].

Similarly but slightly differently, in 1694 Holt CJ said that shopbooks and similar account books were not evidence for the maker, but could be for others[141]. In *Pitman v Maddox* (H1699)[142] Holt said that the 1609 Act did not mean that the shopbook was evidence within the year, without more; but both in that case and in *Price v Earl of Torrington* (T1703)[143] he allowed the books to be used where the entries in question were shown to have been made by deceased employees of the plaintiff tradesman and the employees' handwriting was proved. Whether the use of shopbooks by their makers originally reflected a general ability to use any sort of private document, or an exception to a general rule of using documents as admissions, in these cases the document is being used as testimony by the deceased employee.

An later instance of the use of documents for their makers is that in cases in the 1720s and 30s *obligees'* endorsements for receipt of interest on bonds were admitted to rebut the presumption of payment[144] on best evidence grounds and also on the basis of mutuality, *viz.* that since the receipts would be admissible against the obligee they should be admissible for him or his successors in title[145]. This is clearly an exception to a general rule that documents should not be used for their makers.

c) Conclusion

It is quite possible that originally any species of private documents, and not merely private documents in the nature of admissions, could be used either as proof in equity or as evidence to a jury. In view of the rules for which there is explicit authority, however, I am inclined to doubt that this was still the case either at the time of the 1609 Act on shopbooks or *a fortiori* later in the seventeenth century. The primary use of private documents, it seems to me, is as admissions (or perhaps more precisely as *alii tantum*), and the cases which don't fit into this framework are, at least in the earlier stages, exceptions.

---

140 (P1661) 1 Keb 27.

141 *Anon* (P1694) 1 Ld Raym 745 and *Smartle d Newport v Williams* (P1694) Comb 247 at 249 (Skin 423, 431, 3 Lev 387, 2 Salk 245, 280, Holt KB 478, all not SP). Given the dating it is possible that the anonymous report in Lord Raymond is simply a report of the *dictum* in *Smartle v Williams.*

142 2 Salk 690, 1 Ld Raym 732.

143 1 Salk 285, 2 Ld Raym 873.

144 Below Ch 9 § 2 *(1)*.

145 *Searle v Lord Barrington* (M1724) 1 Ld Raym 370, 8 Mod 278, 2 Stra 826, (KB) aff'd Ex Ch (1728), aff'd HL (1730) 3 Bro PC 593, and following cases cited in the notes to these reports.

However, towards the end of the century and at the beginning of the eighteenth, some judges (and in particular Holt CJ) seem to be engaged in re-theorising some of these exceptions; a process which meant in certain cases allowing in private documents as *testimony,* by analogy with the use of depositions and of the practice of proving the signatures of attesting witnesses. If this interpretation is correct, it may be this re- theorisation (and possibly extension of the sort of documents which could be used) which is at the root of the eighteenth century generalisation of "hearsay" to cover documentary, as well as oral, statements out of court.

3. Proof of documents

Private documents[146] which were to be used as proofs themselves required to be proved. In equity this requirement was stated by Egerton in 1599[147]: documents were not to be read unless supported by the depositions in the cause. This is reproduced by Ballow: "all exhibits proved by the depositions may be read at the hearing"[148]. The requirement that documents should be proved had two basic aspects. The first was that (if possible) the original document should be produced, rather than a copy. The second was that execution of the document must be proved; this meant that (again, if possible) if the document was attested by witnesses, these witnesses should be produced to swear to execution.

a) Documentary originals

The proof of the contents of documents by producing the original gave rise to a substantial body of slightly confusing authority both at common law and in equity in the seventeenth century. Since a part of the activity of equity consisted of relieving against common law rules and in other respects equity may have followed the law, it is necessary to consider the meaning of the common law as well as the equity authorities.

The first question which is posed by these is when, how and in what form the rule appeared. The basic rule that where documents are to serve for proof, the original must be produced, is present in Roman law[149] and therefore in civilian

146 And private copies of public documents; but this is a slightly distinct point, as the requirements of proof were different.

147 Add 20700 f 11. Jones p 236 treats this as an Order establishing a new rule, but it looks rather more like a *dictum:* "Noe written letter shallbe read at the hearinge except they bee justified by some depositions in Court, nor witnesses *viva voce* are to be examined after publication, for the first is noe receivable evidence before a Judge, and the latter ... By the Lord Keeper Oct 1599".

148 P 123.

149 D.22.4.2.

sources[150]. The requirement of profert at common law is, as previously indicated, analogous. Littleton, however, says that documents not available to be proffered may be found by a jury on the general issue[151]. This still seems to have been the rule in 1571, when in *Newis v Lark*[152] the Common Pleas upon full argument decided that the jury was entitled on the general issue to find records of their own knowledge, without any evidence whatever. The first trace of a requirement that the original document be produced to a jury on the general issue is in Coke's report of *Doctor Leyfield's Case* (1611)[153].

There are a number of reasons for supposing that Coke's statement represents merely Coke's own opinion and (subsequently) made new law. It is clearly *obiter*, since the case actually arose on a demurrer on the pleadings and turned on whether profert had to be made of a head title. The only authority Coke cites for it is to "reconcile" some yearbook cases in the *Liber Assisarum*[154], and his statement is expressed in terms that it is dangerous to allow proof of instruments before the jury without producing the original, not that it cannot be done[155]. It is also not easy to reconcile with the *ratio* of *Newis v Lark*. Coke distinguishes records from deeds as being provable by copy because rasure or interlineations in them are not to be presumed[156], but this is not the *ratio* in *Newis v Lark*, which does extend to deeds and does not (unlike Coke's statement) require a copy[157].

Coke's statement did not settle the rule, in two ways. The first is that up to the 1650s some common law courts seem to have continued to prefer the rule in *Newis v Lark*, i.e. that on the general issue the jury could find the contents of documents on any evidence or without evidence[158]. The second is that, even where an explanation of the absence of the original document was required, it is not clear that this was ever limited to the case of destruction by fire given by Coke[159]. Coke's em-

150 Above n 34.

151 § 366, Co Lit 226 f.

152 Plowd 403 at 410a.

153 10 Co Rep 88 at 92b.

154 At 92b: 28 Ass 3, 12 Ass 16 and 26 Ass 2 *semble*. In commenting on *Dr Leyfield's Case* in the preface to the tenth volume of the reports Coke cites two unreported cases, *Small & Blackledge* (M1607) in KB and *Greene & Eyer* (undated) in Star Chamber, which "in circuitu meo annotavi", but these seem from the context to be examples of the dangers of the jury finding deeds which prove on later inspection to be void, rather than authorities for the rule as stated. Cf. also *Robinson v Nethersall* (P1607) Hawarde 319, where a forged copy of a non-existent bond was used to procure a verdict at law, leading to a Star Chamber prosecution for perjury.

155 The fact that Coke's statement does not appear in the other printed reports of the case, 1 Bulst 154 and Cro Jac 317, is not material since Croke's report is a brief note and Bulstrode's is of the original proceedings in KB, while Coke's is in error in the Exchequer Chamber.

156 92b-93.

157 Plowd 411: "by parol, or by copies, or by other argument of truth".

158 *Wright v Pindar* (P1647) Style 22, KB; *Anon* (M1646) Style Prac Reg 161, 162, KB; *Anon* (T1647) Style Prac Reg 114, KB; *Olive v Gwin* (T1658) Hardr 118, 2 Sid 145, Ex.

phasis on destruction by fire seems, in fact, to be closest to the basic texts in the Digest and Code[160].

At the time of *Dr Leyfield's Case* the fact that documents were unavailable or in the hands of the adverse party had been a ground of relief in equity for some time[161], but the sources do not tell us how proof of these documents was made in order to entitle the plaintiff if the defendant in his answer denied the claim or claimed a title himself. The first indication is an anonymous case of 1603 in Cary[162], in which

> A release was offered to be disposed [Harv, Stowe, deposed] that it had been seen by some at the bar, it being affirmed that by casual means it was lost; but the Lord Chancellor said, the oath should be, that he saw it sealed and delivered, not that he saw it after it was a deed: for in Munson [Harv, Mounson, Stowe, Monson], the Justice[163], his case, a deed was brought into the Chancery, and a *vidimus* upon it, being but a counterfeit copy; and after the fraud discovered, and the true deed produced; therefore none allowance to be given of a [Stowe, the] deed, without producing the deed, or proving the execution thereof; and here appeareth what want we have of notaries and their deputies [Harv, Stowe, protocols].

Like Coke's rule in *Dr Leyfield's Case,* this looks, with its awful example of past bad practice, like a new initiative by Ellesmere rather than a statement of existing law. At this period Ellesmere is reported as complaining on several occasions about the "abuses" of the use of *ejectio firmae* to try titles, which drove the defendant to the general issue and hence made it impossible to compel profert of the plaintiff's title deeds[164].

It would seem that at this time there was concern about loose methods of proving transactions and titles both in equity and at law, which is also reflected in rela-

---

159 Coke does say "grand & notorious extremities, *come* per casualtie de fewe que touts les evidence in son meason fuer' arses" (my emphasis) which suggests that there may be other cases, but he doesn't indicate any and later returns to "le dit case del casualtie per le fewe".

160 D 27.7.57 "Chirographis debitorum incendio exustis cum ex inventario tutores convenire eos possent..."; C 4.21.5: "sicut iniquum est instrumentis vi ignis consumptis debitores quantitatum debitarum retinere solutionem...".

161 Avery, 'Chancery before 1460' at 134-5 says that this was a common ground for seeking relief in the first half of the fifteenth century, and Jones 194 says of the Elizabethan period that "almost every bill rested on the foundation of a claim of defective evidence". For deeds in the hands of the defendant in equity, *Diversity de Courtz et lour Jurisdictions* (1526) title *Chancery,* West sig B4 ee; for lost acquittance, West sig Biii,v X cites YB 22 Ed 4, 6, YB 7 Hen 7, 11.

162 (21 Nov 1 Jac) Cary 31, Harv 1090 f25b, Stowe 415 f99b, Lansd 599 f10, all substantially identical; variations given in the text quoted.

163 Presumably Robert Monson, puisne justice of CP 1572-81 (Foss, *Judges* V 524f). The case is probably *Mounson v West* (1588) 1 Leo 132, Gould 92, CP.

164 *Observations* f 460v No 185, f 464v No 209 ("208"), in Chancery; "Memorialles for Iudicature", Knafla 276; *Anon* (M 8 Jac) Add 25207 f13, in Star Chamber, "q[uia] en cest accon home ne poet plead spec[iall] plea de enforce le pl[aintiff] de faire title ...". (Square brackets are expansions).

tion to requirements of writing established by Ellesmere (below Ch 4 § 2 *(1)*). Imposing on equity and on jury trial of the general issue requirements of production of original deeds for proof is one way of tackling this problem. Both Ellesmere's solution (to require proof of execution and delivery as a deed) and Coke's arguments for the requirement that the original be produced (the danger that a copy, or witness evidence, will not show flaws which would avoid the deed) appear to be based on the mediæval common law rules. But the rule eventually created (that the original must be produced, except ...) is closer to the roman-canon rules than to those of the mediæval common law.

Subsequent seventeenth century authority is primarily concerned with the means of proving documents otherwise than by producing the original[165].

One option available to the party seeking to rely on a private document was to produce a public document in which it was established or recited in full, and a good many of the cases are concerned with this option. The public document would itself be primary evidence of the existence and terms of the document, so that *prima facie* if a public document could be used it would not be necessary to give reasons for the absence of the original private document. The authorities are therefore concerned with two issues: the admissibility of the public document, mainly a question of jurisdiction/ authority, which is discussed above, and the means by which a public document could be proved.

Coke in *Dr Leyfield's Case* said that a record could be proved by exemplification, whether under the Great Seal or the seal of the court, or by sworn copy[166]. Gilbert, towards the end of the period, said that public documents can be proved by exemplification, office copy or sworn copy[167]. Exemplifications had been used for some time: exemplifications of patents were made usable for profert by statutes of Edward VI and Elizabeth I, and exemplifications under the Great Seal can be seen to be in common use from the Orders promulgated in 1596 by Puckering LK and Egerton MR for the control of exemplifications[168]. Exemplifications of records of inferior courts were held to be acceptable at law in *Olive v Gwin* (T1658)[169].

---

165 The common law authorities are somewhat obscured by distinctions which are taken in the cases between (1) (a) evidence which can be read to a jury and (b) evidence binding on a jury, i.e. so as to make the jury liable to punishment (attaint, or imprisonment and fine by Star Chamber or the judge) for finding against it; and (2) (a) evidence which can be read to a jury and (b) evidence which can be taken away by the jury when it retires. Cf *Vickery v Farthing* and *Olive v Gwin* for discussion of these distinctions. Another distinction is between evidence under which title is made and evidence which is merely "inducement" (*Eden v Chalkhill* (M1661) 1 Keb 117, T Raym 25, KB); the question here *seems* to be whether the proponent could be required to make profert if the matter had been raised in pleading, but may be another way of stating the readable evidence/ binding evidence distinction. These distinctions are no doubt important in themselves but the details are not pertinent here.

166 At 93a.

167 Pp 11-20.

168 i Sanders 71; Stowe 415 f27b, No 10(?).

Sworn copies seem from several cases in Clayton to have been accepted from the 1630s[170].

"Office copies" are rather less clear. The examples given by Gilbert are (1) the chirograph of a fine, because the chirographer is appointed to give out copies[171]; (2) the endorsement of the enrollment of a deed, because the officer "is intrusted to authenticate such deeds by enrollment"[172]; but not copies made out by officers of the court whose function is not to give out copies, or copies of enrolled deeds made out by the Clerk[173]; and (3) office copies of depositions, as being evidence in Chancery but not at law[174]. In fact, it seems that the Chancery never required depositions to be exemplified before they could be used in its own proceedings[175]. Gilbert's category looks like a pigeonhole constructed to hold these different elements after they had already become admissible in practice.

Presumably as a result of the continued authority of *Newis v Lark*, there was some uncertainty as to whether matter of record could be proved by witness or circumstantial evidence. By the time of Gilbert it seems to be settled that a copy of some sort is required, where the writ is essential to the cause of action or defence[176], but there are some authorities suggesting that circumstantial evidence would suffice[177].

---

169 Hardr 118, 2 Sid 145; citing Dy 276 (= *Anon* (H1564-5) Dy 236a) (and *per* counsel *arg, Whitehead's Case* temp Wilde CB).

170 *Anon* (1638) Clayt 62 pl 108, NP, Berkeley J; *Anon* (1640) Clayt 85 pl 143, NP, Foster J; *Anon* (1647) Clayt 122, NP, Jermyn J; *Beamsley's Case* (1640) Clayt 90, NP, Whitfield J; *Nelthrop v Johnson* (1650) Clayt 142, NP, Thorpe, Rigby BB; and cf *Thurle v Madison* (M1655) Style 462, UB.

171 P 18, citing T. Ass. 1701. Third edition (p 24) cites Plow. Com 110b, actually *Newis v Lark* at 2 Plowd 410, where it is said that the chirograph "is the usual evidence of the truth of such fine", but the *ratio* is that the jurors "may find the fine of themselves, if they know of it, though it be not shewn by any of the parties".

172 P 18, citing 2 Inst = presumably, Coke, *Second Institute* pp 671f, though I have not found any mention there or elsewhere in the book of the question of usability as evidence.

173 Citing 2 Inst = as previous note.

174 Pp 19-20. Third Edition, pp 25-6, cites [Bathurst] Theo.[ry of] Evid.[ence] 14 and [Buller] Tri.[al] at Ni.[si] Pri.[us] 215, but both of these are derived from Gilbert.

175 This is implicit in Egerton's Order of 23. 6. 1596, i Sanders 73, that no copies of depositions or pleadings to be read unless under the hand of the officer, deputy or clerk authorised in that behalf. These office copies could, indeed, be used to supply defects in the records: *Kynaston v Alice Countess of Derby & John Earl of Bridgwater* (H1626/7) i Sanders 155, briefly in Toth 77, 1 Chan Rep 15, depositions burnt in the fire at the 6 Clerks' office; *Tregunnel's Case* (H1677/8) 2 Freem 30, a writ lost from the file, proved to have existed, copied onto the file from a surviving copy. In *Mason v Goodburne & al* (T1678) Rep t Finch 391 a deed was ordered to be brought into Court and both parties to have copies attested by a Master for use at law; but this would probably have been made evidence at law by a special order to consent, rather than being admissible as an "office copy".

176 Gilbert pp 30-31 cites TPP [= *Trials Per Pais* 3rd Edition, 1695] 167 (where a writ is only "inducement" a copy need not be produced, otherwise where it is the gist of the action); [in the MSS] *Greenland v Geer* (T Ass 1701) (a sherriff's bailiff to justify taking goods in

There are relatively few equity authorities on secondary evidence of public documents, and they do not seem to establish a clear course of the court, but they do imply that the same sort of questions were involved in equity as at law. It seems in equity to have been possible to establish records by circumstantial evidence: in *Anon* (T1602)[178] an enrolment of a deed settling the customs of a manor was accepted as a bar to the tenants in spite of the absence of any other records to support it; in *Herbert v Griffith* (1612)[179] in the Wards it was said ("by the three Chief Justices") that a lost record can be given in evidence but not pleaded, which merely follows *Newis v Lark*, and in *Kent v Bridgman* (M1704)[180] a sheriff's bailiff who had failed to produce a copy of the judgment under which he was acting, but had produced related records, obtained relief in Chancery.

On the other hand, in *R v Arundel & Howard* (T1616)[181] the terms of a private Act were said to be provable only by the Parliament Roll, and not by endorsements on it or the Journals of either House, and the fact that no originals were extant was given as a reason to reject exemplifications of depositions before the Council of the North[182]. In *AG, ex rel Inhabitants of Stains, v Taylor* (1695)[183] Somers LK rejected an exemplification of part of a patent on the ground that the statutes for the use of such exemplifications[184] did not authorise their use in evidence, and cited a decision in KB in support of this view. And the decisions on enrolled deeds in *Lady Holcroft v Smith* (T1702)[185] and *Combes v Spencer* (M1704)[186] are fairly clear examples of equity following the law.

---

execution must show a copy of the writ of execution, not merely the judgment and the sheriff's warrant), and *Sibly v Hinckly* (T Ass 1701) per Gold [= Gould J] (in an attorney's action for fees a coroners' warrant is sufficient to show a writ was taken out).

177 *Newis v Lark; Wright v Pindar* (P1646) Aleyn 18; *Knight v Dauler* [Keb *Dancer*] (P1663) Hardr 323, 1 Keb 7, where it is said that the evidence to prove a lost record must be "strong and cogent, slight and ordinary evidence will not serve the turn". *Contra Anon* (1647) Clayt 122, NP, Jermyn J. In *R v Weeden Ford, Warden of the Fleet* (1699) 12 Mod 337 at 341 Holt CJ said that to prove a conviction to disqualify a witness a copy of the record must be produced, and it was insufficient that the witness had been burnt in the hand [sc. on taking benefit of clergy on conviction of felony]; but in *Thurston v Slatford* (1700) 1 Salk 284 (1 Lutw 905, 3 Salk 155, not SP) Holt said that to prove a conviction of recusancy, on proof that the record was lost, other evidence was admissible to prove the "effect" of the record.

178 Cary 21.

179 Lansd 1110 f 11.

180 Pre Ch 233, 2 Eq Ca Ab 159.1, 243.10.

181 Hob 109, Moo KB 832 (more fully in Hob); Ellesmere C, Coke and Hobart CJJ and Caesar MR.

182 The primary reason given for excluding these depositions, however, was that the Council of the North had no jurisdiction in matters of freehold.

183 Pre Ch 59, 2 Eq Ca Ab 395.

184 Above n 168.

185 2 Freem 359, Harv 1105 pp 233, 235, 1 Eq Ca Ab 224.

If absent private documents were to be proved otherwise than by public documents, they had to be shown to be either lost or destroyed, or in the hands of the adverse party.

It is not entirely clear what limits were at first placed on loss or destruction. As mentioned above (p 115), Coke in *Dr Leyfield's Case* refers to "grand & notorious extremities, come per casualtie de fewe". Jenkins, writing during the 1650s, says that

> In cases where charters have been lost by fire, burning of houses, or when robbers have destroyed them: the law in such cases allows the proof of charters without shewing them.
>
> *Necessitas facit licitum quod alias non est licitum.*[187]

On the basis primarily of these statements and *Medlicot v Joyner* (M1669)[188], Wigmore argued that initially only destruction by fire was allowed as an exception to the requirement of production, and that other instances were only gradually added[189].

The basic difficulty with this argument is that as, up to the 1650s, some courts persisted in following *Newis v Lark,* it is difficult to say that there was any settled rule before the 1660s. *Barry & Styles' Case* in the 1620s provides some evidence for common law hostility to bare allegations of loss, as Jones J in that case criticised equitable relief against the requirement of profert in these circumstances on the ground that

> si un surmise on Chancery que il ad perd tiel fait, nest conscience pur le Chancery de aider luy: car devoit il aver looked melius a c[eo][190].

In *Grice v Beaumont* (1647)[191] circumstantial evidence was allowed to prove the terms of a deed to lead the uses of a fine, said merely to be "lost"; but this is not a clear instance, because deeds to lead the uses of a fine were said in the 1690s to be governed by special rules in the context of the parol evidence rule because the uses of the fine could in any event be proved by parol[192]. Nor is *Medlicot v*

---

186 2 Vern 471 (Trevor MR). As *Combs v Dowell* (M1707) 2 Vern 591: a feigned issue was ordered by Cowper LK, and on trial, the original being proved lost, Holt CJ admitted the enrollment as secondary evidence.

187 Jenk 18 case 35, at 19. Jenkins says in his preface that he wrote his book, which is a species of chronological Abridgement with commentary, while in prison. Most of the references in the text in the English Reports text were added by the translator/ editor of the 1734 edition; this passage is clearly commentary.

188 1 Mod 4, 2 Keb 546

189 § 1193

190 Latch 24; undated, but from the judges present must have been between 1624 and 1628.

191 Clayt 121, NP, Jermyn J.

192 *Jones d Bellingham v Morley* (P1694) 4 Mod 261, (T1697) Comb 429, Carth 410, Holt KB 321, Com 29, (H1697/8) 12 Mod 159, 1 Ld Raym 287, Salk 677, Com 47, at 1 Ld Raym 289, 290 *per* Holt CJ.

Joyner clear evidence of a limitation to destruction by fire, since it is clear from the reports that the issue argued is not what sort of loss will let in secondary evidence, but whether a copy not sworn compared with the original is good secondary evidence.

Loss of deeds seems to have been a well established ground for equitable relief[193]. However, in *Lister v Lister* (T1675)[194] and in *Lord North v Lord Gray* (1680)[195] Lord Nottingham denied relief to plaintiffs alleging that their deeds were lost on the ground that they could prove them at law. This implies fairly strongly that by 1675 simple loss was a ground to admit secondary evidence at law. From the 1690s it is clear that simple loss was sufficient[196].

This evidence does not allow the construction of a clear chronology, but it is clear that Wigmore's account of a very gradual extension of the sorts of loss allowable, starting with fire and extending into the eighteenth century, cannot stand[197].

That deeds were in the hands of the adverse party was, again, a well established ground of relief in equity from an early date[198]. The first instance of this being used as a ground to admit secondary evidence at law is in 1633[199], and from the Restoration it seems fairly well settled[200]. During the eighteenth century the com-

---

193 *Barry & Styles Case,* above.

194 Nott CC No 253, ((H1675/6) Nott CC No 403, ((?)H1676/7) R t Finch 285, not SP). R t Finch says that the deed was in fact alleged burnt, but Lord Nottingham has "lost" and the point is what Lord Nottingham thought the law was, not the specific facts. Though Lord Nottingham at No 253 has the plaintiff dismissed, it appears from No 403 and Rep t Finch that a feigned issue as to the existence of the deed was directed and on a verdict for the plaintiff an account ordered.

195 Dick 14, Nott CC 1031. Dickens has "lost", Lord Nottingham that the deed was alleged to have been concealed or destroyed by the defendant's father. The relief sought and denied was examination of witnesses *in perpetuam memoriam.*

196 *Haines Barley's Case* (P1696) 5 Mod 210, KB (cited by Wigmore § 1193 as 3 Mod 210); *R v Culpeper* (H1696/7) Skin 673, Holt KB 293, *per* Holt CJ; *Sir Edward Seymour's Case* (1711) 10 Mod 8, KB, *per cur* (*Seymour v Seymour* (1711) 5 Bro PC 105, connected proceedings in equity).

197 Wigmore § 1193 cites a number of eighteenth century cases which display a more restrictive approach than those of the later seventeenth and early eighteenth century. I suggest that these may actually represent new restrictive rules, comparable to those in the case of documents in the hands of the adverse party (below n 201), rather than the continuation of a restrictive tradition.

198 Above n 161.

199 *Anon* (1633) Clayt 15 pl 24, NP, Vernon J (cited by Wigmore 1199 as *Bradford's Case,* which is actually pl 23 and concerns what needed to be proved to establish a feoffment).

200 *Negus v Reynel* (P1661) 1 Keb 12, KB; *Moreton v Horton* (P1669) 2 Keb 483, KB; *Earl of Peterborough v Lord Mordaunt* (P1672) 1 Mod 94, 3 Keb 1 ((M1673) Nott CC No 37, (P1674) 1 Mod 114, 3 Keb 305, (H1674/5) Nott CC No 200, not SP. Criticised by Guilford, Add 32518 f 6b); *Ecclestone v Petit alias Speke* (M1689) Carth 79 at 80, Comb 156 at 157 (variously spelled. 3 Mod 259, Holt KB 222, 1 Show KB 89, not SP); *Lynch v Clerke* (H1696/7) 3 Salk 154 (this date is not in Salkeld, but though the overall arrangement is by

mon law courts appear to have restricted the availability of secondary evidence in this case by requiring the party seeking to rely on it to give notice to the adverse party to produce the document at trial[201], but in our period there is no trace of this rule at law or in equity.

A number of questions arose on the issue of what secondary evidence was acceptable. The straightforward case was a copy sworn by a witness to have been accurately copied from and/ or compared with the original[202]. There was discussion in the cases, however, of the use of counterparts; recitals in other deeds; and oral evidence; and a rule appeared in the later seventeenth century prohibiting the use of a "copy of a copy".

Counterparts of indentures might, in principle, have been regarded as originals (i.e. all parts of the indenture as of equal weight)[203]. However, around the turn of the sixteenth and seventeenth centuries the Common Pleas in *Yelverton v Cornwallis*[204] decided that covenant would not lie on a counterpart of an indenture; and the logic of the explanation of the primary rule given by Coke in *Dr Leyfield's Case* was that the counterpart might not be sufficient, since the first part might have been razed or interlined after execution and this not appear on the counterpart[205]. The later seventeenth century common law authorities certainly seem to treat counterparts as secondary evidence, usable in the case of old deeds[206].

Recitals of documents in other documents are said by Wood and Domat not to be evidence of the documents recited[207], unless either the adverse party was a party

---

subject, the case is among a group of cases in this term and this date is given to it by Viner (Vol 12, in several places), KB; *Earl of Sussex v Temple* (H1697/8) 1 Ld Raym 310, 5 Mod 384, KB; *Anon* (M1698) 1 Ld Raym 731, KB, *per* Holt CJ; *Sir Edward Seymour's Case* (1711) above n 190. *Carver v Pinkney* (1683) 3 Lev 82, cited by Wigmore § 1199 as an example of this, is actually on a statutory exception to profert in debt sur obligation.

201 *Bartlett v Gawler* (T1737) 7 Mod 343, KB, and Wigmore 1202 ff and cases cited there.

202 Above nn 166-7 and text there.

203 This seems to be the approach in Littleton, § 370, and reasserted by Coke, Co Lit 229. Cf also Wigmore § 1233.

204 Noy 54, temp Walmsley J (1589-1611). The arrangement of Noy does not allow more precise dating.

205 Cf also Bracton f 398b, Thorne ed p 242.

206 *Garrett v Lister* (P1661) 1 Lev 25, 1 Keb 15, KB; *Anon* (M1704) 6 Mod 225, 1 Salk 287, Holt KB 301,KB *per* Holt CJ. In this case Holt CJ cites *Mayo v Combe* temp Hale as establishing this point, but the point is not in the printed reports of that case ((P1674) 3 Keb 477, 1 Freem 396, KB, Pollex 164, Ex Ch). In *Brisco v Earl of Banbury* (M1675) R t Finch 237 at 239 (Nott CC 331 not SP; (T, M1676) Nott CC Nos 445, 522, 572, 602, 1 Ch Cas 287, 1 Freem 15, 2 Freem 8, *Earl of Banbury v Brisco* (H1680/1) Nott CC No 1081, 2 Ch Cas 42, subsequent proceedings on other points) Lord Nottingham decreed a counterpart to be admitted as an original, which implies that it would not at that time be treated as an original without an order.

207 Wood 320; Domat 3.6.2.12. Cf also Covarruvias QP Ch 21 § 2: mention of a document in a notarised instrument is not an original but does give rise to a presumption. A slightly distinct point is in Cotta 31-2 and Gaill i Obs 37 No 12: recitals of boundaries are no

to the reciting document or there are other special reasons, i.e. reasons to admit secondary evidence[208]. The rule at common law seems to have been the same, with the (possible) difference that recitals in deeds are evidence against privies as well as parties: recitals seem not to have been acceptable primary evidence[209], but were admitted against privies[210], and where supported by long possession in accordance with the title recited[211].

In *Sir Edward Seymour's Case* (1711)[212] the King's Bench under Parker CJ said that oral evidence was not admissible of a deed which was lost, but was admissible of a deed which was in the hands of the adverse party. The nearest thing to an antecedent to this decision is *Ecclestone v Speke* in 1689[213], where evidence given at a former trial where the defendant had produced a deed containing a pedigree was allowed to be given orally on the ground that the defendant had the deed and so could controvert the witnesses, if they stated its terms wrongly, by producing it[214]. There is some indication of a similar view that the contents of deeds ought not to be proved by witnesses in the equity case of *Earl of Suffolk v Greenvill* (1631)[215], but there cannot be any more direct connection, as *Earl of Suffolk v Greenvill* was a case in which the deed in question was alleged to be in the hands of the adverse party.

The origin of the "copy of a copy" "rule" is obscure. It first appears in *Faulconer's Trial* for perjury (1653)[216] as an argument by the defence counsel[217] against

---

evidence against third parties, unless the document is old, in which case they can stand as evidence of *communis opinio* (local reputation).

208 Domat cross-refers to his preceding section (3.6.2.11) which is on this point.

209 *Rowe v Huntington* (H1669/70) Vaugh 66 at 74-5.

210 *Ford v Lord Grey* (H1703/4) 6 Mod 44, 1 Salk 286, KB. The printed text of Gilbert at p 72 has the same point citing *Fitzgerald v Eustace* (1718), Ex (I), per Gilbert CB, but this is absent from the MSS. Wigmore 1257 as well as *Ford v Lord Grey* cites *Earl of Sussex v Temple* (H1697) (above n 194), which is actually on the recital of a deed *in hæc verba* in an answer in Chancery, and *Sherwood v Adderley* (1699) 1 Ld Raym 734, (actually *Anon* of the same date), which is on a will recited in the admission to a copyhold. In both cases the point is different, since the answer and the admission are public documents.

211 *Anon* (1667) Add 32518 f 87b, NP.

212 Above n 196.

213 Above n 200.

214 At Comb 157, Carth 80. In *Anon* (1664) 3 Ch Rep 17 (probably *Sewel v Freeston* 1 Ch Cas 65) a defendant demurred to a bill based on the defendant's possession of a note, which would allegedly have given the plaintiff a defence against the defendant's action at law, on the ground that the bill was after verdict, but also that the plaintiff in equity had been allowed to lead (presumably oral) evidence of the "effect" of the note at the trial; this suggests that oral evidence could at this stage be given of the contents of a document in the hands of the adverse party, but not the other branch of the rule.

215 Below n 228 and text there.

216 5 St Tr 323.

217 Wyndham, Latch, Letchmore, Haggat, at 356.

a copy of the defendant's deposition before the Commissioners for Sequestrations, which had been made from a copy in the Commons' Journal which, in turn, was derived from a copy sent by the Commissioners to the Council of State. The argument was evidently unsuccessful, since Faulconer was convicted[218]. It appears again in *Elwaies v Coteswell* (P1675)[219] where it is used as an argument to reject a copy of a lease out of the Dean & Chapter of Lincoln's Ledger Book, on the ground that the book itself is merely a copy, and in *Anon* (P1684)[220], *per* Jeffreys, as a ground for the inadmissibility of a probate of a will of lands.

The "rule" is repeated as a legal commonplace in Locke's *Essay Concerning Human Understanding* (1689)[221]. Curiously, however, the instance given by Locke, that a copy of a copy of a record cannot be used, does not appear in this or in the subsequent cases in which "copy of a copy" is treated as a commonplace[222]. Apart from *Faulconer's Trial,* in which the argument fails, the standard example is probate of lands, and for this the original explanation is the want of jurisdiction[223]. The rule is stated by Covarruvias, who says that "exemplo exempli credendum non sit", giving, however, an account of academic controversy on the point and several exceptions.[224] Since Covarruvias is cited by Hale in his *Pleas of the Crown,* not much later, it is a reasonable inference that his general rule is the source of the expression at common law.

If it were not for *Faulconer's Trial, Elwaies v Coteswell,* and Locke's statement, the natural interpretation would be that "copy of a copy" was a subsequent rationalisation of the original rule about jurisdiction applied to probate of realty. It does, however, appear to have had an independent civilian origin and some operative effect.

The equity authorities do not, on their own, display anything like this degree of complexity. In fact, those from the later seventeenth century seem, to some extent,

218 The report is not clear, so that the whole argument on both sides is somewhat obscure. But it seems that the defence counsel objected to this copy at an early stage, though on what grounds do not appear; whereupon the prosecutors proved elaborately by witnesses the transmission of the copy at each stage from the Commissioners, to the counsel of state, to the Commons' journals; and concluded by arguing that the original was in Faulconer's hands, so that if the copy was false he could produce the original. The "copy of a copy" argument then surfaces in the defence opening, presumably to persuade the jury not to rely on the copy.

219 TPP, 3rd edition, 230. (*Elways v Cottesford* 3 Keb 457 SC but not SP).

220 Skin 174.

221 Book IV, c 16, § 10; ed. Nidditch, Oxford, Clarendon paperback ed., 1979, pp 663-4. This particular argument is not in Versions A (ed Aaron & Gibb, OUP, 1936) or B (ed Nidditch, Sheffield University, 1982), so presumably dates from the 1680s.

222 *R v Haines* (1695) above nn 89, 100-1 and text there; *Smartle v Williams* (1695) above n 141; *Hoe v Nathorp* (1696) 1 Ld Raym 154, 3 Salk 154; *Worrall v Holder* (1696) Skin 672. It does appear in Gilbert, p 7, but this is of no assistance since no authority is cited in the MSS; Gilbert probably took the point from Locke.

223 Above n 86.

224 *PQ* Ch 21 §§ 4-5. Cf also Wood 323, rather later.

to assume principles used at common law, while varying from these principles at some points. I have already noted a number of instances of equitable relief against the rules at law, or refusal to give relief, as evidence for the contemporary rules at law[225]. *Barry & Styles' Case,* referred to above, indicates that loss and possession by the adverse party were grounds of relief, and therefore presumably to let in secondary evidence, in equity[226], and there are a range of subsequent authorities on possession by the adverse party[227].

As to secondary evidence, there are only scattered authorities. In *Earl of Suffolk v Greenvill* (1631)

> the Court held it very dangerous to admit the contents and sufficiencies of deeds to be proved by the testimony of witnesses, the construction of deeds being the office of the Court; and the Fact touching execution pertained only to the proof of witnesses[228].

This could mean that either (a) the original was always required, which seems implausible, (b) more probably, oral evidence of the contents of a deed was unacceptable, but some sort of copy at least ought to be produced.

---

225 Above nn 190, 194-5 and text there; and cf also *Lord Gorges v Foster* (1661) Nels 82, a copy of a probate of realty decreed to be evidence, and *Norwich v Sanders* (T1677) Rep t Finch 302, copy of a deed to lead the uses of a fine decreed to be evidence.

226 For loss cf also *Anon* (M1603) Cary 31 (other refs above p 116 n 156), "lost by casual means", the objection taken by Ellesmere being to the secondary evidence, not loss as a ground to let in any secondary evidence.

227 As a ground for relief: *Lake v Prigeon* (1633) Nels 27; *Meriel v Wymondsold* (M1661) Hardr 205, 1 Eq Ca Ab 24.1; *Anon* (1662) 3 Ch Rep 5, 1 Ch Cas 11, 2 Freem 160, Harv 1105 p 140; *Kinaston v Maynwearing* [Nels *Kingston v Manwaring*] (P1664) Nels 94, 1 Ch Cas 47, with *Quære*'s by the reporters because the existence of the deed allegedly detained was not proved. To let in secondary evidence: apparently not accepted on the ground of insufficient secondary evidence, *Earl of Suffolk v Greenvill* (1631) 3 Ch Rep 89, Nels 15, 2 Freem 146, Harv 1105 p126; *Norwich v Sanders* (T1677) Rep t Finch 302; *Eyton v Eyton* (1700) Pre Ch 116, (1706) 4 Bro PC 149, HL; rejected on grounds not shown ever in the adverse party's hands, *Earl of Peterborough v Germaine* (1702) 3 Bro PC 539, HL (on appeal from *Earl of Peterborough v Duchess of Norfolk* (1702) Pre Ch 212, 2 Freem 264, Harv 1105 p238, Wright LK, but this point not reported there; (1709) 6 Bro PC 1, HL, not SP); *Winne v Lloyd* (1707) 2 Vern 603, (1709) 2 Bro PC 374, HL; *Hampden v Hampden* (1709) cit 1 P Wms 733, Trevor MR, Cowper C; 13 Viner 540 ca 1; 3 Bro PC 550, HL.

228 3 Ch R 89, Nels 15, 2 Freem 146, Harv 1105 126, Harg 174 f 18, Coventry LK assisted by Hutton and Whitelock JJ. Text as quoted is the version in Chan. Rep.. Nelson has "the sufficiency of a Deed to be proved by the single oath of such a witness, especially since the construction of Deeds...", Harg 174 "the contents and sufficiency of a Deed to be proved by the testimony of one witness, the construction of Deeds...", and Freeman and Harv 1105 "dangerous to admit any one to swear the the contents of a Deed ...". These formulæ obviously echo the statement in *Anon* (M1603) Cary 31, cited above p. The Nelson and Harg 174 versions suggest that the singularity of the witness is an important element of the argument, and the Freeman version might be interpreted in this way ("any *one*"), but the subsequent argument that the construction of deeds is the office of the court implies that the point is more general.

The remaining cases are from the reign of Anne. The recital in a settlement after marriage of a bond given before marriage to make such a settlement was rejected in *Willson v Pack* (T1710)[229]. A copy of counsel's abstract of a deed was rejected as evidence to prove the contents of the deed in *Earl of Peterborough v Germaine* (1702)[230]. However, copies made by a person now dead were accepted where a document had been torn while in the possession of the adverse party in *Winne v Lloyd* (1707)[231], and oral evidence and presumptions were said to be sufficient where a document was in the possession of the adverse party in *Hampden v Hampden* (1709)[232], and in *Newburgh v Newburgh* (1712)[233] old rentrolls and correspondence were accepted to prove a title where the title deeds were lost. These decisions are generally consistent with the common law authorities.

In general this area displays considerable consistency between law and equity. There is, however, no significant lapse of time between the emergence of the rule at common law and in equity; the first reported expressions of the need for a rule are in 1603 in equity, 1611 at law, and the next clear case in equity is as early as the next common law cases. Moreover, the issue debated at law in the early stages of the rule is not what sort of rule to apply to control the jury, but (following *Newis v Lark*) whether the jury is bound by rules which would bind the court (albeit in a different form). And though the rule becomes considerably elaborated in the later seventeenth century common law, its starting point is strikingly similar to civilian formulations.

b) Proof of execution

This topic can be dealt with fairly briefly. The requirement that private documents should be proved by witnesses is present in the civilian authorities[234] and in mediæval common law authorities[235]. The mediæval common law rule would seem to be that where a deed is disputed on the pleadings its execution must be proved, *prima facie* by the attesting witnesses, who will be summoned with the jury[236], but if they are unavailable by comparison of hands or seals, or by verdict[237]. *Prima facie,* therefore, the rule in *Newis v Lark* ought to have applied to

229 Pre Ch 295, 1 Eq Ca Ab 155.2.

230 Above n 227.

231 Above n 227.

232 Above n 227.

233 3 Bro PC 553, HL(I).

234 Above nn 30, 33 and text there.

235 Glanvill X.12 (Hall ed p 127); Bracton *Of Warranty* ff 396-400 (Thorne ed Vol IV pp 235-243); YB 7 Hen 5 pl 3 at p 5 *per* Cockaigne CJ.

236 Bracton cited at previous note; Thayer pp 97-102; 12 Viner 43-5.

237 Bracton cited above n 235, Co Lit 6b.

proof of execution of documents given in evidence on the general issue as much as to production of originals. However, there is no trace in the printed reports of the sort of doubts which are found in relation to documentary originals: the requirement of proof of execution seems to have been applied from an early date[238].

If the document was attested, proof of execution was prima facie to be done by producing the attesting witnesses. If, however, there were no attesting witnesses, or the attesting witnesses were unavailable[239] or, at least from the later seventeenth century, denied their attestation or that the document was executed by the party[240], execution could be proved by other witnesses or by comparison of handwriting[241]. In the civilian sources comparison of handwriting was generally only a half proof; the only trace of this view at common law or in equity is the controversy about its use in criminal cases resulting from its use to convict Algernon Sidney in 1683[242].

Old documents, unless suspect, did not require proof of execution. Gilbert explains this rule as based on the view that after a certain lapse of time the witnesses to execution could be presumed to be dead[243]. However, it was restricted to cases where the old deed was supported by possession going along with it, and clearly an element in the reasoning is the presumption of regularity, *ex diuturnitate temporis omnia præsumuntur rite et solemniter esse acta*[244].

---

238 In *Rolfe v Hampden* (T1542) 1 Dy 53b the plaintiff proceeds to attaint on the failure of the jury on the general issue to accept proof of a will by witnesses, which suggests (no more) that witnesses were required to be produced. Co Lit 6b cites *Anon* (P1612), CP on Statute of Bankrupts for the exception for old deeds (below), which again implies that the primary rule was in force.

239 Bracton loc cit n 235; Co Lit 6b; *Goodrick's Case* (1647) Clayt 118, NP, Jermyn J; *Phillips v Crawly* (1673) 1 Freem 83; *Smartle v Williams* (P1694) (above n 141) at Comb 148 (other reports not SP); *Wood v Drury* (1699) 1 Ld Raym 734; *Dillon v Crawly* (P1701) 12 Mod 500, Holt KB 299, KB; *Key v Gordon* (P1701) 12 Mod 521, Holt CJ; *Anon* (M1701) 12 Mod 607, NP, Holt CJ.

240 *Hudson's Case* (1683) Skin 79; *Dayrell v Glasscock* (1694) Skin 413, Holt KB 742; *Blurton v Toon* (1696) Skin 639; *Osborne v Hosier* (P1704) 6 Mod 167, Holt KB 194.

241 Cases cited in the last two notes.

242 (1683) 9 St Tr 817, 854, objected to by Sidney at 879. Holloway J doubted whether it was admissible in the *Seven Bishops' Trial* (1688) 12 St Tr 183 at 304; the Act reversing the attainder of Sidney declared it not to be legal evidence (9 St Tr 996), and it was rejected, at least if uncorroborated, in *Crosby's Trial* (1695) 12 St Tr 1291, 5 Mod 15, 12 Mod 72, Skin 578, Holt KB 753, 2 Salk 689, 1 Ld Raym 39, at 12 St Tr 1297, Skin 579, 12 Mod 72, 1 Ld Raym 40. Gilbert p 41 takes the same line, i.e. that in criminal cases it is evidence if corroborated, but not on its own.

243 Gilbert p 73 cites T.Ass Kent 1700, but this is not in the MSS.

244 Gilbert p 73 cites Ass 1702 per Hasset (MSS ruled by Baron Hassell). Co Lit 6b has the rule together with the maxim; cf also *Isaack v Clark* (H1614/5) 2 Bulst 306 at 314, 1 Rolle 59, 126 at 132, *per* Coke CJ; *Anon* (1648) TPP (2nd ed, 1682) 244, KB; *Wright v Sherrard* (T1665) 1 Keb 877, KB. This rule did not apply to documents which were *ex facie* suspect: *William Mettam's Case* (1639) Clayt 80, NP, Henden B; Gilbert p 74 cites Ass 1700 in Kent and *Chattel v Pound* (Hil Ass 1701) in Kent = *Chettle v Pound* (1701) 1 Ld Raym 746, on a slightly different point.

Public documents in general, including deeds of bargain and sale enrolled, would "prove themselves" and not require proof by witnesses[245]. Moreover, from the 1690s it was held that where deeds were enrolled their execution could not be disputed by parties and privies. This rule was applied to deeds which were enrolled for safekeeping, as well as deeds of bargain and sale enrolled under the Statute of Enrolments[246], and for this purpose was explained as a species of admission.

The bulk of these specific rules are derived from authorities at common law. There are very few authorities in equity on the point, and these seem merely to indicate the same basic approach[247].

4. Privity and mutuality

Some part of the requirements of privity and reciprocity/ mutuality which were applied to estoppels was clearly applied in the early modern period to the use for proof or in evidence to a jury of documents of a party and party character; i.e not only records and deeds but also other documents, and not only private documents but also such "party and party" judicial proceedings as equity answers[248] and depositions[249], depositions from other courts[250] and verdicts in previous trials[251].

---

245 Gilbert pp 15-16, and cf the cases cited on public documents above pp 97-102. On deeds enrolled, Gilbert pp 71-3 and citations there (*Fitzgerald v Eustace* passage not in MSS).

246 *Smartle v Williams, per* Holt CJ at Comb 248.

247 The need for proof was explicitly stated by Egerton in 1599 (above p 113) and is implicit in *Anon* (M1603) and *Earl of Suffolk v Greenvill* (1631). *Bloxton v Drewit* (1696) Pre Ch 64, Trevor MR, illustrates the practice of proving documents by witnesses and the availability of comparison of hands if they could not be produced.

248 For the use of answers in previous proceedings cf above Ch 2 § 2 *(2)* & n 194, and for their use against co- defendants Ch 2 § 2 *(3)* (b). Cf also *Ireland's Case* (1632) Clayt 106 (NP), inventory exhibited by executor in the ecclesiastical court does not affect co-executor merely *de son tort*.

249 In equity: *Tolson v Lamplugh* (1669) 2 Ch Rep 43; *Backhouse v Middleton* (M1669, T1670) 3 Ch Rep 32, 1 Ch Cas 175, 2 Freem 132, 2 Eq Ca Ab 2.2, (H1670-1, T1671) 1 Ch Cas 208, at 1 Ch Cas 175; *Cook v Fountain* (M1686) 1 Vern 413 (Trevor MR) ((1674) 1 Mod 107, ?2 Vent 347, (1675-6) 3 Swans 585, Nott CC Nos 273, 500, not SP); *Earl of Peterborough v Duchess of Norfolk* (1702) 2 Freem 264, Pre Ch 212 (Wright LK), aff'd HL 3 Bro PC 539 ((1709) 6 Bro PC 1 not SP); *Allibon v AG* (1707) Colles 393 (HL, affg Ex(E)). At law: *Aldbroke's Case* (1632) Clayt 9 pl 17 (NP, Davenport CB); *Ecclestone v Speke* (M1689) Comb 156, Carth 79 (KB); *Tilley's Case* (M1703) 1 Salk 287 (CP).

250 2 Rolle Ab 679.9, depositions before commissioners of bankrupts, excluded because different parties so not opportunity to cross-examine, stated as a rule; in equity, cited, Nott Proleg 29.7, and followed, *Greenwood v Knipe* (M1677) Nott CC No 754 (No 878 not SP); hence the witnesses can, exceptionally, be re-examined, *Perrat v Ballard* (M1681) 2 Ch Cas 73, 1 Eq Ca Ab 53.7 (Lord Nottingham C); at law, depositions before JPs excluded on the ground of absence of opportunity to cross-examine, *R v Paine* (1696) Comb 358, 5 Mod 163,

However, mutuality appears mostly in connection with judicial proceedings[252], and it seems that some documents could be used against parties and privies which would not, because of the requirement of reciprocity, have created estoppels[253]. It cannot therefore be safely assumed that the pleading doctrine was simply transplanted, but the scope of the early modern doctrine remains unclear.

III. Conclusion

If we review the general conditions for the use of documents as proof what we find in the first place is some underlying structural similarities. Civilians, common lawyers and equity lawyers all alike made a structural separation between proof by documents and proof by witnesses. Within proof by documents, the distinctions between public and private documents found in the civilian sources is found also in the mediæval common law in the form of the distinction between records and deeds; and it is found in a form in some ways closer to civilian approaches in the early modern law of evidence to a jury and of equity proof. Equally, the mediæval common law and civilian doctrine were similar in limiting the effect of documents to parties and privies, and treating private documents primarily as admissions. Here, however, roman-canon ideas were more flexible, giving some limited weight to third party documents; this latter characteristic seems to be shared by early evidence law and equity proof.

A similar parallelism of principle can be seen in the requirement that the original document must be produced. Absolute in the case of deeds in the mediæval common law, the rule is qualified in various ways with exceptions for unavailability by civilian sources; and similar exceptions were found in equity and developed in seventeenth century evidence law. Likewise, the requirement that private documents be proved by witnesses exists in the roman-canon sources and (if the document is controverted) in the mediæval common law; it is found in equity proof and early evidence material in a form closer to the roman-canon materials, since it is not limited to controverted documents and shares the exceptions for old documents.

---

1 Ld Raym 729 (KB); and witnesses to be re- examined on appeal from commissioners of excise, *Breedon v Gill* (M1696) Comb 414, 5 Mod 265, 2 Salk 255, 1 Ld Raym 219 (KB).

251 All common law authority: *Brounker v Atkins* (M1681) Skin 2, 15 (KB); *Lock v Norborne* (M1687) 3 Mod 141 (KB); *Pyke v Crouch* (M1696) 1 Ld Raym 370 (KB); *R v Weeden Ford, Warden of the Fleet* (M1700) 12 Mod 337, 2 Salk 690, (H1703-4) Colles 332, at 12 Mod 339 (KB) (*per cur,* as a ground to admit an interested witness in criminal proceedings, the verdict being excluded in subsequent civil proceedings because the parties are different); *contra, City of London v Clerke* (H1691) Carth 181, Holt KB 283, where the verdict is admitted as evidence of general custom.

252 Cf cases cited above nn 248-251.

253 *Ford v Lord Grey* (M1703) 1 Salk 285, 6 Mod 44 (KB), recitals in a deed (for the point that recitals would not make an estoppel, Holdsworth HEL IX 156).

At the same time it is necessary to register certain fundamental differences. The effective absence of notaries and notarised instruments from mediæval common law practice was accompanied by a difference in the paradigm case of a public document, which for the common lawyers was a document recorded in a central official archive. This difference seems to be reflected in the discussion of public documents in the later seventeenth century. If Ellesmere's comments in 1603 represented a temptation to introduce notaries, it was no more than a passing thought; records remained the central case of public documents, deeds the central and strongest case of private documents, down to the time of Gilbert and after. These features were shared by equity, which thus to a significant extent followed the law.

However, in the development of the new rules which governed evidence to a jury and of the rules of proof in equity, the chronology does not allow the inference that all the rules in equity were developed by imitation of the common law rules. In some cases the evidence for the rule in equity is earlier (ability to use equity's own proceedings, relief on lost documents), in others it is contemporaneous with the first evidence at common law.

Moreover, the new body of rules shared the structural similarity of the common law pleading rules to the roman-canon concepts, distinguishing public and private documents, requiring production of the original and proof of private documents, and privity/ mutuality. In addition it was not a simple transposition of the common law pleading rules, but was in several respects closer to the roman-canon system, notably in the extension of the usability of public documents other than records and private documents other than deeds, and the recognition of exceptions to the rule requiring the production of the original document.

The relationships involved are obviously complex. But the evidence does tends to suggest acceptance of the *leading principles* of the roman-canon system both in equity and at law in this period.

Chapter Four

The Weight of Documentary Proof

Between the sixteenth and the eighteenth centuries the laws of much of europe moved from theoretically preferring witnesses to documents, to preferring documents to witnesses and for many transactions requiring writing. At the same period, the english laws of evidence to a jury and of equity proof saw the development of a rule of preference for documents over witnesses – the parol evidence rule – and the enactment in the Statute of Frauds (1677) of a body of requirements of writing. On the face of it, this is a strikingly parallel development. There is, however, a fundamental difference: the medieval common law, unlike the european *jus commune*, preferred documents to witnesses (more exactly to jury trial). The development of preference for writings in seventeenth century England may, therefore, be seen less as an innovation than as a reaction to a brief period in the sixteenth century in which the scales were tipped towards testimony.

These developments are critical areas for the relationship of equity and law, and for the origins of the common law of evidence. Wigmore established an orthodoxy in arguing that the rules of preference for, and requirements of, documents, were established to control the defects of jury trial; and were only gradually and partially received into equity, where there was no jury. In this chapter we will see that this view is false. The development of rules of preference for writing in equity proof and in evidence to a jury is contemporaneous, and that of requirements of writing is earlier in equity proof than in evidence to a jury; and the equitable exceptions to the rules are not founded either on a general preference for testimony, or on the idea that equity is free from defects peculiar to jury trial.

I. Writing preferred

1. Estoppel and relief against it

The common law rules of estoppel by record and by deed fairly clearly indicate a preference for writing. The extent and elaboration of these rules mean that it is obviously impractical to discuss them here; it is also unnecessary to do so in any detail in order to discuss the equitable rules[1].

Relief against estoppel is an early aspect of equity; the standard example given is payment of a debt secured by a deed without obtaining an acquittance[2]. This might suggest a preference in equity for witness evidence. However, equitable relief against estoppel is limited in ways which make this less clear.

In the first place, though there are instances of relief against records, the question of whether relief was available against records was a controversial one throughout this period. The most notorious aspect of this controversy was that over equitable relief after verdict and judgment at law[3]. This concerns *res judicata* rather than proof by documents in the narrow sense, and it is inapropriate to deal with it here[4].

There was, however, also an episodic argument about whether equity could relieve against fines and common recoveries. St German says that these are estoppels in equity as well as at law[5]; and this is followed by Crompton and West, who also give statutes merchant and staple as another instance of records as bars[6]. However, in certain circumstances relief does seem to have been obtainable against fines[7],

---

1 Cf above Ch 3 § 1 *(2)* (a) & references cited there.

2 St German, SGCS p 110f; Crompton, 45b cites YB 7 Hen 7, 11; *Observations* f 467v No. 224 ('124') *per* Egerton LK citing YB 9 Ed 4, 14a.

3 For this see Baker, (1969) 4 *Irish Jurist* 368, Gray, "The Boundaries of the equitable function", 20 *AJLH* 192, and authorities cited there. The controversy was by no means dead in the later seventeenth and early eighteenth century: Holdsworth *HEL* i 464; Macnair, "'Where the Court of *Chancery* is regular in its remedy, why is that not Law?' – Common Law and Statutory Imitations of equitable relief under the later Stuarts", forthcoming in C. W. Brooks & M. Lobban ed., *Communities and Courts.*

4 St German says that no relief is available in equity against a false wager of law or against a false verdict in attaint: *Doctor & Student*, 91 SS 108-9, 116-7; or against a false certificate by a Bishop: ib. 186-7. This latter point is confirmed by *Bloomer's Case* (H1603/4) Cary 26, Lansd 599 f 6b (Egerton C).

5 D&S 146/7, 205-6 (fine), 157-8 (recovery, though with extensive doubts, 156ff).

6 Crompton p 43; West sig ?B5v, X-aa, sig ?B7, qq, sig C1v, 19. Crompton p 43 and West B3, X both cite YB 22 Ed 4, 6 (for this cf Yale's note, Nottingham *TT* p 213 n 1) for the proposition that there can be no relief on payment without acquittance in the case of a statute because it is a record. Lord Nottingham denies this rule (Proleg. VII.1,2, *TT* p 213), but on the ground that the defendant's *confession* is a good ground for relief, thus side-stepping the question posed by Crompton & West's authority of the dangers of a record being avoided by *witnesses;* cf below p 142. On a fine with proclamations, cf also *Thynne v Townsend & Cary* (H1638/9) W Jon 416, Coventry LK assisted by judges; and a deed enrolled is treated as an estoppel in *Anon* (T1602) Cary 21.

7 *Paramore's Case* (1561,71) Cary 4 (fine levied by an infant); *Welby v Welby* (1595) Toth 99, Egerton MR (fine obtained by fraud; compensation ordered); *Arundel v Arundel* (n.d.; 1597 x 1603) *Observations* f 456v No. 161, defective fine given for consideration; *Solly v Whitfield* (H1675/6) Nott CC No 415, R t Finch 277 [as —— *v Hawkes*] 1 Ch Cas 273 (Nott CC No 169 not SP), Lord Nottingham (rent accidentally extinguished by fine decreed); *Wilkinson & al' v Brayfield* (M1693) 2 Vern 367, 1 Eq Ca Ab 258.1 (fine proved to be in trust, or by fraud; conveyance to devisee ordered); *Clerk v Ward* (1700) Pre Ch 150, 2 Eq Ca Ab 474, *per cur* reconveyance can be ordered after a fine procured by fraud.

and a case went to the House of Lords on this issue in 1706[8]. Ballow says that fines and common recoveries will bar in equity as well as at law on the ground of their character as common assurances, but that "if a Fine is unfairly obtained, Equity will order a Reconveyance"[9].

Secondly, if the practice of relief against estoppel by deed represents a preference for witness evidence[10], in the seventeenth century this was not unambiguous. Ellesmere's Orders of 1614 provided *inter alia* that

> "Bills to staie payment of debts which are due by statute recognizance *obligation or bill* are not to be allowed unless it is in speciall cases where there is no willful default or grosse negligence. *And the like for conditions broken upon leases mortgages &c*" [my emphasis, MM][11].

Bacon's Orders of 1618/19 took a slightly different approach to the same problem, limiting relief by injunction against suits at law and relief after arrest for debt at law largely, but not entirely, to cases where grounds for relief were confessed in the defendant's answer or appeared by record or writing[12].

Bacon's rules were repeated in the Parliamentary Commissioners' collection of Orders in 1649[13], and the Cromwellian Chancery Ordinance of 1654 not only repeated the first rule but absolutely prohibited relief against bonds which were merely for the payment of money[14]. Neither rule appears in Clarendon's Orders of 1661[15], but the first, on interlocutory injunctions, is repeated by Lord Nottingham in his *Practice*[16].

Nottingham also says, in the Chapter of his *Prolegomena* headed "Equity relieves in many cases, where the printed books deny it", that

8 *Clerk v Ward* (1700) Pre Ch 150, 2 Eq Ca Ab 474, Wright LK, refusing relief, aff'd HL (1706) 4 Bro PC 70.

9 P 125.

10 It is arguable that estoppel would not be a ground for relief in itself (which would be the implication of saying that there was a real preference for witness evidence) but some positive equity against the instrument would have to be shown. Cf e.g. *Anon* (M1614) Lansd 1110 f13b (no court given, but most of these reports are in the Exchequer so probably Ex (E)) "The plaintiff relieved against his own release... the plaintiff being a simple man and the release gotten by fraud"; SP at *Observations* f 475r No 264. Cf also, however, the discussion of the rectification jurisdiction in Sheppard, *Faithful Counsellor* 624-8, which founds the jurisdiction on the underlying contract.

11 i Sanders 86.

12 i Sanders 112, No 21, injunctions (or where the debt is old); 113, No 25, relief after arrest (or where the principal is brought into court).

13 i Sanders 233, Nos 49, 50.

14 i Sanders 260, No 28 (interlocutory injunctions), 262, No 43 (relief against bonds).

15 i Sanders 296 ff.

16 XII.2, *TT* p 143.

"And it is against a maxim too to avoid a statute or bond under hand and seal by a naked averment of payment without acquittance under hand and seal. *Vide* in the former case [VII.1., on statutes]. These are rules by the common law. But if a man who sues a bond will confess in Chancery 'tis paid, or he that is sued in Chancery on lost bond will confess the money due, shall there therefore be no relief?"[17]

This is a clear statement that relief against estoppel was available in cases in which it was heavily restricted by Ellesmere and attempted to be prohibited by Cromwell's Ordinance. Nonetheless, it is ambiguous, because the ground offered for relief is the defendant in equity's confession, and this ground is consistent with the general preference for records and deeds over witnesses which is the ground of the basic common law rule, as the confession would be a higher form of proof (above, Ch 2) .

There are in the later seventeenth century a number of statements in the context of the parol evidence rule that parties are not to be relieved on witness evidence against deeds, or particularly against their own hand and seal (below); and in *Davies v Beversham* (M1661)[18] the common law doctrine that the tenant is estopped from denying his landlord's title was applied in equity, and there are several cases in which a deed under seal is treated as *sufficient* proof of a binding agreement without proof of consideration[19]. These all imply that the ambiguity of Nottingham's statement reflects a real ambiguity in the practice of the period.

Thirdly, there is one clear situation in which a writing could be pleaded in bar in equity. This is the case of an account stated. The first appearance of this rule is in 1636 in *Lumley v Garrett*[20]: "When merchants and co-traders have made an accompt, shall not be compelled here to make a new accompt". In the Restoration the rule is clearly a settled one[21] and there is some authority on exceptions to it.

17 VII.2, *TT* p 213.

18 3 Ch Rep 4, Nels 76, 2 Freem 157, Harv 1105 p 133, Clarendon C assisted by Grimstone MR.

19 See the cases from this period cited in my article "Equity & Volunteers" (1988) 8 Legal Studies 172 at 173-7.

20 Toth 2; *Lumley v Carrott* Harg 281 f100. Egerton had said, c. 1600, that he was "much against this course of exhi[bi]ting bills in C[h]anc[ery] against Accomptants to examyne Accompts in C[h]anc[ery]" (*Observations* f 460v No 184), and his *Orders* of 1614 had contained the rule that "Marchants accompts and such like are not to be examined in the Chancery for none is to accompt upon oath but to the King onely" (Sanders 86), but this is not repeated in subsequent collections; the rule and the reason are both denied by Nottingham, Proleg VII.12 and VII.6, *TT* pp 216, 214-5.

21 *Proud v Combes* (M1663) 1 Ch Cas 55, Nels 100, 3 Ch Rep 18, Harv 1105 164, Grimstone MR (*Combes v Proud* (T1664) 1 Ch Cas 54, 2 Freem 182, 1 Eq Ca Ab 174, Harv 1105 163, bill of review, not SP); *Holstcomb v Rivers* (P1669) 1 Ch Cas 127, Nels 139, 1 Eq Ca Ab 5.1, [*Holcomb v Ryves*] Nott Proleg XIX.1, Bridgman LK, Rainsford, Wilde BB; *Tilsley v Jevon* (H1673/4) Rep t Finch 66; *Beak v Beak* (H1674/5) Rep t Finch 190; *Foot v Tresilian* (H1674/5) Nott CC No 194; *Wright v Cox* (T1675) Nott CC No 231, [*Coxon*] 1 Ch Cas 262, 1 Eq Ca Ab 12; *Hardwick v Price* (T1675) Nott CC No 247; *Gold v Chambers* (M1675) Nott

For the rule to apply the person sought to be bound must be a party to the account stated[22], and in one case the party's signature was required[23]. No exceptions should have been taken at the time of the account[24]. The account stated must be set out in full in the plea, so that any exceptions alleging specific errors could be taken[25]. It is not entirely clear whether the party seeking to overturn the account was limited to errors appearing on its face, or could also allege extraneous facts[26]. As with all other possible bars, the account would be no bar if it was collusive or fraudulent[27].

In *Fashion v Atwood* (M1679)[28] it was argued that the basis of the rules on accounts was mercantile custom. It is perhaps similarly on the basis of mercantile custom that a note admitting liability is assumed to be capable of being "conclusive" in *Trist v Buckeridge* (H1673-4)[29] and a promissory note in *Trowel v Evans* (M1710)[30]. *Trist v Buckeridge* comes most clearly close to the idea of a "conclusive proof" in this context, with the note directed (on the basis, it seems, of undue influence) to be admitted in evidence on a *quantum damnificatus* but "not to conclude" the party[31].

CC No 317; *E.I. Co v Maniston* (T1676) Nott CC No 521, 2 Ch Cas 218, *Maniston v E. I. Co* (P1677) Nott CC No 651; *Chandler v Dorsett* (M1679) Rep t Finch 431, 1 Eq Ca Ab 12; *Fashion v Atwood* (M1679) Nott CC No 983, 2 Ch Cas 6, 1 Eq Ca Ab 8.5; *Knight v Bampfield* (T1683) 1 Vern 179, 1 Eq Ca Ab 12.6, North LK; *Sherman v Sherman* (M1692) 2 Vern 276, 1 Eq Ca Ab 12.10, 375.2, Lords Commissioners; *Carr v Boulter* (M1697) 2 Freem 217, [*Boulton*] Harv 1105 p 194, Trevor MR.

22 *Gold v Chambers* (M1675) Nott CC No 317, so not against an executor; for an argument for this point cf Nott Proleg VII.6.

23 *Hardwick v Price* (T1675) Nott CC No 247. This is only a brief note, and it is possible that the point is that the facts gave rise to suspicion of fraud.

24 *Holstcomb v Rivers,* above n 21. *Tilsley v Jevon,* above n 21, seven years' acquiescence; *Sherman v Sherman,* above n 21, no objection by the second or third post.

25 *Chandler v Dorsett,* above n 21.

26 In *Proud v Combes* (above n 21) illegal compound interest was deduced by the Court taking judicial notice of arithmetic. In *Wright v Cox* (above n 21) the matter appears in Lord Nottingham's report to be an error on the face (double entry of the same item) but Lord Nottingham says that the burden of proof is on the party seeking to overturn the account, which suggests extraneous facts, in Chan. Cas. it is said to be extraneous facts (mistaken admission when accounting due to lack of access to own records). In *E.I Co v Maniston, Maniston v E.I. Co* (above n 21) allegation of extraneous facts was allowed, but the case seems to be an exceptional one turning on the position of the East India Co. In *Knight v Bampfield* (above n 21) a general allegation of fraud and collusion was said by Lord Guilford to require allegation of specific errors in the account, which might seem to show that errors could be averred on the basis of extraneous evidence. Compare the civilian authorities cited above Ch 2 § 2 *(2)* n. 178, confession based on a proved specific error of fact can be revoked.

27 *Foot v Tresilian,* above n 21.

28 2 Ch Cas 6 at 7.

29 (H1673-4) Rep t Finch 47.

30 (M1710) 1 Eq Ca Ab 375.3.

31 Rep t Finch 47 at 48.

On the face of it the availability of equitable relief against common law estoppels suggests that equity might have treated proof by witnesses as at least equal to documentary proof. But on closer examination this does not seem to be the case in our period. Equity was willing to relieve against estoppels in certain cases, but this relief was in some cases based on a positive equity against the instrument rather than mere contradiction, in others restricted by the Chancery itself. And some documentary estoppels were accepted as such in equity. This suggests a preference for writings shared with the common law, if subject to more exceptions than existed in common law pleading.

2. The parol evidence rule

The parol evidence rule (i.e. the rule that the terms of a transaction in writing are not to be varied by witness evidence[32]) is, as a rule, clearly based on a preference for documentary evidence.

Wigmore and Holdsworth argued that the basis of the rule was a generalisation from the rules of estoppel by record and deed[33]. Wigmore saw this generalisation and the rules of estoppel themselves as influenced by roman-canon theory[34], in the shape of the concept of writings being of higher nature than witnesses and the *regula iuris* that *nihil tam naturale est quam eo genere quidquid dissolvere quo colligatum est*[35]; this is one of the few areas in which he sees the common law of evidence as being influenced by this theory.

Much as it would suit my argument to accept this view, there are two problems with it. The first is that, as already indicated, the medieval *jus commune* preferred

32 Wigmore, Book I Part IV (§ 2401 & f) treats the topic as a group of rules including requirements of writing; this approach may be analytically desirable but is not helpful for present purposes. Ballow, pp 125-6, treats the issue of deeds and writings as a question of estoppel, and refers to "parol declarations" in the context of wills (pp 126-7). The later seventeenth century equity cases (below), however, seem to use objections to parol evidence to vary terms in the context of agreements and deeds as well as wills rather than referring to them in this context in terms of estoppels, so it is more convenient to treat these topics together.

33 Wigmore § 2426, 3rd ed Vol X pp 88-91; Holdsworth HEL IX pp 176-7, 219-221.

34 Wigmore loc cit.

35 D. 50. 17. 35; cited by Coke in his report of *The Countess of Rutland's Case* (below) from Bracton "Book 2 fo. 28"; the relevant references in Thorne's edition of Bracton are i 289, SP in different terms, iii 124, same, iii 167-8, direct quotation of the first words of this text. Coke therefore cannot have simply quoted Bracton, but must have followed up the reference in the Digest. Wigmore loc cit at p 88 and n 33 cites Pollock & Maitland *HEL* ii 205-222 (222), D.46.3.80, (SP in different terms) and this text. Wigmore's account of the rules of estoppel and profert in this section is confused by failure to distinguish (1) interests lying in livery from interests lying in grant, and debt *sur contract* from covenant and debt *sur obligation*, and (2) the rules of pleading from the rules as to what can be found on the general issue (though in this latter point there is a close connection).

witnesses to documents, and the issue was by the sixteenth century an area of theoretical controversy and variation between jurisdictions. The second is that the transition from estoppel rules affecting proof by pleaded documents, to the parol evidence rule affecting jury trial, was not seamless. Just as the courts had held in *Newis v Lark* that the *profert* rule did not bind the jury, so in 1584 in *Goddard's Case* and *James' Case* the Common Pleas held that estoppels by record and deed did not bind the jury[36]. The parol evidence rule generalised to cover evidence to a jury was therefore an innovation of the 1590s and 1600s.

The first appearance of the rule is in relation to wills, in *Lord Cheyney's Case* (1591) in english bill procedure in the Wards[37], where Wray and Anderson CJJ decided after a judicial conference that proof by witnesses was not admissible to show the testator's intention in relation to a wills of lands, "for the will concerning lands, &c, ought to be in writing, ... " and also on the policy ground that to allow testimony would make it impossible to advise on a title which included a will[38]. The same emphasis on the statutory requirement of writing is found in the first of two statements of the rule by Egerton LK, sometime between 1597 and 1603:

> My Lo[rd] Keep[er] said that of Lands that were not deviseable at the Co[mm]en Lawe but are made deviseable by the Statute of 32 & 34 H 8 in writinge noe averm[en]t shalbe received ag[ains]t the very L[ette]re of the will as thus for the purpose I will that my Lands shallbee & his heires, the scrivener gets downe I will that my Lands shallbe to J. S. though many witnesses were present and can testifie that I willed my lands to J. S. and his heires yet this averm[ent]shall not be receaved but of Lands deviseable by the Co[mm]en Lawe if they be devised by p[ar]oll or a Legacy of goods there you may take averm[en]ts ag[ains]t the will[39].

The second statement asserts the agreement of the common lawyers with him on this point and distinguishes the case of deeds in equity:

> ... he said it was the opinion of all the Justices in England concurring w[i]t[h] him, that noe averm[ent] in a will or to suply a will shalbe received in any plea, neither can the Chanc[er]y aid it by any meanes. But the Chancery will aid intentions of p[ar]ties in their deeds by averm[en]t. As if a man makes a lease of a house w[i]t[h] th[e] appurtenances although p[er]adventure noe Land will pass but only [th]e use of the house yet in Chanc[er]y if it may be proved [th]e intentione of the p[ar]ties was that other things should passe, [tha]t shall be decreed according[40].

---

36 *Goddard's Case* (*Goddard v Denton*) (H1583/4) 2 Co Rep 4b (3 Leon 100 not SP), estoppel by deed, and *per* Coke's report by any record other than that in the case tried; *James' Case* (T1584) Moo KB 181.23, deed.

37 (M1591) 5 Co Rep 68a, Wards (Moo KB 727 not SP).

38 Id. at 68b. Coke's report goes on to discuss latent ambiguity as an exception, drawing on medieval law relating to fines, but there is no strong reason to suppose that the court would have discussed the point.

39 *Observations* ff 462r-462v No. 196.

40 *Observations* f 469r No. 230.

In relation to wills, the rule thus fairly clearly appears first in english bill jurisdictions[41]; and it is based on statutory requirements and policy considerations, not general theory.

In relation to agreements and deeds, the earliest authority is clearly at common law. In *Countess of Rutland v Earl of Rutland* (1604)[42] a piece of double conveyancing had occurred, probably inadvertently, with the result that a manor intended for the dowager countess' jointure had been included not only in this but also in a general settlement on the eldest son in tail; there were thus two contradictory deeds to lead the uses of the fines levied, executed at about the same time and with overlapping trustees. The dowager sued in trespass[43], and the case was tried at bar, probably on the general issue[44]. The case is thus a clear one of a rule governing evidence to a jury rather than estoppel. Coke reports a fairly elaborate direction to the jury. The uses of a fine can be proved by parol, but if they were settled by deed, evidence of a parol agreement to vary the terms of the deed is in general excluded on the basis that

> Every contract or agreement ought to be dissolved by matter of as high nature as the first deed, *nihil tam conveniens est naturali aequitati, unumquodque dissolvi eo ligamine, quo ligatum est.* Also would be inconvenient, that matters in writing made by advice and on consideration, and which finally import the agreement of the parties, should be controlled by averment of the parties to be proved by the uncertain testimony of slippery memory[45].

The first of these arguments is the *regula iuris* cited above. The second certainly expresses a general preference for documents. The formula of "slippery memory" is markedly similar to one used in West's explanation of the origin of contractual documents, that "at the first godlie wise men (seeing the slippperinesse and weaknesse of the memorie of men ...) invented first these instruments ..."[46]. The idea that "memoria hominum labilis est" was a civilian one, discussed by Cotta and Gaill[47]. Notwithstanding these arguments, parol evidence was allowed in the in-

---

41 Though there is a gap in the equity authority between the two *dicta* quoted above and the first case in the printed reports, *Fry v Porter* (P1670) 1 Mod 300, Bridgman LK assisted by CJJ and CB, at 307 (Vaughan CJ), 310 (Hale CB) 313 (Kelyng CJ) ((M1669)1 Ch Cas 138, Grimstone MR, (P1670) 1 Ch Cas 138, 1 Ch Rep 26, *Porter v Fry* (undated) Nott Proleg XXIX.14, *TT* 318-9, *Williams d Porter v Fry* (P1672) 1 Vent 199, 1 Freem 31, T. Raym 236, 2 Lev 21, 2 Keb 756, 787, 814, 867, 3 Keb 19, KB, not SP).

42 *Countess of Rutland's Case* (T1604) 5 Co Rep 25b at 26, 26b, Cro Jac 29, KB.

43 After an unsuccessful attempt to litigate in the Wards, blocked by an outstanding life interest: (M1592) Moo KB 723.

44 The reports make clear that we are concerned with a ruling on evidence on trial at bar. If any issue other than *not guilty* was being tried it is likely, though not absolutely certain, that the reports would tell us the issue.

45 5 Co Rep 26b.

46 *Symboleographia* (London, 1591) Lib 1 § 1, sig. q1v.

47 Cotta 574-5 uses classical literary sources; Gaill ii Obs 104 No 2 cites to D. 41.2.44 where "infirmitatem memoriae" is referred to. If West derived it from Vulteius, it was not either in the discussion of contracts, or that of proof and procedure.

stant case, as the fines actually levied were inconsistent with either deed, and parol evidence was allowed to explain this inconsistency.

As reported by Coke this case appears to have established the parol evidence rule for contracts and deeds on a clear basis independent of estoppel doctrine. Croke's report of the same case, however, reports the direction as being that if the fine is consistent with the deed, "the indenture is directory to the fine", but where there is inconsistency, "it is but evidence". This amounts to the proposition that the deed and fine if consistent are pleadable as a single entity, i.e. as an estoppel; the inconsistency prevents this, making the deed merely evidence. The direction would then involve no more than the rejection of *Goddard's Case* and *James' Case*, to hold that the jury *is* bound by the estoppel[48]. Even on these terms, the decision did not wholly settle the rule: it was still arguable much later that the jury was not, or was only in some circumstances, bound by the estoppel[49].

The Chancery can be found preferring deeds to witnesses in the 1630s[50]. Given the background of relief against estoppel, and the controversy round it, which continued at least into the 1690s[51], this is an unexpectedly early appearance of preference for documents in equity; and a fairly 'classic' statement of the parol evidence rule as applied to contracts and deeds can be found in 1673[52].

Wigmore argued that the rule was only gradually received into equity, and that this was attributable to the rule being partly based on the unreliability of juries[53]. It would be more exact, however, to say that equity courts displayed the same ambiguity in their attitude to this generalised rule as they already already displayed in relation to documentary estoppels (noted above); with the difference that the equi-

---

48 *Altham's Case* (M1610) 8 Co Rep 148 at 155-155b, CP (1 Brown & Golds 162 not SP), which is cited by Holdsworth for the parol evidence rule, is a pleading (estoppel) decision argued on demurrer; the reason given by Coke is that the interpretation of documents is a question of law from which the jury is excluded.

49 *Trevivan v Lawrence* (M1704) 1 Salk 276, 3 Salk 151, 6 Mod 256, Holt KB 282, 2 Ld Raym 1048 (P1704) 2 Ld Raym 1036 not SP); and later cases cited in n (D) to *Goddard's Case* at 76 *English Reports* 397.

50 *Lake v Phillips & Lake* (1636) 1 Ch Rep 110, proof contrary to a deed of trust, "which goeth beyond all witnesses" disregarded; *Vesey v Vesey* (1638) Harg 174 f 6, Coventry LK, demanding a high standard of proof. which suggests that at this time relief was at least in some cases available.

51 In *Parawick's Case* (M1610) 1 Rolle Ab 379 T.1, CP, (cited by Nottingham, *Proleg* XXVII.6) the rule was made a ground for a prohibition to the Requests. The Cromwellian Chancery Ordinance of 1654, Firth & Raitt ii 949 at s 45, p. 959, prohibited relief in Chancery on averments of the intention of parties to deeds "other than what doth appear by the deed it self", and the common law judges attempted to get this clause re-enacted in 1690: Historical Manuscripts Commission 13th Report (House of Lords MSS) v 128-141 (for the context see Macnair, "Imitations" above n. 5).

52 *Bell v Hemmings* (T1673) Nott Proleg XXVII.8, *TT* 310-1.

53 § 2426 p 91 nn 46, 47.

ty rules become more systematised in relation to the admission of parol evidence to vary the terms of instruments.

In the first place, the relationship alleged by Wigmore, between the different approach of Chancery to the rule and the fact that proof in Chancery was before a judge alone, not by jury, cannot be supported on the evidence. It may well be that there is a connection in the most general sense between the perceived unreliability of juries and the origins of the rule, in the sense that the rules of profert and estoppel by deed, from which the parol evidence rule is descended, are related to ideas of what lies within the cognizance of the country. Wigmore's immediate argument, however, is based on *dicta* in *Litton Strode v Lady Falkland* (P,T1708)[54], and rests on a misunderstanding of the point taken there. The true point is that in Chancery evidence which is *prima facie* inadmissible may be read *de bene esse,* in case, when read, the circumstances show it to be in reality admissible; because, unlike a jury, the court is then able to disregard it if in the upshot it remains inadmissible[55]. As a result, the rule was not generally pleadable to bar proof, but the benefit of such a plea would be reserved to hearing[56].

Secondly, the cases do not show so much a *gradual* reception of the rule in Chancery, as the recognition from the outset of a range of exceptions to it – some of which can be said to have survived from earlier practice. For this purpose it is necessary to distinguish between agreements and settlements on the one hand and wills on the other.

The rule that parol averments were not in general to be received against or to vary the terms of deeds is, as has already been indicated, found in Chancery cases from the 1630s[57]. Nonetheless there are a number of situations in which the terms

---

54 *Litton Strode alias Litton v Lady Falkland & al'* 3 Ch Rep 169, 2 Vern 621, 1 Eq Ca Ab 210, Cowper C assisted by Trevor MR, Trevor CJ, Tracy J, most fully in 3 Ch Rep, at 3 Ch Rep 176-7; (H1708/9) 3 Bro PC 24, HL, not SP; cited by Wigmore as *Strode v Russell* (Wigmore's citation for this point, n 26, is actually to the report in Chan. Rep., though he does not cite this report).

55 Cf also on the same point *Newton v Preston, Briggs & al'* (M1699) Pre Ch 103, *per* Powell J.

56 *Earl of Feversham v Watson* (M1677) Nott CC No 773 ((P1678) Nott CC No 823, 2 Freem 35, Rep t Finch 445 not SP), *Bellasis v Benson* (H1685/6) 1 Vern 369, 1 Eq Ca Ab 229.9, Jeffreys C (*Benson v Bellasis* (T1681) Nott CC 1124, 1 Vern 15, (1681-5) 2 Ch Rep 252, not SP).

57 And cf also *Lewis v Lewis* (?1672) 2 Ch Rep 77, [*Lewys v Lewys*] (T1673) Nott Proleg XXX.72, *TT* p 347, Shaftesbury C assisted by Wyndham & other JJ; *Turner v Pearl* (H1674/5) Nott CC No 180, witnesses "not to be heard" to an alleged statement not included in the conditions of a bond; *Earl of Feversham v Watson* (P1678) Nott CC No 823, 2 Freem 35, Rep t Finch 445, Lord Nottingham assisted by North CJ and Montague CB (reversed HL apparently on the ground that the HL is free to act on non- legal grounds, Nott CC No 823) ((M1677) Nott CC No 773 preliminary point on pleading); *Jason v Lady Eyres* (T1680) Nott CC No 1043, 2 Ch Cas 33, 2 Freem 69; *Seymour v Fotherley* (P1685) 1 Vern 320, Guilford LK; *Tidcombe v Cholmley* (1700) Pre Ch 143, Somers LK (compromised after argument in HL, (1701) Colles 166; *Clavell v Littleton* (M1710) Pre Ch 305, Harcourt LK.

of deeds were not conclusive. (1) The mediæval common law rule that an ambiguity could be supplied by parol evidence seems to have been applied in equity[58]. It is possibly in connection with this that parol evidence is sometimes let in as an aid to construction, particularly of general words in agreements and deeds[59]. (2) It seems that collateral matter confessed by the defendant in his answer could be decreed[60]; the logical basis of this might be that the answer, as a confession in court, was of a higher nature than the deed[61].

(3) Where a settlement or conveyance was made in pursuance of precedent articles of agreement in writing, the settlement or conveyance would be construed, or if necessary rectified, by reference to the articles[62]. This approach was questioned on the basis that the final conveyance was conclusive and the precedent agreements were displaced by it, but this view does not seem to have been accepted[63].

---

58 For the rule and for its mediæval origins, *Lord Cheyney's Case* above; Bacon *Maxims* Regula 25, cited by Holdsworth HEL IX 221. For application in equity, *Goring v Bickerstaff & al'* (M1661) Grimstone MR, (H1661/2) 1 Ch Cas 4, 2 Freem 103, Pollex 31, Clarendon C assisted by Foster CJ, Wyndham J, Hale B.

59 *Coldcot v Hill* (M1662) 1 Ch Cas 15, 2 Freem 173, 1 Eq Ca Ab 27; *Fielder v Studley* (H1673/4) Nott CC 67, Rep t Finch 90; *Garnam v Fox* (1674) Nott CC 146, Rep t Finch 172 (Nott CC 276 not SP); *Knight v Coke* (H1680/1) Nott CC 1084, 2 Ch Cas 43; *Lee v Henley* (H1681/2) 1 Vern 37, this principle not applicable on a voluntary conveyance.

60 *Tyler v Beversham* (1673) Rep t Finch 80, that land not parcel of a manor sold; *Garnam v Fox,* Rep t Finch at 74, similarly to restrict general words. Similarly, some of the cases where parol evidence was let in were cases where the point was not taken, or not taken in time, by the adverse party: *Proud v Combes* (M1663) 1 Ch Cas 55, Nels 100, 3 Ch Rep 18, Grimstone MR, not argued at all, and on bill of review *Combes v Proud* (T1664) 1 Ch Cas 54, 2 Freem 182, 1 Eq Ca Ab 174, argued only that the proof of the agreement was insufficient; *Balch v Tucker* (H1880/1) 2 Ch Cas 40, "the court said we came too late" to seek a new feigned issue on this ground after the bill had already been dismissed; *Benson v Bellasis* (1681-6) 1 Vern 15 ((1681) Nott CC 1124, *Bellasis v Benson* (1685) 1 Vern 369, not SP), a parol "collateral warranty" varying a marriage settlement decreed by Lord Nottingham, incidentally to his primary decree that the settlement barred the widow's customary rights, by consent of the adverse party; after Lord Guilford had reversed the primary decree and Jeffreys C restored it, Jeffreys C also restored the decree on the parol agreement, over the adverse party's objections.

61 Cf Nott Proleg VII.2, cited above n 17 and text there.

62 *Cheek v Lisle* (T1674) Nott CC No 95, Rep t Finch 98 ((H1673/4) Nott CC No 45 not SP); *Read v Read* (P1679) Nott CC No 934 ((P1678) Nott CC No 816 not SP). *Beachinall v Beachinall* (T1684) 1 Vern 246, (Guilford LK reversing a decree of Lord Nottingham's) in which Lord Nottingham's original decision appears *prima facie* to display variation of agreements by witness evidence, but looks on closer examination more like the use of *secondary* witness evidence of the contents of articles which were unavailable. Similarly, an *ex facie* absolute bond or grant could be alleged to be merely a collateral security: *Lockner v Strode* (H1680/1) 1 Ch Cas 48 (bond), *Hales v van Berchem* (M1708) 2 Vern 617, assignment of an annuity.

63 *Bellasis v Benson, per* Jeffreys C obiter, but not reflected in his final decree; *Earl of Plymouth v Hickman* (T1690) 2 Vern 167, *per* counsel *arg* but rejected by Trevor, Rawlinson, Hutchins LCssrs; *Herbert v Earl of Winchelsea* (1714) 1 Bro PC 145, *per* counsel *arg* but rejected by HL affg. Harcourt C.

(4) At least until the Statute of Frauds, and thereafter at least in relation to personalty, it was possible to aver a trust against a deed or other conveyance[64]. This possibility goes back to the early equity jurisdiction, and could be justified on the basis that the trust was collateral to the deed. The same sort of argument might justify the fact that relief was also available on the ground of fraud[65]. Where a resulting trust would be presumed, parol evidence could accordingly be introduced to rebut it[66]. In relation to trusts of land, the enactment of s 7 of the Statute of Frauds obviously did not prevent proof of a trust by a declaration *in writing* outside the conveyance. It did, however, give rise to doubts in the 1690s and 1700s about whether there could be a resulting trust of land on the basis of payment of the purchase money, and therefore whether trust funds could be traced into land[67].

Finally, manor court rolls were not conclusive and could be corrected by other evidence of the real transaction. This rule is a genuine anomaly, but not one specific to equity; when the Lords Commissioners stated it in 1689, they justified it on the basis that this was the rule at common law[68].

If anything there may have been movement in equity away from the rule in this context in the early eighteenth century. It is fairly commonly referred to in the later seventeenth century, but in Ballow the exceptions seem to have swallowed up the rule, as they are generalised on the basis that

> So in natural Justice, Deeds and Writings are consider'd only as Memorials of the Contract, not as a substantial Part of them; and therefore any other Proof is as well, and the Estoppel will not in Equity be regarded against the Truth[69].

In relation to wills, in the Restoration the rule continued to be justified in terms of the requirement of writing for a will of realty under the Statute of Wills[70] and later the Statute of Frauds[71]. In relation to wills of personalty, though writing was

---

64 *Okeover v Pettus* (M1675) Nott CC No 347, Rep t Finch 270; *Harvey v Harvey* (M1680) Nott CC No 1066, Lord Nottingham, (M1686) 2 Ch Cas 180, Jeffreys C.

65 *Read v Read* (P1678) Nott CC No 816 ((P1679) Nott CC No 934 not SP).

66 *Rundle v Rundle* (1692) 2 Vern 252, 264, 1 Eq Ca Ab 119.9; *Lamplugh v Lamplugh* (M1709) 1 P Wms 111, 2 Eq Ca Ab 415.3.

67 Below § 2 *(2)* (b) n 199 and text there.

68 *Towers v Moor* (P1689) 2 Vern 98, Lds Cssrs, *per cur; Hill v Wiggett* (P1706) 2 Vern 547, 1 Eq Ca Ab 232.8. Cf also Lord Nottingham's comments on Taunton Deane copyholds in his speech against the registration proposals, 79 SS at 976.

69 P 125. This section, Book VI c2 3, gives, without citation, the decisions in *Dr Coldcot v Hill, Tyler v Beversham, Harvey v Harvey* and the dictum in *Towers v Moor* as support.

70 32 Hen 8 c 5 s 1. *Fry v Porter*, per Hale CB; *Falkland v Bertie* (H1696/7) *per* Holt CJ at 2 Vern 339, Holt KB 231 (other reports not SP). Cf the argument of Sjt Crawley in *Jones v Lord Sheffield and Ratcliffe* (1623) 1 Rolle 416 at 422 ([*Lord Sheffield v Ratcliffe*] Hob 334 SC but not SP)

71 29 Car 2 c 3 s 5. *Towers v Moor* (P1689) 2 Vern 98, *per cur; Falkland v Bertie* (H1696/7) 2 Vern 333, 3 Ch Cas 129, 12 Mod 182, Holt KB 230, 1 Salk 231, *per* Treby CJ at 2 Vern 337, Holt CJ at 2 Vern 339, 3 Ch Cas 130, 12 Mod 182, Holt KB 231 (Salk *per cur*)

not required, it might be analogously required that the terms should be proved in the church court[72]. However, collateral proof was said to be available in relation to wills of personalty[73], though in 1695 Somers C said that the proof in such cases should be "plain and indisputable"[74].

Parol proofs were let in in three ways. The first was that it was said that though they could not be read *against* the will, they could be read in cases of ambiguity (as had been accepted in Coke's report of *Lord Cheyney's Case*)[75]; and to support interpretations which could be argued from the words of the will[76]. This latter is perhaps an argument which could become somewhat tortured to let the evidence in.

Second, as with conveyances, a trust could be averred[77], i.e. what would now be called a secret trust. Cases on this point display already the different explanations of this phenomenon offered in modern times: proof in the church courts is not needed because the trust is outside the will[78]; alternatively, the secret trustee is made liable on the ground of fraud[79].

((H1697/8) Colles 10, HL, (1715) Dick 25, Cowper C, not SP); *Dormer v Bertie* (1699) Colles 98, HL, *per* Poley for the respondents *arg* (the decision below was affirmed) (Pre Ch 94, 2 Eq Ca Ab 430, 434, Somers C, not SP); *Oldham v Litchford* (T1705) 2 Vern 506, 2 Freem 284, 1 Eq Ca Ab 231.4, 2 Eq Ca Ab 44, Harv 1105 259, *per* counsel *arg* at 2 Freem 285, Harv 1105 260; *Litton Strode v Falkland per* Northey *arg* at 3 Ch Rep 173, Tracy J at 184.

72 *Rogers v Bamfield* (M1677) Nott CC No 724 (Rep t Finch 460 not SP) for the point that in general the terms of a will must be proved in the church court, *Hawtre v Lady Wallop* (1666-7) 1 Ch Rep 265 ([*Hawtry v Trollop*] Nels 119 not SP) *per* counsel *arg* as an objection to the use of a paper to aid construction, *Bowyer v Birds* (T1675) Nott CC No 285 (2 Ch Rep 98, SC has decree opposite to Lord Nottingham's report) for this as an objection to a trust; *semble* this is also a point in *Pring v Pring* (P1689) 2 Vern 98.

73 Eg *Bowyer v Birds*, above n 72; *Fane v Fane* (H1681/2) Nott CC No 1144, 1 Vern 30; *Gainsborough v Gainsborough* (1692) at 2 Freem 188-9.

74 *Petit v Smith* (P1696) 1 P Wms 7 ((M1695) 5 Mod 247, 1 Ld Raym 86, Comb 378, Comyns 3, KB, not SP).

75 *Hawtre v Wallop* may be an instance of this, though the report is not explicit; *Re Darrell* (1700) 1 Eq Ca Ab 231, Wright LK (2 Vern 378, 1 Eq Ca Ab 297 not SP), (1701) Colles 163, HL; *Pendleton v Grant* (M1705) 2 Vern 517, 1 Eq Ca Ab 230.2; *Hodgson v Hodgson & Fitch* (1707) 2 Vern 593, Pre Ch 229, 1 Eq Ca Ab 231.5. For *Lord Cheyney's Case*, above n 37 and text there.

76 *Lampen v Clobery* (M1683) 2 Ch Cas 155, North LK, *semble* (*Clobery v Lampen* (1677) Nott CC Nos 674, 704, 2 Freem 24, 2 Eq Ca Ab 539 not SP); *Gainsborough v Gainsborough* (1692) 2 Vern 252, 1 Eq Ca Ab 230.1, 2 Freem 188, Harv 1105 168, at 2 Freem 189, Lords Commissioners, aff'd HL (1 Eq Ca Ab 230.1).

77 *Chamberlaine v Chamberlaine* (P1680) 2 Freem 52, 2 Eq Ca Ab 41.5 (*Chamberlain v Chamberlain* (P1678) Nott CC No 819, 2 Freem 34, seems from the facts not SC), has the possibility of alleging a trust stated as an exception by Lord Nottingham.

78 *Bowyer v Birds*, above n 72, on the ground that the church courts have no jurisdiction over trusts. Compare *Newton v Jackson* (M1601) *Observacons* f 472v-473r No. 251, no relief against executor for a legacy because of ecclesiastical jurisdiction, otherwise if the legacy is "transmitted into a fforein hand out of the hand of the executor".

Third: during this period the equity courts developed a presumption that surplus personal estate undisposed of by will was not to go to the executor beneficially (the rule at common law) but to be held on trust for those entitled on intestacy[80]. Parol evidence was allowed to be used to support and to rebut this presumption, and several cases were extensively argued on this point in the 1690s and 1700s[81]. Analogously, parol evidence was admitted to support or rebut the presumption that legacies were given in satisfaction of portions and similar precedent duties[82].

On parol evidence in relation to wills, Ballow says that

> However the later Resolutions have been very cautious of admitting parol Evidences, because they encourage Suits and Litigations and introduce the very Mischiefs that the Statute [sc. of Frauds – MM] intended to prevent[83].

This, however, seems to refer primarily to parol evidence to support and rebut presumptions[84]. As with deeds, it is not a matter of *gradual* acceptance of the basic rule in Chancery, but of recognition of the basic rule from the outset together with exceptions; here one of the exceptions is proving to be inconvenient and therefore cut down.

The lapse in time between the appearance of the generalised parol evidence rule in common law authorities and in equity authorities is not, therefore, as great as was suggested by Wigmore; indeed, in relation to wills equity came first. His argument that what took place was a gradual reception in equity of a rule designed to control juries cannot be sustained. Rather (as with documentary estoppels) equity

---

79 *Thynn v Thynn* (1684) 1 Vern 296, Guilford LK; *Devenish v Baines* (H1689/90) Pre Ch 3, Lords Commissioners; *Oldham v Litchford* above n 71.

80 Below Ch 9 § 2 *(3)*.

81 *North v Crompton* (H1670/1) 1 Ch Cas 196, Nott Proleg XIII.4, is said by Hutchins LCssr, 2 Vern 253, to have decided that parol evidence could be used to support the legal estate in the executor; though this point does not appear as decided in Chan Cas or Lord Nottingham's report, it does appear as a point at issue in Chan Cas. The main body of cases starts with *Cunningham v Mellish* (M1691) 2 Vern 247, Pre Ch 31, 1 Eq Ca Ab 273; *Gainsborough v Gainsborough* (1692); *Lady Bellasis v Crompton & al'* (T1693) 2 Vern 294, 1 Eq Ca Ab 381.5; *Smith v Goodman* (P1707) 2 Vern 586, *Quære* (no decision); *Docksey v Docksey* (1708) 2 Eq Ca Ab 429, Cowper C, (1710) 3 Bro PC 39, HL; *Lady Granville v Lady Beaufort* (1709) 2 Vern 648, 1 P Wms 118, Cowper C, (1710) 3 Bro Pc 37, HL; *Wingfield v Atkinson & Myres* (M1711) 2 Vern 673; *Littlebury v Buckley* (1711) 1 Eq Ca Ab 244.9, rejected by Recorder King, but rvsd HL 3 Bro PC 43; *Gale v Crofts* (1713) Dick 23, 2 Eq Ca Ab 415, 494, rejected by Harcourt C.

82 *Bromley v Jefferies & al'* (H1700/1) 2 Freem 245, 2 Vern 415, Pre Ch 138, 1 Eq Ca Ab 18, rejected by Wright LK & Trevor MR; *Hassell v Knatchbull* (1703) Colles 305, HL, admitted; *Cuthbert v Peacock* (M1707) 2 Vern 593, 1 Eq Ca Ab 204.8, 232.6, Cowper LK,admitted; *Chapman v Salt* (H1709/10) 2 Vern 646, Trevor MR, admitted.

83 Bk VI. c2 § 5, p 127

84 The point is made at the end of the section on the use of parol evidence to support and rebut presumptions, and is followed by sections on its use to deal with ambiguities and to support the construction of the will.

recognised the rule, but accepted a wider range of exceptions to it than the common law.

These exceptions, in both cases, do not indicate denial of the underlying rule, or that documents were not in general seen as offering stronger proof of the terms of transactions than witnesses. On the contrary, by their very character as exceptions they "prove the rule" itself: in general documents (at least records, deeds and wills) were seen as a higher form of proof than witness proof.

II. Writing required

Requirements that transactions should be in writing or be proved by writing indicate a preference for proof by writing, no less obviously because they do so slightly indirectly. The passage of the Statute of Frauds in 1677 was a landmark in this area, and the Statute and its effects have been extensively discussed. Accordingly, it is necessary to divide the discussion of requirements of writing into (1) what requirements of writing there were in equity before the passage of the Statute of Frauds, and (2) the Statute itself and its effects in equity.

1. Before 1677

The background to requirements of writing in equity before the Statute of Frauds is the basic rules at common law. Wigmore in his treatment of this subject says that there were essentially no requirements at common law[85], but this is inexact. In the first place, incorporeal hereditaments "lay in grant" and would not pass without a deed[86]. Secondly, no action of covenant or debt *sur obligation* would lie without a deed[87]. Leases could be created by parol, but there would be problems with remedies on a lease so created until entry into possession[88]. While estates in land in possession would pass by livery and copyholds by surrender and regrant whether or not this was actually recorded in writing, these were in theory solemn, formal and public conveyances[89], and in the action of debt *sur contract* on informal contracts the defendant was protected from fraudulent (and genuine) claims by his right to wage his law[90].

---

85 § 2454, 3rd Ed Vol X p 172.

86 Co Lit 9b. It may also be said that Crown grants had to be by record, i.e. (usually) letters patent, but this point is marginal to my present concerns.

87 Simpson, *Contract* pp 10ff (covenant) 88ff (debt sur obligation).

88 Covenant would not lie because there was no deed, and ejectment would not because, being trespassory in nature, it was founded on possession.

89 Bacon's Abridgment tit. Feoffment, introductory para; Blackstone, Commentaries II 315-6; Holdsworth HEL III 221-6.

The relevance of these "unwritten formalities" is that it is a trite story that equity, by enforcing uses and contracts merely consensual, subverted all these formalities; that this formed part of the argument for the Statute of Uses, and that one result was the Statute of Enrolments of 1535 and the requirement of writing in the Statute of Wills of 1540; that the extensions of assumpsit are connected with competition between common law and equity for business; and that at the turn of the sixteenth and seventeenth centuries some lawyers thought that the movement towards informality had gone too far or ought to be restrained[91]. It is in this context that requirements of writing begin to appear in equity.

The first instance to appear seems to be refusal to relieve on parol leases which had not taken effect in possession, which appears in the early 1580s[92]. Then in 1597 Egerton announced that he would not relieve on parol leases in general, "for avoiding perjuries and other abuses"[93].[94] There was still some uncertainty about the rule, as in *Observations* Egerton is reported as saying that

> Leases p[ar]olls and indorsed Surrenders or Assignm[en]ts are not simply of theselves discountenanced in equity, but whereas they come to be sett on foote after many yeares past[95].

But by 1603, perhaps as a result of a series of Star Chamber cases on perjury by witnesses to parol leases, he was taking a tougher line, saying that

> he neither would help leases parol in Chancery; and that it was good for the commonwealth, if no lease parol were to be allowed by law, nor promises to be proved by witnesses, considering the plenty of witnesses nowadays, which were *testes diabolices, qui magis fame quam fama moventur*[96].

90 Simpson *Contract* 137 f.

91 Simpson *Contract* 276-80 for subversion of the common law requirements in relation to covenants and connection, or possible connection, with assumpsit for nonfeasance; Ibbetson 4 OJLS 295 at 310- 315 for the policy arguments in this connection around *Slade's Case;* Baker, 94 SS Introduction *198* citing Audley's Reading of 1526, for subversion of formalities for conveyances of freehold and objections to this process; above Ch 3 pp 116-7 for Ellesmere's objections to the new methods of trial of titles weakening the necessity of *profert.*

92 *Page v Spencer* (1581-2) Ch C Ch 148, Stowe 415 f 136b, dismissed; *Williams v Moore* (1582) Ch C Ch 158, Stowe 415 f 139, *Quære* & no order; *Nicholls v Lovell* (1583-4) Ch C Ch 171, Stowe 415 f 143, dismissed.

93 Cary 7, Harg 281 f 13b; probably same statement differently reported, *Observacons* f 440v No. 35. In *Harrison v Cholmeley* (1560-1) Cary 51, Stowe 415 f 107b, where the plaintiff on a parol lease had entered and sowed corn, he obtained only an injunction for the corn, which slightly suggests that the rule goes back to Bacon LK, but this is fairly weak evidence compared to Egerton's explicit pronouncements.

94 Contemporary examples of "perjuries and other abuses" in connection with alleged parol leases can be found in the Star Chamber perjury prosecutions in *Ridgly's Case* (P1596) Hawarde 40 and *Beverley v Pittes* (M1597) Hawarde 83.

95 ff 452r-v at f 452v.

96 Cary 27, Stowe 415 f 98b, Lansd 599 f 7b; in Cary as *Anon* but looks like a *dictum* in *Musgrave's Case* immediately before.

The refusal of relief on parol leases is repeated by Bacon's Orders[97], by Norburie (quoted below) and by Powell[98], in *The Practice of the High Court of Chancery* (1651) (quoted below), and by Lord Nottingham in 1674[99].

Again, Egerton is reported in *Observations* as saying that "he would never aide a nuncupative will nor give any favor unto it"[100]. This rule is similarly repeated by Bacon's Orders, and in that form by Powell,[101] by Norburie and by *The Practice ...* (quoted below). It made equity considerably more rigorous than the common law on this point: the common law courts held that instructions for a will taken down in writing by a witness, the testator dying without executing the will (which would be nuncupative in the canon law, according to Swinburne[102]) was a good will in writing to pass land under the Statute of Wills[103]. The Star Chamber in 1596 rejected this rule, but this rejection was not followed at common law, and, indeed, by 1622 the Chancery was following the law on this specific point.[104] It is not found in Lord Nottingham, and the fact that a nuncupative will will suffice to pass personalty was used as an argument in the later seventeenth century in the context of the parol evidence rule (above § 1 *(2)*).

Under Egerton, again, we find the beginnings of a rule that equity will not enforce a parol contract for the sale of land. The rule stated in *Observations* is that

> If two doe treate about the purchase of land and doe conclude of the manner of the bargaine and of the price & doe appoint a time that the Counsell on both sides shall meete to make Conveyance that this will not binde either p[ar]tie except some p[ar]te of the money w[hi]ch is to be paid for the purchase be delivered to the seller (& not other money in earnest) or that the Agreem[en]t be set downe in writing[105].

Tothill collected a number of cases which probably define the limits and operation of this rule as it related to part payment and performance[106]. Yale[107] follows

---

97 No 15, Sanders p 111; together with a mixed bag of matters objectionable on public policy grounds (perpetuities, marriage brocage, wagers, sale of offices, usury and simony).

98 208, quoting Bacon's Order.

99 *Rothwell v Hussey & al'* (M1674) 2 Ch Cas 202 ((H1673/4) Nott CC No 68 not SP).

100 f 402r No. 193

101 Same Order and quotation as above on parol leases.

102 Part I § 11.2; though he subsequently cites Dyer for the common law position.

103 *Brown v Sackville* (M1552) 1 Dy 72.

104 Rejected in Star Chamber, *AG v Harward* (H1595/6) Hawarde 28. Common law rule followed in equity, *Re Stoddard* (1622) Toth 31, argument about whether a rent could be created by a nuncupative will (of this type), but decreed; *Forrester & Cowden* (H1677/8) Nott CC No 784. Reversed by the Statute of Frauds s 5.

105 f 479v No 285, MN "Ex relat R Moore".

106 *Moyles v Horne & al'* (?T1602) Toth 5, decreed because £200 deposited towards payment; *Clarke v Hackwell* (1605) Toth 162, decreed on £5 paid; *Miller v Blandist* (1605) (3 Jac; printed text has 30 Jac, which is impossible) Toth 24, 55s paid in hand, dismissed; *Cooke v Trewman* (T1606) Toth 69; *Ferne v Bullock* (1611) Toth 141, 162, 10s in hand, decreed; *Otway v Hibblethwaite* (T1613) Toth 163, promise in consideration of marriage,

Sugden[108], who argued that some of these early cases in which plaintiffs seem to have been relieved on mere "earnest money", which would not have been accepted as part performance in the Restoration, were attributable to the failure of the defendants to demur[109]. However, the rule it must have been fairly new and may well have remained not entirely settled, as it was still possible in the 1590s to repeat without qualifying it the traditional position that equity gave relief on covenants without specialty[110], and *Williams v Nevill* in 1596, a clear case for this rule, is decided on jurisdictional grounds[111].

By the time Norburie was writing, the rule appears to have become generalised from the case of sale of land; he includes in "Matters not relievable in Chancery":

> A debt without specialty against an Executor, unless it be in very special cases.
>
> Leases and bargains paroll, verball promises, and wills nuncupative. [112]

Though these general rules on parol contracts do not appear in Bacon's or Coventry's Orders or the Parliamentary Commissioners' collection of 1649, *The Practice of the High Court of Chancery* (1651) has among "Suits denied help in the Chancery", "suits grounded upon wills nuncupative or leases paroll ... verbal agreements not executed (on either part)"[113]; and the part performance rule is discussed by William Sheppard in his *Faithful Counsellor* (1651)[114]. Lord Nottingham in his *Prolegomena* says that:

> ... equity will never compel the performance of a parol agreement *in specie*, unless it have been in part executed or executed on one side.[115]

---

performed, decreed; *King v Burrell* (H1626/7) Toth 66, decree in the Requests on a verbal promise confirmed "because the plaintiff is ancient tenant, and been at costs in building".

107 73 SS cii-ciii.

108 *Vendors & Purchasers* pp 202 f.

109 As in the anonymous case in 2 Freeman, below n 116.

110 West, sig Biii Y, Z and *The cases of Conscience* Stowe 415 f 146, repeat the statement in *Diversitie de Courtz* that relief is available in equity on covenants without specialty.

111 (T1596) Toth 72, Harl 1576 f 163b, [*Nowill*] Stowe 415 f 206, "A bill laying a promise to assure lands for 10s in hand and £2100 (Stowe £100) at a day, demurred and allowed [Harl allowed, Stowe overruled] because it was but a preparation for an action on the case".

112 P 432. It is possible that the generalization also dates back to Egerton, since Norburie's tract appears to be a Chancery parallel to Hudson's *Star Chamber*, aimed to induce Williams to return to the good old ways of Egerton, allegedly departed from by Bacon. (For Norburie as addressed to Williams, Holdsworth *HEL* v, 271-2; for Hudson's call for a return to the practice of Egerton, Barnes, "Mr Hudson's Star Chamber" in Guth & McKenna (ed) *Tudor Rule & Revolution* (Cambridge, CUP, 1982) 285 at 298f).

113 P 48.

114 Pp. 619-621.

115 XVII.3, *TT* p 310.

That this rule was applied in practice is confirmed by several cases, including some of Lord Nottingham's own decisions[116] and by *dicta* after the Statute of Frauds as to what the rule in equity was before the Statute was passed[117].

There is a curious parallel between this development and the account given by Ibbetson[118] of the development of the requirement of a deed in the action of covenant in the later thirteenth and early fourteenth century, also starting from a requirement of a deed in the context of a lease. Ibbetson attributes this to civil law influence[119]. There is no clear evidence, however, that the later equity development is anything more than parallel.

The overall effect of these rules was that during the seventeenth century equity, at least in the Chancery, required writing (or part performance) in some cases in which the common law did not, i.e. leases and agreements. These rules cannot, however, be seen as a matter of direct roman-canon influence. Rather, the new rules introduced in this area in the late sixteenth and early to mid seventeenth century seem to be modelled on a conservative conception of the common law rules.

In spite of the provision of relief on the basis of part performance, these requirements of writing tend to reinforce the indications in relation to estoppels and the parol evidence rule that in equity in this period documentary proof was preferred to proof by witnesses.

2. The Statute of Frauds

The origins of the Statute of Frauds have been fairly extensively studied[120]. For my purposes the issues of interest are (1) the relation of the origins of the Statute to (a) roman-canon conceptions and continental legislation, and (b) the prior development of requirements of writing in equity (above); and (2) whether, as Holdsworth, following Wigmore, argues, the equity courts can be said to have placed a restrictive construction on the Statute and in some respects even amended it[121].

---

116 *Simmons v Cornelius* (1663) 1 Ch Rep 241, bill dismissed; *Anon* 2 Freem 128 (probably 1669-70, from associated cases; quite likely to be *Voll v Smith* (M1669) 3 Ch Rep 28, where SP is decreed on very similar facts but without explanation) Grimstone MR, the rule accepted but SP decreed on the ground that the defendant had failed to demur; *Pelham v Honeywood* (M1674) Nott CC No 122, *per cur; Russell v Russell & Downing* (H1675/6) Nott CC No 380 at 73 SS 258; *Reasby v Smallwood* (T1677) Nott CC No 685; *Taylor v Badderley* (T1678) Nott CC No 845; *Cope v North* (T1678) Nott CC No 861.

117 *Wheeler v Newton* (H1690/1) Pre Ch 16, 2 Eq Ca Ab 44.5, *per* Rawlinson LCssr; *Marquis of Normanby v Duke of Devonshire* (M1697) 2 Freem 216, Harv 1105 193.

118 4 Law & History Review 71 at 81 f.

119 Ib 83-4.

120 Summarised in Holdsworth *HEL* VI 379-397 and Simpson *Contract* Ch 13. Cf also Hamburger 27 *AJLH* 354, Youdan [1984] *CLJ* 306, Teeven 9 *Adelaide Law Rev.* 252.

121 HEL VI 393-5.

a) Origins

Rabel argued in 1946[122] that the introduction of requirements of writing in the Statute was a part of a general development of statutory requirements of writing in European law. He supported this view by suggesting that Nottingham's original formula for what subsequently became ss 4 and 17 (parol contracts) was influenced by seventeenth century interpretations of the French Ordinance of Moulins (1566)[123]. The idea that there might be some relationship between the Statute and continental legislation had been very tentatively suggested by Hayes (1929)[124], and this approach is also taken in Gilissen's general outline survey of development in proof in early modern european laws (1959)[125].

This is not, however, the dominant view in anglo-american legal history. Rabel's argument has been sharply criticised by Simpson, and several alternative explanations of the origin of the Statute have been advanced by different writers.[126]

(1) The "common-sense" view suggested by the title and preamble is that the Statute became necessary because of a growth in fraud and perjury. This view has received some support from Ibbetson and Baker[127].

(2) Probably the "orthodox" view is that offered by Holdsworth, following Thayer and Wigmore[128]. This is that the root of the Statute was the problems with jury trial at this period and the underdeveloped or problematic state of the rules of evidence at common law. This view is also adopted by Simpson[129] and by Teeven[130].

---

122 63 LQR 174.

123 Ib. pp 177-8.

124 *Le Statute of Frauds en Droit Anglais*, Thèse, Paris 1929. This is the barest glancing reference; the bulk of the thesis is on eighteenth and nineteenth century interpretations of the statute.

125 "La Preuve en Europe du XVIè au debut du XIXè siecle" in Receuils de la Société Jean Bodin Vol XVII (1965) 757-833 at 820-7 collects together the relevant provisions in the different European laws, merely assuming that the English statute is a part of this general process.

126 Christopher Hill has suggested, *en passant,* a class approach to the motivation of ss 1 and 2 of the Statute, as under these provisions "So far were copyholders from winning security of tenure, an Act of 1677 extended their insecurity to small freeholders except in the unlikely event of their being able to produce written title to their estates" ("A Bourgeois Revolution?" in *Collected Essays,* III (Brighton, Harvester, 1986) 94 at 101; the same point is made in slightly different terms in *Some Intellectual Consequences of the English Revolution* (London, Weidenfeld & Nicolson, 1980) p 35). As it stands this argument, which is not supported by evidence, seems manifestly unsound; but it is not directly relevant to my present concerns.

127 Ibbetson 4 OJLS at 313, though the point is not there specifically directed to the origins of the Statute; Baker, *Introduction to English Legal History* (3rd edition, London, Butterworths, 1990) p 396, applying the point to the Statute.

128 HEL VI 388-393, citing Thayer 180, 430, 431 and Wigmore § 3426.

129 Pp 604-5.

(3) More recently, Hamburger has argued that the Statute, read as a whole, addresses problems of fraudulent conveyances and undiscoverable incumbrances on titles, and that it represents an alternative solution to these problems to that offered by the scheme of compulsory registration of title which was being promoted in the run-up to the passage of the Statute. Hamburger's argument extends to suggest that the mechanisms employed derive from earlier proposals by Hale in connection with the law reform debates of the 1650s[131].

There are two aspects to these arguments. The first is the motivation for the Statute; the second the source of its drafting, i.e. whether the formulas used were simply pulled out of the heads of Nottingham, Guilford and Jenkins[132], or had some prior antecedents. Rabel's and Hamburger's arguments address both issues, but they are in principle distinct. It would be perfectly logically consistent, for instance, to combine any of the arguments as to motivation with the view that the mechanisms used to deal with the problem were (a) pulled out of the draftsmen's heads, (b) borrowed from previous reform proposals, or (c) borrowed from continental models. It is also possible that different sources or none were used in relation to different sections or parts of the Statute. The question of motivation also poses two issues: why? and why at this time?

The Statute contains, in essence, three parts: a body of requirements of writing (ss 1-9 and 17); a group of reforms to the law relating to real securities and their priorities (ss 10-16 and 18); and a set of reforms to the law of nuncupative wills applied in the church courts (ss 18-23), essentially designed to restrict nuncupative wills[133].

Technically, only the requirements of writing are relevant to the present discussion, and Holdsworth regarded these as the important parts of the Statute, seeing the other parts as "not intimately related to the clauses which carried out the main purposes of the Statute"[134], while Simpson says that "The Statute was in fact a general measure of law reform"[135]. Hamburger's argument, however, suggests that at least the first and second parts formed part of a single coherent project; and it is obvious that restrictive rules for nuncupative wills are naturally associated with requirements of writing.

None of the arguments is entirely satisfactory. Firstly, the "common sense" view that the Statute was made necessary by a rising tide of fraud and perjury, or at least motivated by the perception that there was such a problem, should not be ruled

---

130 9 Adelaide Law Rev at 252-266.

131 27 AJLH 354.

132 Identified by Holdsworth, following Hening 61 U Penn LR 283, as the principal authors.

133 Nobody has suggested that s 25, which "explains" 22 & 23 Car 2 c 10, is anything but an entirely separate provision merely tacked.

134 HEL VI p 387.

135 P 601.

out. It is obviously impossible or very difficult at this date to get any clear impression of the actual incidence of perjury in judicial proceedings in the seventeenth century, let alone of whether it tended to increase or decrease[136]. In fact, since political history tends to suggest that there was never a period in which perjury (at least of promissory oaths) was not commonplace[137], the thesis of an *actual* increase in perjury needs to be treated with extreme caution. It is, however, clear that there was widespread concern in the seventeenth century about the sanctity of oaths and a *perceived* growth in oath- breaking[138], and this perception and concern may well have contributed both to the introduction of requirements of writing in equity in the earlier part of the century, and to the requirements of writing and restrictions on nuncupative wills in the Statute of Frauds.

This could, then, be a partial answer to the question "why?". But it is not really an answer to the problem "why at this time?" except in the broadest possible sense. The Ibbetson- Baker suggestion supplies this defect by reference to the abolition of Star Chamber[139]. But this is subject to the same problems of evidence. It would need to be shown that (1) the Star Chamber was extensively used to control *genuine* cases of perjury (as opposed to allegations of perjury being made to give jurisdiction) and also that (2) the statutory remedy was felt to be ineffective. Both of these propositions may be true[140]; and yet, as we have already seen, in equity requirements of writing were introduced in the early part of the seventeenth century, at a time when Star Chamber was still in extensive use.

For these reasons, I would suggest that the most that can be made of the problem of fraud and fear of perjury is as a general backdrop to the introduction of the Statute, not a sufficient motive for its introduction.

---

136 For the limitations of contemporary records of criminal proceedings as a source of evidence for the incidence of crime cf Cockburn in Cockburn (ed) *Crime in England 1550-1800* (London, Methuen, 1977) at 50-51, and Introduction to *Calendars of Assize Proceedings* (HMSO, 1985) 84-5, Sharpe, *Crime in Seventeenth Century England* (Cambridge, CUP, 1983) 9f, Beattie, *Crime & the Courts 1660- 1800* (Oxford, Clarendon, 1986) 15 f. The printed Calendars of Assize Records contain a total of six indictments for perjury in eleven volumes, which is obviously meaningless.

137 See e.g. the celebrated story of Harold Godwinsson's oath to uphold William of Normandy's claim, and numerous subsequent instances in the middle ages of oaths broken or dispensed with.

138 See the discussion in Staves, *Players' Scepters* Ch 4. But it may be that this is merely a perennial grumble: the commonness of perjury in judicial proceedings is complained of in Elyot, *The Book Named the Governor* (1531) (Everyman edition, London, 1962 p179f).

139 *loci cit* above n 127.

140 There are 27 perjury cases in Hawarde, which suggests that Star Chamber was doing a fair amount of business on this head, but not all of these were serious allegations. The statutory remedy was provided by 5 Eliz I c 9 s 6 (discussed by M.D. Gordon, 'The Invention of a Common Law Crime: Perjury and the Elizabethan Courts' (1980) 24 *AJLH* 145-170). The lack of indictments, above n 136, does tend to suggest that this remedy was ineffective in the late sixteenth and early seventeenth century.

Secondly, the Wigmore/ Holdsworth/ Simpson view that the statute addressed problems with evidence in trial by jury plainly will not hold water.

The evidence in support of this view consists basically of the general view of these writers that the law of evidence in trials by jury was at this time primitive, in particular in excluding the parties from giving evidence. Two specific items of evidence have been advanced to show contemporary recognition of this problem as an element in the introduction of the Statute. Firstly, Holdsworth refers to the injustice capable of being worked by the exclusion of the parties as witnesses, and in this point to a story about Guilford in Francis North's *Life* of him in which the demeanour of the plaintiff induced Guilford to examine a receipt closely and find it forged[141]. This story is one of forgery of written evidence, and therefore does not primarily suggest the introduction of requirements of writing.

Secondly, Simpson refers to *dicta* of Hale CJ in 1671-2[142] criticising the effect of *Slade's Case* and suggesting the introduction of formal requirements in contract. In view of Hale's known opinions on the general merits of jury trial stated in his *History of the Common Law*[143] it seems problematic to attach these *dicta* to Holdsworth's general argument, as Simpson does.

A third possible item of evidence along these lines could be added. Guilford in his commonplace book suggested that in contractual matters the defendant should be regularly required to plead on oath at common law as in equity[144], and this might at first be taken as showing recognition of the problem. But in reality Guilford's proposal is aimed to save costs; and moreover (as elsewhere) Guilford addresses the problem he sees directly; on the Wigmore/ Holdsworth/ Simpson interpretation, the Statute is an *indirect* attempt to solve problems with jury trial.

I will return later to the correctness or otherwise of Wigmore and Holdsworth's claim that the Statute was construed restrictively in equity, which might be taken to corroborate the view that it was "aimed at" jury trial. Even if this basic claim was correct, the further inference from it that the Statute was "aimed at" jury trial would not follow, in view of the requirements of writing in equity *before* the Statute.

The crucial item of evidence against the "jury trial" interpretation of the Statute is the content of the Statute itself. Even allowing that the second part (priorities of incumbrances) may be treated as tacked, the third part (nuncupative wills) addresses problems with proof *per testes* in the church courts, and even if this part is

---

141 HEL VI p 389 n 3 referring to North I pp 146-7.

142 Simpson pp 603-4 cites *Buckridge v Shirley* Treby's Reports, Middle Temple MSS at 651, and anonymous cases in the same reports at 747 and 775.

143 Gray edition pp 163-4, quoted below ch 8 § 2.

144 Add 32518 at f11b: "... Why may not the def[endant] at com[mon] law be compelled to plead upon Oath, in Civil Contracts. To avoid charg of tryall, but then must doe it in person".

treated as tacked, the requirements of writing in the first group of sections, and in Nottingham's original draft[145], include matters of pure equity (trust or no trust and assignment of equitable interests) which Nottingham thought ought not to be tried by jury but proved *per testes* in equity[146]. It therefore seems highly improbable that the primary motivation of the Statute was problems with jury trial.

The basic strength of Hamburger's argument that the Statute was aimed to deflect the agitation for registration of title consists in the fact that it coincides with the clearest piece of evidence as to the motivation of the Statute that we have, namely Nottingham's speech against the register proposal in February 1670/1[147]; and thereby explains the *apparent* tack of the provisions relating to priority of incumbrances.

I think, however, that Hamburger overstates the specificity of the bill's objects and their relationship to Hale's previous scheme of extending the use of enrolment under the Statute of Enrolments[148], and is too much inclined to see the "non-conveyancing" elements of the Statute as merely tacked. Hamburger himself admits that the Statute did not lead to a large increase in enrolments[149], and, indeed, the voluntary enrolment of deeds made only a limited difference to their evidential status[150]. Moreover, Nottingham's speech, which is closer to the Act than Hale's scheme, *opposed* voluntary registration (which was the essence of Hale's scheme) on the ground that it would *de facto* compel registration[151].

I would suggest, therefore, that (1) Hamburger is probably correct to argue that the Statute was introduced at the time that it was as a consequence of the registration agitation, and that the sections on incumbrances are therefore not merely tacked. But (2) the "project" of the Statute was not to carry into effect Hale's scheme, but rather to tackle some particular problems of fraud and perjury which had been used by advocates of registration – *and to do so primarily by introducing requirements of documentary proof of certain transactions.* If this is the case, then we can see how the contemporary concern about oaths and perjury fits into the result, and the critical question is why proof by documents was perceived as representing a solution to these problems.

It is at this point that the contemporary european law context comes back into the picture. Simpson criticised Rabel's argument on the ground that he gave too

---

145 Holdsworth HEL VI Appendix I at p 375.

146 Nott Proleg 8.3, 11, discussed below Chs 6, 10.

147 79 SS 966 at 978; Yale comments, n 2, that "this paragraph contains legislative germs of many provisions of the Statute of Frauds".

148 Hamburger at pp 365-6.

149 Hamburger at pp 379-80. On the Statute of Enrolments itself cf Kaye 104 LQR 617, who suggests that the Statute was not, in fact, aimed primarily at producing publicity of conveyances.

150 Above Ch 3 nn 172-173.

151 79 SS at 974.

much weight to the contemporary continental legislation as a motive for the Statute, and that the French *Ordonnance* of 1667 was too different in character to have served as a motive or model for the Statute[152].

One of the items of evidence cited by Rabel for his view was that in Nottingham's 1675 draft s 4 (i.e. what became ss 4 and 17) set a limit to the damages recoverable without proof in writing[153], and that the most plausible origin of this formula is to have been modelled on the continental legislation and in particular either the French Ordinance of Moulins or the Perpetual Edict in the Spanish Netherlands, both of which used formulae of this type[154]. Baker appears to accept this analysis[155]; Simpson's objection that the purposes of the Ordinance of Moulins were different from those of the Statute misses the point of Rabel's argument, i.e. that the *seventeenth-century interpretation of* Moulins was consistent with the purposes of the Statute of Frauds[156].

However, Rabel was not able to find continental models for the final version of the Statute on this point, or for any other part of it, and, indeed, he suggested that other elements were influenced by mediaeval common law[157]. This fact very much weakens any claim of a direct and specific influence of european civilian ideas in the motivation of the Statute.

Moreover, Gilissen's survey makes clear that the introduction of requirements of writing was by no means universal[158]. Apart from England, he finds evidence for the existence or legislative introduction of requirements of writing in contracts in Naples (1306), Bologna (1454), Milan (1498), France (Moulins, 1566), Lithuania (1588), and the Spanish Netherlands (Perpetual Edict, 1611, said[159] to be modelled on Moulins). Such requirements were not, however, present or introduced in the common law of the Holy Roman Empire[160], in Switzerland, Spain[161], the Papal States, or the Scandinavian countries. Gilissen does not refer to the law of the Dutch Republic, but Bosch's survey of the history of proof in the law of the Netherlands[162] does not mention any requirements. This evidence again weakens the

---

152 Simpson pp 608-9.

153 Holdsworth HEL VI Appendix I pp 673-4.

154 Rabel 177-8.

155 Baker *Introduction* p 397.

156 Rabel 178.

157 Rabel 184-7.

158 Gilissen 820-6.

159 Gilissen 824.

160 Requirements were introduced in Prussia in 1770 (Gilissen 825) but this is not relevant in the present context.

161 Gilissen refers, p 823, to royal ordinances in Aragon and Portugal cited by Danty, *Traite de Preuve par temoins en matière civile* (Paris, 1727) but from Gilissen's account of these provisions they refer to conclusivess of instruments, not to requirements of writing.

162 "La preuve dans l'ancien droit néerlandais" in Receuils de la Société Jean Bodin Vol XVII 453-480.

inference that the Statute involved direct emulation or imitation of the european laws. In the light of Simpson's criticisms and of Hamburger's argument it does seem that the suggestion that the Statute was motivated by direct emulation of the French (codifying) *Ordonnance* of 1667 is both weak and unnecessary.

There are, however, two points in favour of european influence, albeit perhaps more indirect. The first is that English law may have been unusual at this period in allowing title to land to be affected by merely oral transactions, and certainly one of the arguments for registration was the use of registers in Holland and France[163]. Thus the registration debate, in motivating requirements of writing in transactions connected with land, may be said to display a european influence.

The second point is that the idea that writings were preferable to witnesses does seem to be more general in the european laws of the period than requirements of writing. I have already cited Egerton's reference to the usefulness of notaries, which must reflect the influence of continental practice[164]. In this indirect sense it may be said that the solution adopted by the Statute to the problems it addressed, i.e. requirements of writing, may have been influenced by the european evolution towards preference for writings. But this should not be overstated, in view of the fact that (as indicated above) preference for writings is actually *earlier* in the mediaeval common law than in some other european laws.

A more immediate probable influence, which should be blatantly obvious from the previous discussion of requirements of writing in equity before 1677, is these requirements. Equity refused relief on parol leases; the Statute cut down the effectiveness of parol leases at law. Equity required a deed or part performance in contracts; the Statute introduced a variety of requirements of writing in contracts. Equity refused relief on nuncupative wills; the Statute required wills of land to be by signed and attested writing and introduced new controls on nuncupative wills of personalty. In equity court orders took effect from the date of the order; the Statute modified the common law rules under which orders might "relate back" to the beginning of the law term.

In this perspective, the major substantive innovation in the Statute as compared to the prior equity rules is ss 7-9 on the creation of trusts and assignment of equitable interests. This, however, had its own precedent. The Cromwellian Chancery Ordinance of 1654 provided (s 44):

> That no trust or agreement made or declared after the 25 day of March 1655, concerning lands, or any other thing in the realty shall be relieved in Chancery, unless it be contained in writing, and so averred in the bill, save in such cases where the possession hath gone along with the party claiming the trust.[165]

---

163 See Nottingham's response to these arguments, 79 SS at 975-6.

164 Above Ch 3 n 96 and text there.

165 i Sanders 254 at 262.

This is not to suggest that the prior equity rules on requirements of writing provided the models for the drafting of the Statute. This is plainly not the case.

The point is, to pull the threads of the argument together, (1) There was in the period a general background fear of fraud and perjury and doubt about the force and effectiveness of oaths. (2) There was pressure in Restoration England – following from pressure which had been at its strongest in the Interregnum – for greater certainty of title, which it was argued could be achieved through a registration scheme. Advocates of a scheme were able to point to aspects of the existing law which made purchasers and creditors vulnerable. (3) Nottingham, who opposed a registration scheme, suggested as an alternative reform of the specific problems, and a few years later produced an initial draft bill, which, extensively amended, ended up as the Statute of Frauds. (4) Though Nottingham probably borrowed his initial draft formula on contracts from French law, and though there is no direct relationship between the final formulae and the equity rules, the basic core solutions of the Statute assimilate the common law rules to existing requirements of writing in equity. (5) In this context there is certainly a parallelism with the introduction of requirements of writing in continental Europe, and possibly some influence from the general european development of the idea that writings were preferred to witnesses. The primary significance of the Statute (at least for my purposes) is as evidence of the weight of this idea in England at this period.

b) The application of the Statute in equity

Holdsworth, following Wigmore and Thayer, said that

> "The court of Chancery was inclined to construe [the Statute's] clauses in a somewhat restrictive fashion, and even to modify them materially. ... No doubt this restrictive method of interpreting the statute was due to the fact that the causes which made the provisions of the statute so useful in the courts of common law did not operate in the Court of Chancery. The Court of Chancery did not depend upon a jury to ascertain the facts, nor were the parties debarred from giving evidence."[166]

If correct, this view of the interpretation of the Statute would reinforce the argument that the Statute was "aimed at" problems with jury trial. It would also suggest, as Wigmore[167] does suggest, that the preference for documentary evidence was very markedly weaker in Chancery than at common law.

However, this Wigmore/ Holdsworth view is *a priori* questionable. I have already criticised the argument that the motivation of the Statute is primarily problems with jury trial. It should in addition be said that (1) while matters of fact in equity were primarily decided by proof to a judge *per instrumenta* or *per testes*,

166 HEL VI p 393, citing (n 4) Thayer 431, Wigmore § 3426.

167 Wigmore § 2426 (3rd ed Vol IX p 91).

not by trial by jury, in the same period as the Statute and its immediate aftermath the equity courts were making some use of feigned issues in order to send issues of fact to juries[168]. (2) The use in equity of the answer on oath and the occasional availability of other forms of interrogation of parties and in some cases of the oaths of parties is by no means the same thing as the modern general use of the evidence of parties. The most that can be said of this point is that in equity the plaintiff could more easily obtain a confession by the defendant, which might then be a way around the Statute[169].

Holdsworth's evidence for his view consists of (a) the development soon after the passage of the statute of the doctrines of secret trusts and of part performance[170] and (b) the conflicting views of judges in the mid to late eighteenth century as to the merits of the statute and whether it should be construed restrictively[171].

The second of these points, the eighteenth century disputes, would only be relevant to the present study if the absence of evidence from the later seventeenth and early eighteenth century made it necessary to make inferences backwards, i.e. to assume that the mid to late eighteenth century disputes were a continuation of earlier differences. In fact, however, there is a good deal of evidence about the application of the Statute in equity and the attitude of equity judges to it in the earlier period, and on balance this evidence suggests that the eighteenth-century difference of approach discussed by Holdsworth, if it was a difference between law and equity, was one which arose in the eighteenth century rather than a continuation of earlier differences[172].

In our period it is possible to point to four items of evidence in favour of the view that the Chancery construed the Statute "restrictively" in the sense of limiting its operation. These are (1) the rule that a plea of the Statute was not "peremptory", i.e. did not release the defendant from the obligation to answer the bill; (2) the rule that a confession of the agreement in the answer, without pleading the Statute,

---

168 Below Ch 10 § 1 *(3)*.

169 Above Ch 2, below Ch 6 § 4 *(1)* (c). On both these points cf also Youdan [1984] CLJ 306 at 308-10.

170 Loc cit above n 166.

171 Pp 394-5.

172 Holdsworth's references are actually to differences between Lord Mansfield and subsequent judges, with the exception of a dictum of Gilbert CB in *Whitchurch v Whitchurch* (1724) Gilb R 168 at 171, quoted p 394 n 6, to the effect that such statutes have been construed restrictively. The trouble with this quotation is that the context makes clear that "restrictively" means "strictly", i.e *not* so as to give effect to the intention of the settlor; the actual decision being that the trust of a term settled to attend the inheritance was realty in equity and so subject to the requirements of s 5 of the Statute. The date given in Gilb.Rep., 1721, is false; the case is also reported in 2 P Wms 235 and 2 Eq Ca Ab 763.10 (Jekyll MR), 1 Stra 619 and 9 Mod 124 (Lords Commissioners Gilbert and Raymond), but the point taken by Gilbert only appears in his own report and more briefly in Strange. I have indicated above in connection with the parol evidence rule that there may have been some movement towards admitting parol proofs more freely in the first half of the eighteenth century.

barred the defendant from subsequent reliance on the Statute; and (3) part performance and (4) secret trusts, which are referred to by Holdsworth.

However, (1) the rule that a plea of the statute was not peremptory *prima facie* merely reflects the general course of the Chancery practice of saving the benefit of pleas to the hearing, relatively few pleas being peremptory[173]. If it is more than this, it is merely a consequence of the existence of the doctrine of part performance; the points appear to be connected in *Alsopp v Patten* (1687)[174].

(2) The rule that a confession of the agreement without pleading the Statute bars subsequent reliance on the Statute is probably a consequence of the doctrine that a confession in court is the highest form of proof[175]. In any event, it cannot represent a difference with the common law, since a defendant at law who confessed the agreement without pleading the Statute would be far more clearly barred by the rules of pleading from subsequently relying on the Statute[176].

(3) It is far from clear that the doctrine of secret trusts *considered as an exception to the Statute*[177] is separable from the doctrine of part performance. The leading case on the point, *Thynn v Thynn*[178], is cited by Fonblanque in his edition of Ballow (1793-4) as an instance of part performance[179]. It is now difficult to conceive of *Thynn v Thynn* as a contract case, (a) because of the obvious privity problem, and (b) because the plaintiff is a volunteer, so that a fully constituted trust is required. But in the 1680s the leading case on privity in assumpsit in this context was *Dutton v Poole* (1677)[180] in which the beneficiary-plaintiff succeeded, and the principle that equity will not assist a volunteer did not at this time have its modern form and extent[181]. Given these circumstances, the most straightforward way to interpret the early post-statute "secret trust" cases is as instances of part performance, rather than as representing an independent restriction on ss 5 (wills) and 7 (declaration of trust).

---

173 Yale, *Introduction* to *TT* at 57.

174 1 Vern 472, 1 Eq Ca Ab 22.13, Jeffreys C: "the agreement being in part executed, the Court ordered the defendant to answer, and saved the benefit of the plea to the hearing".

175 Above Ch 2.

176 In fact the Statute was normally taken at trial on the general issue: *Lee v Bashpole* (M1689) Comb 163: "this is never done in pleading, but ought to be proved on the trial" so that writing need not be averred by the plaintiff (after the New Rules it was suggested that the defendant ought to plead the Statute; it was conceded that this would not have been necessary before: *Buttermere v Hayes* (1839) 5 M & W 460). This may explain how the "pleading" rule in equity subsequently came to be seen as problematic (cf Fonblanque's edition of Ballow (1793-4; reprint, New York, Garland, 1979) Vol I p 168 (&f) n *(d)*).

177 The doctrine appears to exist before the Statute as a ground for equity jurisdiction in relation to wills of personalty: above § 1 *(2)*.

178 (H1684/5) 1 Vern 296, 1 Eq Ca Ab 380.6.

179 Vol I p 173 n 5.

180 Discussed, with collection of the references, Simpson 479, 481 f.

181 Macnair "Equity & Volunteers" (1988) 8 LS 172 at 173-7.

The evidence in favour of a "restrictive" attitude of equity to the Statute is therefore reduced to the development of the doctrine of part performance as an exception to s 4 (contracts). This is certainly a substantial divergence from the terms of the Statute, and one which appears very early, in the time of Lord Guilford, who himself had a major hand in the drafting of the Statute.

How and why the doctrine arose remains unclear. In the first place, the words of s 4 ("no *Action* [my emphasis] shall be brought") did not in terms affect English bills for specific performance, which were not "actions": i.e. s 4 may simply not have applied[182].

However, the Statute was considered at an early date to have affected the law relating to bills for specific performance, at a minimum (notably) by eliminating the older requirement that in the absence of part performance a contract to be specifically enforceable must be under seal[183]. And if it had been generally assumed that bills for specific performance were outside the section, it is not obvious why the 1680s and 90s should have seen a steady flow of cases in Chancery on the issue of what constituted sufficient memoranda and/ or sufficient acts of part performance[184].

An eighteenth century explanation of this, which is accepted by Yale[185], is that before the time of Somers the Chancery would only sustain a bill for specific performance where an action at law would lie, and even required plaintiffs to go to law to establish the validity of their contract. While the procedural aspect in this explanation may be questioned[186], the doctrinal point seems plausible in view of

182 Costigan 26 Harv LR 329 at 343-4 said that the section was not intended to apply to the equity jurisdiction, but on the basis of the Thayer/ Wigmore argument as to its purpose; on this cf above § 2 *(1)*. Yale Introduction to 73 SS, ciii, makes the rather different point that it was "a matter of assumption, quite correctly, that the Statute did not apply where the contract had been executed in part".

183 *Wheeler v Newton* (H1690/1) Pre Ch 16, 2 Eq Ca Ab 44.5, *per* Rawlinson LCssr at Pre Ch 17; *Normanby v Devonshire* (M1697) 2 Freem 216, Harv 1105 193, "said".

184 *Leake v Morris* (1682) Dick 14, 2 Ch Cas 135, *Hollis v Whiteing* (H1682/3) 1 Vern 151, 1 Eq Ca Ab 19.1, *Hollis v Edwards* (P1683) 1 Vern 159, 1 Eq Ca Ab 19.2, *Heighter v Sturman* (M1683) 1 Vern 210, 1 Eq Ca Ab 21.2, *Lowther v Carill* (H1683/4) 1 Vern 221, 1 Eq Ca Ab 21.11, *Butcher v Stapeley & Butcher* (H1685/6) 1 Vern 363, 1 Eq Ca Ab 21.9, *Alsopp v Patten* (M1687) 1 Vern 472, 1 Eq Ca Ab 22.13, *Cookes v Mascall & Cookes* (H1687) 2 Vern 34, (H1690) 2 Vern 200, 1 Eq Ca Ab 22.28, *Douglas v Vincent* (H1690/1) 2 Vern 202, *Wheeler v Newton* (H1690/1) Pre Ch 16, 2 Eq Ca Ab 44.5, *Cass v Waterhouse* (M1691) Pre Ch 29, *Halfpenny v Ballet* (H1699/1700) 2 Vern 373, Pre Ch 402, 1 Eq Ca Ab 20.6, *Finch v Resbridger* (M1700) 2 Vern 390 (*Lord Guernsey v Rodbridges* (1708) Gilb R 3, 2 Eq Ca Ab 518, subs procs), *Lester v Foxcroft* (1700) Colles 108.

185 Yale Introduction to 73 SS, cii cites Clarke MR in *Dodsley v Kinnersley* (1761) Amb 403 at 406, where he says that patent cases are like "agreements before Lord Somers' time: the party was sent to law, and if he recovered an thing in damages, this Court entertained the suit".

186 This is the sort of procedural point which is commonly reported or included in practice books, so it is odd that the only evidence for it appears to be three highly ambiguous cases at

the analogous refusal of Chancery to relieve volunteers on contracts not enforceable at law[187]. If so, this would explain the apparent assumption that s 4 did apply in some way to bills for specific performance; and the part performance doctrine then could not be explained as *mere* continuance of the pre-Statute practice in equity.

If so, the doctrine of part performance does fall to be explained as an exception to s 4 constructed in equity. However, so far as the early cases give any explanation of the doctrine, (which is not common) it is not in terms either of the evidential advantages of equity, or of the argument advanced by Ballow in connection with the parol evidence rule that in natural law the gist of the matter is proof, not form[188]. Rather, the one explanation offered is that relief is given on the ground of fraud[189], the implicit assumption being that it is fraudulent to lead the other party on to perform their side of the bargain and then refuse to perform yours. Domat, who prefers writing to testimony, gives fraud (as well as duress and forgery) as an exception to this preference[190], and relief on the ground of fraud was a well-established branch of the equity jurisdiction[191]. It could also have been argued (though this does not appear in the cases) that if fraud was established there might have been a liability in damages for deceit at common law[192], so that equity was merely offering a better remedy.

---

the very beginning of the part performance doctrine (*Leake v Morris* (1682) Dick 14, 2 Ch Cas 135, *Hollis v Whiteing* (H1682-3) 1 Vern 151, 1 Eq Ca Ab 19.1 and *Hollis v Edwards* (P1683) 1 Vern 159, 1 Eq Ca Ab 19.2) and a *dictum* of Clarke MR seventy-eighty years after the event. It is also difficult to see how the strict procedure could be reconciled with the use of bills to get the defendant's answer to establish contractual liability at law. It therefore seems to me that Clarke MR's statement probably does not represent an oral tradition, but rather an *ex post facto* theorisation of *Leake v Morris* and the two *Hollis* cases. The reference to law in *Hollis v Whiteing* may be merely an unusual way of putting what was in substance a feigned issue to establish the facts. Ballow Bk I c 3 § 9 explains the cases as turning on s 1 (parol leases) rather than s 4.

187 Macnair, "Equity & Volunteers", above n 181.

188 Book VI c 2 § 3.

189 Besides the explicit references to fraud in *Thynn v Thynn* (H1684/5) above n 178, *Devenish v Baines* (H1689/90) Pre Ch 3, 2 Eq Ca Ab 43.4, *Floyd v Buckland* (M1703) 2 Freem 268, 2 Eq Ca Ab 44, Harv 1105 243, *Lammmas v Bayley* (M1708) 2 Vern 267, 1 Eq Ca Ab 22.14 and Cowper C's account, Pre Ch 402, of *Halfpenny v Ballet* (above n 184), it is possible that the requirement of a promise to enter a contract in writing in *Leake v Morris* (above n 184) and *Hollis v Whiteing* (above n 184) is an application of the idea which appears in more general terms in *Anon* (H1683-4) Skin 159, that the plaintiff can't rely on the defendant's fraud where he could have discovered it by due diligence; obviously, in the absence of a promise to make a contract in writing, the plaintiff would in substance be relying merely on his own ignorance of the law. Bacon's Abridgement, Title *Fraud,* subtitle (E) (fraud in equity) gives many of the part performance cases as instances.

190 Domat 3.6.2.5.

191 Jones, Ch 12.

192 Holdsworth HEL V 292, 416-7, VIII 67f; Bacon's Abridgement Title *Actions on the Case,* subtitle (E).

The "fraud" argument was still being used to justify the doctrine of part performance in the 1700s[193], by which time there was a substantial body of authority both in favour of the doctrine, and on what acts would or would not amount to part performance[194]. This latter body of doctrine pointed in the direction of part performance as an evidential substitute for writing; this first appears explicitly in the time of Lord Cowper[195].

It is possible either that what was really going on was in part simply a continuation of the existing equity rule, i.e. of allowing performance on one side as an alternative to writing, which then had to be *justified,* in response to arguments from the Statute, by reference to fraud; or, alternatively, that the Statute cut off the older doctrine and part performance then developed anew out of the general jurisdiction to relieve against fraud. However, neither scenario lends much support to the Wigmore-Holdsworth view of the Chancery adopting a "restrictive" construction of a statute addressed to jury trial problems. "Part performance" before the Statute was an exception to a requirement of writing *created in Chancery itself;* and the jurisdiction to relieve against fraud was absolutely general and only tenuously connected to problems of proof.

On the other side of the argument, i.e. to support the view that the Chancery did *not* take a particularly "restrictive" attitude to the Statute, are also five items of evidence.

(1) The Statute was on several occasions cited in equity to support a tough approach to the parol evidence rule[196]. This shows if anything a disposition to extend the operation of the Statute.

(2) There are thirteen cases on the "note or memorandum... signed by the party to be charged" required by s 4[197]. These cases certainly liberalised the previous rule in equity, but not so as to go beyond the words of the Statute; some of them

193 *Floyd v Buckland, Lamas v Bayley,* above n 189.

194 Cases cited above n 184, and *Pyke v Williams* (H1703) 2 Vern 455, 1 Eq Ca Ab 21.9, *Floyd v Buckland, Lamas v Bayley, Lord Pengall v Ross* (M1709) 2 Eq Ca Ab 46.12, *Hall v Butler* (H1710) 1 Eq Ca Ab 20.7.

195 *Hall v Butler,* above n 194: must be able to ascertain the terms of the contract.

196 *Towers v Moor* (P1689) 2 Vern 98, Lords Commissioners, *per cur; Falkland v Bertie* (1696) 2 Vern 333, at 337 per Treby CJ, at 339 per Holt CJ, as connected to the reasons for the Statute; *Strode v Falkland* (1708) 2 Vern 621, 3 Ch R 169, at 3 Ch R 184 *per* Tracy J. Wigmore, § 2426, saw the parol evidence rule as becoming generalised *as a result* of the Statute, and refers to the last two of these citations in that context, but this argument does not fit the chronology; for this question cf above § 1 *(2).*

197 *Moor v Hart* (1682) 1 Vern 110, (1683) 1 Vern 201, 2 Ch R 284, *Bird v Blosse* (P1683) 2 Vent 361, *Lowther v Carill* (H1683/4) 1 Vern 221, 1 Eq Ca Ab 21.11, *Hatton v Grey* (T1684) 2 Ch C 164, 1 Eq Ca Ab 21.10, *Cookes v Mascall & Cookes, Douglas v Vincent, Wheeler v Newton* above n 184, *Wanchford v Fotherley* (M1694) 2 Freem 201, 2 Vern 322, 1 Eq Ca Ab 22.17, *Holtham v Ryland* (P1697) Nels 205, 1 Eq Ca Ab 18.8, *Normanby v Devonshire* above n 183, *Coleman v Upcot* (H1706/7) 5 Viner 527.17, *Hall v Butler* above n 194, *Hodgson v Hutchinson* (1712) 5 Viner 522.34, 2 Eq Ca Ab 47.14.

make a point of distinguishing between contractual and pre-contractual documents[198], which shows an effort to apply the principles of the section rather than simply grabbing at anything to satisfy it.

(3) In the 1690s-1700s a line of cases suggested that the requirement in s 7 that a declaration of trust affecting land be "manifested and proved by some writing ..." had the effect either of abolishing or severely restricting the resulting trust arising from provision of purchase money, or of preventing the tracing of trust funds into realty, or both[199]. In view of s 8 (saving trusts arising by implication or construction of law) this is again an extension, rather than restriction, of the terms of the Statute.

(4) The trust of a term attendant on the inheritance was held to be realty and so subject to the provisions of s 5 in relation to wills of realty[200]. This was a logical construction, but not one strictly required by the terms of the Statute, which *prima facie* applied only to estates of freehold[201].

(5) In other cases on s 5 the Chancery was invited to find loopholes in the Statute and refused to do so – for instance, refusing to allow bad wills to be validated as appointments to charitable uses under the statute 43 Eliz c 4[202].

Taken together, I would argue that this evidence more than balances the evidence for restrictive construction of the Statute. It suggests, rather, that Chancery judges up to the reign of Anne continued in Lord Nottingham's view[203] that the

198 *Moor v Hart, Bird v Blosse, Cookes v Mascall & Cookes* before Jeffreys, (1687) 2 Vern 34, *Douglas v Vincent, Cass v Waterhouse.*

199 *Kirk v Webb* (M1698, T1699) 2 Freem 229, Pre Ch 84, Harv 1105 205, 2 Eq Ca Ab 743, Somers C assisted by Trevor MR and Powell J, *per* Powell J at Pre Ch 87, Somers C concurring, Trevor MR dissenting as to the reasoning, aff'd HL (Pre Ch 88); *Newton v Preston & al'* (M1699) Pre Ch 103, Powell J; *Halcott v Markant* (T1701) Pre Ch 168, 2 Eq Ca Ab 744.3, Trevor MR distinguishing *Kirk v Webb* but dismissing for inadequacy of proof; *Kinder v Miller* (M1701) Pre Ch 171, Trevor MR distinguishing *Kirk v Webb* but reversed, *Kendar v Milward* (M1702) 2 Vern 440, Wright LK; *Shales v Shales* (1701) 2 Freem 252, 1 Eq Ca Ab 382.9, Harv 1105 226, *per* Wright LK not possible after the Statute of Frauds to rebut presumption of advancement except by declaration in writing; *Skett v Whitmore* (P1705) 2 Freem 280, Harv 1105 255, Wright LK, *semble.*

200 *Tiffin v Tiffin* (H1680/1) Nott CC No 1091, (T1681) Nott CC No 1114, & other refs there; *Whitchurch v Whitchurch* (1724) above n 172; discussed Yale 79 SS Introduction, *154.*

201 "...Lands or Tenements, devisable either by Force of the Statute of Wills, or by this Statute, or by Force of the Custom of *Kent,* or the Custom of any Borough, or any other particular Custom ...". So wills of copyhold or leasehold were held to be outside the section: *AG v Baines* (M1707) 3 Ch R 150, 2 Vern 597, Pre Ch 271, Gilb R 5, 1 Eq Ca Ab 97.7.

202 *AG v Baines,* above n 201; *Jenner v Harper* (T1714) Pre Ch 389, Gilb R 44, 1 P Wms 247, 1 Salk 163.

203 "Of which the Lord Nottingham said that every line was worth a subsidy" – North, i, 141; & cf Nottingham's argument for narrowing the scope of trusts implied by law in the light of the statutory exception, *Elliot v Elliot* (M1677) at 79 SS 568, *Woodman v Morren* (T1678) at 79 SS 693 (2 Freem 32, HLS 1105 p 25, Atkins J).

Statute was an important measure of reform which required a purposive construction.

III. Conclusion: Preference for writings

Overall, therefore, considering both the specific rules of preference for writings and the requirements of writing both before and after the Statute of Frauds, it seems clear that in the seventeenth century there was in equity proof a fairly marked general preference for writings over witnesses. Documentary estoppels, though relieved against in certain circumstances, were accepted in others. The general parol evidence rule was recognised early, and the exceptions to it are fairly clearly exceptions. Equity developed its own requirements of writing before the Statute of Frauds, and in some respects the Statute may be regarded as carrying rules developed in equity into the common law. And the interpretation of the Statute in equity diplays overall a wish to implement its aims, in spite of the development of the part performance exception to s 4.

This preference for writings is not without exceptions, but some of these may have been based on the idea that the defendant's sworn confession in the answer was the highest form of proof. It is consistent with the roughly contemporary evolution of the european laws, but not dependent on it. But in the light of it, the Wigmore- Holdsworth argument that the parol evidence rule and the Statute of Frauds provided instances of a jury-free Chancery only gradually and partially accepting rules introduced at law to control the jury seems unacceptable.

Chapter Five

Proof by Witnesses – Principles and Procedure

Proof by witnesses is an aspect of the system of proof in equity which is procedurally most obviously akin to the system used in the learned laws[1], and both english civilians[2] and advocates of common law procedure[3] characterised it as such. However, some modern historians think that contemporary observers were misguided on this point. Wigmore argued that in relation to the competence of witnesses equity followed rules pragmatically developed in jury trial[4], and that the rule requiring two witnesses to make a proof was heavily diluted in equity by comparison with the learned laws[5]. More recently, Dawson argued that the mode of examining witnesses in Chancery was developed pragmatically and only bore a superficial similarity to the roman-canon system[6].

In this and the next three chapters, I aim to show that Wigmore's arguments in this respect were false, and that Dawson's, whether or not it is true of the late mediaeval origins of the equity jurisdiction, is not helpful in consideration of the early modern law of proof. In this period, equity followed essentially the same general principles in relation to witnesses as the roman-canon system.

The bulk of the material necessitates a division into several chapters. This Chapter gives an outline of the principles and procedure of proof by witnesses in the learned laws, and considers the procedure applied in the examination of witnesses in equity and the principles involved in this procedure. Chapter 6 covers the law relating to exceptions or objections to witnesses; Chapter 7 the compulsion of witnesses and its exceptions; and Chapter 8 the principles applied in determining the weight of testimony.

---

1 Cf Langdell 773, Millar "Prolegomena" in Engelmann at 60-1, 78.

2 Cosin III 53; Duck 329.

3 Sir Robert Atkyns, *An Enquiry into the Jurisdiction of the Court of Chancery* (London, 1695) 31; Gilbert, *Evidence* 44-5 (and the whole discussion of the topic in Gilbert *FR* 115-150 is founded on the belief that the Chancery procedure is a variant of the civilian procedure).

4 Below Ch 6 § 1.

5 Below Ch 8 § 3.

6 Dawson 145 f.

I. The principles of proof by witnesses in the learned laws

As already indicated in Chapter 1, the central rule of the roman-canon law of proof was the rule that two witnesses make a full proof[7]. Around this rule developed the general hierarchy of proofs; but also an extensive body of rules governing proof by witnesses. The object of these rules was to ensure that the "full proof" of two witnesses was of the highest possible standard.

(1) To make a full proof the witnesses must be *omni exceptione maiores*, not subject to any objection. There was a substantial body of the law about exceptions to witnesses, which might be based on status, intellectual incapacity, bad character or bias; some exceptions completely disqualified the witness, while others depended for their effect on the discretion of the judge. This topic is discussed further in Chapter 6.

(2) Witnesses were required to be sworn[8], and were liable to punishment for perjury[9], thus providing both spiritual and rather more immediate sanctions against perjury.

(3) The witnesses should be interrogated to establish the grounds and detail of their knowledge[10]. Their evidence must show internal consistency[11], and for a full proof the depositions of the required two witnesses must agree[12]. The latter rule reflects the two-witness rule: the fact that the witnesses corroborate one another is an important element in the weight of their testimony.

(4) Not merely the witnesses, but their testimony, must be independent of the parties. This principle found expression in a body of procedural rules designed to prevent perjury and subornation of perjury. (a) witnesses are compellable, and they must be compelled to attend rather than merely attending voluntarily[13]. Compulsion to testify and its exceptions is discussed further below Ch 7.

---

7 Discusssed further below Ch 8 § 3.

8 'Alciatus' 214v No. 5, form of oath 214v-215r; Maranta 561.1-3, 563-4.19; Cotta 868-871; Covarruvias *VR* ii c 13 No 3; *Reformatio* 245 c 5, form of oath 246 c 9; Gaill ii Obs 101 (form of oath at No 2); Vulteius 372r, 504v; Andrewes 81 cites Heb. 6, 16; Cosin i, 84; Clerke 43, 44; Fulbecke *PLN* 80r-v; Zouch *EI* 98, 99; Wiseman 17; Conset 113; Wood 317; Ayliffe 390-1, 536.

9 Fulbecke loc. cit. last n. says punishment for perjury is universal; Covarruvias *QP* 449-50 No. 8.

10 Maranta 562.9-18; Cotta 865-8, 880-1; *Reformatio* 254-5 c. 42, 259 c. 55; *Principia Quaedam* 29, 75; Vulteius 371v-372r; Zouch *EI* 90; Wood 319.

11 *Summa Angelica* 346 No 21 (cited *F&C* f 546r); Lyndwood 304, v. *Testium receptionem;* 'Alciatus' 208v Nos 22, 23; *Reformatio* 249 c 18; Vulteius 508r; Clerke 209-211; Conset 140; Wood 319.

12 Discussed below Ch 8 § 3..

13 'Alciatus' 213v-214r No. 1; Maranta 561.14; *Reformatio* 244 c 4, 247 c 13; Gaill ii Obs 100 No 1; Vulteius 503v; Cosin I 69, 72 (citing Lev. 5, 1), 74; Clerke 43, 49-51; Ridley 107; Zouch *EI* 98; Conset 109; Wood 317; Ayliffe 539.

(b) The witnesses are to be examined by the judge[14], or, where this is impractical, by officers (in the english civilian courts the Registrar) or commissioners appointed by the court[15], rather than by the parties. The extensive character of Clerke's discussion of commissions indicates that this was the normal practice in the Arches.

However, the procedure – at least that of the english civilian courts and the civilian sources used here – was not normally fully inquisitorial. The parties nominated the witnesses[16], and were in general entitled to be present, or at least cited to attend, when the witness was sworn (though not during the examination)[17]. The basis of the judge's examination of the witness was the articles served by the party proponent, and the adverse party had the right to serve interrogatories[18].

The interrogatories were subject to judicial control[19], and the judge or commissioners were to draw out the circumstances and grounds of the witness' knowledge, i.e. were not strictly limited to the words of the articles or interrogatories[20]. On the other hand, the witnesses are only to be examined to points at issue between the parties, and hence can only regularly be examined after *litis contestatio,* though there were exceptions to this rule[21].

(c) The witnesses are to be examined separately and secretly[22].

(d) The witnesses' testimony was written down in the form of depositions[23], which were then kept secret until the court ordered publication[24]. Witnesses were

---

14 Maranta 562.6; Wood 318.

15 'Alciatus' 214v No. 8; *Reformatio* 247 c 11; Clerke 54ff, 235-6; Wiseman 16; Conset 120 ff. The ultimate authority is *Novel* 90, 5. Cf also Cotta 611, notary cannot take oaths without a commission.

16 *Reformatio* 244 c 3.

17 'Alciatus' 214v No. 5; Maranta 561.1-3; Covarruvias *VR* ii c 13 No 15; *Reformatio* 245 c 5; Gaill ii Obs 94.4, 96.5, 102; Vulteius 372r-v; Clerke 43; Ayliffe 536.

18 For articles see above Ch 2 § 1, and 'Alciatus' 215r Nos 1-2. For interrogatories, 'Alciatus' 215v; Maranta 492.18-19, 583; *Reformatio* 245 cc 5, 6; Gaill ii Obs 95, esp No. 4, 102 No 2; Vulteius 503v; Clerke 43-4; Conset 114; Ayliffe 537.

19 Gaill ii Obs 95; Clerke 47, 49; Conset 144-7; Ayliffe 536, 541.

20 Above n 10; Gaill ii Obs 95 Nos 1, 7, and *Reformatio* 259 c 55, explicitly; but *contra,* 'Alciatus' 208v No 20, to disregard answers going beyond the interrogatories; Ayliffe 537, to hold the witness to the interrogaties exclusively.

21 'Alciatus' 209v No. 30; *Reformatio* 243-4 c 1; Gaill ii Obs 92; Vulteius 494r-v; Conset 106, 108.

22 'Alciatus' 209v No 38, 216v; Maranta 621.7; *Reformatio* 246 c 10; Gaill ii Obs 96 No 9; Vulteius 504v-505r; Clerke 47-8, 60; Conset 115-6, 127; Ayliffe 536. Lake, *Notes Touching the Amendment of Laws* (1663) 119 argues for the extension of the rule to the common law.

23 *Reformatio* 254 c 39; assumed elsewhere. This practice, though general, does not appear to be dictated by any principle of the law of proof, but rather by practical considerations, viz. (1) the examination of witnesses by persons other than the judge, whether examiners or commissioners (above n. 15), (2) the possibility of further witnesses being called during the

not generally to be re-examined[25]. After publication there could be no further examinations to the same articles[26].

The rules relating to exceptions and to the consistency of depositions were enforced by a procedure called *reprobatio*[27]. The parties could take exceptions to or protestations against the witnesses or to their depositions, which might then themselves be proved by further examinations[28]. A party could not impeach his own witness[29]. The proponent party could respond in support of the witness or impeach the impeaching witness, but the process was not allowed to go any further: *in testem testes et in hos, sed non datur ultra*[30].

The principles disclosed by the roman-canon rules are, then (1) that the witnesses should be reliable (*omni exceptione maiores*); (2) that their testimony should be internally consistent and corroborated; (3) that they should be sworn; and (4) that the taking of testimony should be independent of the parties, controlled by the court or officers appointed by it and kept secret from the parties. The first of these principles is discussed in Chapter 6, the second in Chapter 7. It remains to see how far the equity procedure for the examination of witnesses conformed to the remaining two; and (a separate but related question) whether the procedure for taking exceptions to witnesses conformed to the *reprobatio* procedure.

---

proof due to the exhibition of new positions and articles (above Ch 2 § 1), and (3) the possibility of appeals, and in this context the rule that all judicial acts must be notarised (Ayliffe 27).

24 On publication, 'Alciatus' 217r-v; Maranta 620-1; *Reformatio* 257 cc 50, 51; Clerke 67, 205-6; Ridley 80; Conset 134-5. On secrecy before publication, Maranta 618.56, 619.60.

25 The general rule and exceptions to it can be found at Lyndwood 304 v. *testium receptionem;* 'Alciatus' 208v No 15; Maranta 492.19; Cotta 876; *Reformatio* 251 c 28, 258 c 52; Conset 118-9; Ayliffe 541.

26 Lyndwood 313 v. *purgatio admittatur;* 'Alciatus' 209r-v No 29; Maranta 564.22; Cotta 877-8; *Reformatio* 227 c 9, 258 cc 52, 53; Covarruvias *QP* 448-9 No. 6; Gaill ii Obs 71 No 12, 105; Vulteius 503r; Clerke 217-9; Ridley 80; Conset 136-7; Ayliffe 541.

27 'Alciatus' 218v-219; *Reformatio* 249 c 55; Covarruvias *QP* 448.5 (not on appeal); Gaill ii Obs 105 Nos 8, 17; Vulteius 503r; Ayliffe 545. Maranta 623-7 calls the process 'testium repulsa'; Wood calls it 'objections' to witnesses.

28 The majority of our authors say that protestations against witnesses must be made before publication: 'Alciatus' 218v; Maranta 624.2; Covarruvias *QP* 448.5, (in appeals); *Reformatio* 245-6 c 8; Clerke 45; Conset 114; Ayliffe 537, 545. Clerke, however, says at one point that they may be made after publication. It is possible that the solution to this contradiction is the distinction between exceptions to the person of the witness and exceptions to the deposition.

29 Maranta 626.10, (exceptions) 11, 12; Vulteius 508r; Cosin i, 82 (used rhetorically); Clerke 45, 209-11; Ayliffe 539, 540. Maranta 625.4 and Ayliffe 540 add that protesting against a witness bars you from using anything he says in your favour.

30 Maranta 625.3 (cited *F&C* f 546v); Clerke 214-6, 221; Conset 139, 143-5; the quotation is at Clerke 216, Conset 145; also quoted by Hudson, 200, and Lord Nottingham, Prac. V. 6, *TT* 109.

II. The examination of witnesses in equity

The examination of witnesses gave rise to a large body of case-law. My concern here is not to examine this authority in detail (most of it concerns small points of procedure), but to draw out the principles it expresses. It is therefore convenient to proceed *prima facie* on the basis of the accounts of examination given by Jones for the early part of the period and Gilbert's *Forum Romanum* for the later part, only referring to the cases to the extent that it is necessary to supplement these accounts. The rules for examinations can also usefully be supplemented by consideration of the rules for the use of depositions from previous causes, which broadly speaking applied the same principles, but also showed some differences between equity and law.

In general the equity procedure for taking testimony is very similar to the forms of the roman-canon system[31]. More importantly, the principles applied seem to be broadly the same, though with some variations. (1) Examinations must be on oath, i.e. on a lawful oath, so the proceedings must be fully regular. This point is perhaps given rather more emphasis than in the roman-canon system. (2) The parties must not be given any opportunity to lead the witnesses or manufacture evidence. Accordingly (a) examinations must be by officers of the court, i.e. impartial persons appointed by the court; (b) they are to be on written interrogatories which are in principle to be checked by the Court for compliance with various rules, in particular that they are not to be leading; (c) they must be secret from the parties until the date of publication, when all the depositions are published; after publication no further depositions are to be taken; and (d) witnesses are not to be re-examined to the same point to "improve" their evidence. (3) The adverse party must have the opportunity to cross-examine. This rule is given more emphasis than in accounts of the roman-canon system, at least in the later part of the period.

1. Regularity of examination

The witnesses must be examined on a lawful oath. This implies that the court must have jurisdiction of the subject-matter of the examination[32], and that the parties must be properly at issue. This implied that depositions could not be taken until the pleadings in the cause were complete. In practice in the Elizabethan period examinations in Court could begin after the defendant had put in an acceptable answer, but a commission could not issue until after the plaintiff had replied and

31 Gilbert *FR* Ch 7 prefaces his account of examinations in equity with an account of the roman-canon procedure, drawn from various civilian sources, particularly Maranta and Gaill.

32 *R v Arundel & Howard* (T1616) Hob 109, Moo KB 832, at Hob 112. Cf Gaill ii Obs 101 No 7, consent of the parties will not cure want of jurisdiction in the court where depositions were taken.

served the defendant with a *subpoena ad rejungendum*[33]; by the early eighteenth century the *subpoena ad rejungendum* was necessary to all examinations[34]. The concern for regularity is not solely addressed to the lawfulness (and hence binding effect) of the oath; until the parties were effectively at issue, it would be (in theory) impossible to ascertain what questions were relevant or to examine completely[35].

It appears from the authorities that in practice these rules mainly affected the use of depositions from other courts (where there might be objection to the jurisdiction) and from previous proceedings[36]. It is convenient to distinguish the two issues of (a) jurisdiction and (b) joinder of issue.

a) jurisdiction: Gilbert says that

> "Depositions taken in the Spiritual Court in a Cause relating to Lands can't be read, because they are no Oaths at all, in as much as the Spiritual Courts have no Authority to take Depositions relating to Lands; but it seems they may be read when taken in a Cause in which they have Authority, as far as relates to that Cause, in as much as these are lawful Oaths, and a Man may be indicted for the Violation of them, though they be not Oaths in a Court of Record"[37].

The rule that the court where the depositions were taken must have jurisdiction dates back to the early seventeenth century[38], but the rationale given by Gilbert is not given elsewhere[39].

---

33 Jones p 239. See also Add 20700 f11b, no examinations before answer "*quia nulla lis contestata est*"; *Observations* f 452r No 131, f 470v No 238, f 472v No 250.

34 Gilbert *FR* 122, Bacon p 297 (This section of Bacon is clearly derived from Gilbert, *FR* Ch 7). In the later seventeenth century cases on depositions the objection is usually that the depositions were taken before answer.

35 Gilbert *FR* 115-6, discussing the romano-canonical rules; more briefly Bacon p 297.

36 It may be that when examinations were accidentally taken early the parties did not usually object, in order to save the cost of a new commission, unless there was some other objection. These reasons would not affect depositions from prior causes and other courts.

37 *Evidence* 67-8. MSS sidenote "Oath in a spiritual Court" and cite 2 Sid 454, March 20, Style 10; printed text March 120, Style 1, and adds Cro Jac 463, [Nelson] L.E. 115 pl 80. The references in the printed text are more accurate than those in the MSS; but only March 120 (below n 32) and that in the MSS to Siderfin are relevant: *Anon* (P1670) 1 Sid 454, perjury in the ecclesiastical court is punishable on indictment. Cro Jac 463 and Style 1 concern the admission of sentences in the ecclesiastical courts, and the reference to Nelson cites 2 Rol. Abr. 679.3, depositions before commissioners of bankrupts excluded on the ground of want of cross-examination.

38 *R v Arundel & Howard* (T1616) Hob 109 (depositions before the Council in the North excluded in Star Chamber by Egerton C, Coke and Hobart CJJ, and Caesar MR for want of jurisdiction on the matter examined to; though in Star Chamber, the case was cited as an authority in Chancery (Nott Proleg 29.2, *TT* p 316).

39 Some common lawyers in the early to mid-century excluded depositions in the ecclesiastical courts altogether on the ground that they were not taken in a court of record: *Anon* (M1641) March 120, per Banks CJ; but this comes to the same point, since Chancery depositions, which were not records unless exemplified, were admissible, so that the point of saying the ecclesiastical court is not of record must be to take it out of the Statute of Perjury so that

b) Joinder of issue: In general to make depositions in previous Chancery causes admissible it was necessary to produce bill and answer[40]. Problems arose because if the defendant delayed answering and the plaintiff was afraid his witnesses might die he could have them examined *de bene esse* by leave of the court before the answer came in[41]. The common law courts seem at first to have taken a fairly strict attitude to these depositions. In – *v Brown* (M1662)[42] the witness had been examined by the defendant before answer and had died twenty days after answer without being re-examined. The Exchequer took the advice of all the judges and ruled that the deposition could not be read because it had been taken before issue, the witness could have been examined after issue, and the defendant did not appear to be in contempt. In *Marsden v Bound* (T1685)[43] on a bill to examine witnesses for use at law the plaintiff examined witnesses *de bene esse* before answer in Michaelmas vacation; the defendant, who, though the parties were not at issue, had sent commissioners to the examination, answered in Hilary term, and one of the witnesses died five weeks later; on being told that the deposition would be excluded at law, Lord Guilford ordered the defendant not to oppose its admission at the trial.

In *Howard d. Langford v Tremaine*[44] two witnesses who had been examined *de bene esse*[45] died before the defendant put in an answer[46]. Their depositions were admitted at *nisi prius* but judgement stayed for the opinion of the Court, and the

---

(on one view) a false oath would not be punishable. In most cases it is hard to see how depositions in the church court could be used, since if the church court was properly seised of the matter the sentence would be conclusive one way or the other; but cf *Danby's Case* (1638) Clayt 62 pl 107 (church court depositions admitted in case (defamation? contract?) against a parish clerk.

40 *In equity: semble,* since special reasons are given to admit depositions without bill and answer, *R v Arundel & Howard,* supra n 31 (Star Chamber); *Floyer v Strachley* (1631) Nels 13 (Chancery, Lord Coventry assisted by all the judges); *Backhouse v Middleton* (M1669) 1 Ch Cas 173, 2 Freem 132, 3 Ch Rep 39, at 1 Ch Cas 175 *per* counsel *arg. At law: Aldbroke's Case* (1632) Clayt 9 pl 17; – *v Brown* (M1662) Hardr 315 (Ex (L), citing *Colt v Dutton* in KB (probably SC, but not SP (M1657) 2 Sid 2)); *Bray v Whitelage* (undated) T. Raym 335 (commission of review, per Ellis J citing *Colt v Dutton*); *Marsden v Bound* (T1685) 1 Vern 331 *per* Maynard Sjt *arg; Howard v Tremaine* (1692) Carth 265, 1 Salk 278, 4 Mod 146, 1 Show KB 363. Gilbert *Evidence* 63-6 discusses the whole issue (p 65 para 2 to p 66 para 1 in the printed text appears from the MSS to be transposed with p 63 para 2 to p 65 para 1).

41 *Jennings v Sayler* (M1575 or 6) (M18 Eliz) *The Practice of the High Court of Chancery* (1651) p 9; *More v More* (1645) Harl 1576 f 229, ——— *v Brown,* above n 40. Compare Gaill ii Obs 92 Nos 2-7, Vulteius 494r-v, Wood 318, all giving examination *in perpetuam memoriam* as an exception to the rule against examination before *litis contestatio*.

42 Above n 40.

43 Above n 40.

44 (T,M1692) 1 Salk 278, 4 Mod 146, 1 Show KB 363, (H1692-3) Carth 265.

45 According to Salkeld (p 278), with the defendant joining in the commission and cross-examining.

46 According to Modern (p 146), the answer did not come in until two years later, but according to Carthew (p 265) the plaintiff had not taken out any process of contempt.

case was extensively argued. The plaintiffs argued essentially on the basis of the Chancery practice and the inconvenience of excluding the depositions[47]. Tremain Sjt for the defendants argued that the witnesses could not be prosecuted for perjury because there was no issue for their answers to relate to, and that depositions cannot be admitted without an answer[48]. At first Holt CJ was inclined to exclude the deposition, on the basis that before the parties are at issue the court cannot have power to examine the witnesses, so that the point is the same as that of jurisdiction[49], and Dolben J "doubted", while Gregory and Eyre JJ favoured admissibility, Eyre J arguing that refusal to admit depositions in these circumstances would defeat the purpose of examination *in perpetuam rei memoriam*[50]; eventually the Court seems to have agreed that they were admissible on this ground[51].

Gilbert[52] in the *Evidence* identifies the objection as the lack of an opportunity to cross-examine, and says that depositions in these circumstances are not admissible at law, but that it is possible to obtain an order from Chancery to compel the adverse party to consent to the their being read. In the *Forum Romanum* he does not discuss the question of admissibility at law, but explains the possibility of examination *de bene esse* by reference to the existence of examination *in perpetuam memoriam* in the civil law[53]. The interest in this point is not the procedural point itself, but the conflicting effects of the principles of jurisdiction/ regularity and cross-examination/ mutuality, and the influence of the equity practice on the common law, in *Howard v Tremaine*[54].

---

47 Modern p 146, Shower p 363.

48 Shower p 363.

49 Shower p 364.

50 Shower. Modern has a different account of what the court said at this stage:
"Nothing can make it evidence but the necessity of the thing. It is true, in cases of wills it may be necessary to examine witnesses to perpetuate their testimony, but in this case the plaintiff was nonsuited upon evidence *viva voce*, and afterwards exhibited a bill, and obtained these depositions upon examination of his own witnesses, which is but paper evidence at best, and therefore they inclined not to allow it. *Tamen Quaere.*"

51 The editor of the third edition of Gilbert cites this case as an example of the best evidence rule.

52 p 47.

53 FR 140-1, Bacon 304-5. For examination *in perpetuam memoriam* in equity cf Jones 254-263 and below Ch 10 § 1 *(1)*.

54 Two other points can be noted. There had to be an answer at some stage, because otherwise it was not possible to say that the issue was the same as the present issue: *Aldbroke's Case*, above n 40. And the depositions were admissible if the bill was dismissed for want of equity, but not if it was dismissed for irregularity: *Backhouse v Middleton*, above n 40; *Smith v Veale* (1700) 1 Ld Raym 735.

2. Control of examination by the court and safeguards against subornation

a) Examination by officers of the court

In the learned laws, witnesses were required to attend for judicial examination, not merely to give evidence by letter[55]. The same rule was applied in Chancery under Egerton: 'testimonials' for overseas were unacceptable, and so were 'depositions' by letter sent to the commissioners[56].

The equity courts never deviated in theory from the principle that the examination of witnesses was to be by officers of the court and not by the parties or their agents. There was an official Examiner in Chancery from the early Tudor period and two from the 1530s[57]; examinations in the Exchequer were in theory before the individual Barons, in practice before examiners appointed by them[58]. From the later sixteenth century these officials handled only examinations in London and its immediate vicinity. Chancery had from an early date made use of lay commissioners to take answers and examinations of witnesses who were unable to attend the court for examination[59], and in the later sixteenth century and the first half of the seventeenth examination by commissioners became the norm outside London[60].

The use of commissioners was Dawson's primary argument for a sharp distinction between equity proof and roman-canon proof. In fact, however, this argument is misplaced: commissions to examine witnesses were regularly used in the learned laws[61]. Authority to use them was founded on *Novel* 90, 5, which *inter alia* allowed what would now be called letters of request to judges in other provinces to examine witnesses resident within their jurisdictions. From this starting point, two types of commissions had developed in the practice of the Court of Arches, as described by Clerke. The first was the commission out of the jurisdiction, which was addressed to the judge having jurisdiction where the witnesses resided[62]. The second was the commission to examine witnesses who lived remote from the court, though within the jurisdiction, and for some reason could not attend to give evidence in court. Here the court appointed commissioners, but by the 1590s the prac-

---

55 D. 22.5.3.3 & 4; reproduced, *Reformatio* 251 c 26, Covarruvias *VR* ii c 13 No 6, Gaill ii Obs 100 No 21, Zouch *EI* 99, Domat 3.6.3.18, Wood 317.

56 *Observations* f 439r No 23 for 'testimonials', 479r No 284 for depositions by letter. *Forme et Certenty* f 545r cites the roman rule from the *Leges Visigothorum* (II, 4, 7).

57 Jones pp135-6; Jones pp 135 ff discusses the examiners and their contest with the Six Clerks for control of examinations by commission, and the settlement of the geographical limit on commissions.

58 Bryson pp 135-6.

59 Dawson, Lay Judges p 150.

60 Jones, loc cit above n 57.

61 Above n 15.

62 Clerke 235-6 tit. 167; Conset 121-2. Cf also Vulteius 505r.

tice was for the parties to nominate four each and the court to select two from each side[63]. In this feature, the seventeenth century practice of the equity courts was identical[64].

Dawson's claim that the law of proof could not be applied because the commissioners were laymen[65] cannot be supported: in the first place the control in the learned laws of the legal effect of the examinations operated either before the examination, by judicial control of articles/ interrogatories[66], or after, by *reprobatio/* exceptions to witnesses[67], and secondly, ordinances cited by van Espen make clear that the european church courts had problems not unlike those faced by equity of the commissioners producing useless depositions[68]; and comments by Clerke indicate the that problems could arise in examinations by the, *professional*, Registrar of the court due to incomprehension of complex interrogatories[69].

However, it does seem that during the seventeenth century there was in Chancery there was something of a shift away from a view of commissioners as judicial officers, to one of them as perhaps somewhat suspect party nominees. According to Jones, up to the Elizabethan period commissions for examination seem to have had something of the same inchoate character as the commissions of the peace and of assize[70]. The commissioners for country examinations would at this period in Chancery be local county notables[71], and commissions often included a large number of commissioners, with a quorum of two, though a common number was four[72]. Commissions to hear and determine the cause were often combined with commissions to examine witnesses[73]. In the Star Chamber, commissioners were Justices of the Peace[74]; so it is possible that Jones' county notables were Justices

---

63 Clerke 54-6 tit. 45 (the practice of party nominations, said to be recent and to give rise to abuses, at 55-6); Conset 122-5. Cf Gaill ii Obs 96 No 1; Vulteius 501v-503r.

64 Stowe 415 f 197 says that the parties name commissioners in turn. The normal practice from the seventeenth century was for four to be nominated by each side, two of whom would be struck out leaving a total of four: for Chancery, Bryson 130 for the Exchequer, Tothill *Proceedings* 9 (1649), Gilbert FR 126, Bacon 197 ; for Star Chamber, Hudson 182; the total number also appears to be four in Isaack Cotton on Star Chamber Practice, Add 41661 f 87.

65 At 154-5.

66 Above § 1 nn 18-19; below § 2 *(2)* (b).

67 Above § 1 nn 27-30; below § 2 *(4)*.

68 3.7.6.37, Mechlin provincial ordinances, not to make depositions unnecessarily verbose; ib. 8, not to say merely that the witness corroborated another or said that the article in question was true. On the second of these points cf also Gaill ii Obs 104 No 5.

69 Clerke 49; Conset 117.

70 Jones 240-1.

71 Jones 240.

72 Jones 240.

73 Jones 141.

74 Isaac Cotton on Star Chamber practice, Add 41661 f 85b-6, 87b. Hudson 182 says that commissioners to take the defendant's answer must be 'gentlemen of credit and worship', but

of the Peace or equivalent, too[75]. In this case the commission would be a form intermediate between the civilian commission out of the jurisdiction, addressed to a local judge, and commission within the jurisdiction (since the Justices of the Peace' jurisdiction was not one autonomous from the central jurisdictions)[76]. Justices of the Peace are not exactly 'laymen' in the examination of witnesses, at least for the tasks required of commissioners in civilian procedure.

By the end of the period commissioners were "generally country attorneys"[77] rather than county notables. It is possible that there is a connection between this decline in social status and the indications of distrust of commissioners which may be found in the later part of the period[78], both on the basis that they are nominated by the parties[79] and because, unlike the examiners, they were not sworn to keep the depositions secret[80]. Paradoxically, the varying frequency of reported cases of irregularities tends to suggest that the 'country attorneys' were less prone to misconduct due to bias than were the 'gentlemen of quality' of the Elizabethan and Jacobean period. They were certainly no more 'laymen' than Justices of the Peace were.

Nonetheless, examination on commission was still to be considered as examination by persons authorised by and under the control of the court. Though the commissioners were nominated by the parties[81], in theory they were required to be impartial, and various exceptions relating to bias could be taken to the nominees[82].

---

at 183 that the default position if the plaintiff fails to join in commission is for the court to appoint four JPs living near the defendant. The assumption that they were JPs appears in *Lord Dudley's Case* (H1593/4) Hawarde 10, St. Ch., where quarter sessions is said to be no excuse for the non-attendance of commissioners at examination because the parties could have chosen another date, and in *Peacock's Case* (T1611) 9 Co Rep 70b, where a commissioner was removed from the commission of the peace for misconduct in Star Chamber examinations.

75 In *Moor v Foster* (P1605) Cro Jac 65, a defamation case, for a Chancery commissioner to hear & determine to take bribes is said to deserve "to be put out of every commission".

76 A Chancery form more exactly analogous to the commission out of the jurisdiction was the commission to a foreign Christian country, which went to the court having jurisdiction and could, therefore, be granted *ex parte* ('on petition'); in contrast, commissions to non-Christian countries required a motion, because the court had to appoint commissioners. See *Observations* f 441r No. 37.

77 Gilbert FR 135, Bacon p 301.

78 Notably the introduction of new rules tying the examiners more closely to the interrogatories (below nn nn 99-101 and text there) and the different approach of the court to new examinations after examination in the office and after a commission (below nn 79, 80).

79 *Andrews v Brown* (P1714) Pre Ch 385, Gilb R 41 (SR).

80 *Pearson v Rowland* (H1715-6) 2 Swan 266n. A General Order of 1722 required commissioners to be sworn in the same terms as the examiners: Bacon p 302.

81 Above n 64.

82 Stowe 415 f 197, Tothill *Proceedings* 21, Brown *Praxis* 17; cf Cotton Add 41661 f 87; solicitor to party not to be commissioner, *Fortescue & Coake's Case* (1613) Godb. 193, *per cur;* nor solicitor's clerk to be clerk to commissioners, *Newton v Foot* (1686) Dick. 793. On the other hand, it was misconduct for the plaintiff's commissioners to examine on the defendant's interrogatories or *vice versa*, *Observations* f 477r No. 22.

b) Examination on interrogatories

The drafting of the interrogatories was (at least in theory) the only contribution of the parties, or rather their lawyers, to the examination of the witnesses. In theory in the late sixteenth and early seventeenth century interrogatories were supposed to be filed with the court and checked by a Master before examinations began or a commission was issued[83]. They were not to be irrelevant or scandalous[84], to be designed to discredit witnesses[85], or to be leading[86], Jones says, however, that this system seems to have broken down in practice[87]; and Gilbert says of the interrogatories that "by consent of the parties they are delivered to the commissioners at the opening of the commission"[88], which rather excludes any prior checking. According to *Baker v Cole* (1612)[89] the commissioners were not entitled to decide that interrogatories were irrelevant.

The back-up was for the witness to demur to objectionable interrogatories[90]. This suggests that the witnesses were either knowledgeable about the law, or advised by lawyers in answering, or prepared in advance by the parties with a view either to a genuine objection, or to make possible a re-examination, since if, after publication, the demurrer was rejected, a re-examination would be necessary[91]. It seems from *Hawtre v Lady Wallop* (1666-7)[92] that by the 1660s witnesses were not allowed either copies of the interrogatories or the assistance of counsel, since the court there permits these advantages to defendants who are to be examined to perfect their answers[93]. By 1683 it was not possible to demur to interrogatories as irrelevant[94]; however, the demurrer to interrogatories continued to be used to raise questions of privilege up to the early nineteenth century[95].

In his report of *Peacock's Case* Coke says that the Examiners and Commissioners are "not strictly tied to the words of the interrogatories, but to explain every

---

83 Jones 242-3; cf above n 19.

84 Jones 243-4; for relevance, cf. civilian sources above nn 18, 21; for scandal, above Ch 2 § 2 *(1)* (b), below Ch 7 § 3 *(1)*.

85 Jones 244.

86 Coke Fourth Institute p 279; Jeffreys' Order of April 1687, i Sanders 374; *Despard v Ormsby* (1713) Colles 459 (complained of by counsel for the appellant); Gilbert FR 148-9, Bacon 303-4.

87 Jones p 243.

88 Gilbert FR 126, Bacon p 299.

89 (H1611/12) *The Practice* (1651) p 14, Cotton Add 41661 f 136b.

90 Jones p 243.

91 Ib.

92 Nels 119; 1 Ch Rep 265 not SP.

93 Compare (& contrast) Maranta 551 No 16, on examination of parties advocates & proctors not allowed, making an exception in the case of 'in rustico vel ideota'.

94 *Ashton v Ashton* (P1683) 1 Vern 165, 1 Eq Ca Ab 41.11 (North LK).

95 *Parkhurst v Lowten* (1818) 2 Swanst 194 (and notes there).

thing also which necessarily riseth thereupon"[96] and in the Fourth Institute he says that the commissioners or Examiner ought not to interrupt the witness and ought to read the deposition over to the witness and "suffer them to explain themselves"[97]. Hudson, commenting on *Peacock's Case,* attributes the rule to the civil law[98]. In 1649, however, the Parliamentary Commissioners made a General Order requiring the commissioners to hold the witness strictly to the interrogatories and not permit departures[99]. This Order was adopted by Clarendon[100] and subsequently followed. It implies a decline in the status or authority of commissioners and (whatever abuse promoted it) must have contributed considerably to the decay of the system[101].

c) Secrecy

The object of the secret examination of witnesses was the same as that of the examination of witnesses by impartial officers of the court: to prevent the parties tampering with the witnesses to "improve" their evidence in the knowledge of what had been said on the other side[102]. The rule itself was simple. The examiners were sworn on taking office to keep depositions secret until publication[103]; at least in the Exchequer, the witnesses were sworn on giving evidence not to reveal the evidence they had given until publication[104], and after 1722 the commissioners and their clerks were sworn to keep the depositions secret until publication[105].

96 9 Rep 70b. Cf, for slightly different wording, 4th Inst p 278. The case was citable by civilians on church court procedure: Helmholz, *Roman Canon Law*... 131 n 32.

97 Fourth Inst p 278.

98 P. 203. Compare Gaill ii Obs 95 Nos 1, 7; Vultieus 503v.

99 i Sanders 227-8.

100 i Sanders 302; cf Nott Prac. Title V No 8, *TT* p 110. In contrast, however, Lord Nottingham includes the rule stated in *Peacock's Case* (Title IV No 12, TT p 107, Title V No 6, TT p 109).

101 Holdsworth HEL IX p 355-6 describes the terminal decay of the system from the evidence given to the 1826 Chancery Commission, and in particular problems stemming from the incomprehensibility of the interrogatories to the witnesses. Interrogatories seem already to have been phrased in legalese in the late sixteenth century (Jones p 238; & cf Clerke, above n 69 for the same problem in the ecclesiastical courts); the disappearance of the commissioners' discretion as a result of the Order of 1649 must have exacerbated the problem.

102 See Clerke 47-8, Conset 115-6, Ayliffe 536; and compare the common-law rule that witnesses are to attend outside court until called (Wigmore § 1837). It seems that a similar rule applied to examinations on commission in the later seventeenth century, since there are two decisions that commissioners could themselves be witnesses, but in this case must be examined before the other witnesses: *Anon* (M1681) 2 Ch Cas 79; *Bright v Woodward* (H1686) 1 Vern 369, 1 Eq Ca Ab 225.9 (Jeffreys C).

103 Jones 139.

104 Bryson 139 gives no date, but it seems unlikely that so obvious a loophole would have been left alone by the Order of 1722.

105 Above n 80. 1726 in the Exchequer: Bryson p 130.

After publication there were to be no examinations without leave of the Court[106]. In practice parties could obtain an order to postpone publication on affidavit of not having seen the depositions[107], and in certain circumstances leave to examine after publication[108]; these rules became the basis for various procedural manoeuvres designed to delay the cause or embarrass the other party[109]. The principle remained, and also gave rise to subsidiary rules about additional examinations of new witnesses, or of the same witnesses on new interrogatories, before publication but after a commission had been executed[110].

d) Re-examination

Like the rules for "official" examination and secrecy, the purpose of this rule was to prevent the parties tampering with the witnesses. The rule is generally stated as a flat prohibition on re-examining the same witness to the same interrogatory or matter[111]. A logical limit on it was that where the witness' prior depositions were suppressed for irregularity or otherwise inadmissible, it was possible to obtain leave to re-examine[112]; a corollary was to bar cross-bills after publication and new examinations on bills of review on new matter and new bills brought after previous bills had been dismissed without prejudice[113].

The basic rule itself was problematic in practice in view of the defects of the system of examination on interrogatories. Civilian doctrine generally allowed the witness to correct him or her self immediately, but whether re-examination for this purpose after publication was acceptable was arguable[114]. A note in "Keilwey"

---

106 Jones 248-250; Bacon LK's Orders, Sanders 119; Hudson 211-214; Order of 17 November 1635, Sanders p 179; 1649 Orders, Sanders p 229; Lord Clarendon's Orders, Sanders 301.

107 *Tilney v Johnson* (n.d.) *Observations* f 443r No. 51; Stowe 415 f 197b, Gilbert *FR* 144-6, Bacon p 298. Cf 'Alciatus' 217r-v; Clerke 67, 205-6; Conset 134-5.

108 Gilbert FR 146, Bacon pp 298, 303 says that it is possible to obtain an order to postpone publication after publication is already passed, (cf Nott Prac V.13, *TT* p 111) and also (pp 301-2) that it is possible to examine witnesses at or after the hearing to prove exhibits.

109 *Anon* (M1684) 1 Vern 253, 1 Eq Ca Ab 233.5; *Allanson v Doulben* (1703) Colles 299, HL; 1 de G F & J 477, 479n, (LK) not SP; Gilbert *FR* 146-7.

110 *Hungate v Crooke* (1613) Toth 190; *Lewis v Owen* (1637) Toth 112, Dick 2, i Sanders 201; *Andrews v Brown* (P1714) Pre Ch 385, Gilb Rep 41, 1 Eq Ca Ab 233.6, 2 Eq Ca Ab 490.5; *Pearson v Rowland* (H1715-6) 2 Swans 266n.

111 Nott Prac V.13, *TT* p 111.

112 Hudson 211-2; *Exton v Turner* (M1681) 2 Ch Cas 79 ((T1679) Nott CC No 1043 not SP). Cf Maranta 492 No 19, 583-4, if no cross-examination; Gaill ii Obs 105 Nos 12, 13.

113 *Observations* f 443r No 52; Nott Prac V.13, *TT* pp 111-2.

114 Lyndwood 304 v *testium receptionem;* 'Alciatus' 208v No 15; Cotta 876, 877-8; *Reformatio* 258 c 52; Conset 118-9. Ayliffe 541 says that re-examination is in the discretion of the judge and not allowed after publication.

says that new proofs can be taken to explain obscurities (though not in contradiction of previous depositions)[115]; but in *Chamberlaine v Pope* (1597)[116] it is said that a mistaken deposition cannot be amended after publication, and in *Randal v Richford* (1663)[117] a special commission to re-examine a deaf witness who realised before publication that he had mistaken his evidence and the depositions taken on it were suppressed. However, in *Callow v Mince* (M1704)[118] counsel *arg* says that a witness is not to be examined twice to the same matter *without leave of the court,* and the editor of *Equity Cases Abridged* (1730s) notes against *Randal v Richford* that in his time the practice was, by motion producing an affidavit that the witness had been "surprised" at the examination, to have the witness examined by the examiner in Court or viva voce at the hearing[119].

3. Cross-examination

The rule requiring that the adverse party should have the opportunity to cross-examine corresponds to the civilians' requirements of notice and opportunity to present interrogatories[120]. The requirement of an opportunity to cross-examine finds expression in the requirement that the parties should be at issue[121], in procedural rules requiring notice to be given to the adverse party of examinations in the office and of commissions[122], and in the requirement for admissibility of depositions in prior causes that the party against whom the depositions are to be used must either have himself had the opportunity to cross-examine, or claim under someone who had the opportunity to cross-examine[123].

Examples of this rule were that depositions taken in bankruptcy proceedings could not be used[124], because the proceedings were not inter partes; that deposi-

115 Keilw. 96; cited *F&C* f 546v, Nott Proleg 29.6, *TT* p 317.

116 Toth 77.

117 Nels 92, 1 Ch Cas 25, 2 Freem 178, 1 Eq Ca Ab 102.3. That the witness was deaf appears from a note in Freeman.

118 Pre Ch 234, 2 Vern 472, 1 Eq Ca Ab 223.2.

119 1 Eq Ca Ab 102.3. There is no discussion of this point in Gilbert *FR*.

120 Above nn 18, 19.

121 Above § 2 *(1)*.

122 Gilbert *FR* 125-6, 135, Bacon pp 298, 300, 301.

123 Nott Prac V.18-21, *TT* pp 113-4; *Tolson v Lamplugh* (1669) 2 Ch Rep 43; *Backhouse v Middleton*, above n 40; *Lambert v Bainton* (M1670) Nott Proleg 29.1, *TT* pp 315-6, *per* Finch *arg; Gargrave alias Fan v* —— (H1677) 2 Ch Cas 250 (Delegates; the cross-examination in Chancery barring an exception to the witness); *Barstow v Palmes* (M1704) Pre Ch 233, 2 Eq Ca Ab 490.2 (co- defendants can use depositions against one another in a subsequent cause). Gilbert *Evidence* p 47 says that depositions can only be used against former parties. A party's own deposition as a witness in a prior cause could presumably be used against him as a confession (above Ch 2 § 2 *(3)*).

tions taken against a tenant for life or in tail could not be used against subsequent tenants in tail, remaindermen or reversioners, because these did not claim under the former party[125]; and that if a husband refused to join in his wife's bill to examine witnesses *in perpetuam memoriam,* he would have to be made a defendant so that the depositions could be used against him[126]. It seems that the depositions must also be usable against the proponent, for reasons of mutuality[127].

4. Reprobatio?

In the civilian procedure, exceptions to witnesses fell into two classes, those to the person and those to the deposition[128]. Objections to the person should be taken by protestation before the witness was sworn, though this was subject to exceptions[129], while those to the depositions fell to be taken after publication (obviously). Exceptions to the person which involved bad character could not be established by cross-examination, since witnesses were not obliged to answer incriminating or defamatory interrogatories[130]. These exceptions, and others which could be taken after publication, fell to be proved by the process called *reprobatio*, a special probatory term to impeach witnesses or their depositions[131]. Gilbert in the *Forum Romanum* describes a substantially identical procedure as applying to exceptions to witnesses in Chancery, but says (in effect) that it is obsolescent[132]. The immediate picture that would be derived from this is of a *reprobatio* procedure originally being applied but subsequently decaying. The difficulty is that the earlier authorities are not as clear as this, and Gilbert's account may be given a spurious clarity by his general assumption that the equity procedure is *simply* civilian in origin[133]. The earlier authorities do, however, suggest that some sort of specific procedure was followed.

---

124 Nott. Proleg. 29.7, *TT* p 317, citing Rolle Abridgment, *Trial* B pl 9; *Greenwood v Knipe* (M1677) Nott CC No 754, 79 SS 571.

125 *Earl of Peterborough v Duchess of Norfolk* (1702) 2 Freem 264, Pre Ch 212, (Wright LK) aff'd HL *Earl of Peterborough v Germaine* 3 Bro PC 539 (6 Bro PC 1 not SP).

126 *Bowyer & Tufton v Tufton, Welsh & al'* (H1662) Nott Proleg 29.15, *TT* p 319.

127 *Rushworth & al' v Countess of Pembroke and Currier* (H1667-8) Hardr 472 (Ex(E)); *Lambert v Bainton,* above n 123 (Bridgman LK); Gilbert *Evidence* p 47. Not all the cases seem to fit well with this rule, but it was always possible for the party who wished to use the depositions to consent to their use against him, as Finch did in *Lambert v Bainton.*

128 Lyndwood 304 v *testium receptionem;* Maranta 624 No 2; *Reformatio* 259 c 54, 287 c 20; Vulteius 507v; Conset 140; Wood 319; Ayliffe 254-5, 588.

129 Above n 28.

130 Below ch 7 § 3 *(1).*

131 Above nn 27-30 and text there.

132 *FR* 147-8, Bacon 303.

133 Compare *FR* 124-5 where he deduces from this view that examinations were originally by the Master of the Rolls as a judge of the court and on the basis of the bill serving as a

A note in "Keilwey" says generally that exceptions to witnesses must be taken before publication[134]. *Observations* says in one place that parties may move before or after publication for leave to examine to the bad character of witnesses, but elsewhere that exceptions to witnesses may be established either by cross-examination or by regular examination of other witnesses[135]. In 1599 Gawdy J sitting in Chancery ruled that though there were to be no interrogatories to credit, if a case on examination depended on the evidence of one or two witnesses, examination to credit *ad informandam conscientiam judicis* might be allowed[136]; this implies that such examinations will be after publication, as it is only at this point that the special circumstances will emerge. Bacon's Orders of 1618 provide for examinations to credit only on special order to be sparingly granted[137]. Isaack Cotton on Star Chamber similarly has the rule that examination to credit is to be only on special order; also that if it is proposed to suppress depositions for procedural irregularity this must be moved before publication[138], which implies that other objections could come after publication. In *Nurse v Mossam* (M1635)[139] it was ruled that the party seeking to examine to credit must set down exceptions in writing and obtain leave, and this was followed in the 1649 Orders, Clarendon's Orders, and Lord Nottingham's *Practice*[140].

Lord Nottingham, in addition, (1) restated the rule in "Keilwey" that exceptions must be taken before publication[141], and applied it[142], and (2) wrote that after examination to credit there could be a further examination to impeach the impeaching witnesses, but no more[143]. Hudson says of the Star Chamber that "it is a firm and constant rule, as well in this court as in all laws, that no man shall be received to except against a witness as incompetent, if he examine him also himself"[144]. The civilian sources I have used do not have this rule, though it may be derived

libellus articulatus; contrast Dawson 150, commissions used from the 1450s, and 151, Master of the Rolls examining a witness *on interrogatories,* Jones 55f for uncertainty about the judicial status of the Master of the Rolls in the later sixteenth and seventeenth centuries.

134 Keilw. 99.

135 f 452r No 133; f 460r No 183.

136 *Anon* (M1599) Add 20700 f 11b, "and the whole court", cited Jones 244. The first point, no interrogatories to credit, is attributed to Lord Keeper Williams in 1622, but the two points are thoroughly intermingled.

137 i Sanders 118.

138 Add 41661 f 90b, because if depositions are suppressed for this reason the party may re-examine.

139 Harl 1576 f 229.

140 1649 No 25, i Sanders 228, Clarendon at i Sanders 302, Nott. Prac. 5.4, *TT* 109.

141 Prac. 5.4, Proleg. 29.6.

142 *Roberts v Aylway* (1676) Nott CC No 565, but not in the instant case where the hearing (after which examination to credit was sought) was *ex parte.*

143 Prac. 5.6, Proleg 29.8.

144 201.

from the rule against impeaching one's own witness[145]. However, it was said in argument at the Delegates in 1677[146], and ruled by Lord Guilford in *Sutton Coldfield v Wilson* (M1684)[147] that where the adverse party cross-examined an exceptionable witness on the merits, he was taken in Chancery to have waived the exception. This rule was also applied at common law[148]; if consistently followed it would have made it highly unlikely that any exceptions would be taken unless the opponent was certain of their success.

However, in *Lord Culpeper v Fairfax* (T1700)[149] objection was taken to a witness on interest grounds and the court "put off the hearing" to allow the plaintiff to examine witnesses to prove release of the interest; and in *Needham v Smith* (M1704)[150] it seems that counsel argued that it was permissible to examine to credit but not to competence after publication (the issue being whether the witness' answer in another cause, taken after hearing, could be read on hearing to prove interest), and Powell J rejected this distinction, saying that such examinations were possible in both cases[151]. This case strongly implies the existence of a procedure of the type described by Gilbert.

This evidence suggests that Gilbert's account of an obsolescent procedure of taking exceptions to witnesses conforming to the roman- canon procedure is not accurate. Rather, it suggests that exceptions to witnesses became a substantial issue in the 1590s (which, as will be seen below Ch 6, fits with the evidence as to the appearance of some of the exceptions). The context was a court which was (a) inundated with business[152], and (b) concerned about abuses of process, whether in the form of the use of process as a means of defamation[153], or of the use of procedural devices to procure delay[154]. There was therefore a persistent judicial hostility to procedures for taking exceptions to witnesses, which could easily be abused in both these ways[155]. In this context proving exceptions by cross-examination is re-

---

145 Above n 29; and in particular the rule stated by Maranta and Ayliffe, noted there, that if I except against a the person of a witness I cannot use his statements in my own favour.

146 *Gargrave alias Fan v* ——— 2 Ch Cas 250, above n 123.

147 1 Vern 254, 1 Eq Ca Ab 224.3. In Roger North's copy of his commonplace book the cryptic comment "que cross examine set up witness" appears under the title "Abus".

148 Cf *Pyke v Crouch* (M1696) 1 Ld Raym 730, Holt CJ.

149 2 Vern 375, 1 Eq Ca Ab 223.

150 2 Vern 463, 1 Eq Ca Ab 224; *Anon* (M1704) 12 Viner 12 *Evidence* F 37, probably SC, & F 38 abridging Vernon's report. Wright LK assisted by Trevor MR, Holt CJ and Powell J.

151 2 Vern 464. 12 Viner 12 as well as this point has the additional objection that it was improper to bring a bill against the witness, but should have been done by cross examination or articles (exceptions) and proof; the court responding that though the bill might have been demurrable on self-incrimination grounds this objection was waived by answering it.

152 Baker (1969) 4 *IJ* at 386.

153 Above Ch 2 pp § 2 *(1)* (b), & cf Hudson 208-9.

154 Jones 309 f.

155 Cf Maranta 626 No 7, "repulsa est odiosa et restringenda".

jected on self-incrimination grounds[156], and examinations to impeach witnesses only allowed in exceptional cases, therefore after publication.

Examinations on exceptions to witnesses are clearly common enough for rules on this subject to be incorporated in general orders in 1618, 1649 and 1660. Lord Nottingham tries to cut them down by insisting on exceptions and examination on them before publication, and Lord Guilford by treating cross-examination to the merits as waiving the objection. But by the 1700s a procedure more or less similar to that described by Gilbert is at least theoretically in place, though the cases suggest that the practice is not as clearly settled as Gilbert's account makes it appear. The picture that emerges is one of an evolution over the period *towards* the romano-canonical procedure, tempered by judicial hostility to the taking of exceptions to witnesses[157].

III. Conclusion

As I said at the beginning of this chapter, Dawson argued that the similarity between the examination of witnesses in equity and in the learned laws was merely superficial and accidental, that the procedure was originally merely a pragmatic administrative device, and in particular that the use of commissioners to examine witnesses ruled out any systematically civilian approach to proof. It is certainly *possible* that this was true of the earliest uses of witnesses in Chancery in the early to mid fifteenth century: for this period the sources are too thin to rule out any explanation. By the later fifteenth century, however, as Pronay has shown, the Chancery was a court staffed by trained civilians and canonists; and from 1507 and 1508 come two rulings in 'Keilwey' on re-examination and on exceptions to witnesses, which are consistent with the civilian sources and assume a fairly complex and developed context of procedural doctrine. From the late Elizabethan period on, when the sources are better, they show a body of technical law which is closely parallel to civilian doctrine.

More specifically, Dawson's comparison of the procedure of witness examination in Chancery with the *enquête* in the Parlement of Paris, focussing on the use of lay commissioners as a distinction, was misconceived. The use of commissions was common in the learned laws and in particular in the Arches, the English nearest civilian parallel; the commissioners in Chancery should not be thought of as legally ignorant; and the application of the law of proof did not depend on the particular *enquête* technique.

---

156 Below Ch 7 § 3 *(1)*.

157 There may be a connection between this circumstance and the lack of equity authority on exceptions grounded on bad character, below Ch 6 § 4.

As far as the procedure for taking testimony was concerned, therefore, contemporaries were right to see the equity courts as civilian in their fundamental character, and in contrast to the common law. The procedural rules in equity were not identical to those outlined by Clerke for the Arches; which is hardly surprising. But they were markedly and not merely superficially similar; and the evidence strongly suggests that this similarity was attributable to an application of the same underlying principles as the roman- canon system: examination on oath and under the control of the court with the examination to be by officers of the court, on interrogatories supplied by the parties, with the results to be kept secret until publication and reexamination of witnesses and examination after publication generally prohibited. It remains to be seen whether the same was true of the exceptions which could be taken to witnesses, the rule of compulsion and its limits, and the rules for assessing the weight of testimony.

Chapter Six

Exceptions to Witnesses

In the modern law there is not much law relating to the competence of witnesses[1], and though Wigmore discusses at length grounds on which the credibility of witnesses can be impeached[2], in English law this matter is only subject to limited and specific regulation[3]. The roman-canon system, however, contained a very extensive body of law about exceptions to witnesses, and the early modern period saw the development of a substantial body of law about the competence of witnesses at common law, which was largely swept away in the nineteenth century.

There is no doubt that at this period there was also a body of law concerning exceptions to witnesses in equity: it is this body of law which is my primary concern in this chapter. This area was one of the central elements of Wigmore's argument that equity followed the law in matters of evidence[4]. He argued in particular that witness competence rules were developed pragmatically at *nisi prius* over the course of the seventeenth century[5]; and he denied that the rules were copied either from the learned laws, or from the existing law relating to challenges to jurors. It was these rules developed at law which were then followed in equity.

Neither of these arguments can hold. In the first place, though Ballow (1737) says that equity follows the law in relation to witnesses[6], and there is some contemporary and earlier evidence that the rules were the same in equity as at law[7],

---

1 Cf Cross, Ch 6.

2 Book I Part I Title 2 Subtitle 2, §§ 874 ff.

3 Cross Chs 8 & 9.

4 § 4.

5 § 575.

6 P 122.

7 *Manning v Lechmere* (1737) 1 Atk 453, West t Hard 174, *per* Lord Hardwicke "the rules as to evidence are the same in equity as at law" (according to West t Hard this point not in Hardwicke's notebook), and *Henly v Phillips* (1740) 2 Atk 48, *per* Lord Hardwicke "the rules of evidence in this court as to witnesses are exactly the same as at law". Gilbert FR 147 says that "... (for the rule of evidence is the same in equity as at law). If the party cannot be a good witness at law, no more can he be in equity." Lord Nottingham in *Cook v Fountain* (T1675) Nott CC No 273, 3 Swanst 585 (in KB, probably *Anon* (P1674) 1 Mod 107 (dated 1680, but probably really this case) 1 Vent 347; not SP, (P1676) Nott CC No 500, (M1686) 1 Vern 413) allows a witness in equity on the basis that he has been allowed in previous proceedings at law, and counsel for the plaintiff argues on the assumption that the rules are the same in

the evidence does not support an inference that the rules in equity were *taken from* rules previously developed at law.

Secondly, there is some direct evidence of influence from the learned laws, and, in spite of important divergences, a greater degree of parallelism between exceptions recognised in equity and at common law and at least the leading principles of the roman-canon exceptions than Wigmore would allow.

We can approach this question in two ways. The first is through the logical soundness of Wigmore's argument *prima facie*. The second is through the concrete development of the rules in equity and at law and their relationship to one another and to civilian doctrine on exceptions to witnesses.

In general there is less authority in equity than at common law, and in some cases (infancy, lunacy, infamy) there is effectively no equity authority. However, I would argue that this reflects two circumstances: (a) as has already been indicated in Chapter 5[8], the equity courts made it difficult to take exceptions to witnesses, especially on grounds of bad character; and (b) in any case the discussions of these topics at law tend to be theoretical (and reflect direct civilian influence) rather than driven by practice.

I. Wigmore's arguments

Wigmore argued on several grounds that the common-law disqualifications were introduced pragmatically in individual cases over the course of the seventeenth century, rather than copied from the challenges to jurors or the civilian or canonical exceptions. (In point of fact the general structure of these bodies of law was quite similar; unsurprisingly, as Glanvill tells us simply that the challenges to jurors are the same as the canon law exceptions to witnesses, so that the inference that they were copied from them is irresistible[9].) Wigmore's arguments against transfer of the rules for challenges rest on the absence of some of the challenges from the list of disqualifications, and also on the long delay between the beginning use of witnesses in jury trials in the fifteenth century and the emergence of rules about the qualifications of witnesses in the seventeenth century reports. His argument against "reception" of the romano-canonical exceptions rests again on the absence of some of the rules, and also on the jurisdictional conflicts of the early seventeenth century making conscious borrowing unlikely.

Callow v Mince (M1704) 2 Vern 472, Pre Ch 234, 1 Eq Ca Ab 223.2; Pre Ch at 234, this point not in Vern.

[8] Pp 206-9.

[9] ii.12, Hall ed 32.

None of these arguments is really satisfactory. It is *prima facie* implausible that the common lawyers should have laboriously built up a system of rules as to the competence of witnesses case by case when there was an existing system readily available either next door in the civilian and canonist jurisdictions or upstairs in the lumber-room in the form of rules about challenges to jurors. If lawyers were minded to borrow from them, the antiquity of the rules relating to challenges (which had not gone completely out of use at this period[10]) would hardly have deterred a generation which was apt to quote ancient precedents and statutes in constitutional debate[11]. It is clear that the challenges were not simply lifted *en bloc*[12], but it is also clear that there was some influence at least in the area of infamy (below § 4 *(1)*).

Secondly, the absence of some of the romano-canonical rules, and differences in detail, do not in themselves imply there was no borrowing, for reasons indicated above Ch 1: what may have been (and I would argue most probably was) involved was use of the *leading principles* of the learned laws, and some partial use of specific rules.

It is true that there are relatively few instances of reference to the learned laws in the authorities[13], and it is said as early as the 1580s[14] that the rules in Chancery are different from those of the civil law in this matter. On the other hand, the use of the romano-canonical language of "exceptions against witnesses" in *Earl of Suffolk v Greenvill* (1631)[15] in equity and *Onbie's Case* (1642)[16] at law, and by Hale[17], Lord Nottingham[18] and Lord Guilford[19] writing in the 1670s, is suggestive of an influence of the learned laws.

---

10 The topic is discussed extensively by Coke (Co Lit 156b f) and in Rolle's Abridgement Vol II pp 645f, though most of the precedents cited are mediæval. There are occasional instances of challenges in the 1680s in Skinner (82, 91, 101, 229) and in the 1690s in Holt KB and Salkeld (both at title *Challenge*).

11 For examples cf Pocock, *The Ancient Constitution and the Feudal Law* (Second edition, Cambridge, CUP, 1987) passim.

12 Co Lit 6b says explicitly that the rules are different.

13 Though see in particular Hale's use of Covarruvias, *Trial of Treasons, Whyte v Oxenbridge* and *Wyly v Vincent*, and *Bulwer v Levet*, discussed below.

14 *Prawnce v Hodilow* (1581-2) Choyce Cas 156, relatives said to be excluded by the civil law and hence in the Chancellor's court at Cambridge University, but competent in Chancery.

15 3 Ch Rep 89, Nels 15, 2 Freem 146 Harg 174 f 18r; this point only in Hargrave MS and Ch Rep.

16 March NC pl 136.

17 *History of the Pleas of the Crown* (London, 1736, reprint, London, Professional Books, 1971) Vol II pp 276-7.

18 Practice, Examinations, No 4 (no examination to credit without an exception filed); Prolegomena c 29 No 7, exceptions to witnesses to be before publication, citing Keilw. 99.

19 Add 32518 at f 113b.

II. The classification of exceptions

Exceptions to witnesses are sometimes listed in contemporary accounts in a highly disorganised way. Thus among the civilians 'Alciatus' offers a long outline list in no particular order[20] and Ayliffe wanders from topic to topic[21]; among common lawyers the same disorganisation is apparent in Coke[22] and *Trialls per Pais*[23], though in these authors this is a general feature. The problem with these treatments is that all exceptions appear to have the same weight and practical significance. Other evidence, however, suggests both that the effect of exceptions varied, and that there were certain underlying principles which in the early modern period informed the particular exceptions and enabled them to be grouped into larger classifications. Recognising the existence of these classifications helps us in understanding the extent and the limits of civilian influence on exceptions to witnesses in equity and at law.

1. Classification by effect

In the common law there is a fundamental distinction between objections to witnesses which disqualify the witness as incompetent, so that the witness is not heard by the jury, and grounds of impeachment which can be used by counsel to attack the weight of the evidence given by the witness, but which are left to assessment by the jury. This distinction was already known to common lawyers in the later seventeenth century[24].

On the face of it, this distinction concerns the functions of judge and jury and is therefore specific to evidence to a jury. Closely analogous distinctions can, however, be found both in the law of challenges, and in some civilian sources. In the law of challenges, the distinction is between 'principal' challenges, which exclude the juror automatically if proved, and challenges 'to the favour', which involve matters of degree of bias and therefore require trial by 'triers' appointed by the court[25].

In the civilian sources, the distinction is variously drawn. Lyndwood distinguishes exceptions which lead to the rejection of the witness before examination,

---

20 207v-211r.

21 536-544.

22 Co Lit f 6b.

23 Ch 11 of the first to fourth editions mix witnesses with other evidence points in no particular order. In the fifth edition ch 15 pp 307-330 segregates cases on witnesses, but still does not classify them.

24 Hale HPC II 276-7; Francis North, 'A Fragment' at 143.

25 Co. Lit. 155-158; the same principles applied to challenges to the array based on bias in the sherriff, and the two topics are discussed together.

which are those of conspiracy and capital enmity, from exceptions taken after examination, which are to the quality of the testimony (single, contrary, varying obscure, etc)[26]. Cotta says that one witness of undoubted good character can counterbalance the defects of another witness, so that the two together make a full proof; and that affinity does not exclude the witness but makes him suspect, so that this rule can operate[27]. Covarruvias, in discussing the use of corporation members as witnesses for the corporation , says that in those cases where they are admitted their credibility is affected and subject to judicial discretion[28]. The *Reformatio* says that all witnesses except excommunicates are to be heard though there are exceptions to their persons[29] and goes on to distinguish exceptions which lead to the rejection of the witness (infamy, capital enmity, domesticity, dependence, parents, proxies and solicitors of causes) from those which affect the weight of the evidence in the discretion of the judge (suspicion of crime, 'mercenarii amici', women, relatives within the prohibited degrees, and persons who have previously testified for the adverse party)[30]. Vulteius similarly distinguishes some witnesses who are repelled (interested persons, parties, their spouses and immediate relatives) from other exceptions which do not lead the witnesses to be repelled, but still leave them not *omni exceptione maiores* (consanguinity and affinity, friendship and enmity, advocates and proctors in the cause, proxies, and hearsay witnesses)[31]. Swinburne says that if exceptions are "lighte, or slender, such as do in part diminish the credite of their testimonie, as the exception of friendship, domesticitie, or of suspition of some small fault; there the number dooth supplie the defect, . . ."[32]. Some exceptions, however, do completely eliminate the witnesses subject to them, such as conviction of perjury, or insanity, and the same is true where the witness is subject to more than one exception[33]. Similarly, Swinburne says that consanguinity and affinity, dependence, interest, and bias affect the credit to be given to the witness' testimony proportionately to the degree of the relevant relationship[34]. For Domat, infancy and insanity, infamy, interest, consanguinity and affinity, dependency, and having been employed as an advocate in the cause lead to the rejection of the witness; in contrast the exceptions for "mere" bias, based on friendship to the proponent or enmity to the opponent, "depends on the prudence of the judge" or are "causes for doubting" the evidence of the witness[35].

---

26 304 v. *testium receptionem.*

27 The general rule is at 512-5 and 864-5, the application to affinity at 879-80.

28 *QP* 447-8 No. 4.

29 247 c 12.

30 248 c 17; further exceptions and their limits are discussed in the following cc.

31 507v-508r.

32 P 186.

33 Swinburne loc cit.

34 P 187.

35 3.6.3.9; 3.6.3.10 (Strahan's translation).

This varied use of the distinction means that we cannot say with certainty which side of the line any particular exception would fall. It is important, however, to note the presence of the distinction in adjudication of facts by judge alone. Its presence also makes it possible that some civilian exceptions to witnesses which did not have parallels as disqualifications in the later common law of evidence were initially present in equity and/ or at common law but withered away as being exceptions to credit rather than to competence[36].

2. Classification by grounds

The various exceptions to witnesses could be classified in different ways, which indicate the underlying principles which were thought to apply. Coke classifies challenges to the polls under four heads: *propter honoris respectum* (the exclusion of peers), *propter defectum* (aliens and serfs), *propter affectum* (bias) and *propter delictum* (bad character)[37]. Swinburne makes a tripartite basic distinction:

> ... onely I will remember three speciall causes whereby the witnesses are not omni exceptione maiores : the first is dishonestie in manners: the second is want of iudgement or understanding: the third is affection more to the one partie then to the other.[38]

Ridley, Zouch, Wiseman and Pufendorf all omit intellectual incapacity and dichotomise the qualifications of witnesses into good character and absence of bias[39]. Vulteius and Wood start with a general dichotomy between general disability, and disability in relation to the cause in question (the various heads of bias). Vulteius then subdivides general disability into natural (infancy, insanity, and physical disability of perception) and legal (criminality)[40], while Wood does not subclassify but lists particular exceptions[41].

Gilbert adopts the basic dichotomy that witnesses are exceptionable either on grounds of intellectual incapacity, or on moral grounds, i.e. that they are liable not to tell the truth[42]. He then divides moral incapacity into bad character and bias[43]. Other common lawyers were less sophisticated. Rolle divides the authorities he collects between "Testimonies – Persons Interested" and "Testimonies – Quel per-

---

36 There is some suggestion that this might be the case, at least for equity, in the discussion of lesser "objections or articles" related to minor bad character in Gilbert *Forum Romanum* 147, quoted below § 4 *(3)*.

37 Co. Lit. f 156b.

38 P 186.

39 Ridley 79-80; Zouch *EI* 89-90; Wiseman 18; Pufendorf 5.13.9.

40 372v, 507v.

41 314-5.

42 *Evidence* 86, 103-4. The same approach seems to be implicit in the organisation of Domat's treatment, 3.6.3.3-5.

43 Domat 3.6.3.5, Gilbert loc cit above n 28

sons poient estre testimonyes" (status rules, spouses and bad character)[44]; Nelson divides them among interest, infamy and "Witnesses in general"[45].

For my present purposes, Swinburne's tripartite classification is most convenient, into intellectual incapacity, bad character and bias. I am not concerned, as Vulteius, Wood and Gilbert seem to be, to force an ultimately dualistic classification. I leave exemption from testifying on the grounds of high status to discussion as an issue of compulsion, in Chapter 7, and treat exclusion on the grounds of low status as an issue of bad character, which is one of the approaches of the contemporary authors to the issue.

III. Intellectual incapacity: Children and lunatics

Swinburne gives both these exceptions and says that in these cases adults can give evidence of events during their childhood, and recovered lunatics of what happened during their lunacy[46]. There is no equitable authority, and the common law authority appears to be in substance abstract discussion influenced by the civil law. Coke says that a witness may be excluded if "... of non-sane Memory, or not of Discretion ..."[47]. Hale[48] says that lunatics who have lucid intervals may be witnesses while lucid, and that children of over 14 may be sworn, that in some cases younger children are sworn for the Crown in criminal cases, and that in some cases of offences against children they may be examined without oath.

This identification of a "child" as someone under 14 is interesting. D.22.5.20 disqualifies persons under the age of 25, but D. 22.5.19 *pupilli*[49], and D.22.5.3 *impuberes*[50], both of which mean children under 14, the age given by Hale[51]. Wood and Ayliffe say that 14 is the relevant age in civil and 20 in criminal proceedings[52]. The age of majority in socage had been 15 in the time of Glanvill[53], and 14 was (for canon-law reasons) relevant to the validity of marriage in the middle ages[54],

---

44 ii 685-6.

45 Chs 2 (witnesses in general), 3 (infamy), 4 (interest).

46 187-8. Vulteius 372v, 507v, and Wood 314, give the general exception. On evidence of events during childhood cf Wood 314; Ayliffe 537, more cautiously.

47 Co Lit 6b.

48 HPC II 278-9, 283-4.

49 Followed by Ayliffe 537.

50 This authority is followed and cited by 'Alciatus' 208r (also giving lunacy generally) and Domat 3.6.3.3.

51 *impuberes* cf J. Inst I.22, *pupilli* Lee, *Elements of Roman Law* (London, Sweet & Maxwell, 1956) 350.

52 Wood 314; Ayliffe 536.

53 Pollock & Maitland *HEL* ii, 438-9.

54 Helmholz, *Marriage Litigation*, 98-9.

but the age of 14 was without practical significance in the common law when Hale was writing[55]. Gilbert[56] says that

> "As to those who are excluded from Testimony by the Want of Skill and Discernment, and they are Ideots, Madmen and Children under the Age of common Knowledge; they are perfectly incapable of any Sense of Truth, and are therefore plainly excluded.
>
> Children under the age of 14 are not regularly admitted as Witnesses ... There is no Time fix'd wherein they are to be excluded from Evidence, but the Reason and Sense of their Evidence is to appear from the Questions propounded to them, and their Answers to them]."

Hawkins[57] simply cites Coke and Hale for the proposition that want of discretion is an exception. It seems clear that apart from Hale's discussion of the evidence of children, and Gilbert's latter comment on this point, the discussions of these issues are entirely academic. No case-law or practice is cited, and the (slightly different) practices sketched by Hale and Gilbert in relation to children have little relation to the theoretical rule stated by both writers[58].

IV. Bad character

1. Infamy

Most of the civilian sources state as a general rule that any offence creating infamy will exclude a witness[59]. The detailed civil law as to offences and conduct giving rise to infamy is not relevant here, as it was clear from an early stage that the primary english equivalent was felony[60]. Conviction of perjury gave rise to permanent exclusion[61], and this was also an early exclusion in the common law,

---

55 Co Lit 157 says that it is a good challenge to a juror that he is under 21; but his only authority for it is the *Mirror of Justices*.

56 Pp 103-4.

57 ii, 434, § 26. Citations to passages already cited.

58 It seems clear that there was no rule in the 1530s, in view of the awful story reported by Spelman (*Corone* 40, 93 SS 60) of a child procured to give evidence to convict his father of murder. In *Harris v Scott* (1568) 101 SS 78 the reporter thought it worthwhile to note that one of the witnesses to the jury was a child (i.e. the child was admitted, but the reporter thought this was noteworthy). In *Anon* (1572-3) Dalison 104 pl 44 counsel excepted to a witness on the ground that he was under 20, but this was rejected by Catlin CJ. In *Young v Slaughterford* (T1709) 11 Mod 228, KB, the modern rule that a young child (under 12) is qualified if he "knows the danger of the oath" was applied.

59 'Alciatus' 207v, 210 Nos 55-7; Cotta 879; *Reformatio* 248 c 17; Vulteius 372v, 507v; Swinburne 187; Wood 314; Ayliffe 538. Cf also Lyndwood 304 v *testium receptionem* (implied, as infamous witnesses are exceptionally admitted in heresy); Covarruvias *QP* 447 No 1 (implied, as *infamia facti* where there is no conviction needs discussion).

60 Co Lit 6b.

61 *Reformatio* 219 c 7; *Principia Quaedam* 5, 6; Swinburne 187.

being expressly provided by the 1563 Perjury Act (ss 5, 6). In other cases, however, a period of subsequent good behaviour, three years according to some authors, would restore the offender's character[62]. *Forme et Certenty* extracted Maranta on this point, and Egerton referred to this view and said that seven years good behaviour would do[63].

Suspicion, as opposed to actual condemnation, of crime could have varying results: Cotta, the *Reformatio* and Swinburne say that this goes to credibility rather than excluding the witness altogether[64], Covarruvias and Gentili that the witness is excluded in criminal but not in civil proceedings[65]. There is similar variety on the question of accomplices to crimes and frauds: 'Alciatus' says that they are exceptionable[66], the *Reformatio* that they are excluded in criminal causes[67], Gentili that they are acceptable in cases involving conspiracy because they speak against themselves[68], Wood that they are exceptionable unless "the publick security is immediately concerned"[69]. Ayliffe that they are excluded except in conspiracy cases[70]. There is some overlap with the more general rule which allowed the use of witnesses who were otherwise exceptionable in *maiestas* (treason), heresy, and other cases where there were inherent difficulties in proof (discussed below § 5 *(1)* (b))[71].

There is, again, no equity authority directly in point[72], though there is some at the turn of the seventeenth and eighteenth century on the subsidiary question of accomplices. Coke[73] offers a long list of disqualifying offences, which appear to be simply copied from his account of challenges to jurors[74]. They consist of

62 Maranta 625.3, 3 years; *Reformatio* 251 c 25, without any definite time; Swinburne 187, 3 years.

63 *F&C* f 546v; Egerton, *Observations* f 462v No. 198.

64 Cotta 512; *Reformatio* 248 c 17; Swinburne 187.

65 Covarruvias *QP* 447 No 1; Gentili ii 144, adding only so far as credible.

66 208r.

67 249 c 19.

68 ii 144.

69 314.

70 537.

71 Lyndwood 304 v *testium receptionem;* Cosin II 114-5; Gentili ii 143; Ayliffe 536. Maranta 577 No 65 and the *Reformatio* 249-50 c 21 apply the principle to 'domestic' witnesses. The heresy rule stated in Lyndwood and elsewhere was controversial in England in the 1530s: see St German, *A Treatise Concerning the Division between the Spiritualty and the Temporalty* 189, More *Apology* 138, & Trapp *Introduction* lxxx-lxxxi, in *The Works of St Thomas More* Vol 9 ed. J.B. Trapp (New Haven, 1979); St German, *Salem & Bizance* 359-364, More, *Debellacyon of Salem & Bizance* 146-167 & *Introduction* lviii-lxviii, in id. Vol 10 ed. J. Guy, R. Keen, C.H. Miller & R. McGugan (New Haven, 1987).

72 Unless we are to count *Willy v Thomas,* Chan, sidenoted by Gilbert 101; below n 83.

73 Co Lit ff 6-6b.

74 Co Lit 158a. The only difference is that outlawry is not mentioned at 6b.

(1) felony, (2) various other offences involving interference with the administration of justice, and (3) the punishments of cropped ears, standing on the pillory or tumbrel, and branding. He also says that *Allegans suam turpitudinem non est audiendus*[75], a point also taken by Cotta[76].

Hale[77] goes into slightly more detail on the disqualifying offences. He also says that (1) an approver is not to be sworn as a witness, as being a felon by confession, "but only his general oath, that he taketh at the time of his becoming an approver, shall be taken". This might be an example of *allegans suam turpitudinem*, i.e. alleging his own disqualifying infamy; but Hale doubts the rule about approvers, though he cites no authority for it[78].

(2) A pardon removes the disqualification[79], but does not remove the challenge to a juror. It is still possible to attack the credit of a pardoned felon, and exceptions which go to credit in the cases of witnesses may be good challenges to a juror. And (3) following the statute 4 Hen 7 c 13 a felon cleric in orders, and following that of 18 Eliz I c 7 a felon who pleads clergy and is burned in the hand, are competent[80]. The effect of these two points is to remove felony from the list of disqualifications for practical purposes, with the exception of the case of the approver, since a felon who neither successfully pleads clergy, nor is pardoned, will be hanged. What is left are the offences involving interference with the administration of justice and the "infamous punishments", the latter of which become an anomaly.

This is more clearly reflected in Gilbert's account of infamy, which reflects the treatment of this issue in cases after 1689. Gilbert identifies Coke and Hale's list of miscellaneous offences other than felony involving interference with the course of justice with the civilian *crimen falsi*[81]. On this basis the list is extended to include "Forgery, and the like"[82], i.e. offences involving fraud, but on the other hand restricts the disqualifying effect of the "infamous punishments" to cases where these punishments are imposed for "*Crimen falsi*, as for Perjury, Forgery, or the like"[83].

---

75 Fourth Institute p 279, citing *Sir Richard Raynham's Case* (T1571) in CP. At this point the text of the Chapter has degenerated into a series of latin tags about witnesses and proof, which were presumably intended as notes for points to be made more fully.

76 893: "Turpitudinem suam alleganti, non creditur".

77 *HPC* ii, 277-8.

78 Ib at 277.

79 Ib at 278 citing *Cuddington v Wilkins* (M1614) Hob 67, 81 (KB), *contra* to Coke in *Crashaw's Case* (M1613) Bulst 154 (KB).

80 HPC II p 278, citing *Searle v Williams* (T1618) Hob 288 (which decides that 18 Eliz c 7 operates as a statute pardon so that all effects of the conviction are wiped out, but not referring to competence as a witness).

81 Gilbert pp 100-101; cf C.9.22.5.

82 Gilbert pp 100, 101; "Felony or Cheating", p 101.

83 Gilbert p 101. The MSS start this para. "The common punishment that marks the Crimen falsi", not "works", as in the printed text; have "Perjury, or Forgery and the like", and cite *Willy v Thomas,* Chan, where the printed text cites *Welby v Chan.* Hill 79 cites Salk 689, 90,

Gilbert also explains the effect of a pardon in terms reminiscent of the civilian view of credit restored by subsequent good behaviour: i.e. that the pardon gives rise to a presumption that "he hath repented of his fault, and hath returned to a better Mind, [and therefore that his Evidence is not dangerous to the Life, Liberty or Estate of the Subject]"[84].

The picture this suggests of disqualification by infamy is of the rules for challenges to jurors as an initial starting point, modified in practice and then re-theorised in more directly romano-canonical terms of the *crimen falsi* and restored good character in the 1690s and 1700s. The practical problems arise in connection with (1) pardons, (2) the extension of the disqualification to a wider class of offences, and (3) the problem of witnesses who, though unconvicted, give evidence which implies that they are guilty of a disqualifying offence. These are the cases of accomplices in criminal proceedings and *allegans turpitudinem suam.*

Though the phrase *allegans turpitudinem suam* appears in Coke[85], it does not do so in any of the other discussions of the topic. Wigmore[86] collects under this head the cases of accomplices, obligors who give evidence which would invalidate their own instruments, attesting witnesses who claim that they attested falsely, and witnesses who claim that their former testimony was perjured. It is probable that to the extent that this was seen as a ground for an exception, only the first and possibly the last cases would have fallen under this head. The exclusion of obligors to invalidate their own instruments is seen by Coke[87] and subsequent writers[88] as a case of disqualification by interest. The objection to attesting witnesses claiming that they attested falsely, which seems from the authorities cited by Wigmore never to have been accepted[89], seems to be based on *contraria allegans non est audien-*

Ld Raym 39, LE 42,3,5,8, all of which are probably later than the text. Otherwise the only MS citations are Co Lit 6 and *R v Crosby.* The statement in the text is clearly drawn from the argument of Ward AG, Trevor SG and Cowper in *Crosby,* reported at Skin 578, Holt KB 753, 1 Ld Raym 39, 5 Mod 15, 12 St Tr 1295 f. Samuel Eyre J accepted this argument (Skin 578, 12 Mod 72), but Holt CJ rejected it and decided that the witness (the Whig solicitor Aaron Smith) was qualified on the basis of the Act of Indemnity of 1690 operating as a general pardon (this point in all the reports already cited and also at 2 Salk 289). The court, including Holt, is reported as saying that it is the nature of the offence and not of the punishment that disqualifies in *R v Weeden Ford, Warden of the Fleet, ex p Leighton* (M1700) 2 Salk 690, 12 Mod 337; but this was to extend the disqualification to an offence of barretry which had been punished only by a fine, rather than to take away the "infamous punishments" (this was an issue at KB bar directed on a *monstrans de droit* out of Chancery. Other points are reported at 3 Salk 155, Holt KB 133, 1 Eq Ca Ab 128, (M1703) 6 Mod 18, (1703) Colles 332, HL; in the end the case seems to have been compromised.

84 P 102. Bracketed words absent from MSS.

85 4th Institute p 279.

86 § 523 f.

87 Co Lit ff 6b-7.

88 Hale HPC II p 280, Gilbert pp 126-7, Hawkins II pp 433-4.

89 *Hudson's Case* (1683) Skin 79, *Dayrell v Glasscock* (1694) Skin 413, *Blurton v Toon* (1696) Skin 639, Holt KB 290 SR, *Austen v Willes* (1700) Buller Nisi Prius 264.

dus, and the exclusion of witnesses who allege that their former testimony was perjured is probably primarily on this basis: thus Gilbert:

> ANOTHER Thing that derogates from the Credit of a Witness is, if upon Oath he affirmed directly contrary to what he asserts; then if the Matter be Civil, you may give in Evidence the [civil proceedings, if criminal you must give in evidence the] criminal Proceedings, and swear what he gave Evidence at the Trial; and this takes from the Witness all Credibility, inasmuch as Contraries cannot be true."[90]

Some counsel in the 1690s and 1700s seem to have attempted to exclude "accomplices" in civil proceedings, i.e. witnesses whose evidence implicated them in frauds. In *Oldbury v Wynne* (1698-9)[91] Turton J, sitting in Chancery while Somers C was ill, refused to allow a deposition (essential to the defendant's case) to be read *inter alia* on the ground that the witness "had sworn himself guilty of a very great fraud", but Somers C reversed the decree on a rehearing, and Somers' decree was affirmed in the Lords. In *Tidcombe v Cholmley, Boddington & al'* (1700-1)[92] counsel argued in an appeal to the Lords *inter alia* that the answer of one defendant (an agent for both sides) admitting a parol assurance collateral to a contract in writing ought not to be credited because if there was such a contract this defendant was guilty of defrauding the other defendants by bringing an unqualified contract to them for execution. Nonetheless the Lords "seemed disposed to reverse the decree" and the case was settled. In *May v Harman* (1709)[93], an appeal to the Lords from the Irish Chancery, Jekyll and Turner, for the appellant, argued that the deposition of the assignor of a bond showing both himself and the assignee to have had notice that it was paid (and hence to be conspiring to defraud the obligors) ought not to have been read *inter alia* because it was a confession to fraud. Harcourt and Spencer Cowper for the respondent replied that "*particeps criminis* in case of fraud is the most proper person to discover and prove it, especially when as here what he proved was to his own detriment"[94].

This argument is in line with the common law authorities. Though *An Essay on the nature of Oaths, and Judicial Evidence* (1715)[95] argues forcibly that accomplices should not be received on grounds both of interest and of bad character, this seems to be special pleading for political reasons; the majority view being that accomplices, whether in crime, tort or fraud, are receivable on the ground of necessity[96] notwithstanding bad character and interest.

---

90 Gilbert p 153. Bracketed words in MSS, not in printed text.

91 (1699) Colles 91, HL. The prior proceedings appear from the arguments of counsel in the HL.

92 (1700) Pre Ch 143 (Wright LK), (1701) Colles 166 (HL). Cf above Ch 2 nn 244-6 and text there.

93 4 Bro PC 156.

94 4 Bro PC at 158.

95 By a Gentleman of the Inner Temple, London, printed for H. Carpenter, 17pp. This pamphlet appears to be directed to a critique of the treason trials after the Jacobite uprising of 1715.

2. Infidels

Gilbert says that "by the rules of the Civil Law *Judaei et Haeretici contra Orthodoxos produci in Judicio Testes nequeunt*"[97]. This is a quotation from the Code of Justinian[98]; the doctrine was shared by the medieval canonists[99], and 'Alciatus', Wood and Ayliffe follow these sources[100]. However, it is less clear that the doctrine was generally or strictly applied. Gentili argues that Turks are unacceptable against Christians, but the context makes clear that the argument is against the use of depositions which have already been taken in another jurisdiction[101]; and, indeed, Hale says that

> "Yea, the oaths of idolatrous infidels have been admitted in the municipal laws of many kingdoms, especially *si juraverit per verum Deum creatorem,* and special laws are instituted in Spain touching the form of the oaths of infidels. *Vide Covarruviam. Tom.* I. Part. 1. *de juramentiforma*"[102].

Wood, in spite of listing infidels among exclusions, says later that "Such Oaths ought to be imposed on *Heathens* and *Jews*, which they allow to be Obligatory"[103]. Moreover, it is possibly significant that this head of exception is absent from the *Reformatio* and from the discussions of the topic by Swinburne, Pufendorf and Domat[104].

Coke says that an infidel cannot be a witness[105]. In the Fourth Institute he seems to connect the question with the nature of an oath and the possibility of punishment for perjury:

> "An Oath ought to be accompanied with the fear of God, and service of God for advancement of truth, *Dominum Deum tuum tibemis, & illi soli servies, & per nomen illius jurabis.*(1)

---

96 *Anon* (Aug 1647) Clayt 115; cases cited by Hale HPC II p 280; *Dockwra v Dickenson* (P1696) Skin 640, Comb 366, (trover, admission of participants said to be *ex necessitate rei*); Hawkins II p 432, (accomplices admitted on the ground of general necessity).

97 103.

98 C 1.5.21.

99 X 2.20.21; Lyndwood 304 v *testium receptionem* allowing the use of heretic in heresy proceedings implies rejection in other cases.

100 'Alciatus' 208v; Wood 314; Ayliffe 448, 536, 544.

101 i 114.

102 HPC II p 279; the citation is to his *In Constitutionis Secundae ex rubrica de Pactis* lib 6 § 1 *De Iuramenti forma* No 24; "Tom. I Part. 1" in *Omnia Opera.*

103 323; he footnotes to the form of oaths for Jews in Germany and the English Act of 1696 permitting Quakers to affirm, 7 & 8 Will. 3 c 34.

104 It is also absent from Maranta and Covarruvias, but neither offers a systematic account of exceptions to witnesses; and from Ridley, Zouch and Wiseman, but these are not more than brief indications of general heads.

105 Co Lit 6b.

Bracton(2) saith that an Alien born cannot be a witnesse: which is to be understood of an alien Infidel.... *Testis falsus non erit impunitus.*

Nocte dieque suum gestat sub pectore testem:

His conscience always gnawing and vexing him. *Vox simplex nec probationem facit, nec praesumptionem inducit.*(3)

Testium numerus si non adjicitur, duo sufficiunt.(4)

Jurato creditur in judicio."[106]

Hudson says that a Turk and Pagan cannot be a witness because he cannot swear on the gospels[107]. Hale says that in his opinion Jews are to be sworn *tacto libro legis Mosaicae* in cases of necessity such as "forein contracts"[108], and in *Anon* (M1684)[109] a Jew's answer was taken on an oath on the Pentateuch by special order. In contrast in *Anon* (M1677)[110] when a Quaker was brought to the bar in contempt for not answering a bill for tithes and refused to swear, Lord Nottingham told him that if he did not swear, the bill must be taken to be true. The objection is not to the mere fact of his being a dissenter, but to his refusal to swear.

Gilbert says that neither an excommunicate nor a recusant may be a witness[111]; the first of these was a canon law rule[112]. The later disappearance of these two objections is probably attributable at least in part to practical considerations. On the analogy of infamy, it would presumably be necessary to produce the record of a conviction of excommunication in the church courts, or of recusancy, to make

---

106 Fourth Institute p 279. Bracketed numbers are my references to sources so far as I have been able to trace them, as follows: (1) Paraphrases Deut. 10, 20. (2) Coke does not give a reference for this; I have not found it in Bracton, and in view of what is said about aliens in the period in P&M HEL I 458f the attribution seems implausible. Rolle Ab II 657 cites YB 14 Hen 4, 19 (f 19 pl 23) for the proposition that an alien is not to be a juror. (3) Bracton f 400b, Thorne ed. p. 248. (4) D. 22.5.12.

I take the train of thought to be: nature of an oath; you are to swear by the one God alone; hence the exclusion of aliens is only of alien infidels; a false witness will be punished, i.e. by the torments of conscience, i.e. the importance of religion; a bare voice (i.e. without oath) is neither proof nor circumstantial evidence (presumption); the second meaning of this tag, that more than one witness is required; only two are required unless more are required by the specific law; what is under oath is to be believed in judicial proceedings. It would probably be wrong, however, to make too much of these loose notes.

107 207.

108 HPC II p 279. The admission of Moslems was settled by *Blake v Lynch* (H1743) CP, reported in Lincoln's Inn Hill MS 79 (Gilbert) pp 134-5, and that of other theists by *Omichund v Barker* (1745) 1 Atk 21.

109 1 Vern 263.

110 2 Ch Cas 237, 2 Freem 27. Not reported by Lord Nottingham.

111 P 103, citing 2 Bulst 155 = *Brown v Crashaw* (H1613/4) 2 Bulst 155 at 155 *per* Coke CJ, *AG v Griffith & al'* (H/1613/14) 2 Bulst 155 also *per* Coke CJ. The MSS also cite 2 Rolle Ab 155, but this seems to be an error.

112 Lyndwood 304 v *testium receptionem*; 'Alciatus' 208r; *Reformatio* 247 c 12; Zouch *DIE* 42.

good the objection. After the civil war ecclesiastical discipline over the laity largely broke down[113], and the prosecution of recusancy tended to decline[114]: so the relevant proof would be hard to come by. Practical considerations may similarly explain the disappearance of the civilian exclusion of heretics cited by Gilbert; a mere allegation of heresy against a witness would hardly suffice to exclude him, and from the thirteenth to the sixteenth century, convicted heretics were liable to the death penalty, and so hardly likely in practice to be produced as witnesses.

In any event it seems clear that the origin of such rules as did exist in England on this topic is not the result of "pragmatic" development, as Wigmore would argue, but of theoretical reflection on the need for evidence to be given on oath and the nature of oaths, coupled with the modification in practice of rules generated by theory.

3. Other bad character

The *Digest* instructs the judge to consider the general character of the witnesses[115]. In consequence, in civilian doctrine exceptionable bad character was not limited to the specific cases discussed above but covered a wide field[116].

The same approach seems to have applied at this period both in equity and at law. In *Talbot v Wood, Earl of Shrewsbury v Talbot* (1595) in Star Chamber exception was taken to the credibility of a witness (among other objections) on the ground of his practising medicine without a license or degree[117], and in *Observa-*

---

113 Cf Hill, *Society & Puritanism in Pre-Revolutionary England* (London, Mercury, 1966) Chs 8-11.

114 See Kenyon, *The Popish Plot* (London, Penguin, 1974) Ch 1 for variations in the policy of Charles II's administrations on this. James II's policy is well known, but William III also tended to discourage prosecutions on the penal laws against Catholics as well as against dissenters: S.B. Baxter, *William III* (London, Longman, 1966) p 251 refers to a "consistent refusal to enforce the penal laws", & Horwitz, *Parliament, Policy & Politics* (Manchester, MUP, 1979) gives the government's perceived leniency to Catholics as a motive for the 1700 bill against Catholic landholding, citing Vernon Correspondence II 428-9. The intellectual climate after the Revolution of 1688 was also not likely to favour the disqualification of witnesses on religious grounds, and Quakers were admitted to affirm by 7 & 8 W 3 c 34. The admission of the evidence of avowed catholics in *Whitebread* (1679) 7 How St Tr 311, 361, 379 and *Oates* (1685) 10 How St Tr 1079, 1172, though it may have affected the later law, is not very helpful as to the regular practice of the courts at the time, since both cases were political show trials.

115 D 22.5.3 pr.

116 *Reformatio* 248 c 17, "de criminibus suspecti"; Clerke 209, "infames, criminosi" and 211; Swinburne 147, "infamous by their evill life"; Gentili ii ch 5; Ayliffe 538. Conversely, statements that witnesses must be of good character are found in Ridley 79-80, "of honest fame and name", Wiseman 18 "honest", Pufendorf 5.13.9 pp 568-9; and the Digest proposition is directly reproduced by Zouch *EI* 89, Domat 3.6.3.15, and Ayliffe 536.

117 Hawarde 13.

tions exceptionable witnesses are described as being "an infamous or notorious knave", "a suspected person", or "had lived in evill conversation or of bad fame"[118]. In the *Forum Romanum* Gilbert says that

> "If the party cannot be a good witness at law, no more may he be in equity; or these articles may be founded on the party leading a lewd life, or being a common drunkard, or swearer, or of ill repute and character in his neighbourhood, a common vagabond, a man not known, or who hath no abode, or such like (though these latter objections seldom come to anything), for notwithstanding all this, the man is a legal witness, therefore the court will hear his evidence, and judge of the credibility of it accordingly."[119]

There is also one later seventeenth century Chancery case which seems to show criminal misconduct put in proof to show bad character to attack credit. In *Okeover v Lady Pettus* (1675)[120] Lord Nottingham said, on the distinct but related question of the credit to be given to the defendant's answer, that

> Besides, it is in proof that deeds have been razed by her and her husband's name counterfeited, and that she solicited an attorney, whom she would have corrupted, to do the like. After this any circumstance to prove a trust is enough to outweight the Lady's credit.[121]

At common law, there is an indication of a wide conception of bad character as an objection to witnesses at the end of Coke's chapter on commissioners to examine witnesses in his Fourth Institute, where among a collection of latin tags he includes *De crimine in Lupanari commisso, lupanares testes esse possunt* (brothelkeepers can be witnesses to crimes committed in brothels) and *Qui prodit in scenam mercedes ergo, infamis est* (whoever appears on stage for reward is therefore infamous), both of which seem to be romanistic[122].

Wigmore collected a number of cases in the State Trials of impeachment of the credit of witnesses by bad character insufficient to disqualify[123]. However, proof was a problem. In *Onbie's Case* (1641) it is said that "in examining of a witness Counsel may not question the whole life of the witness, as that he is a whoremaster, &c. But if he hath done such a notorious fact which is a just exception against him, then they may except against him"[124] and in *Reading's Trial* (1679) and *Cook's Trial* (1696) it seems to be agreed that a witness could not be required to

118 f 452r No. 133, f 460r No 183, f 462v No 198.

119 147.

120 Nott CC No 347, (73 SS 236) R t Finch 270, aff'd HL (T1678) Lo Jo 13 267.

121 73 SS at 238.

122 Fourth Institute p 279. Cf D.3.2.1; The tag about brothels is also to be found in *Sir Antony Ashley's Case* (M1611) Moo KB 816 pl 1105, Star Chamber (Egerton, Coke), & Hudson 201; cf also below § 5 *(1)* (b) (iv). A lay perception of prostitutes as exceptionable witnesses is indicated in Marlowe's *Jew of Malta,* where Barabbas, when accused in Act V scene i, says "She is a curtezan, and he a thief/ And he my bondman. Let me have law".

123 *Bushnell's Trial* (1656) 5 How St Tr 633 at 641, *per* prisoner *arg,* and cases cited below.

124 March NC 83.

answer defamatory questions[125]. Hale said that disqualifying infamy had to be proved by producing the record of the conviction[126]; but this rule seems not to have been applied to the use of specific criminal acts in order to discredit witnesses; these could be proved by other witnesses[127], though it is possible that these witnesses would then be liable to be sued for slander[128].

By the end of the seventeenth century, therefore, it was clear that general bad character went merely to credibility. It was, nonetheless, as in the learned laws, a ground of formal exception to witnesses in equity.

4. Status rules

Both mediaeval civilian doctrine on exceptions to witnesses, and the common law challenge rules, contained a body of rules excluding witnesses on social status grounds, essentially affecting women and slaves (villeins in the challenge rules)[129]. These rules could be variously explained either on the ground of intellectual incapacity (women and slaves are too stupid to give evidence)[130] or of bad character (women and slaves are prone to lie)[131]. In both evidence to a jury and equity the exclusion of women is absent, and social status is relevant only to credibility (discussed below Ch 8 § 4). If, as Holdsworth thought[132], these rules still had full force in early modern civilian doctrine this would be an important variation. In reality the position was less clear.

---

125 *Reading* 7 St Tr 259 at 296; *Cook* 13 St Tr 311 at 334-8 *per* Treby CJ, Powys B, Trevor AG and Cowper arg.

126 HPC II 278.

127 *Faulconer* (1653) 5 St Tr 323, 354, character of the defendant in a perjury prosecution; *Whitebread* (1679) 7 St Tr 311, 357; *Earl of Stafford* (1680) 7 St Tr 1293, 1384-5, 1391-2,3,4; *Lord Delamere* (1686) 11 St Tr 509, 570; *Harrison* (1692) 12 St Tr 833, 861, 863; *Cranburne* (1696) 13 St Tr 221, 261; *Vaughan* (1696) 13 St Tr 485, 518, 519 (Salk 634 not SP); *Fielding* (1706) 14 St Tr 1327, 1355-7; *Willis* (1710) 15 St Tr 623, 636; *Francia* (1716) 15 St Tr 898, 967 f. *Contra Rookwood* (1696) 13 St Tr 139, 209-12; *Layer* (1722) 16 St Tr 93, 246, 256. All cited Wigmore § 986.

128 *Turberville v Savage* (1667) 12 Viner 39 ((1669) 1 Mod 3, 2 Keb 545, not SP and *semble* not SC). Cf Clerke 199-204, may sue the party who made a defamatory exception which failed in proof.

129 Co Lit 156. Women did not serve on juries, but there does not seem to be any authority for the proposition that they were challengeable. The civilian rules extended more widely to cover a range of occupations.

130 E.g. Ayliffe 537-8, and implied in 'Alciatus' 208r No 9, where women are grouped with children and lunatics.

131 This argument is reported in relation to women (without agreement) by Swinburne 188.

132 *HEL* IX 186, 187.

The formal exclusion of slaves presumably declined in practice with the decline of serfdom. Though present in 'Alciatus' and Ayliffe (who here as elsewhere draws mainly on mediaeval sources)[133] it is absent from the *Reformatio*, Swinburne, Ridley, Wiseman, Zouch, and Domat; and Pufendorf assimilates the rule to dependency and identifies its class basis from Roman sources[134]. Cotta and Wood both say that poverty is exceptionable because the poor are more easily corruptible, but both limit the case to poverty attributable to bad character[135].

The case of women is slightly more complex. Though 'Alciatus' says that women are excluded[136], other authors take more varying views. The *Reformatio* says that the exception to women affects credibility[137]. *Principia Quaedam* says that women cannot witness wills in civil law, but can in canon law[138]. Vulteius has the gnomic statement that "Sed nec foeminis in causis promiscue omnibus & quibusvis testibus esse licet"[139]. Swinburne says that "divers do write, that a woman is not without all exception", but that in reality "their testimony is so good, that a testament may be proved by two women alone ..."[140]. Domat follows the Digest in saying that women are generally acceptable in civil and criminal proceedings, except in the particular case of attesting wills[141]. Ayliffe, on the other hand, says that women are competent in civil causes but excluded in canon law criminal ones unless their evidence is required by the difficulty of proof or the importance of the case[142]. These varying opinions will not support the idea of a sharp contrast between civilian doctrine and equity and evidence rules in relation to the testimony of women – or in relation to status objections generally.

V. Bias

Apart from "simple" bias arising from friendship or enmity to one of the parties[143], bias as a ground of exception may be subdivided into three areas: the par-

133 'Alciatus' 208r Nos 9, 13; Ayliffe 538.

134 P 568.

135 Cotta 662; Wood 315. The argument was also used to justify property qualifications for jurors: J. Oldham, 'The Origins of the Special Jury' (1983) 50 *U Chic. LR* 137.

136 208r No 9.

137 248 c 17.

138 75.

139 372v.

140 188.

141 3.6.3 pr, Strahan 447, and 3.6.3.3; D 22.5.18.

142 537.

143 For friendship and enmity as exceptions in the learned laws, 'Alciatus' 207v, 210r; Cotta 420-1; Covarruvias *QP* 447.3; Vulteius 507v-508r; Clerke 209; Swinburne p 187; Ridley 79-80; Zouch *EI* 89-90; Conset 140; Domat 3.6.3.9,10; Ayliffe 541-2. Lyndwood 304 v

ties and other persons interested in the outcome of the cause; affinity to one of the parties; and dependence on one of the parties.

1. Parties and persons interested

In the civil law *Nullus idoneus testis in re sua intellegitur*, no-one can be understood to be a suitable witness in his own cause[144]. In the romano-canonical system this proposition means that the oath of a party is not the evidence of a witness for the purpose of proof by witnesses. It does not imply that the court is never concerned to take the oaths of the parties. As well as using examination on the positions with a view to obtaining a confession (discussed above Ch 2), the romano-canonical system inherited from the later roman law the ideas of the the decisory oath tendered by one party to another, and the oath imposed or awarded by the judge to be taken by one or another party, as means of concluding the cause; later classified as the *decisory* oath tendered to the adverse party and the *suppletory* oath available as a type of proof where one side had some, but insufficient, proof[145]. *Nullus idoneus testis in re sua intellegitur* as applied to parties is therefore basically definitional. The oath of a party is *not the same thing as* the deposition of a witness for the purposes of proof. This definitional aspect is made explicit by Vul-

---

testium receptionem and the *Reformatio* 248 c 17 refer only to 'capital' enmity as a ground for complete exclusion; Ayliffe 541-2 distinguishes capital and lesser enmity and friendship. Cotta 420-1 says that these exceptions are subject to judicial discretion because it may be collusively arranged; Vulteius 507v-508r that they do not lead to the complete rejection of the witness. There are two equity authorities which suggest exclusion on grounds of bias *per se*. In *Earl of Suffolk v Greenvill* (1631) 3 Ch Rep 89, Nels 15, 2 Freem 146, HLS 1105 p 126, Harg 174 f 18, Lord Coventry, sitting with the assistance of Hutton and Whitelock JJ, said *inter alia* that the plaintiff could not be relieved on the evidence, as to the contents of an instrument allegedly detained by the defendant, of a witness who was (on their analysis of the facts) interested, and "there being other exceptions against him, in respect of former and continued differences between the defendant and him". (This point appears in Chan Rep, Harg 174 and HLS 1105, not in the other reports). In *Dolman v Pritman* (1670) 3 Ch Rep 64 (*Anon* (?M1670) 2 Freem 134 probably SC) Grimstone MR said that if a witness refused to appear for one side, but subsequently appeared for the other side, the party for whom he had refused to appear could have the deposition suppressed on motion. This looks like suppression on grounds of apparent bias, but it may be merely want of mutuality or procedural irregularity, since the adverse party would probably be unable to cross-examine. *Suffolk v Greenvill*, if it is not a mere confusion in the report, looks like an application of the exclusion on grounds of "double exceptions" referred to by Swinburne, but overall these two cases do no more than suggest that bias may be a ground of exception in this sense.

144 D 22.5.10.

145 Discussed, 'Alciatus' 227v-229r; Maranta 596-600, 601 No 30; Cotta 454, 5, 458-62, 465-6; *Reformatio* 230 c 24; Gaill ii Obs 108 (suppletory); Vulteius 368v-369v; Cosin II Ch 3; Clerke 256-7 (suppletory); Ridley 8-9; Zouch *EI* 97, *DIE* 43; Conset 154-5 (suppletory); Pufendorf 5.13.8 p 567 (decisory); Domat 3.6.6 (decisory); Wood 324-5; Ayliffe 391 (suppletory) 392 (decisory).

teius, who defines testimony as "probatio facta per alios, quos causa de qua agitur non concernit"[146].

The same tag from the Digest was used to justify the exception to witnesses interested in the event of the cause[147]. As already indicated, Swinburne took the view that the effect of this exception was a matter of degree[148]. Thus the parties might be regarded as an extreme case of the exception for interest.

The exception to witnesses on the ground that they were parties or interested is one of the more highly developed areas of the case-law in this period both at common law and in equity, and therefore demands extensive discussion.

Wigmore argued that the rules started with an essentially procedural exclusion of parties in the mediaeval common law, which was gradually generalised from the mid seventeenth century to other interested persons, and that the rules so developed began to be followed in Chancery from the end of the seventeenth century[149]. This argument is interconnected with his claim that the rules of evidence at common law and particularly the law of witnesses were developed gradually and pragmatically as a means of controlling the jury, rather than influenced by roman-canon conceptions.

An examination of Wigmore's and other evidence, however, shows that (i) the first clear evidence for the exclusion of the parties from giving evidence to a jury at law is associated with an explanation of this exclusion that it is on the basis of bias due to interest, and the evidence for exceptions to witnesses other than parties on the ground of interest is earlier, and nearer to the first evidence for the exclusion of the parties, than Wigmore suggested, both in equity and at law; and (ii) there were in the seventeenth century a body of exceptions to these rules which tend to point to an approach, both at common law and in equity, similar to Swinburne's view that the effect of the exception for interest is a matter of degree.

a) The dating and origins of the rule

At common law the use of a party's oath in his own favour was limited to wager of law, i.e. to defendants in non-delictual transitory matters not proved in writing by the plaintiff (detinue, debt sur contract, certain pleas in account[150])[151]. In the

---

146 371v.

147 E.g. Zouch *EI* 89; Domat 3.6.3.6.

148 Above n 34 and text there.

149 § 575.

150 Baker IELH 445 (detinue), 366 (debt), Milsom HFCL 254 (debt) 278, 281 (account).

151 The romanistic expression "non-delictual" used here is merely for comparative purposes, not to suggest civilian influence. (The distinction between local and transitory matters is contemporary common law, where it affected the rules of *venue* for pleading and trial). It should also be noted that in the local courts the purgatory oath of the defendant was used in

seventeenth century common law parties of record could not be witnesses to a jury, subject to certain exceptions (below). Gilbert explains this exclusion of the parties as an instance of exclusion of the ground of bias due to interest[152].

Wigmore, however, argued that the exclusion of parties arose originally in the middle ages on procedural grounds, that is, that to swear the parties would involve mixing modes of trial, i.e. wager of law and trial by jury, and was only a good deal later generalised to exclude interested persons who were not parties of record[153]. In a certain sense this is to say no more than that the distinction between party oaths and witnesses was at common law, as in the roman-canon system, definitional.

Wigmore did not offer evidence for an early exclusion of parties, but argued that it went without saying[154]. Baker, in his Introduction to Vol II of Spelman's Reports, says that parties were incompetent in the early sixteenth century[155], but the authority he cites for the proposition, *Diversitie de Courtz*, seems to be merely saying (with emphasis) that in the cases at hand wager of law is not available[156].

In an assault case of 1572-3 in Dalison[157], the plaintiff was produced as a witness; after an exception had been taken to him as a witness as being under 20, and rejected, he was sworn; the defendant later realising that this witness was the plaintiff asked for the jury to be discharged. Not, however, on the ground that an incompetent witness had been heard, but on the ground that the proceedings were irregular because the plaintiff was under age and had not appeared by guardian. There may be a practical or procedural explanation for the failure to object to the plaintiff appearing as a witness[158], but the fact that the plaintiff was produced at all is hard to reconcile with the view that the exclusion of the parties was an ancient procedural rule so obvious it went without saying.

At a meeting of all the judges in 1556 to discuss trials for treason was said that

> "by the civil law accusers are as parties, and not as witnesses; witnesses ought to be indifferent, and not come until they are called, but accusers offer themselves to accuse, for 'tis a good challenge to witnesses, to say, that he was one of his accusers."[159]

---

delictual (i.e. criminal and tortious) matters: P&M HEL II 634-7; J.S. Beckerman, 'Procedural Innovation and Intellectual Change in Medieval English Manor Courts' (1992) 2 *L&HR* 197-252 at 203-212.

152 P 94.

153 § 575 point 1 (b).

154 § 575 at II 582

155 94 SS *110*

156 "1523" edition sig C vii r. I have not been able to consult the other editions cited by Baker, but the 1526 and subsequent editions on microfilm in the STC series have the same text on this point as the "1523" edition.

157 *Anon* (15 Eliz) Dalison 104 pl 44.

158 Cf the later rule that cross-examination to the merits waives the objection, above ch 5 § 2 *(4)* nn 146-8 and text there. Or it may be that since there were other witnesses, the admission of an incompetent witness would not have been seen as fatal.

This is discussion of the statutory provisions of the reign of Edward VI requiring two witnesses in treason[160]; but it indicates awareness of exclusion of parties as a principle at least where witnesses are required by law.

The first clear evidence of the exclusion of parties of record is from the 1580s: a decision in the Exchequer to receive the testimony of defendants who have no interest and were joined merely to disqualify them[161], a Chancery decision to issue a common injunction against a suit at law where this had been done[162], an argument in Chancery that a defendant had been joined merely to disqualify him[163], and a refusal by the Common Pleas to receive the plaintiff's prior oath before a Justice of the Peace as evidence in an action on the Statute of Winchester[164]. The cases on joining to disqualify suggest a long-established rule, beginning to be re-theorised in terms of bias due to interest, which was Wigmore's argument for an early dating of the exclusion of parties. The Common Pleas case, however, is more ambiguous. Wyndham J argued that such an oath had previously been received, and that the party's own oath was received in wager; Peryam J responded that

> That's an ancient law, but we will not make new presidents, for if such oath be accepted in this case, by the same reason in all cases where is secrecy, and no external proof, upon which would follow great inconveniences: and although such an oath hath been before accepted of, and allowed here, yet the same doth not move us; and we see no reason to multiply such presidents.[165]

This suggests fairly new law being made on policy grounds; in addition, exactly contrary to Wigmore's argument, the existence of wager is used as an argument *for* admitting the party's oath as evidence to a jury.

On this evidence, (1) the first evidence for the rule of exclusion of the parties is the distinction made between "accusers" and witnesses in the discussion of trials of treasons in 1556, where it is derived from the civil law; and (2) it is definitely established both at law and in equity in the 1580s, but may at law be relatively new law at that time.

---

159 Bro NC 50 (Bro *Corone* 219), at 51-2. Compare van Espen 3.7.6.6, voluntary witnesses suspect.

160 1 Ed 6 c 12 ss 19 & 22, 5 & 6 Ed 6 c 11 s 12.

161 *Dymoke's Case* (1582) Savile 34, Exchequer, defendants "envers que nul cause d'action est, & ceo est per Covin a toller lour testmoigne, que si appiert issint sur evidence, les Justices poent & doent receive lour testimonie"; cited by Wigmore 575 n 21. Since we are told that the *judges* are to receive their evidence this is probably on the equity side.

162 *Angrome v Angrome* (1583-4) Choyce Cas 176.

163 *Hollingworth v Lucy* (1580) Cary 91, (part of an argument about improper procedure in examination on commission).

164 *Firrell v The Hundred of B.* (T1586) 2 Leo 82 (*Terrets v The Hundred of &c* 4 Leo 51, otherwise SR; *Tirrell v A Hundred in Essex* Gould 24, SC but not SP), CP.

165 2 Leo 82; 4 Leo 51 at 52, with slight variations.

Wigmore argued that the starting point of the disqualification by interest of persons other than the parties of record at common law was the publication of Coke upon Littleton in 1628, and that the 1640s is the *terminus post quem* for the exclusion of interested persons other than parties. This dating gave a long gap between the emergence of the disqualification of the parties (on his argument dating from mediaeval times and well established in the reign of Elizabeth) and the generalisation to other interested persons. His evidence for this view is (1) the absence of cases in the Abridgements or in the State Trials, (2) instances of the reception of interested witnesses, in particular YB 27 H 8 f 20 pl 110 (1535) (Lord Cobham, party of record's employer, received to prove his own title) and *Anon* (1612)[166] (attesting witness to a feoffment received though he had subsequently become a tenant at will under the feoffee); and (3) statutory provisions; thus 27 Hen 8 c 4 (1535) recites the disqualification of interested parties in the Admiralty (inter alia, and very much in passing) as a reason for giving the common-law courts jurisdiction to try piracy, and James I's act for trial of offences committed on the borders (1606)[167] makes special provision to disqualify (inter alia) biassed witnesses; both implying that interested persons are not then disqualified at law. To these could be added (1) the statute 22 Hen 8 c 11, which gave the party robbed a right to restitution in the criminal proceedings if he gave evidence against the robber, and (2) the act of 1548 (2 & 3 Edw 6 c 29) re-enacting the Act of Hen 8 (25 Hen 8 c 6) against buggery (repealed by the Act of Grace at the beginning of the reign). This took away the forfeiture of property usual in felony, but then (s 2) felt it necessary to exclude witnesses who would gain by the decease of the accused.

Just as the dating of the emergence of the disqualification of parties seems rather early, so, too, Wigmore's dating of the objection on the ground of interest seems rather late. The 1535 case is actually of no assistance, since Wigmore misunderstood the report, which does not in reality suggest that Lord Cobham was sworn as a witness[168]. The absence of the objection from the State Trials can be disregarded, because these are mostly trials for treason or felony, to which the rule as it developed at common law only ever had a limited application[169].

166 1 Bulst 202.

167 Stat 4 Jac I c 1, s 16.

168 In replevin the defendant justified as bailiff to Lord Cobham, distraining for rent on land he claimed to be held by rent and fealty. After the court had rejected an ancient document and evidence of seisin of the rent alone as insufficient, "Purque le *Seignor* passa oustre, & don' evidence, que il fuit seisi del' suite al' Court." "Don' evidence" elsewhere in this report and in other reports means "produced evidence", usually writings, i.e. as a party, not "gave" evidence as a witness. In any event even if Lord Cobham did give evidence as a witness (the report tells us he was present in court, since he engaged in an altercation with Fitzherbert CJ which distracted the judge from the arguments of counsel) he might be regarded as a party. He was represented by counsel, and in 1586 it was arguable (by Walmsley, on a challenge to the array for consanguinity of the sheriff) that the master in replevin was closer to being a party than the lessor of the plaintiff in ejectment: *Anon* (M1586) Gould 42.19.

169 The rule as it developed excluded witnesses who either (a) would gain or lose by the result of instant proceedings, or (b) for or against whom these proceedings would subse-

The statutory provisions are interesting. The Henrician statutes clearly indicate an absence of rules at common law, and in addition that it was not thought there ought to be rules. The Buggery Act of 1548 is double-edged. On the one hand it indicates that there was at that time no rule at common law, on the other that the draftsman (or Parliament) saw interest as an objection. The Act for the trial of offences committed on the borders is particularly interesting, because the Parliamentary history of the provision is avaliable in the diary of Robert Bowyer[170].

It appears that the government's original proposal was to allow Englishmen who committed offences in Scotland and escaped into England to be remanded for trial in Scotland. This proposal was rejected by the Commons on the ground that trial in Scotland was according to the form of the Civil law. The Commons committee on the bill therefore devised a special form of trial for such offenders (s 6) including the provision that the accused should be allowed to have witnesses in his defence, which was a variation from English law[171]. Some government supporters proposed that these witnesses should be subject to exceptions, but this does not seem to have been included at this stage[172].

The King objected to the whole proposal, whereupon a general debate followed which indicates that the nature of the government argument was that (a) trial by jury and trial by witnesses were opposed, and (b) offenders would escape by procuring perjury[173]. The Lords objected to the clause on this latter ground, and Salisbury at a conference between the two houses proposed the compromise which was eventually adopted, viz. that the *jury* should be given the power to reject witnesses[174]. This proposal came to the Commons as a Lords' amendment, and was widely opposed in terms which suggest that the opponents thought that witnesses

---

quently be evidence. For this reason "interested" persons were only ever excluded from testifying for the Crown in criminal cases in those cases where a verdict of guilty would be evidence in their favour in subsequent civil proceedings – an early example of which is *Smith's Case* (T1610) 12 Co Rep 69. Disqualification by interest is therefore unlikely to be found in cases of treason and felony, since the offender's property was forfeited to the Crown, so that witnesses could hardly expect to gain by the conviction. In contrast in the civil and canon laws, where prosecutions criminal in form could lead to civil relief for the victim, the victim was excluded. This is the rule applied to exclude the non-party victim in Star Chamber, where criminal proceedings could similarly lead to civil relief, in *Dr Manning's Case* (P1612) 2 Brownl 151, and stated by Hudson, *Star Chamber* 205, both cited by Wigmore.

170 *The Parliamentary Diary of Robert Bowyer 1606-7* ed DH Willson (Minneapolis, U Minn Press, 1931) pp 300-319, 321, 322-330, 350-6, 358-363. The text of the Act is in SR iv (2) 1134 f.

171 End of s 6, SR iv (2) 1135; Bowyer 309.

172 Bowyer 309.

173 Bowyer 310-319.

174 Bowyer 323-6, Salisbury's proposal at 326: "some mitigation might be had of this clause touching witnesses: but the same not to be referred to the iudge, who is but one, who is but a stranger, who is to greate to beare out his owne doings, but to the jurors, who are 12, who are neighbors, who are not [too] greate to beare out their doings".

were not essential to trial by jury, that there were no clear rules governing who could be a witness, and that such rules were undesirable as tending to turn the jury into a civil law trier of fact[175]. It was, however, eventually carried[176].

What this history shows is that (1) The Act as passed tells us nothing about the exception on the ground of interest (Wigmore's argument) since the exceptions contained in the section are general bias and bad character[177], and the only other exception referred to in argument is domesticity, i.e. dependence[178]. (2) It probably does not tell us much about contemporary common law practice, since it is a proviso to a wholly new departure, witnesses for the defence, in special circumstances. (3) It does tell us, however, that it was at this time a matter of uncertainty and debate what the relation of witnesses to jury trial was. This is obviously parallel to the difference over documents between *Newis v Lark* and *Dr Leyfield's Case* discussed in Chapter 3 above. (4) Supporters of the use of exceptions to witnesses argue not by generalising the case of the party, as Wigmore's argument would suggest, but by direct reference to general bias.

The attesting witness case of 1612 is ambiguous; the objection is taken by counsel, but the court seems to say that it does not apply *to this case*. In the circumstances it could be argued (a) that the interest was trivial – thus Gilbert explains this case by saying that a tenant at will is competent as not really having an interest in the land[179], or (b) that the case of an attesting witness who subsequently takes an interest under the feoffee is out of the rule because conveyances ought to be upheld; the cryptic passage in the report, "being in affirmance of the feoffment" suggests this line of argument[180]. This case could therefore equally be either rejection of interest as an objection, or acceptance of it subject to limitations.

It is true that the main body of authority starts in the 1640s[181], but there is a clear case at common law in 1630[182], a *dictum* in 1617 in a maintenance case in Star Chamber that

---

175 Bowyer 353-6, 358, 359-61.

176 Bowyer 363-4.

177 s 16, SR iv (2) at 1137.

178 Sir Edwin Sandys, Bowyer 309; cf below § 5 *(2)* (b).

179 P 88. Printed texts cite Hale super Lit 6; BL MS cites Hawk Abr CL 6; Linc Inn MS cites [Nelson] L.E. 76, 78. The reference is clearly to this case. For small interests as an exception to the rule in general cf below § 5 *(1)* (b) (iii).

180 Coke's discussion of witnesses, Co Lit 6b, shows that in any case attesting witnesses are a special case.

181 There are 6 cases from the 1640s in Style Prac Reg pp 354-6.

182 *Mericke v King* (1630) Hetley 137. In *Anon* (1639) Clayt 68, (NP, Vernon J or Henden B) the plaintiff made title by a devise of a term with a proviso that the testator's widow should enjoy it for 21 years; the widow was admitted to prove the will "*because* [my emphasis] her term was expired". This ruling appears to suppose the prior existence of disqualification by interest.

"... the tenants might defend the suit on a common charge, and the reason was, that since the title was one against all, it was in effect but one's defence, and one defendant, for trial in one man's case tried all. And therefore the courts of justice do every day deny them to be witnesses one for another in such general cases, as in cases of common[,] modus decimandi, and the like;..."[183],

and a decision in 1610 excluding the obligor in a criminal prosecution for usury, since he would thereby discharge himself of the money owed[184]).

In Chancery, *Observations* (c. 1600) lists among exceptionable witnesses "one that by his oath shall charge the def[endant] or pl[aintiff] and thereby dischargeth himself"[185], a fairly clear general statement of the exception. The next clear case is *Suffolk v Greenvill* (1631)[186]. Earlier, *Hollingworth v Lucy* (1580) and *Angrome v Angrome* (1583-4)[187] on witnesses joined as defendants to disqualify, like *Dymoke's Case* (1582) in the Exchequer[188], suggest theorisation of the exclusion of parties in terms of interest, since parties who are not interested are to be allowed to testify. This impression is reinforced a ruling in Star Chamber in 1598 in *Litleton v Litleton* that where a bill raises multiple and independent issues, codefendants who are not concerned in the same issue may testify for each other[189], and by two certificates from Master Carew in *Wyley v Vincent* (1607) and *Whyte v Oxenbridge* (1608) authorising the examination of defendants as witnesses to matters in which they were not interested, on the basis of the rule (stated in Swinburne) that a legatee can be a witness as to matters other than his own legacy[190]. There is also one

183 *Lord Howard v Bell, Salkeld, Dacre & al'* (1617) Hob 91 at 92, *per* Coke and Hobart. I have inserted a comma after "common" as it seems essential to the sense. Wigmore thought this *dictum* concerned disqualification of the of parties, but it is quite clear that what is being said is that interested non-parties are disqualified, since the action in question is not a representative one; indeed, the possibility of joinder of defendants is an additional reason to allow shared funding of a trial action, and is said to be possible because they are excluded as witnesses, or as a sort of tit-for-tat: they share the burdens of the litigation, therefore they are to share the (possible) benefits.

184 *Smith's Case* (T1610) 12 Co Rep 69, (also cited Co Lit ff 6b-7, where Coke cites Britton f 134 *accord*). Wigmore suggests that the decision is also based on the parol evidence rule, but the Crown would not be estopped by the obligor's act and in any case an invalidity in the creation of the deed which would only appear by parol evidence was a well-known exception to the operation of the doctrine (above Ch 4).

185 f 460r No 183.

186 3 Ch R 89, Nels 15, 2 Freem 146, Harv Freem 126, Harg 174 f 18. This point only in Nelson and Harg 174. In *Hill v Hill* (1631-2) Toth 109 a special order was required to examine a guardian as a witness, but there is nothing to say why this should be so, and the guardian may have been a nominal party; and in *Sherborne v Foster and Towneley* (Toth 187) in the same year it is said that trustees are not to be examined as witnesses against each other, which might possibly be something to do with interest but seems more likely to be some other rule about trusteeship.

187 Above nn 163, 162.

188 Above n 161, probably also equity.

189 (T1598) Hawarde 98.

ambiguous case in Chancery in the reign of Elizabeth which may be a case of disqualification by interest. In *Livers & Oylands v Brend & Brandon* (1579)

> "One Benn being produced to be examined as a witness refused to be examined. An attachment granted, he appeared and shewed that the articles concern a lease of land whereof the said Benn hath the reversion, therefore discharged."[191]

This may be that he is excused because he is not competent on grounds of interest, but could equally be an early example of the one of the rules limiting compulsion, i.e. there may be a forfeiture involved, or the witness may have been a purchaser[192].

The authorities do to some extent suggest a first stage of theorisation of the exclusion of the parties in terms of interest (*Hollingworth v Lucy, Dymoke's Case, Angrome v Angrome, Litleton v Litleton, Wyley v Vincent, Whyte v Oxenbridge*) and extension of the party rule to witnesses who were in substance parties (the obligor in *Smith's Case*, the victim in *Dr Manning's Case*, commoners or parishioners in *Lord Howard v Bell & al'*; but not tenant at will in *Anon* (1612)); though this may be a matter of the courts, like Swinburne, seeing interest as a matter of degree so that small interests went only to credit and only "parties in interest" were actually excluded. To this extent they support Wigmore's argument of a process of generalisation from the case of the party.

However, (1) It is certainly impossible to say on this evidence that the exclusion of parties emerges at common law and is copied in equity, since the equity case of *Hollingworth v Lucy* is as early as the first clear common law authority. (2) It is quite clear that exclusion at common law on the ground of interest does not to any significant extent antedate the exception for interest in equity, so that we cannot suppose equity to have followed the law in this development. (3) The available evidence does not entitle us to suppose a *long* gap between the exclusion of the parties and exclusion for interest at common law. And (4) Wigmore's suggestion that the exclusion of the parties was originally procedural and unconnected with bias due to interest, though it *may* be true, is in substance a pure speculation, and contrary to the earliest evidence, the 1556 discussion of trials for treason, where it is grounded on the civil law.

b) Theory, limits and exceptions

Gilbert accounts for the exclusion of interested witnesses on the ground of the danger of bias. He draws from this the corollary that "he is the best witness that

---

190 *Wyley v Vincent* (1607) Monro 83, *Whyte v Oxenbridge* (1608) Monro 102; Swinburne p 187. It appears from the 1742 edition of Swinburne (p 347, citing, rather inappropriately, *Howard v Bell & al'*) that this rule was later rejected at common law.

191 Choyce Cas 137. Stowe 415 f 133b, *Lyvers & Oylandere v Bonne & Brandon* and the witness' name also Bonne.

192 Above Ch 2.

can be against himself"[193]. He defines interest as "where there is a certain benefit or [dis]advantage to the Witness attending the Consequence of the Cause one way,. . ."[194] and proceeds immediately to discuss the cases of (1) trustees and other fiduciaries; (2) tenants, commoners and witnesses bound by contract to the parties; (3) criminal cases; (4) obligors and mortgagors to the testator as witnesses to wills; (5) members of corporations and inhabitants of other local government areas; and (6) exceptions on the ground of necessity[195], before proceeding to the cases of the parties and their spouses.

Bacon states the rule as

> ". . . not to admit the Testimony of a Witness, who is either to be a Gainer or a Loser by the Event of the Cause, whether such Advantage be direct or immediate, or consequential only."[196]

However, he goes on (unlike Gilbert) to say that

> "From this General Rule several Doubts and Difficulties have arose with regard to those Cases where the Party may be said to have an Interest, and from the extream Difficulty attending certain particular Cases, which seem in several Instances to leave this Matter very unsettled, and which can only be learned from the Nature and Circumstances of the Cases themselves"[197].

Both the general formulation, and the statement that the law is unsettled, come from Hawkins[198]; Bacon, however, makes the point more strongly, and though he cites heavily from Hawkins his account is much more extensive, drawing on reports published in the 1720s (which, nonetheless, deal in the main with cases of the reigns of William and Anne). Like Gilbert, Bacon says that necessity is a ground to admit an interested witness, but unlike Gilbert he does not restrict this rule to statutory cases[199]; also unlike Gilbert, Bacon says that

> "no General Rule can be laid down, but that every Case must stand upon its own particular Circumstances, viz. Whether the Interest be of that Nature, or so considerable as by Presumption to produce Partiality in the Witnesses."[200]

and he discusses the question of witnesses who acquire an interest after being examined but before hearing, or who divest themselves of their interest, which Gilbert does not.

---

193 Pp 86-7, 99.

194 P 87. Bracketed letters absent from the MSS, which also have a full stop and end the para at the final comma.

195 Pp 87ff, in this order, though not analysed this explicitly.

196 P 289.

197 Ib.

198 II pp 433-4.

199 Pp 290-1.

200 P 291, citing Scroggs CJ in the London Quo Warranto trial of 1678, 2 Lev 231.

Ballow follows a different approach. He says that "the Cases where the Party is concern'd in Interest, tho' never so small, have usually prevail'd, unless in special instances"[201] but then proceeds to list seven exceptions, which are (1) necessity, (2) spoliation, (3) length of time, (4) small sums in an account, (5) release of interest, (6) *particeps criminis* to prove matters of fraud, and (7) defendants made parties to take away their testimony; and concludes that

> "this cannot be a general Rule, but every Case stands on its own Circumstances, that is, whether their Interest is so great as it may be presum'd to make them partial, or not; and therefore Alms-people and Servants are good Witnesses. So it is usual for a Legatee of a small Legacy, as 5s. to a private Person, or 5l. to a Nobleman, to be admitted a Witness for the Will."[202]

It seems to me that both this statement and Bacon's, taken together with the existence of several of the exceptions, indicate some uncertainty as to the nature of the rule. The rule which was to become (which was becoming) established was that any interest, however small, was a complete disqualification. But Ballow's and Bacon's statements, and the exceptions, point to a view of the basic rule as a matter of degree – as it was said to be by Swinburne – so that small interests may be disregarded, and in some cases interested witnesses may be accepted where their evidence is supported by a presumption, such as those arising from spoliation and from length of time. In the same period some of these exceptional cases are becoming re-theorised as instances of the admission of *prima facie* disqualified witnesses on the ground of necessity; which in the eighteenth century became the "inclusionary" aspect of the best evidence rule[203]. These questions therefore need slightly more detailed discussion[204].

In addition, the courts of equity, as well as examining parties, particularly defendants, as witnesses in matters as to which they were not concerned[205], made some

---

201 P 122.

202 P 123.

203 For this terminology, and a summary account of the best evidence rule, cf Wigmore §§ 173-5

204 Divestment of interest, and interests acquired after examination, are not relevant here.

205 Co-defendants who had no interest in the cause (so that their addition as defendants was an abuse) *Angrome v Angrome* and *Hollingworth v Lucy,* above nn 163, 162; the *Kingston on Thames Case* (1601-2) Cary 21 may be also on this ground; and cf also *Observations* f 443r No 49, where it is said that in these circumstances D should prefer a cross-bill against P or against the co-D; id. f 457v No 168, however, says that the disinterested co-defendant's answer may be read as testimony. Co-defendants whose interest was limited examinable as to points in which they were not concerned in interest: *Litleton v Litleton, Wyley v Vincent* and *Whyte v Oxenbridge,* above nn 189, 190 and text there. Defendants examinable if they disclaimed: *Oke v Pridieux* (1581) Choyce Cas 148; *Observations* f 449v No 110. Defendants who were bare trustees, or who disclaimed, could be examined by the plaintiff: *Windham v Richardson* (H1675-6) 2 Ch Cas 212, 1 Eq Ca Ab 225.7, Nott CC No 408. By the time of Jeffreys C the examination of defendants *de bene esse,* saving exceptions to the hearing, was an order of course: *Glover v Faulkner* (P1687) 1 Vern 452, 1 Eq Ca Ab 233.1; Bacon

use of party oaths in their own favour which may be analogous with the decisory and suppletory oaths of the learned laws, and this (so far as it has not already been discussed in Ch 2) needs to be considered.

(1) SPOLIATION: Ballow gives no example of this. The usual context of the maxim *omnia praesumuntur contra spoliatorem* is suppression or destruction of deeds[206] leading either to the admission of otherwise inadmissible evidence, or to a simple presumption of title against the despoiler. However, Maranta gives spoliation as a ground to admit a party's oath to *quantum*. This passage was extracted by the author of *Forme et Certenty*[207], and there is a similar statement in Hudson[208]. There are some cases in Chancery in the later seventeenth century which admit the party's oath to prove the measure of damage on this ground. In *Childrens v Saxby* (M1683)[209] the defendant took out execution at law in contempt of an injunction, and the plaintiff alleged that the bailiffs had taken £150 in hidden money and damaged his goods. Lord Nottingham ordered that the defendant pay all the damage the plaintiff would swear to; Lord Guilford affirmed this order and said that *in odium spoliatoris* the oath of the party injured was a good charge on the wrongdoer. In *East India Co. v Evans* (H1684-5)[210] Lord Guilford in deciding a point about discovery of torts and self-incrimination, cited

> "... the case where a man run away with a casket of jewels, he was ordered to answer, and the injured party's oath admitted as evidence *in odium spoliatoris* ..."[211]

In *Eyton v Eyton* (1700)[212] a co-defendant's answer in earlier proceedings is admitted, together with a counterpart, to show a settlement destroyed by a party; though the report is imperfect, this may also be a case of spoliation. There are no instances of this principle at law.

---

pp 287-8, also explaining the procedure, and justifying it on the basis that defendants are forced into the cause, while plaintiffs (who could not be examined on this basis) were liable to costs if the claim failed even if they had no interest; a motion was required suggesting that the defendants it was sought to examine were not interested. However, Tothill has a cryptic precedent from 1632-3 of the examination of a plaintiff as a witness, *Mayor of Bristol v Whitson* (1632-3) Toth 146, and in *Exton v Turner* (M1681) 2 Ch Cas 80 (earlier proceedings, (T1679) Rep t Finch 368, Nott CC No 943) a former plaintiff who had released his interest to the other plaintiffs and was not now a party, was allowed to be examined for the plaintiffs on a bill of revivor. The reporter queries how the release of the interest is to appear judicially to the court, and in *Phillips v Duke of Buckingham* (H1683) 1 Vern 227, 1 Eq Ca Ab 225.7, it is said that a plaintiff who avers that he is a mere trustee is not examinable, otherwise a defendant who answers that he is a mere trustee, because then on oath.

206 Above Ch 3 § 3 *(3)* (a); below Ch 9 § 2 *(1)*.

207 Maranta 601 No 30; *F&C* f 546r. Zouch lists the point as a disputable one: *SQ* cl 9 No 16.

208 206.

209 1 Vern 207, 1 Eq Ca Ab 15.2, 229.11.

210 1 Vern 305.

211 Ib. at 308.

212 Above Ch 2 nn 242-3 and text there.

(2) LENGTH OF TIME: Again, the commonest use of the maxim *ex diuturnitate temporis omnia praesumuntur rite et solemniter esse acta* is in connection with documents[213]. The maxim is also used, however, in Chancery accounts to permit parties to prove items in old accounts by oath. The first authority is *Peyton v Green* (1640)[214] (defendant's oath to prove an account 20 years old); this doctrine was followed by Bridgman LK in *Holstcomb v Rivers* (1669)[215] and *West v Throgmorton* (1671)[216]; by Lord Shaftesbury C in *Mason v Herbert* (1672)[217]; and by Lord Nottingham in *Love v Browne* (1674)[218]. The doctrine does not apply where the accountant has destroyed his books himself or never kept any, on grounds of spoliation[219]. As with the case of spoliation, there are no instances of this rule at law.

(3) SMALL INTERESTS: Ballow[220] treats the rule that the party can discharge himself of small sums in an account (discussed above Ch 2), and this rule that small interests do not disqualify, as separate rules; it is possible, however, that the account rule is a branch of this rule. If so, the cases on small sums in an account would be the first instances of this rule[221]. As said above, there is a marked similarity between the rule as stated by Bacon and Ballow and Swinburne's statement that

> "Wherein (as in many things els) very much is attributed to the discretion of the judge, who as ... the commoditie of the witnes is to reape, more or lesse: So the wise Iudge ought to give more or lesse credite to their saiyngs and depositions."[222]

The more general proposition that small sums do not disqualify first appears at common law, in 1647:

> "One that hath a small Legacy given unto him by a Will, may be allowed as a Witness to prove that will; but he that hath lands given unto him, by a Wil, may not be allowed for a Witness to prove that Will. P 23 Car B.r. For that were to suffer one to swear his own title, but in the former case the Law will not intend that any one will forswear himself for a small matter."[223]

---

213 Above Ch 3 nn 123-4, 243-4 and text there; cf also below Ch 9 § 2 *(1)*.

214 1 Ch Rep 146.

215 (P1669) 1 Ch Cas 127, Nels 139, 1 Eq Ca Ab 5.1, Nott Proleg c19.1; with the advice of Rainsford and Wylde JJ.

216 Nott Proleg c 19.2.

217 (T1672) Nott Proleg c 19.10.

218 (T1674) Nott CC No 120.

219 *Acourt v Chambers* (H1669) Nott Proleg 19.3, 9; *Hide v Petit* (P1673) 3 Swan 295, Nott Proleg 19.13.

220 Pp 122-3.

221 The rationale of the small sums rule does not appear in the cases on it, but the fact that it was doubted and restricted in the later seventeenth century, at the same time as the small interests rule seems to have been restricted, suggests a connection.

222 P 187.

223 Style Prac. Reg. 354-5.

A small legacy is also the hypothetical example given by Ballow[224], and this is drawn from the view expressed by Lord Guilford obiter in *Sutton Coldfield v Wilson* (M1684)[225], that "if it was an inconsiderable legacy as 5s (or 5l to a man of quality) that he should nonetheless be a witness to prove the will". Similarly Lord Nottingham in *Cook v Fountain* (T1675)[226] said that "6s. 2d. per annum seem no such great matter as should bias the witness". The "small interests" rule was controversial in the second half of the seventeenth century in the context of its application at common law to borough corporations, parishes, counties and hundreds[227]. The cases are collected in Gilbert[228] and Bacon[229]; they seem to show a movement away from the "small interest" exception. By the 1690s it was possible for it to be said in equity that "the cases, where the party was concerned in interest though never so small, have always prevailed" so that parishioners were disqualified to prove misapplication of charitable trust funds[230]. At the same period specific statutory provisions were made to admit parishioners in the analogous situation of misapplication of poor relief funds[231], and in 1702 it was also felt necessary to pass an act to enable inhabitants to be witnesses in cases of indictments etc against the relevant local authorities for failing to repair bridges[232]. This suggests that the small interests rule, as a general rule, has effectively disappeared, though it may have been resurrected later[233].

224 P 123.

225 1 Vern 254, 1 Eq Ca Ab 224.3.

226 Nott CC No 273, 73 SS 185. Earlier proceedings at law probably *Anon* (P1674) 1 Mod 107. This or another trial at law, 2 Vent 347, dated by Ventris to H1679-80. It appears from Lord Nottingham's report that the decision at law was to admit the witness, an executor of the plaintiff's grantor; Modern is accord, Ventris contra. Hearing and decree, (P1676) Nott CC No 500, 3 Swans 585 (not SP); subsequent proceedings before Trevor MR (M1686) 1 Vern 413, not SP.

227 The civilians also took varying views on the acceptability of corporation members in corporation causes. Covarruvias *QP* (447 No 8) says that they are excluded in relation to rights of pasture but acceptable, though their credibility is affected, in boundary cases. The *Reformatio* (249 c 20) says that they are acceptable unless the witness' individual right is in question. Wood (315) says that they are excluded if they would gain individually, but acceptable if the only gain would be to the corporation as a whole. Ayliffe (544) says that they are excluded.

228 At pp 91-3, not mentioning "small interests".

229 Pp 291-2.

230 *Dowdeswell v Nott* (P1694) 2 Vern 317, 1 Eq Ca Ab 225.12, in Chancery; it does not appear from the report whether Somers LK or Trevor MR.

231 3 & 4 William & Mary c 11 s 12.

232 1 Anne c 18 s 13

233 Bacon's authorities are all from the later seventeenth century. However, the 1832 edition of Bacon gives some authorities from the later eighteenth century in support of the rule. It may be that despite *Dowdeswell v Nott* the long-established small sums rule in account meant that the general exception survived in Chancery.

Spoliation, length of time and small interests have in common that they appear to be based, not on the logic of the rule excluding interested persons as stated by Gilbert, but on its underlying rationale. The underlying cause of exclusion of interested witnesses is, as in the civilian authors, the danger of bias. In general witnesses are to be believed because they are on oath; what is said upon oath is presumed to be true[234], or, in the tag used by Coke, *jurato creditur in judicio*[235]. In the case of biassed witnesses, however, this presumption is to a greater or lesser extent weakened or removed[236]. The cases of spoliation and length of time reflect the possibility that the presumptions in these cases buttress the weakened evidence of the interested witness; the case of "small interests" is markedly parallel to the view taken by Swinburne that the exception for bias/interest is a matter of degree.

(4) NECESSITY: As already indicated, Gilbert, Bacon and Ballow all give necessity as an exception to the rule against interested witnesses. The antecedents of this idea were much wider both in the civil and the common laws. The *regulae iuris* in the *Digest* include the proposition that *Quae propter necessitatem recepta sunt, non debent in argumentum trahi*[237] and *Principia Quaedam* collects several necessity maxims: *Cessat lex ubi advenit necessitas; Necessitas non habet legem; Necessitas non paret legi, sed legem parit; Quod alias est prohibitum, ex necessitate tolleratur*[238]. The principle of necessity appears in civilian discussions of exceptions to witnesses as a general exception to rules of exclusion[239].

At common law the necessity principle could be found in public law[240], and as a defence in tort[241]. Coke uses *quod necessarium est licitum est* to justify the effect of common recoveries[242], and Jenkins, writing during the civil war and interreg-

---

234 Below Ch 8.

235 Fourth Institute p 279.

236 Cf Gilbert 101 on infamy, discussed above § 4 *(1)*.

237 D 50.17.162.

238 19-20.

239 Generally to admit unsuitable witnesses, *Singularia??* cited *F&C* 546r; Hippolytide Marsiliis in *Singularia Francofurti* (1596) i 608-9 No 73, Autunius Columbetus in id. ii 310 No 1; Paulo Fusco, *Singularia in Iure Caesario et Pontifico* (Frankfurt, 1600) 356 No 24. Applied to heresy and treason, Cosin III 114-5; to admit dependent 'domestic' witnesses in adultery and other matters where witnesses unusual, *Reformatio* 249-50 c 21, and Gaill ii Obs. 102 Nos. 7-9; to allow domestics and *famuli* to prove highway robbery, Maranta 567 No 65; to admit witnesses of bad character in robbery, piracy and other fraudulent conspiracies, Gentili ii 143; general proposition, Wood, note at 316.

240 G. Burgess, *Absolute Monarchy and the Stuart Constitution* (New Haven, 1996) 49-51 and sources cited there. But note that though Burgess claims that the necessity maxims he cites are common law doctrine, he does not either trace these latin tags into the Year Books, or consider possible civilian sources; so that it is quite possible that they are sixteenth and seventeenth century borrowings by common lawyers from civilian sources.

241 *Case of Saltpetre* (1606) 12 Co. Rep. 12, 13.

242 *Dormer's Case* (P1593) 5 Co 40a at 40b.

num[243], applies this tag to several exceptions to procedural rules[244] – and to the rule in *Dr Leyfield's Case* that in case of destruction by fire, etc, a deed may be proved by secondary evidence[245]. The admission of interested witnesses on grounds of necessity first appears explicitly in *Benet v The Hundred of Hertford* (M1650), an action on the Statute of Winchester:

> "nul person est d'estre un testimonie en son cause demesne mes pur necessitie, come sil mesme ad estre robbe coment que il soit plaintife uncore il poet estre un bon testimonie a prover luy mesme d'estre robbe, & de que summe ou choses, & auxi a prover que il done notice al prochein vill & levie hue & crie, pur ceo que ceo est de necessitie pur default de auter profe."[246]

Hudson has this rule, but explains it in terms of spoliation[247]. In *Ipswich v –* (1669), an action for a fine for refusing to renounce the Covenant under the penal legislation of the 1660s, the same rule was applied to a case which might equally have been regarded as one of "small interests":

> "the Town-Clerk (though a Freeman) was allowed a witness to prove Election, Refusal, &c, and the Fine set, which is for necessity, for that none other are or ought to be present at those Acts."[248]

Both these cases fit in with Gilbert's restriction of this exception to cases "Where a Statute law could receive no Execution unless a Party interested were a Witness"[249].

The necessity principle was applied in equity by Lord Nottingham in *Morley v Morley* (H1678-9)[250] to admit a trustee to prove that money stolen was trust money, and by the 1690s it appears to be perfectly general, being applied to admit

---

243 Preface to his *Eight Centuries of Reports* (1661) cited by Holdsworth HEL V 354.

244 "Quod est necessarium est licitum": eg 76.XLV, 85.LXV, 207.XXXVIII.

245 Above Ch 4 pp 116ff; Jenkins 18.XV at 19 and 280.V (the latter citing *The Prince's Case* (1606) 8 Co 1 [at 28a] (no plea of *nul tiel record* against a general act, which may be proved *aliter*).

246 Rolle, *Abridgement* II 685,6. This argument was raised and rejected in CP as a ground for using the party's oath before a JP, required by 27 Eliz c 13 s 11, in *Firrell v The Hundred of B* (T1586) (references above n 109) on the ground cited there. However, in *Wincope's Case* (1635) Clayt 35 at nisi prius Berkeley J held that "his [the party robbed's] own oath before a justice is sufficient within the Stat. 27 Eliz and no contradictory proof shall be received against that oath that he knew any of the robbers, for when he hath once denyed it upon oath this is all required by the law to inable to bring this action as to that point"; the reporter adds, quod nota.

247 206; above n 208.

248 (Summer Ass 1669) per Rainsford J, *Trials Per Pais* (second edition, 1682) p 186.

249 93. In contrast, in *Garrard v Lister* (P1661) 1 Keb 15, KB (*Garrett v Lister* 1 Lev 25, SC but not SP) it is said that "The lord may be admitted to give evidence for the lessee or copyholder, though the Court would have spared him had there been other" which suggests the necessity rule; but the context is very unclear.

250 "He cannot possibly have other proof" – 2 Ch Cas 2; not in Nott. CC.

participants in trover[251] and fraud[252], a prisoner to prove a voluntary escape though the effect was to avoid a bond given by him to the gaoler[253], the master of a ship seized in trover[254] and the victim of a fraud in a criminal prosecution[255]. Several of these cases might have been regarded as instances of small interests or spoliation. It is possible, therefore, that the increased prominence of necessity at this period reflects a hardening of the general rule excluding interested witnesses, for which there is some independent evidence in relation to the "small interests" principle. At this period the principle is still described as "necessity" or "*ex necessitate rei*"; it is not until later that it became attached to the best evidence rule[256].

c) Party oaths in equity

As indicated above[257], the roman-canon system at this period used parties' oaths in their own favour in two ways: the decisory oath, which finished the cause, and the suppletory oath taken by the party who had some but insufficient proof. There are two direct references in contemporary authority to these roman-canon concepts. A sidenote in Cary describes the conclusive effect of the examination of the defendant on interrogatories as *juramentum delatum a parte*, i.e. decisory oath[258]; and Egerton, around 1600 characterises the use of witnesses examined after publication *ad informandam conscientiam judicis* as "Iuramentum Supplemento[rium]" (*sic*, as reported in *Observations*) i.e. suppletory oath. At about the same period *Forme et Certenty* cites Maranta for the propositions that the suppletory oath can be taken after the conclusion in the cause, and that the measure of damage in spo-

251 *Dockwra v Dickenson* (1696) Skin 640, Comb 366.

252 *Oldbury v Wynne* (1699) Colles 91, (Somers C, HL) *May v Harman* (1709) 4 Bro PC 156, HL.

253 *R v Weeden Ford*, above n 83.

254 *Dockwra v Dickenson*, above n 96.

255 *R v Mackartey & Fordenborough* (M1703) 1 Salk 286, Holt KB 300, *per* Holt CJ. 6 Mod 301 gives a different explanation. 2 Ld Raym 1179, 3 Ld Raym 325, not SP.

256 Gilbert does not refer to it as an instance of the best evidence rule, though he uses the rule in several other contexts; nor does Bacon, or Ballow (who does not refer to the best evidence rule at all). In *Searle, administrator of Searle, v Lord Barrington, administrator of John Wildman* (M1724) 2 Ld Raym 1370, Stra 826, 8 Mod 278, aff'd HL (1730) 3 Bro PC 593, Raymond and Fortescue JJ gave it as their opinion that the obligee's indorsements on a bond are "the best and surest evidence of payment of the money", therefore admissible in his administrator's favour to rebut the presumption of payment as well as against him, but this seems to be merely descriptive. It may be that the first application of the phrase "best evidence" in the context of witnesses is the judgement of Lord Hardwicke in *Omichund v Barker* (to admit Hindu witnesses in relation to transactions in India).

257 P 231.

258 Cary 11, Stowe 415 f 93b, Harg 281 f 15. Ballow p 125 starts his discussion of the obligation to answer, Book VI c 3, with the assumption that this obligation is analogous to the oath in the learned laws.

liation can be established by party oath[259]. Beyond these rather limited uses the civilian oath concepts are not discussed in cases, the Chancery Orders, or the practice books.

However, the Chancery in the later sixteenth and early seventeenth centuries made extensive use of examinations of parties[260]. While much of this was probably with a view to obtaining confessions[261], in some circumstances these examinations could be *quasi* decisory or *quasi* suppletory.

In the first place, where the plaintiff relied exclusively on the answer or examination of the defendant, there the defendant's oath would generally be conclusive[262]. The exception to this rule, in cases of fraud or spoliation, proves the general rule[263].

Secondly, in certain cases parties do seem to have been allowed to rely on their own oaths for deficiency of other proof. I have already referred to a number of cases where the party's oath is received in his own favour which involve, or appear to involve, spoliation, length of time, or small sums. In addition, the plaintiff's oath was received to convict the defendant of contempt[264]. This is weak evidence, however, because contempt proceedings were bound to be anomalous[265]. In *Plampin v Betts* (M1684)[266] "After many wrangles in taking the account" Lord Nottingham ordered that if the plaintiff would swear he believed certain questioned sums to be distinct sums they should be taken as such. A bill of review brought before Lord

---

259 f 544r citing 140 nu 29 = 598 No 3; f 546r citing 374 = 601-2 No 30.

260 Jones pp 245-8. Tothill contains various cryptic precedents of the examination of parties on interrogatories (*Mayor of Feversham v Ance* (1569) Toth 85 (defendant), *Cotton v Paget* (1569) Toth 85 (defendant not to be examined upon all interrogatories), *Lambert v Lambert* (1570) Toth 145 (plaintiff), *Burleigh v Shute* (M1594) Toth 85, Stowe 415 f 204v, Harl 1576 f 172r, *Meretvither v Filmer* (1595-6) Toth 190 (*Merywether*) Harl 1576 f 149v (defendant, and the plaintiff left to proofs); at the hearing (*Gwynn v Petty* (P1630) Toth 71 (defendant), *Kent v Banham* (P1630) Toth 146 (plaintiff), *Bradshaw v Bradshaw* (H1632-3) Toth 71 (defendant) and after the hearing (*Lea v Band* (1589-91) Toth 85 (defendant, and plaintiff left to proof), *Pollixfen v Short* (1529-30) Toth 71 (defendant), *Drewry v Watson* (1631-2) Toth 190 (defendant); and some which are even more obscure (*York v Haidon* (1569) Toth 85 (the plaintiff to be examined, "or process to be had against him"); *Bellamy v Radcliff* (1596) Toth 85, Stowe 415 f 204v, Harl 1576 f 172r ("a defendant upon a hearing where the plaintiff's proof served not, appointed to be examined").

261 Above Ch 2.

262 Above Ch 2 § 2 *(4)* (a) nn 220-2 and text there; for the later period *Ireland v Smith* (H1673/4) R t Finch 90, Nott CC No 69, at 73 SS 32. Or after plaintiff's failure in proof, *Williams v Williams* (H1674-5) 1 Ch Cas 252.

263 Bacon's Orders No 70, and *Ireland v Smith,* cited last n; *Harding v Edge* (M1675) Nott CC No 346, 73 SS 234 at 236, suppression of deeds. (This case may also may be affected by the fact that it is in aid of a decree of commissioners for charitable uses).

264 Monro pp 361, 413, 452, 459, 513, (plaintiff) & 352 (defendant serving process for costs on plaintiff); *Nurse v Gwillim* (M1669) 3 Ch Rep 39, 2 Freem 132, 2 Eq Ca Ab 413.

265 Cf Jones pp 234-5.

266 1 Vern 272.

Guilford assigned this and other conclusive oaths in the proceedings as error, and the decree was reversed on the ground that such oaths could only be required "ex abundanti" [cautela?] if there was sufficient proof otherwise. Since the basis of the original decision does not appear, it is not clear whether this represents a change in approach.

Therefore, though there is nothing that can be unequivocally identified with the decisory and suppletory oaths of the romano-canonical system, there are some analogues to these grounds for using party oaths. It would be dangerous to make too much of these. There is, moreover, some slight reason to suppose that the use of the oaths of the parties tended to die out in the late seventeenth and early eighteenth century, apart from the answer itself and those cases (where there was no interest or an exception to disqualification by interest) where the common law allowed parties to be sworn[267]. There may therefore in this respect have been a process of assimilation of equity to common law rules or convergence between the two systems in this period.

This discussion of the exception on the ground of bias through interest has necessarily been very extensive. To summarise its results:

(1) Wigmore's account of the development of this rule as arising through a gradual process of generalisation from the case of the parties, excluded for procedural reasons at law, is still *possibly* true, since it is possible, though there is no evidence for it, that the parties were excluded at law in the late mediaeval period. But on the evidence this account looks less likely than a "reception" of bias as an objection during the second half of the sixteenth and early seventeenth century, with the exclusion of parties as an early result; the process perhaps being delayed by a belief in some quarters that to allow exceptions to witnesses was to undermine trial by jury.

(2) The evidence for the exceptionability both of parties, and of interested non-parties, is as early in equity as at law. But conversely it is not significantly earlier, so that a simple migration of the canon law rules into Chancery in the fifteenth century is not dictated by the evidence[268]. In the later seventeenth century the cases of spoliation and length of time show rules for which the only direct evidence is in Chancery, which also cuts across a view of equity as following the law.

(3) In the later seventeenth century there were a range of exceptions to the exclusion of parties and interested persons, some of these both at law and in equity, others only in equity. Some of these rules tend to indicate a view of the

267 These issues are not discussed in Ballow, Gilbert's *Forum Romanum*, or Bacon's Abridgement.

268 Wigmore § 575 at Vol II p 683 said that the circumstances of variation from the canon law rules, plus later evidence for equity following the law, must mean a departure at some stage from canon law rules originally simply applied. I have indicated above Ch 1 that this need not be the case.

exception for interest as a matter of degree, which conforms to the civilian view stated by Swinburne, and as a rule which can be counter-balanced by other factors. These characteristics do not readily fit with a common law origin for the rule, though there may have been a tendency towards simplification and re- theorisation in perhaps more "common law" terms towards the end of the century. Similarly, it is possible that the later period saw a decline in the use of party oaths in Chancery.

2. Affinity and dependence

In the areas of affinity and dependence the common law of evidence and the law of proof in equity diverged markedly from the learned laws, and from jury challenges. The civilian and jury challenge rules excluded both many relatives, and also servants and dependents of the parties. It seems clear at an early stage that the roman-canon affinity exceptions were not all applied in Chancery[269]; the only relative who came to be excluded was the party's spouse, and most explanations of this rule seem to be in terms of dependence or of interest[270]. There is a slightly stronger trace of dependence as an exception – to the question of spouses can be added a certain amount of evidence that servants were in the early part of the period exceptionable, and *possibly* some influence on the early development of legal professional privilege[271]. This raises three issues: (i) the case of spouses; (ii) evidence for dependence as an exception; and (iii) why, if there was influence of the learned laws, the affinity and dependence rules were not in general accepted.

The area of dependence is marked by a specific feature. This is that quite distinct considerations apply to the admission of the witness *for* the superior on the one hand, and *against* the superior on the other. Dependent witnesses are exceptionable when produced for their superiors on grounds derived from the general bias principle, i.e. that their dependence means that the superior can tell them what to say. The production of the witness against the superior is objectionable on social policy grounds and in a sense analogous to privilege in the modern law: that it is in some sense a breach of duty by the subordinate to testify against the superior. The distinction is made, for example, by Domat in arguing for the exclusion of lawyers in the cause:

> "Whoever have been employed as Advocates in a Cause, cannot be Witnesses in it. For their testimony would be either suspected, if it were in favour of the person whose Cause they had defended, or both uncivil and suspected, if it were against their Client. And it is

269 *Prawnce v Hodilow*, above n 15. But note that an additional and possibly stronger argument to give Chancery jurisdiction in that case was that some of the witnesses lived some way distant from the University and were not amenable to its process.

270 Below § (a).

271 Below § (b).

the same thing as to Proctors and Attorneys, and other persons who should happen to be under the same engagements"[272].

This distinction is apparent in the case-law both on spouses and on servants.

a) Affinity and dependence: Spouses

The first clear decision[273] on the exclusion of spouses is a case in equity in the 1590s:

> The wife not allowed to be a wittnes for her husband *Bulwer con Levet* accordinge to opinions of the Civilians and of the Judges alsoe[274]

i.e., the rule was established after consultation with both civilians and common lawyers. Possibly the same case, though it may be another of the same period, is noted in *Observations:*

> N[ot]a that if the pl[aintiff] or def[endant] doe examyne his owne wife in matt[ers] concerninge his bill or Answere notwithstanding she be neither party pl[aintiff] for def[endan]t, yet my Lo[rd] will give noe regarde to such testimony but it were as good not to have exa[m]i[n]ed at all.[275]

Coke said that spouses were excluded at common law[276], and the subsequent elaboration of the rule and the exceptions to it was in the main at common law[277].

The emergence of the rule seems to have involved more issues than simple consultation of civilian authority. In *Bent v Allot* (1579-80)[278] the plaintiff obtained an order to examine a defendant's wife on the basis that the defendant had examined her; the order was that if the defendant would not consent to examination by the plaintiff, her deposition should be suppressed. This suggests that the primary objection is to examination of the wife *against* the defendant, and that the basis is the

---

272 3.6.3.23, citing D.22.5.25.

273 In two cases from the 1590s spouses were examined: *Lake v Deane* (1595-6) Toth 94, "to discover her husband's deceit" (this may be as a defendant), and *Preston v Powell* (1598-9) (41 Eliz) Toth 86 "The wife to be examined as a witness" (whose wife we are not told). Harl 1576 f 172 has this case as 43 Eliz (1600-1), "by speciall order of Courte examined against her husband for that it was alledged by this said order that the wife wore the breeches".

274 Harl 1576 f 151v; surrounded by cases of M 38 & 39 Eliz (1596) so probably of that date. CUL Gg 2.31 ff 227v, 410v (two copies of the same series) has "A wife not alowed a witnesse for her husband the opinion of the Civilians and the judges too". I have not been able to find a fuller report of this case, but it is no worse than much in Cary & Tothill.

275 f 447v No 101.

276 Co Lit 6b.

277 Gilbert 96-8.

278 (22 Eliz) Cary 94, (*Bourn v Allot & Colston*) Stowe 415 f 121v, (*Benne*) f 134v, (*Ben*) Harg 281 f 93v, (*Bent v Allott & Colyton*) HLS 1090 f 77r.

husband's legal power over the wife; her deposition in his favour is not suppressed as such, but only if he will not consent to her examination by the other side, i.e. on grounds of mutuality. The point is expressed similarly in a note in *Observations*[279] and in *Holman v Awdley* (1612-13)[280]: a wife not to be examined *against* her husband.

There are two later seventeenth century equity authorities for the proposition that a wife cannot be a witness against her husband. In *Collingwood v Basset* (H1680-1)[281] the plaintiff sought to prove a trust by one witness and the admission of the trust by the defendant's wife in her separate answer. Lord Nottingham said that

> "This will not serve, for the answer of a feme covert executrix cannot charge her husband in Chancery, any more than her assent to a legacy without assets shall charge her husband at common law. Therefore prove the trust if you will by some declaration of the wife's before her second marriage, or some other way, for this answer is not to be regarded"[282].

This argument seems to be based less on incompetence of the wife as a witness than on the substantive law of marriage, i.e. that the husband is not bound by the wife's acts in law done without his consent. The result is, however, to hold her incompetent *qua* spouse, since her extra-judicial admissions before the marriage would be admitted. In *Cole v Grey* (T1688)[283] defendants were ordered to be examined on interrogatories to discover an estate on an account, and the wife (who was separated from the husband) having answered more favourably to the plaintiffs than the husband, the plaintiffs got an order from Trevor MR to examine her as a witness *de bene esse*. The master's report, having relied on this evidence, was quashed on exceptions by Jeffreys C on the basis that a wife cannot be a witness against her husband.

Gilbert says that spouses are excluded *for* each other because their interests are identical, and *against* each other both on grounds of mutuality (the wife being excluded for the husband) and on grounds of public policy as tending to break up the marriage relationship[284]. This follows Coke's explanation. In fact, however, these cases seem closer to an argument that the husband is entitled not to have his wife examined against him because she is his dependent.

b) Dependence: Servants and counsel

At the trial of Mary Queen of Scots, she objected to her secretaries being used as witnesses against her, as they were her servants. This gave rise to debate on the

---

279 f 464v No 211.

280 (10 Jac) Toth 96.

281 Nott CC No 1070, 2 Ch Cas 39, 1 Eq Ca Ab 65.9.

282 79 SS 854.

283 2 Vern 79, 1 Eq Ca Ab 65.9.

284 *Evidence* pp 96-7.

propriety of the trial, and its supporters responded, not that parties' servants were perfectly competent witnesses, but that it was questionable whether secretaries were properly servants and in any case that "domestick evidences were to be admitted concerning those things that were done privately and secretly at home"[285], a rule which can be found in the *Reformatio*[286]. This trial certainly was a special case, and it is not authority for anything in either equity or common law. It is, however, evidence of a lay belief that servants were not good witnesses against their masters[287]. This rule did not become established in the later common law[288]; but in *Clerke's Case* (1605) the Star Chamber ruled that a servant's previous answer could only be read to supply gaps in the master's answer, not to contradict it[289]; and in *Gray v Alport* (H1608-9) the Exchequer decided after argument that apprentices, and factors who had been apprentices, could not be examined as witnesses for the Crown in a prosecution of their master, because they were under a duty to keep his trade secrets[290]; and Hudson says that servants can testify *for* their masters in cases of riot, by way of exception – which implies a general rule excluding them[291].

A rather similar line of argument appears in Domat as a ground for excluding counsel in the cause (quoted above). Wood explains the rule not in terms of dependence, but of the lawyer's professional self-interest:

> The same exception lies ... against an Advocate or Proctor for his Client; for Advocates and Proctors may be biassed by an affectation of Fame, and a desire of Conquest.[292]

Gilbert similarly seems to say that lawyers are actually *incompetent* as to information received after retainer:

> "3dly, a Man retained as Attorney, Solicitor or Counsel, cannot give Evidence of any Thing imparted to them after the Retainer, for after the Retainer they are considered as the same Persons with their Clients and are trusted with their Secrets, which without a Breach

285 Camden, *The History...Princess Elizabeth* ... (selected chapters, ed. McCaffrey, London, University of Chicago Press, 1970) pp 253-273, the quotation at 273.

286 249-50 c 21. Cf also Vulteius 507v, *domestici in causa domestici* not repelled but still exceptionable; Wood 315, 'domesticks' usable in matrimonial causes between domestics themselves.

287 Cf also the lines of Marlowe cited above n 122: "and he my *bondman.* Give me law" (my emphasis); and Sandys' suggestion in the debate on the trial of offences on the borders that "domesticall" witnesses should be exceptionable, above n 178 and text there. In *Harris v Scott* (1568) 101 SS 78, CP, the reporter notes the fact that one witness was a servant, which suggests that there was an issue.

288 Cf *Mason v Hogsden* (P1709) 11 Mod 226, NP, Holt CJ, factor qualified if not interested.

289 (M1605) Moo KB 770.1065.

290 (H8&9 Jac) Add 25207 f 13b. The prosecution was for smuggling; the court rejected several contrary precedents on the basis that they were *sub silentio.*

291 206.

292 315-6

of Trust cannot be revealed, and without such Sort of Confidence there could be no Trust or Dependance on any Man, nor any transacting of Affairs by the Ministry or Mediation of another, and therefore the Law in this Case maintains such Sort of Confidence inviolable.

But to what such Persons knew before their Retainer, they may be examined, for in that Case they are in the Condition of any other Person, and should be examined, what they know of their own Knowledge."[293]

By the time Gilbert was writing it seems an oddity to describe counsel as disqualified: almost all the cases treat the matter as one of compellability or privilege[294], and Coke said explicitly that servants and counsel though challengeable as jurors were competent witnesses[295]. However, some of the older authorities in equity do appear to be based, at first, on an objection to competence; sometimes this shades into an objection to compellability in general. The first line of cases, simply to the effect that lawyers in the cause are incompetent, looks most like the civilian exception which is found in the *Digest* and in 'Alciatus' and Vulteius in general terms[296]. The first case in the printed reports is *Breame v Breame* (1571)[297] (counsel's clerk), and the same line is taken a good deal later by *Wilson v Grove* (1630)[298] (solicitor or promoter) and *Thimblethorpe v Thimblethorpe* (1630-1)[299] (counsel in the cause).

It is possible that these are merely defective reports, because *Lee v Markham* (1569) which appears in Tothill as "counsel in the cause not to be sworn" in Monro is clearly privilege, i.e. not compelled to answer questions touching client's title[300], and there are other authorities which are in different ways ambiguous (or suggest movement towards the idea of privilege). One possibility is that lawyers are not compellable; this is suggested by *Bird v Lovelace* (1576-7)[301], *Austen v Vesey* (1577)[302] and *Hartford v Lee* (1577-8)[303]. Almost immediately after these cases come a group of cases which suggest more clearly movement towards the privilege approach, in that they confine the rule to matter of which the lawyer knows from his client, or suggest that the objection is to examination against the client rather than examination *per se*; I will deal with these in connection with privilege[304]. The presence of some authorities to the effect that lawyers for the parties in the cause

293 138-9, corrected by Add 36090.

294 Below Ch 7 §§ 2, 3 *(1)*.

295 Co Lit 6b.

296 D 22.5.25; 'Alciatus' 208v No 28; Vulteius 507v-508r.

297 (13 & 14 Eliz) Toth 48.

298 (T1630) Toth 177.

299 (6 Car) Toth 48.

300 (11 Eliz) Toth 48, (P1569) Monro 228.

301 (19 Eliz) Cary 62.

302 (19 & 20 Eliz) Cary 63.

303 (20 Eliz) Cary 63.

304 Below Ch 7. Cf also *Reformatio* 249 c 19.

are not to be sworn does suggest, however, that the doctrine that lawyers in the cause are excluded may have been present in early cases, together with the other instances of dependency as an exception. If so, relics of the idea of incompetence of lawyers in the cause survive in thought as late as Gilbert.

There is, therefore, *some* evidence – not incredibly strong – for dependence as an objection to witnesses. But in the case-law the dominant element of this seems not to be fear that the servant will be biassed towards his master, but rather an idea that the master has a right not to be betrayed by his servant (or husband by his wife, or client by his counsel).

c) Why were the affinity and dependence exceptions in general not 'received'?

The absence of the exceptions for affinity and dependence was Wigmore's strongest argument against influence of the roman-canon law of proof on the evolution of the common law of evidence and on equity proof. In the case of the exclusion of spouses, however, influence is clear. There may be other influences on the rule (above), but the idea that there was no reference to the learned laws in this context can be ruled out by *Bulwer v Levet.*

Why, then, were the rest of the rules about affinity and dependence not "received"[305]? Two points may be made. The first is that several civilian authorities regard these exceptions as not completely ruling the witness out, but rather affecting their credit proportionally to the degree of the relationship[306]. *Prima facie*, therefore, if translated into common law they would have been matters for the jury; only the closest relationship – marriage – came to be a complete exclusion.

The second point is that these exceptions were inappropriate to the social context. The wider ranging romano-canonical exceptions based on affinity and dependence (and the similar jury challenges) assume that witnesses (jurors) will be so strongly governed by relationships of consanguinity and affinity, or by the influence of their employers or landlords, that they cannot be expected to tell the truth.

---

305 In *R v Lord Dacre & Greystock* (1534) Spelman *Corone* pl 26, 93 SS 54 at 55, trial of a peer for treason, the peers asked to have the prisoner's uncle, in the Tower for the same treason, examined. The Lord High Steward on the advice of the judges ruled this out on the grounds that (1) all the evidence had already been given, and (2) "il ne fuit necessare witnes pur ceo que fuit uncle al senior [the defendant] et ne voit done evidence vers le senior". Baker, Introduction to 94 SS *110* interprets "necessare" here as meaning competent, but the word seems more apt to express compulsion; it could be either (1) the modern sense, he is not necessary (because his evidence if any will add nothing); (2) he is not compellable; or (3) his evidence would not be compelling. Hudson p 205 has the son only exceptionally qualified to testify for his father.

306 Above § 2 *(1)*; compare also Wood's comment on English and other laws on this point, note at 316.

This, however, becomes less likely to the extent that society is governed more by market relationships and the family is "nuclear" rather than extended. Alan Macfarlane has argued that English society was exceptionally "individualistic" and "market-oriented", as compared to other societies in Europe, from a relatively early period of the middle ages[307]; it is unnecessary to accept his full argument, which is controversial[308], in order to accept that the evidence does suggest, at least for the early modern period, a society in which it was not to be presumed that tenants would oblige their landlords, cousins each other, or even children their parents, in the little matter of perjury; a society in which interest was more likely to provide a powerful motive than kindred or alliance; and in which the only relationship thought to be sufficiently powerful to disqualify witnesses by its existence was marriage – as Gilbert argued that "no other Relation is absolutely the same in Interest"[309].

Given the traces of dependence as an exception in the late sixteenth and early seventeenth century, and the direct evidence of roman-canon influence in the case of spouses, this sort of explanation of the absence of wider exceptions for affinity and dependence seems preferable to Wigmore's argument that their absence was evidence against roman-canon influence.

VI. Conclusion

The topic of exceptions to witnesses (testimonial qualifications) was one of the critical elements of Wigmore's argument against roman-canon influence on the early common law, and also provided the context of his earliest authorities for equity following the law in matters of evidence. In this Chapter I think that I have shown that these arguments are wrong.

In the first place, Wigmore's arguments against roman-canon influence were not antecedently strong. Secondly, the variation of the common law rules as to the *competence* of witnesses from the roman-canon *exceptions* to witnesses was not in itself an argument against influence of the learned laws, since in the learned laws not all exceptions to witnesses led to their complete rejection, and accounts differ as to which exceptions led to complete rejection and which merely made the witness suspect.

---

307 *Origins of English Individualism*; (Oxford, Blackwell, 1978), *Marriage and Love in England, 1300 – 1840* (Oxford, Blackwell, 1986).

308 Macfarlane responds to criticisms of *Individualism* in *The Culture of Capitalism* (Oxford, Blackwell, 1987) "Postscript" (p 191ff). On the specific question of family & kinship cf Chaytor, 10 *History Workshop* 25, Razi 93 *Past & Present* 3, Collinson, *The Birthpangs of Protestant England* (London, Macmillan, 1988) 89-90.

309 Gilbert p 98.

Thirdly, and most importantly, a survey of the grounds of exceptions at this period reveals a greater degree of congruity of the exceptions both at common law and in equity to the roman-canon exceptions than is conceded by Wigmore's argument, and some direct evidence of roman-canon influence. Natural incapacity, i.e. infancy and lunacy, appears largely in abstract discussions, and the references to the age of 14 in Hale's and Gilbert's discussions of infants suggest roman- canon influence.

In relation to bad character, though the grounds of disqualification by infamy in Coke upon Littleton are clearly borrowed from the challenges to jurors, in the later seventeenth century infamy is re-theorised in terms closer to the roman-canon concept of *crimen falsi*. There is more evidence than Wigmore conceded of religion as an objection to witnesses, though this is clearly not a simple status rule but is based on the need for an oath; and Hale directly cites a canonist authority on this point. Other bad character appears at an early stage as an exception to witnesses, and Coke's comments in the Fourth Institute on this point are suggestive of influence of the learned laws; there is some reason to suppose, however, that at least in equity and possibly at law difficulties put in the way of proving this exception led to a decline in its importance. The case-law on bad character is mostly at law; this probably reflects the hostility of equity judges to exceptions to witnesses discussed in the last section of Chapter 5.

In relation to bias, Wigmore's argument that the disqualification of witnesses due to interest arose out of a gradual generalisation of an originally procedural disqualification of the parties seems less probable than an original "reception" of bias as an objection to witnesses, first evidenced in 1556 with a direct reference to the civil law, and applied to exclude parties in the reign of Elizabeth. There is some evidence in the early seventeenth century, in the debates on the trial of offences on the borders, of doubts as to whether witnesses to a jury were subject to exceptions at all; this suggests a development at law similar to that in relation to documents, i.e. that the question whether the jury is a means of proof or a trier of fact subject to rules of proof is still arguable. The seventeenth century authorities, particularly in equity, suggest that the exception for interest is understood in this period in terms of the underlying principle of bias and as a matter of degree, as in Swinburne's account of the canon law. In this context there are significant variations between the common law and equity authorities, but some slight indications of a shift towards "common law" thinking in the later seventeenth century.

The absence of the roman-canon exceptions for bias due to affinity and dependence was one of Wigmore's major arguments against roman- canon influence. In fact, however, there is direct evidence of reference to the learned laws in relation to the one case of affinity accepted, spouses, and some later sixteenth and early seventeenth century evidence for dependence as an exception to witnesses. This evidence, however, seems to point less to dependence as a ground of bias, than to a right not to have your dependents used *against* you. In this context the absence of wider exceptions to affinity and dependence may be attributable in part to the fact that in the canon law, according to Swinburne, these exceptions do not necessarily lead to the complete rejection of the witness, and in part to specificities of the English social context.

The overall result, therefore, is a picture of exceptions to witneses strongly parallel to the principles of the roman- canon system, and with some direct evidence of borrowing from the learned laws. Particularly in relation to bias, the equity authorities are contemporaneous with and in some cases earlier than the common law authorities, which is inconsistent with a view of equity merely following developments at law.

Chapter Seven

Compulsion to Testify and its Limits

The compulsion of witnesses to testify, and the limits to this compulsion, gave rise to much less authority in this period than did exceptions to witnesses. However, in these areas it is quite clear that equity authority starts some time before common law authority. The equity authorities on limits to compulsion are broadly consistent with civilian principles, but there are none of the examples of direct citation found in relation to exceptions to witnesses; and, in particular, the evolution of legal professional privilege[1] may represent an autonomous development.

I. Compulsion to testify

Wigmore cites some authority for the view that the question of whether witnesses should be compelled to testify was debateable in the mediaeval canon law[2]. By our period, however, the only relics of this controversy are Àlciatus', who says that in canon law witnesses are compellable in civil, but not in criminal matters[3], and Cosin, who limits the rule about criminal matters to crimes raised by way of dilatory exception to the person of the plaintiff or exception to a witness[4]. Generally our authorities say simply that witnesses are compellable, and, indeed, it was a positive requirement that they should be compelled to attend, as witnesses who ap-

---

1 The expression "privilege" is convenient, how far it is contemporary has been questioned. It does not appear in Gilbert, or elsewhere in discussions of evidence law before Peake's *Compendium of the Law of Evidence* (1801) (reprint, NY, Garland, 1979) Ch 2 § 5 "Of persons who are privileged from giving evidence", applied to self-incrimination. Indeed, the relevant meaning of "privilege" is absent from the OED, and Levy (*Origins of the Fifth Amendment* p viii) claims that the phrase is of twentieth century origin. However, both Lord Nottingham (*Practice,* Title V, No. 23, *Two Treatises* p 114) and Lord Guilford (Add 32518 f 14v) use the term in connection with legal professional privilege, and Jacob's *Law Dictionary* brings this topic under the head 'privilege'; and Lilburne is said to have claimed the right not to answer as one of "all the privileges that do belong to a free man as the greatest man in England" (Levy, p 289).

2 § 2190, Vol VIII pp 67-8.

3 220r.

4 i, 74-5.

peared voluntarily were suspect[5]. The mediaeval common law used the *venire facias* to compel attesting witnesses[6]. But it lacked any means to compel witnesses in general to give evidence to a jury.

It is not entirely clear how early the Chancery made regular use of witnesses[7], but compulsory process to testify, the *subpoena ad testificandum,* is evidenced from the 1450s[8]. By the 1540s at the latest the Chancery *subpoena ad testificandum* was in use to compel witnesses to testify at law[9]. The Perjury Act of 1563 gave an action of debt against the non-appearing witness at law[10], but Chancery subpoenas *ad testificandum* continued to be used after the Act[11]; the *subpoena ad testificandum* issued by the common law courts under their judicial seals was complained of as a recent abuse by Egerton in the 1600s[12], so seems likely to have

---

5 'Alciatus' 231v-214r No 1; Maranta 561 No 1; *Reformatio* 244 c 4, 247 c 13; Gaill ii Obs. 100 No 1; Vulteius 503v; Cosin i 69-75; Clerke 43, 49-51; Ridley 107; Zouch *EI* 98; Conset 106-7; Domat 3.6.3.17; Ayliffe 536, 539.

6 Above Ch 3 § 1 *(2)* (a) n 54.

7 The subpoena requiring a person to attend for examination certainly existed from the fourteenth century, but it is open to question how early it was regularly used for witnesses as opposed to parties. Baildon printed a case of 1408 in which the testimony of Lord Willoughby, described as present in Court, was taken at the request of both parties (*Dent v Gernon,* 10 SS p 88 case 95), but there is nothing to indicate that Lord Willoughby was compelled to attend. He also has an undated case (10 SS p 122 Case 126) in which a subpoena was prayed to testify in Chancery on the ground that the *witness* feared to be thought partisan if not compelled, which suggests that the procedure is not entirely commonplace (though it is concistent with the civilian doctrine noted above). The 1415 petition in Parliament (Rot. Parl. IV 84a) complained that matters drawn into Chancery could only be decided *by the oath of the parties,* which again suggests that the use of witnesses is not entirely regular. By the 1470s it is clear that Chancery is regularly using witnesses, and it seems that some romano-canonical rules are being applied: YB P 16 Ed 4 9b, pl 10 *(contraria allegans non est audiendus),* YB P 22 Ed 4 6b, pl 18 (two witnesses required).

8 Cal. Chan. Proc. I xix.

9 The *Calendar of Chancery Proceedings in the Reign of Elizabeth* prints (Vol I p cxxxiii) a case from the period of the Chancellorship of Lord Paulet (1547-51) of a bill for a subpoena to testify at a trial by jury. An earlier indication is *Anon* (1531) Spelman *Proces* pl 3, 93 SS 185, witnesses in an appeal served with process to testify called subpena "quod nota"; Baker interprets this as use of the Chancery subpoena regarded by Spelman as unusual, but it is possible that what is unusual is either (a) that the proceedings are an appeal of murder, or (b) that the process was in fact issued by the King's Bench itself, rather than the parties going to Chancery.

10 5 Eliz c 9 s 12.

11 As Holdsworth (HEL IX 185) points out, the act does not strictly speaking provide for the common-law courts to use the subpoena *ad testificandum*; rather it says that if the witness is served with any process to appear and testify, and fails to appear, the party grieved may recover a penalty and damages by "debt, bill, plaint or information". i Sanders 34 has two cases from 1569, i.e. after the Act, in which Bacon LK made orders limiting the issue of subpoenas *ad testificandum* to be only to testify before judges of the superior courts or of assize, or commissioners.

12 "Memorials for Judicature", Knafla 274 at 278, dated by Knafla as circa 1609.

developed in the reign of Elizabeth. Compulsion to testify in equity therefore considerably predates compulsion at law[13].

II. Exemptions from compulsion

The civilians recognised certain exemptions from compulsion to testify. These exceptions, however, primarily concern status: thus Àlciatus' refers generally to exemptions on the ground of status, cross-referring to Durantis; the *Reformatio* says that witnesses who "*in majori aliqua dignitate constitute fuerint*" cannot be compelled to attend but should be examined on commission; Gaill discusses a practice of "*nobiles et illustres personae*" giving evidence by signed letter on their honour, a passage cited by Gentili; Domat refers to exemptions on the ground of "*dignité*", and Wood gives some French and German exeptions from formal examination[14]. In the common law, peers were exempt from jury service and hence challengeable *propter honoris causa*[15]. Lord Nottingham in his *Prolegomena* has a rule very similar to these, i.e. that some persons are "of too great quality to be examined"[16]. There are two groups of rules which may represent status exemptions of this sort.

The first is the claim of peers to answer on honour rather than on oath, which Jones suggests results from their original immunity to compulsory process[17]. I have discussed this in the context of the equity answer in Chapter 2; it seems that the peers did not succeed in asserting this privilege in relation to examination as witnesses[18]. Equity authority for the proposition that peers examined as witnesses are to be on oath begins in the time of Egerton[19]; there does not seem to be any common law authority.

A second area is the rule that the King, and in certain circumstances the judges, can testify by signed writing. A rule that the King's certificate is conclusive proof

---

13 This was recognised by Wigmore § 2190.

14 'Alciatus' 220r; *Reformatio* 247 c 14; Gaill ii Obs. 100 Nos 14 15, Obs. 101 No 3, this latter cited by Gentili ii 129-130 as i 101c; Domat 3.6.3.21; Wood 318.

15 Co Lit 156b.

16 29.19, *TT* 320, but qualified "But no man is of credit enough in his own cause".

17 Jones 320-2, citing *inter alia Dacres v Lord Dacre* (1565) Monro 353, peer to exhibit inventory on honour. Compare also the verdict in *Mark Steward's Case* (P1579) 9 Co 99b at 102a, where it is evident that a letter from the Earl of Leicester is received in place of a deposition.

18 *Meers v Lord Stourton* (1711) Dick 20, 1 P Wms 146, 2 Salk 512. Though Lord Nottingham in *Lord Delaware's Case* (1681) Nott CC No 1127 at 79 SS 894 says *obiter* that a peeress cannot be examined in person on oath under a statutory provision, citing YB T 3 Hen 6 f 48 pl 5.

19 Above Ch 2 § 2 *(1)* (a) n 90.

can be found in Bracton's Note Book[20], and letters from the King were accepted as evidence in the Requests in 1613[21] and in Chancery under Francis Bacon[22]. The Lord Chief Justice and the Chancellor of the Exchequer were asked to certify their knowledge in writing, rather than be examined as witnesses, in 1599[23]. Both rules are also given in Hudson's account of the Star Chamber[24]. In 1626 a question arose in the House of Lords about whether the King could be a witness in a criminal cause, and the Lords asked the opinion of the judges, but Charles prohibited them giving an opinion[25] and the proceedings were stopped by the dissolution of Parliament[26]. Rolle denied the rule about the King's certificate[27].

The other areas in which there are authorities for non-compulsion are in the area of dependency, so that there is an overlap with exceptions to the witness. Thus, for example, Pufendorf says that '"*propinqui*" are excluded, and patron and client not compellable against one another, "*ne vel affectus suus, vel conscientiam laedere cogantur*"'[28]. This context means that it is not entirely clear whether the cases are in fact deciding that the witness is not compellable, or rather that he or she is not compellable because not competent. These cases concern parties' wives, and some of the early cases on servants and lawyers. I have discussed these to some extent in Chapter 6[29], and I will return to the cases on lawyers below in connection with privilege.

---

20 Wigmore § 1374 cites Bracton's Note Book Vol 2 No 239.

21 *Lea v Lea* Godb. 198.

22 *Lord Abigny v Clifton* Hob 213, dated by Viner, 12 Viner 190, to "about 9 Jac" but must be in the time of Bacon as "The King, by his letters under his signet manual, certified to the late Lord Chancellor, and also to this...".

23 *Coke AG v Carroll* (P1599) Monro 729.

24 206, though restricting the rule in relation to the judges to cases where they are authorised under the Great Seal to certify a verdict.

25 Cobbett, *Parliamentary History* Vol 2 pp 105-6.

26 *Trial of the Earl of Bristol* (1626) 2 St Tr 1267. Bristol argued, ib. at 1299-1300, that the King could not be a witness in treason or felony proceedings because of interest, but some of the arguments as reported in *Proceedings in Parliament 1626 Vol I: Lords Proceedings* (ed Keeler, Cole & Bidwell, New Haven, Yale UP, 1991) at 381, 384, 392 suggest that the question of the King being too dignified to testify was raised. But there does not seem to be any evidence to support Campbell's claim, *Lives of the Chancellors* (Fourth edition, London, Murray, 1857) Vol 3 214-5, that Coventry LK ruled that the King could not give evidence.

27 Vol II 686. In *Litcot v Backwell* (P1668) 2 Keb 349 ((T1668) 2 Keb 368, 1 Sid 373, (T1669) 2 Keb 538, not SP), "the defendant offered evidence... by Tytus, sent by the King to this purpose, which the Court denied, this being a difference between party and party; but were the matter onely concerning the King, his testimony were good, as a letter in *Sir Gerrard Fleetwood's Case,* and 1 Cr ...". It seems as if this is an oral message from the King offered as evidence, but the whole report is too unclear to make much of (though cited by Wigmore on this point, § 1374).

28 5.13.9, 567-8. Compare also Cotta 877: the defendant can object to *consanguinei* being compelled to testify against him (though this rule is not observed *apud avaros iudices*).

29 §§ 5 *(2)* (a) and (b).

On wives, it should be added that married women were *prima facie* not amenable to process, i.e. not required to answer, without their husbands[30]. The rule that the wife could not be examined against her husband may have been in part a result of this rule: she is not compellable unless he is, and he is not compellable *as a witness*[31]. If the plaintiff wanted the oath of a defendant who contested the suit he would have to comply with the conditions for examination of defendants on interrogatories discussed in Chapter 2[32]; given that the wife was *prima facie* not compellable to answer a bill without her husband, the same rules might have been applied to examination of the wife.

III. Privilege

Wigmore says that at first though a witness could be compelled to attend, it was not clear whether he could be compelled to answer specific questions or interrogatories[33]. His authority for this view is Hudson, who cites Egerton as having said to him during argument that "he knew no law to compel a witness to speak more than he would of his own accord"[34]. This is an extremely odd statement. In the first place, the witnesses were certainly sworn *de veritate dicenda,* i.e. to make a true answer to the questions put to them, before examination – which is a fairly clear "law to compel a witness to speak more than he would of his own accord"[35]. And, secondly, the system of judicial control of interrogatories and the Elizabethan cases, discussed below, on legal privilege, are inconsistent with the view that the witness could refuse to answer questions at will. The context of Egerton's statement, however, involves both dependency and confidential relations and possibly self-incrimination, and it is therefore probable that Egerton's remark is to be limited to this context and that in general a witness was from an early period required to answer the interrogatories put to him.

---

30 *Rone v Bourne* (1583-4) Choyce Cas 170, Stowe 415 f 143, Tothill *Proceedings* 12-13. There were a variety of exceptions: *Trentham v Kinnersley* (1606) Toth 12, "he pretending pleading the jurisdiction of the court"; *Court v Popham* (T1630) Toth 96, "because charged with conspiracy and combination"; *Popham v Portman* (1635) Toth 13, 96, where the husband was overseas.

31 For the defendant as not compellable as a witness cf *Lane v Prannell* (1583-4) Choyce Cas 173, Stowe 415 f 143v, an attachment against the plaintiff for calling up the defendant to be examined as a witness contrary to an order of the court.

32 § 2 *(1)* (a) nn 86-9 and text there.

33 Wigmore § 2190 at pp 66-7.

34 Hudson 209.

35 Hudson quotes the oath at the same reference. Compare in the canon law Clerke 282, failure of the witness to answer articles or interrogatories leads to re-examination.

In this context there were two groups of rules limiting the obligation to answer specific interrogatories. The first, which has clear support in civilian doctrine, is self-incrimination. The second, for which civilian support is less clear, is legal professional privilege and a range of analogous rules depending on obligations to keep information confidential.

1. Self-incrimination

This topic can be dealt with fairly briefly, as I have already discussed it extensively in Chapter 2 in connection with the obligation to answer the bill[36]. *Nemo tenetur seipsum prodere* was readily conceded to apply without significant exceptions to persons produced as witnesses in the canon law[37]. The mechanism by which it was applied in Chancery examination of witnesses was the prohibition of scandalous interrogatories and of cross-examination to credit[38]. Hudson, probably writing around 1620-1, applies the rule to witnesses in Star Chamber[39]; clear common law authority on this point starts from the 1640s[40].

2. Legal professional privilege

Legal professional privilege in its developed form is markedly different from the basic civilian rule that parties' lawyers are to be rejected. There are some reported cases which seem to imply, as is suggested in Chapter 6, that this rule is at some stage applied[41]; but it is also possible that the cases which suggest this view would prove on examination of the records to concern compulsion or privilege[42]. There are also three cases which appear to decide that lawyers cannot be compelled to testify[43], but in the two of these which concern witnesses the decision not to compel appears to be based on the witness lacking any non-privileged knowl-

---

36 Above Ch 2 § 2 *(1)* (b).

37 Covarruvias *QP* 449 No 7; Cosin III 116; Whitgift, 2 St Tr 86; Wood 316; Ayliffe 540-1. On the other hand, the *Reformatio* (245 c 6) allows interrogatories to the character of the witness, which Covarruvias (and the equity procedure) prohibited.

38 Above ch 5 § 2 *(4)*, ch 6 § 4 *(1)*.

39 209-10. For the dating of Hudson see Barnes, 'Mr Hudson's Star Chamber'.

40 Macnair, "The Early Development" 78.

41 Above Ch 6 § 5 *(2)* (b).

42 Jones, pp 318-320, seems to take the view that the rule is from the outset that of privilege.

43 *Windsor v Umberville* (P1574) Monro 411, solicitor, and steward of court, not compelled to answer bill concerning evidences they hold to the use of Lord Windsor; *Strelly v Albany* (P1583) Choyce Cas 163, Stowe 415 f 140b, Monro 519; *Cutts v Armiger* (P1585) Monro 544.

edge[44]; in this situation it would obviously be difficult to distinguish compulsion and privilege. Possibly relevant to the rule in this form is D. 12.2.3.34 on the decisory oath, which says that neither a proctor nor a *defensor* can be compelled to swear; and closer is the rule stated in the *Reformatio:*

> Procuratores, advocati, ceterique negotia alicujus gerentes ad testimonium pro dominis suis non admittantur. At si adversa pars eorum testimoniis uti voluerit, veritatem, quam noverint, post depositum officium dicere cogentur[45].

Similarly, Wood says that

> If the Adversary will produce the Advocate or Proctor in a Civil Cause against their own Client, they ought to answer what they know of their own knowledge, not what was revealed to them by their clients; for a greater regard ought to be had for Truth and Publick Good than to private advantages[46].

The bulk of the early equity authority is fairly clearly founded on privilege, i.e. a right not to answer specific questions[47]. Gaill discusses an analogous rule in relation to confessors[48]; otherwise, the nearest analogy to a rule of this type is the *nemo tenetur seipsum prodere* rule, and it is possible that what is involved is an application of this rule to lawyers: since lawyers are under a legal obligation not to reveal their clients' secrets, by doing so they would subject themselves to liability collateral to the issue[49]. There is some support for this view in the early period in the shape of analogous rules protecting public officers[50], and in the later seventeenth century in some cases on the boundaries of the privilege.

---

44 *Strelly v Albany* at Monro 520, "because the Court thinks it not meet that ... [the witness] ... should be enforced to be examined as a witness, touching anything he knoweth as solicitor; it is therefore ordered that the said Robson shall not be examined in this cause"; *Cutts v Armiger* at Monro 544, "he hath not dealt therein but as a counsellor for the plaintiff; it is therefore ordered, that the said Mr Fuller shall not be enforced to be examined in the cause...".

45 249 c 19.

46 316. The relatively late date and incoherence of this passage makes it possible that it is influenced by the common law and equitable rules, by then well-established.

47 *Lee v Markham* (P1569) Toth 48, Monro 375; *Bird v Lovelace* (1576-7) Cary 62 (*Berd* in the printed text, but uniformly *Bird* in the MSS) Stowe 415 f 110b, Harv 1090 f 51, Harg 281 f 75b; *Creed v Trap* (1578-9) Choyce Cas 121, Stowe 415 f 128; *Kelway v Kelway* (1579-80) Cary 89, Stowe 415 f 120, Harv 1090 f 72b; *Dennis v Codrington* (1579-80) Cary 100, Stowe 415 f 123, Harv 1090 f 81b; *Havers v Randoll* (1581) Choyce Cas 148, (*Haveres v Randle*) Stowe 415 f 136b.

48 ii Obs. 101 No 8; cf also id. Nos 4 (general oath of secrecy is overridden by the witness oath) and 8 (proxies are not compellable unless the parties to the transaction consent).

49 For the common law legal obligation of counsel and attorneys not to reveal their clients' secrets see P. Brand, *The Origins of the English Legal Profession* (Oxford, 1992) 123-5, 137-8.

50 *Tindall's Case* (H1599) Add 20700 f 61, the rule applied to a Master in Chancery; *Sir Henry Spillman's Case* (M1608) Add 25207 f 4b, Ex(E), commissioner examinable touching the taking of depositions, not touching the principal matter; *R v Lord Desmond & al'* (P1621)

Alternatively, and closer both to the shadowy 'dependants' rule and to the modern rule, the rule might be seen as an extension of *nemo tenetur* seeing compulsion of counsel as an indirect and therefore improper form of compulsion of the client. Indications supporting this approach begin only in the later seventeenth century.

The privilege appears to be accorded to witnesses at common law in the same general terms, i.e. that the parties' lawyers can be examined in general, but not on matters they know in their professional capacity, from the 1640s at the latest[51] – a considerable time after the first authorities in equity. In the later seventeenth century there are still relatively few authorities at law compared with those in equity.

The areas of development in the later part of the century seem to be uncertainty as to whom the privilege extends to, and the development of the exception to the privilege in cases of the participation of the lawyer in the client's frauds. The cases arose on bills for discovery, so that an additional complication is that it may be argued that the client (if a defendant) should not escape the obligation to discover deeds which pertain to the plaintiff's title merely by putting them in the hands of his lawyer[52].

The earlier cases are clear that a solicitor has the same privilege as counsel. Two cases of the restoration period, however, cast doubt on this. In *Cutts v Pickering* (P1672)[53], before Bridgman LK and Turner B, a solicitor was ordered to answer inter alia "1. Because dubious if a solicitor has any privilege, *quia non definitur in lege quid sit.*"[54]. In *Bulstrod v Letchmere* (T1676)[55] Lord Nottingham is said to have described the privilege as "of the bar", and "made it a doubt, if a thing were revealed, to one that was not a barrister, whether or no he would oblige him to answer"[56].

Since Lord Nottingham's *Practice*[57] says clearly that solicitors have the privilege, the doubt must arise from *Cutts v Pickering*. In *Legard & Ux' v Foot & Cossens* (H1673-4)[58], on a bill to discover matters relating to the estate of a deceased

Noy 154, Star Ch., privy councillor not examinable to matter he knows only as Privy Councillor.

51 *Onbie's Case* (1642) March NC 83, *Waldron v Ward* (1654) Style 449, *Sparke v Middleton* (1664) 1 Keb 505. Possibly *contra* is *Anon* (M1646) Style Prac Reg 353-4, where it is said that counsel may be examined if compelled by process, because the legal obligation is to be preferred to his obligation to his client.

52 *Long v Earl* (T1711) HLS 1105 p 5n; *Stanhope v Nott* (T1714) HLS 1105 p 4n.

53 3 Ch Rep 66, Nels 81, Nott Proleg c29.9 (TT pp 317-8) (3 Keb 2 not SP; 1 Vent 107, at law). Chan. Rep. and Nelson date the case to 1671, but Lord Nottingham's report is fuller and therefore (and in any case) more likely to be accurately dated.

54 Nott. Proleg, *TT* at 317.

55 1 Ch Cas 277 (*Bulstrode v Lechmore*), 2 Freem 5, HLS 1105 p 4.

56 2 Freem 5.

57 Title V No 23.

58 Rep t Finch 82.

person the privilege was allowed to the deceased's "attorney and solicitor", and in *Kington v Gale* (T1676)[59] the privilege is allowed to an attorney, who is to discover the existence but not the contents of his client's deeds.

The question of other confidential relationships seems to have been more doubtful. The most persistent claimants were scriveners, who at this period were engaged among other things in banking, estate agency and conveyancing and legal drafting work. Lord Nottingham's *Practice* says that the privilege has been denied to scriveners[60]. In *Shalmer v Tresham* (1669)[61], the plaintiff sought discovery of the deeds relating to lands, alleging that they were held upon trust to pay debts and that a debt he demanded was mentioned in a schedule. The defendant pleaded that as a scrivener freeman of London he had taken an oath not to discover the secrets of his clients' business. The plea was rejected *inter alia* on the ground that "the oath of a scrivener doth not oblige from discovery, more than the oath of any other freeman of London" (sc., presumably, a general oath not to disclose trade secrets)[62]. In *Bulstrod v Letchmere* another case *temp* Bridgman LK, *Morris v Clayton*, is cited for the proposition that scriveners do not have the privilege[63]. On the other hand, in *Gregg & al' (Governors of Tonbridge School) v Cotton & al' (The Skinners' Company)* (M1673)[64] a plea by the clerk to the Skinners' Company that he was sworn under the Company's ordinances not to reveal their books without their consent was allowed, on the basis that he was under oath[65]; and in *Harvey v Clayton* (T1675)[66] Lord Nottingham allowed a plea by a scrivener. The plaintiff's father had mortgaged land to a scrivener; the plaintiff sought a discovery of whose money was secured by the mortgage, i.e. the name of the scrivener's client. The defendant answered that he was ready to receive the principal and interest and give a discharge, or in the alternative to continue the mortgage, but pleaded that "he is a scrivener and trusted with men's estates" and ought not to discover. Lord Nottingham said that

> "it is safer for the plaintiff to be ignorant of the trust than to have notice of it, but it may be a ruin to the defendant in his trade to discover it, for no man hereafter will employ him. And what if it be the money of a recusant convict, or a person outlawed, &c; shall the debtor be revenged on his creditor and wound him through the sides of the scrivener?"[67]

---

59 Rep t Finch 259.

60 Loc cit above n 57.

61 2 Ch Rep 29.

62 The case is also decided on the basis that on the facts in question counsel would have been ordered to answer.

63 2 Freem 5.

64 R t Finch 24.

65 And also that the other defendants could be compelled to produce the relevant books.

66 Nott CC No 282, 73 SS 191.

67 73 SS 191.

Nonetheless, in *Atterbury v Hawkins* (P1677)[68] Lord Nottingham said that the privilege is not available to a scrivener, for

> "a scrivener is not a civil confessor as a lawyer is nor to be so treated, but rather a person suspected in law as apt to make unlawful concealments, and therefore is within the Statute of Bankrupts"[69].

The common law authorities are not much help; all that there is on this point is a case in Clayton excluding the evidence of a grand juryman on the ground that he is sworn not to reveal the secrets of the grand jury[70], and a *dictum* of Holt CJ in 1693[71] to the effect that a communication made in the course of seeking advice from a gentleman or a parson would not, unlike the case of counsel, be protected. It is possible that the point is that the existence of the privilege requires a legal obligation[72] not to disclose the information sought. This would explain both the doubt about solicitors "*quia non definitur in lege quid sit*" and the varying results in relation to other confidential positions. It would also help to explain the exclusion from the privilege of matters known otherwise than *qua* lawyer and of frauds.

This latter rule seems to be established fairly early in the Restoration, if it is not already in existence before it. In *Cutts v Pickering*[73] part of the reason for refusing the claim of privilege is "2. *Quia turpis causa,* and no secrecy due to the client in crimes"[74] (here forgery of a will). In *Rothwell v King, Hussey & al'* (1674)[75] Lord Nottingham applied the principle to suppression of deeds or wills. In his *Practice* he states the rule as "if the matter entrusted to their secrecy be scandalous and unfit for them to be trusted in, as the suppression or concealment or razure of a deed or will"[76]. It is possible that *Shalmer v Tresham*[77] in deciding that the privilege would not in that case be available to counsel goes on the same principle, but it is not clear from the report[78].

There is one decision at common law which appears to be on this point. In *R v Weeden Ford, Warden of the Fleet, ex p Leighton* (1700)[79] a former attorney for

---

68 Nott CC No 663, 79 SS 498.

69 79 SS at 498-9. On confessors cf Gaill, cited above n 48.

70 *Anon* (1640) Clayt 84, at nisi prius before Foster J.

71 *Anon* Skin 404.

72 Here including an equitable obligation.

73 Above n 53.

74 *TT* 317.

75 (H1673-4) Nott CC No 68, 2 Swanst 194; (M1674) 2 Ch Cas 202, not SP.

76 V. 23, *TT* 114.

77 Above n 61 and text there.

78 Equally unclear is Guilford's comment in his commonplace book, placing "priviledg d'attorney & councell in fforgery" under the heading "Abus" (Add 32518 f 14v).

79 12 Mod 337. For other reports and points cf above Ch 6 n 83.

the defendant was called against him and the question arose whether he was compellable. Darnell (presumably for the plaintiff) argued that "this being a criminal matter he should; but not so in a civil matter". Pratt, *contra,* said that

> "If he be sworn we must ask him his whole knowledge, and perhaps he cannot discover that without charging himself; for if one's declaration generally may be made use of against him, a fortiori what he says upon oath shall"[80].

So far the argument seems to be: Darnell: Legal professional privilege does not cover criminal matters[81]; Pratt: But if he is compelled to answer he may be compelled to incriminate himself. The reporter says that "this seemed to weigh with the court". But Holt CJ then said:

> he was of opinion against his brothers some years ago, in case of one Holford, that anything an attorney knew, otherwise than quatenus an attorney, he ought to declare it; but his brothers held, that an attorney ought not upon any account to be compelled to reveal his client's secrets. ... If a client bring a forged deed to counsel, counsel ought to prosecute him; and he had known such a thing done[82].

The argument here seems to be that it is unnecessary to decide on the point of the relation to the exception to legal privilege for crimes to the privilege against self-incrimination, because the court is bound by authority to deny the exception to legal privilege in the first place; though Holt himself disagrees with this view, and emphasises his disagreement by saying that counsel should prosecute his client in such a case. It is clear from the subsequent proceedings that the attorney was not, in fact, examined[83].

The view of the rule as *nemo tenetur* for the lawyer is rather suggested by those cases which appear to limit the application of the rule to cases where there is a legally binding obligation of confidence. The obstacle in the way of this view, however, is the *dicta* of North CJ in Common Pleas in *Lea v Wheatley* (1679)[84] that the privilege is the client's and can be waived by the client, and the converse decision of the King's Bench in 1712 in *Lloyd d Fiennes & Mignon v Lord Saye & Sele*[85] that it cannot be waived by the attorney[86]. The view of it as *nemo tenetur*

---

80 12 Mod 337 at 341.

81 It cannot be that it does not apply in criminal cases, since the instant proceedings were civil in character.

82 12 Mod 337 at 341.

83 Colles 332 at 334, where it is said for Ford that the verdict passed on the evidence of a single witness – to whom a different objection had been made.

84 Jacob, *Law Dictionary,* s.v. *Privilege* 2; 4 Bac. Abr. 230; 20 St Tr 574n; cited, Wigmore § 2290.

85 (M10 Anne) 10 Mod 40, citing an earlier unreported and undated case, *Holbeche's Case.* There was also a self-incrimination point. (1 Salk 341, 4 Bro PC 73 not SP).

86 Wigmore says, on the strength of eighteenth-century authority, that the privilege is at first the lawyer's, not the client's, i.e. waivable by the lawyer over the client's objection

for the client is suggested by this case and to some extent by Lord Nottingham's comment in *Harvey v Clayton*[87]. It is difficult, however, to reconcile this view with the fact that lawyers cannot be compelled to discover some matters which their clients, if sued directly, could be compelled to discover[88]. I think it most probable that the later seventeenth century courts, having inherited the privilege without any theoretical explanation, were concerned to set some bounds to it and did so from case to case without very much theorising[89].

IV. Conclusion

On the basis of the evidence discussed here it is quite clear that both provision for compulsion to testify, and the rules providing exemptions from compulsion, were developed first in equity and only subsequently applied at common law. This was recognised by Wigmore in relation to compulsion, but the implication (this is another area in which equity does not at this period follow the law) is not[90].

The existence of both compulsion and exemptions from compulsion is consistent with the learned laws in a very general sense, and there are some indications of an exemption for high social status akin to that discussed by Domat. Other possible exemptions from compulsion in equity are more shadowy and appear closer to exceptions to competence (wives) or privilege (lawyers).

The right not to answer incriminating or defamatory questions is consistent with the canon law rules. The privilege accorded to lawyers and to some other relationships in which there is an obligation not to reveal secrets has only limited support in the civilian authorities I have consulted, but it is possible that at least in the earlier period it is to be linked either to the rules about dependence, or to self-incrimination.

(§§ 2290, 2334). This fits with the view of *nemo tenetur* for the lawyer, but not with *Lloyd v Saye & Sele*.

87 Above n 66 and text there.

88 Cf eg *Gregg & al' v Cotton & al'*, above n 64 and text there.

89 Wigmore also suggested (§ 2294) on the basis of eighteenth century authorities that the privilege was originally confined to communications in connection with the instant litigation. On the assumption that Wigmore's interpretation of the eighteenth century authorities is correct, this appears to have been an eighteenth-century innovation, as the factual circumstances of the majority of the seventeenth century authorities make it quite impossible that the privilege should have been regarded as confined to communications relating to the instant litigation.

90 § 2190. For instance, in the same section Wigmore cites Hudson as if he was referring to the common law, and in relation to wives, § 2227, and legal privilege, § 2290, he cites equity cases without taking the point that they are prior to the first common law cases.

If, then, this area of the law of proof in equity is not one which is strikingly close to civilian conceptions, and does not show evidence of direct citation, it is also not markedly inconsistent with them. On the other hand, it is an area in which, on the evidence, equity cannot be supposed to have followed a development in relation to jury trial; on the contrary, here jury evidence law clearly followed a prior development in equity proof.

Chapter Eight

The Weight of Testimony

What makes testimony credible? In the first part of Chapter 5 I discussed the principles which underlay the weight given to proof by witnesses in the learned laws: the standing and independence of the witnesses, governed by the law of exceptions to witnesses; the oath; the quality, circumstantial detail and internal consistency of the deposition, and corroboration (the two witness rule); and the independence of testimony from the parties, governed by the rule of compulsion and the procedural rules for examination (judicial control, secret and separate examination). In contrast to this approach, there was a strand of opinion among common lawyers which saw witness demeanour under adversary cross-examination in open court as providing the most effective test of the value of testimony.

I have already discussed the equity procedure for the examination of witnesses (Ch 5), exceptions to witnesses (Ch 6) and compulsion (Ch 7). Here I will draw some of these threads together in discussing the overall basis of the probative value of testimony. In the first place, the fundamental basis of the value of testimony at this period in England was the weight of the oath. In this respect there is a degree of variation from the learned laws, in which the weight of the oath was not so prominent. In other respects, however, tests for the value of testimony in equity were closer to the roman-canon concepts than to the "common law" test of demeanour under adversary cross-examination. This can be seen from specific consideration of the purpose of cross-examination in equity; the application in equity of the rule requiring two witnesses to make a proof; the methods of dealing with conflicts of testimony; and the treatment of oral hearsay and opinion.

I. The weight of the oath

The learned laws required an oath to testimony[1]. However, this requirement is not absolutely central to the basis of testimony. Thus the *Reformatio* says explicitly that unsworn testimony is acceptable by consent[2], and Domat derives the force of testimony as proof as much from the concurrence of the depositions as from the oath:

1 Above Ch 5 § 1 n 8.

2 246 c 9. Cf also Gaill ii Obs. 101 Nos. 3, 5.

> "It is certain that two persons who have Reason, and who are not byassed by some impression of Hatred, Revenge, Interest or some other Passion, can never agree to bear false witness together in a Court of Justice, and that upon Oath. And we may conclude certainly from the natural Principles of our Actions, that Witnesses who swear that they will say nothing but the Truth, do really tell it, if nothing changes in them the Natural Order"[3].

In Gilbert's account of testimony at common law, however, the oath is absolutely central. Gilbert says that

> "Now this in the first Place, is very plain, that when we can't see or hear any Thing ourselves, and yet are obliged to make a Judgment of it, we must see and hear by Report from others; which is one Step farther from Demonstration, which is founded upon the View of our own Senses, and yet there is that Faith and Credit to be given to the Honesty and Integrity of credible and disinterested Witnesses, attesting any Fact under the Solemnities and Obligation of Religion, and the Dangers and Penalties of Perjury, that the Mind equally acquiesces therein as on a Knowledge by Demonstration, for it cannot have any more Reason to be doubted than if we ourselves had heard and seen it; and this is the Original of Tryals, and all Manner of Evidence"[4];

and in discussing disqualification by infamy:

> "Now there are several Crimes that so blemish the Reputation that the Party is ever afterwards unfit to be a Witness ... and the Reason is very plain, because every plain and honest Man affirming the Truth of any Matter under the Sanction and Solemnities of an Oath, is intitled to Faith and Credit, so that under such Attestation the Fact is understood to be fully proved.
>
> But when a Man is convicted of Falshood and other [Add 36090 "those"] Glaring Crimes against the common Principles [Add 36090 "Privileges"] of Honesty and Humanity, his Oath is of no Weight, because he hath not the Credit of a Witness, and there is equal or greater Presumption against him than can be on his Behalf; for the Presumption is benign and humane to every Man produced as a Witness, that he will not falsify or prevaricate in Matters of such Importance as all Affairs of Justice are, but where a Man is a notorious and publick Criminal, this Presumption fails him ..."[5]

"Credible" witnesses, in the first quotation, probably refers not to the modern (common-law) conception of credibility as assessed on the basis of demeanour under examination and cross-examination, but to the exclusion of infamous witnesses referred to in the second quotation.

This view that witness evidence takes its essential force from the oath is also reflected in the anonymous *Essay on the Nature of Oaths, and Judicial Evidence* (1715)[6]. I have not found any judicial statement directly supporting the view that the oath really was the essential basis of the probative value of witness evidence.

---

3 3.6.3. pr., Strahan's translation at 437.

4 *Evidence* 3.

5 *Evidence* 100-1.

6 Above Ch 6 § 4 *(1)* n 95.

In fact it would be unlikely that such a statement would be made; the point is so basic that it is unlikely to be directly argued[7]. However, the structure and development of the rules makes sense on the assumption that Gilbert's argument does reflect the general attitude of the courts in the period. In addition to the matters discussed below, some corroboration may be found in the various areas in which the oath is given special weight: as adding to the conclusive force of a confession in the answer against the defendant[8], as an explanation for the two-witness rule[9], and in the use of the parties' oaths in their own favour in equity[10].

One corollary of the principle was the idea that a witness cannot properly swear to a negative[11] (a rule which had civilian antecedents)[12], and hence a negative cannot be proved, so that, finally, a party cannot be put to prove a negative[13]. Another is the view that if the presumption arising from the oath is absent (because the evidence is unsworn, the witness infamous or not a religious believer), or is countered by a contrary presumption (where the witness is concerned in interest in the cause) the evidence is worthless[14]. The existence of limits on compulsion to swear and disputes about it will also serve as evidence that, in spite of common moans about the prevalence of perjury[15], the oath was taken seriously: seriously enough for compulsion to swear to be regarded as problematic[16]. Not only did the peerage re-

---

7 Though cf Coke, Fourth Institute p 278, "jurato creditur in judicio".

8 Above Ch 2 § 2 *(2)*.

9 Above Ch 2 § 2 *(4)* (c), below § 3.

10 Above Ch 2 § 2 *(4)*, Ch 6 § 5 *(1)* (c).

11 Coke, *Second Institute* p 662; *Trott v Le Cle* (1702) Colles 219, (counsel arg).

12 'Alciatus' 208v No 19, to reject the deposition; Cotta 871-2, with limits; Vulteius 372r; Ayliffe 541, "touching a deed", 544, affects weight, but distinguishing a negative "coarcted with circumstances" or directly perceptible "As for example if I see you not to have a cap or Hat on your head"; & cf Harl 1576 f 236v, "Negativa qua non est cuarcta [illegible] et tempore p[ro]bari non potest".

13 *Mullineux' Case* (M1581 or 2) Moo KB 178 pl 316, negative not triable; *Dent v Reeve* (M1623) Benl 139, *quaere* whether negative provable; Coke Second Institute 662, negative not provable; Doderidge, *The English Lawyer* (London, 1631), 111, issue to a jury cannot contain a negative pregnant; *Colwell v Child* (P1667) 1 Ch Rep 195, 1 Ch Cas 86, 2 Freem 154 (Grimstone MR), plaintiff not to be put to prove a negative; Gilbert p 104, citing D. 22.3.2. The printed text is garbled; the text in Add 36090 (at p 142) is:

"the affirmative ought to be proved ffor it is not suffic[ien]t barely to Deny what is affirmed unless the contrary be proved ffor a Negative regularly cannot be proved, is not, cannot come regularly into proof, for words are but the Expressions of Facts and therefore where nothing is done nothing can be sayd to prove it, And this is a Rule both in the Comon and Civil Laws".

Cf also Cotta 8, 599; Wood 309-310.

14 Above Ch 6 *passim*.

15 Cf above Ch 4 nn 96, 127, 136-8 and text there.

16 For general discussions cf Silving, "The Oath, Part I" 68 YLJ 1329, and Susan Staves, *Players Scepters: Fictions of Authority in the Restoration* (University of Nebraska Press, 1970) Ch 4 "Oaths and Vows".

sist compulsion to swear, claiming a privilege by status[17]; but also at the opposite end of the social spectrum, the plebeian Quaker movement which arose in the 1650s refused to swear on grounds of principle, and their objections were appeased by an Act of 1695[18] making provision for affirmation in civil cases. Oaths in ecclesiastical courts were the subject of an extensive political struggle[19]. Oaths were not, therefore, a mere matter of form, but a serious obligation; and in the peculiar weight given to the oath has to be placed in this context.

II. Equity examination and the purpose of cross-examination

The civilians saw a part of the purpose of judicial examination as drawing out details from the witness which would strengthen or weaken his or her testimony[20]. Demeanour under examination was in theory valued[21], but the practice of delegated examination means that it cannot have been seen as indispensable. Similarly, the purpose of cross-examination by interrogatories was partly to try to obtain a confession of bias, partly to draw out evidence favourable to the party cross-examining.

A full statement of the merits claimed for examination and cross-examination in open court as a test of the veracity and accuracy of testimony, as contrasted with the roman-canon procedure, is given by Hale in his *History of the Common Law*[22]:

> "Ninthly, the excellency of this open Course of Evidence to the Jury in the Presence of the Judges, Jury, Parties and Council, and even of the adverse Witnesses, appears in these Particulars:
>
> 1st, that it is openly; and not in private before a Commissioner or Two, and a couple of Clerks, where oftentimes Witnesses will deliver that which they will be ashamed to testify publickly
>
> 2dly, that it is Ore Tenus personally, and not in writing, wherein oftentimes, yea too often, a crafty Clerk, Commissioner, or Examiner, will make a Witness speak what he truly never

17 Above Ch 2 p 37, Ch 7 pp 271-2

18 7 & 8 Wm III c 34; cf Holdsworth *HEL* VI p 200, n 11.

19 Cf Macnair, "The Early Development" and authorities cited there.

20 'Alciatus' 208v-209v; Maranta 562.9 – 536.16; Cotta 865-8; *Principia Quaedam* 29, 75; *Reformatio* 251 c 40; Vulteius 371v-372r, 508r; Zouch *EI* 90; Wood 319.

21 Covarruvias *Var. Res.* ii c 13 No 6; Zouch *EI* 99, following D 48.18.10.5 and 22.5.3; Wood 318.

22 First published in 1713, but obviously written sometime before Hale's death in 1676; cited here from the 1971 University of Chicago Press edition, ed CM Gray, at pp 163-4. This is not the first statement of these views; compare Fortescue, *De Laudibus* 59-77 (1460s), though the argument there is that publicity will restrain perjury and that the jurors will have personal knowledge of the credibility of witnesses, Smith *De Republica Anglorum* 99-100 (1560s), and Popham's speech in the *Case of the Union of the Realms* (1606) Moo KB 790 at 798.

meant, by his dressing it up in his own Terms, Phrases, and Expressions; whereas on the other Hand, many times the very Manner of a Witness's delivering his Testimony will give a probable Indication whether he speaks truly or falsly; and by this Means also he has Opportunity to correct, amend, or explain his Testimony upon further Questioning with him, which he can never have after a Deposition is set down in Writing.

3dly, That by this Course of personal and open Examination, there is Opportunity for all Persons concern'd, viz. The Judge, or any of the Jury, or Parties, or their Council or Attornies, to propound occasional Questions, which beats and boults out the Truth much better than when the Witness only delivers a formal Series of his Knowledge without being interrogated; and on the other Side, preparatory, formal, and limited Interrogatories in Writing, preclude this Way of occasional Interrogations, and the best Method of searching and sifting out the Truth is choak'd and suppress'd".

There are number of reasons for supposing that the purpose of cross-examination in equity is to ensure completeness and bring out any points which might favour the defendant, rather than (as in Hale's argument) to test the veracity of the witness, the accuracy of his recollection, etc. In the first place, the system of examination on interrogatories and secrecy meant that the parties were not supposed to know what evidence the witness gave, so they could hardly be intended to test this evidence by cross-examination. Secondly, although commissions were supposed to be as far as possible carried out all at once, examination and cross-examination together[23], the reason for this is the danger that the evidence given will be disclosed[24], and there was nothing to stop parties examining witnesses *ex parte* in the examiners' office provided they gave the adverse party the name and address of the witness so that they could cross-examine at some subsequent date[25]. Thirdly, Gilbert in the *Forum Romanum* directly says that

"the Defendant ... might ... put such Cross Interrogatories to them, as might bring out Circumstances in his favour ..."[26]

and it is a commonplace of the various praises of common-law cross-examination and the evidence of demeanour that this is not available in civilian or canonist systems or in the equity courts[27].

---

23 Gilbert *FR* 127, Bacon p 300

24 Ib.

25 Gilbert *FR* 127, Bacon p 298. And cf *Pearson v Rowland* (H1715/6) 2 Swan 266n for examination on commission followed by cross-examination in the office. This would clearly have been an irregularity in the civilian procedure, which required the adverse party to be cited to see the witness sworn (above Ch 5 § I n 17); and cf also Hudson 200, commenting on this as a defect of equity as opposed to civilian procedure.

26 *FR* p 116, Bacon p 297. The discussion is actually of the civil and canon law, but the reason is said to be the same in Chancery.

27 As well as Hale, cited above, cf *Case of the Union of the Realms* (1606) Moo KB 790 pl 1091, *per* Popham CJ at 798; the absence of demeanour evidence given as a reason for Star Chamber to decline jurisdiction in *Darcy v Cook & Leigh* (1619) Hob 325 at 325-6; Gilbert *Evidence* 59-60.

"Cross-examination" in equity should, therefore, probably not be seen as a sort of defective common-law cross-examination, that is, as a test of the veracity of the witness,[28] but as governed by different principles, those of completeness and mutuality. Gilbert in the *Evidence* says[29] that depositions are weaker evidence than evidence *viva voce* (though stronger than oral evidence of what a witness said at a former trial) because the credibility of the witness is not tested, and are therefore only usable where the witness is dead or otherwise unavailable. This is a common law view; the only trace of it in equity proceedings is the (allegedly) increased use of feigned issues, where the common law rules would apply[30]. As far as its own procedure for taking testimony was concerned, the Chancery continued in the later seventeenth and early eighteenth century to insist on the principles of judicial control of examinations[31] and of secret examination[32] which it shared with the roman-canon system.

III. The requirement of two witnesses

The rule requiring two witnesses to make a full proof was pivotal to the roman-canon law of proof by witnesses. It required two unexceptionable witnesses, and it required their depositions to agree with each other in all particulars[33]. On this basis arose the distinctions between those witnesses who might, if corroborated by additional witnesses, make a proof, and those who were not to be heard at all[34]. Outside of the context of capital crimes, however,the rule was not absolutely rigid. A single credible witness could be a half proof[35], and as such could be supported by other half proofs, as, for example, presumptions[36], or by the suppletory oath[37]. Two wit-

28 There is a tendency towards this view in Holdsworth HEL IX p 355.

29 44-5, with a discussion of the (alleged) evolution of the equity method of taking evidence from the civilian method and the deficiencies of both compared with jury trial

30 Though the equity courts would dispense with some common law rules by ordering the parties to consent to the admission of depositions which would be usable in equity.

31 Jeffreys made orders requiring counsel to sign interrogatories, with a view to control of irrelevant and leading interrogatories (29 Apr 1687, i Sanders 374) and prohibiting Masters from receiving ready drawn depositions or deputing examination to their clerks (23 June 1688, i Sanders 382), and the first of these orders was revived by Wright LK (15 Jul 1700, i Sanders 416).

32 Order of 9 Feb 1721/2, i Sanders 454-6, requiring commissioners and their clerks to keep depositions secret.

33 *Summa Angelica* f 346v No 24 (cited *F&C* f 546r); 'Alciatus' 219v; *Reformatio* 254 c 40, 256 c 47; *Principia Quaedam* 96; Ridley 191-3; Wiseman 17; Domat 3.6.3.13, 14; Wood 316-7; Ayliffe 541.

34 Above Ch 6 § 2 *(1)*; Domat, 3.6.3.14 for supplying witnesses who disagreed by additional witnesses.

35 'Alciatus' 206r; *Principia Quaedam* 75; Zouch *EI* 90; Conset 108.

nesses deposing to separate facts which tended to prove the same general point was acceptable at least in some cases[38]. A half proof, hence a single witness, would be acceptable in some summary causes[39]; and Ayliffe says that a single witness is good against his proponent[40].

The common law did not apply the two-witness rule to matters triable by jury[41]; though supporters of the common law, following Fortescue, generally regarded this as a virtue, there were episodic outbreaks of concern over the possibility of a criminal conviction being secured on the evidence of a single and perhaps not very reputable witness[42]. The equity courts certainly from the point at which we have clear authority required two witnesses to found a decree on any matter which was sought to be proved by witnesses[43]. The problem which this poses is how far the equity rule corresponded to the rule of the law of proof requiring two unexceptionable witnesses whose depositions concurred.

How far did the rule in equity conform to the romano-canonical rule? Wigmore said that "it is not to be doubted that the rule was followed from the beginning. Probably the simple and direct form of the ecclesiastical rule was in the beginning unchanged; but in later development there came alterations both in the scope of the rule and in the reasons given for it"[44]. The assumption that the canonical rule

---

36 Ridley 193, though critical; Gentili ii 146; E. Lake, *Notes Touching Alteration of Some Lawes*, 115; Wood 316-7 ("circumstances").

37 *Reformatio* 254 c 40; Maranta 563.14; Wiseman 17; Ayliffe 444, also giving the example of one witness and *fama*.

38 Lyndwood 304 v *testium receptionem*, in a general inquiry into heresy; Cotta 860-4, diversity merely verbal; *Principia Quaedam* 75; Vulteius 371v; Gentili ii 146; *F&C* f 546r, (source citation illegible).

39 Maranta 224 No 43; extracted *F&C* f 546v.

40 540. At 541, however, Ayliffe says that a nobleman though a single witness makes a full proof, a proposition which is explicitly denied by other sources; Wood 317 says that a public officer's testimony makes a full proof though single.

41 The explanation given for this by Fortescue (p 74) was that proof at common law was by the oaths of twelve jurors *omni exceptione maiores*, so that the rule was inapplicable. In the middle ages the rule did apply to matters triable otherwise than by jury, such as questions of fact arising on points of procedure. In *Reniger qui tam v Fogossa* (H1549/50) 1 Plowd 1 on a demurrer to evidence Bradshaw AG for the plaintiff argued (at 8) that two witnesses were required by natural law and that therefore the depositions must agree; Atkins (at 8) and Brook (at 12) for the defendant opposed this argument on the ground that the jury could find a verdict of its own knowledge without or against the witnesses. The proceedings were stopped before judgment by royal order, but Plowden (at 20-21) says that this was because the Crown anticipated defeat.

42 Chiefly around treason: Wigmore § 2036, L.M. Hill, (1968) 12 *AJLH* 95; and on accomplice evidence, Langbein 50 *U. Chic. LR* 96-100, Beattie, *Crime and the Courts in England 1660-1800* (Oxford, Clarendon, 1986) pp 369-373. For a contemporary civilian argument as to the common law argument see Lake, *Notes Touching Alteration of Some Lawes* 115-6.

43 Cf the authorities cited below; for the continued existence of the rule up to the nineteenth century, Maddock, *Treatise on the Principles and Practice of the High Court of Chancery* (1815) Vol 2 pp 332f; Wigmore § 2047, citing Gresley, *Evidence in Equity* (1837) 4.

was followed from the beginning rested, however, on Wigmore's acceptance of Langdell's view that the equity procedure was from the outset modelled on the canon law procedure, which has been challenged by Dawson.

It will appear from what I have already said that I think that at least in the seventeenth century, the general parallelism between procedure and proof in equity and the romano-canonical system is a good deal closer than Dawson's argument suggests. Nonetheless, this does not settle the question of the two-witness rule, because in civilian terms, it might legitimately have been argued that proceedings in the equity courts, being generally summary, hence required only a half proof[45].

The earliest direct authority in Chancery is *Witherall & Gourney* (c. 1600), reported in *Observations:*

> Note by Mr Phillips who tould mee that [th]e Court of Chancery will nev[er] Decree for the Pl[ain]t[iff] where he p[ro]ve his Bill by one Wittness onely but they will dismisse him to the Com[m]on Lawe[46].

At the same period in Star Chamber, in *Talbot v Wood* (1595) the court held "that in criminal cases 'one wytnesse suffysethe not' but *testes luce clariores et omni exceptione maiores* may bring proof"[47].

Before and contemporary with these direct authorities there is some indirect evidence. There are two relevant cases in the Year Books, one from 1476[48] in which the Chancellor appears to apply the rule that the depositions must agree, and one from 1482[49] in which Fairfax and Hussey assume in argument that two witnesses are required; St German in *Doctor & Student*[50] said that there could be no decree without sufficient proof; *Forme et Certenty* cites several authorities on the two witness rule[51]; and there are two cases in *Observations* in which the language of *semiplena* and *plena probatio* is used[52].

On the other hand, Tothill provides three examples of decisions taken on the evidence of a single witness. However, of these *Sands v Knighton* (1637-8)[53] is a statement that one witness is sufficient to prove a contempt, and this was consistent with civilian views, since contempts were summary[54], and another, *Eland v Wright*

---

44 Wigmore § 2047, Vol VII at p 291.

45 Above Ch 1 nn 64, 108-110 and text there; and cf Maranta, 224 No 43, above n 39.

46 f 440r No 32; sidenoted, "testis singularis noe Decree".

47 Hawarde 13 at 15-16; Baildon's translation from the Law-French, except the phrase in single quotation marks and the latin tag.

48 YB P 16 Ed 4 9b, pl 10 (LC).

49 YB P 22 Ed 4 6b, pl 18 (Exchequer Chamber, the judges advising the Chancellor).

50 91 SS pp 108-9.

51 Above nn 33, 38, 39; and also f 545r, to Cotta *Memoralia.*

52 f 445v No 66, f 457v No 170; though the reporter evidently had some trouble with the expressions.

53 Toth 41.

(1634 or 1612)[55], "a decree upon one witness appeareth by the Judge's certificate" appears to be on a trial at law (why else the judge's certificate?). There remains *Swan v Atkins* (1574)[56], " a decree upon one witness which proves his pedigree, from whence he claims"; this is too sketchy to draw much from it.

In *Earl of Suffolk v Greenvill* (1631)[57] two reports say that "the Court held it dangerous to admit the Sufficiency of a Deed to be proved by the Single Oath of such a witness"; and in the later seventeenth and early eighteenth century the rule is being subverted by the use of feigned issues, and some judges regard this as an abuse[58]. This does not fit well with the rule being a recent development.

Nonetheless in the late seventeenth and early eighteenth century the rationale given from the rule differed from the civilian rationale, and the rule itself was being diluted in two ways. The rationale given was that the defendant's answer, being on oath, was entitled to weight as such, so that one witness to support a matter positively denied by the defendant's answer was merely "oath against oath"[59]. This rationale does not appear in Lord Nottingham's treatises or Reports, though the two-witness rule does[60]. The formula "one witness against the defendant's answer" appears first in the time of Lord Guilford[61] and reference to the defendant's oath in that of the Lord Commissioners of 1689-93[62].[63]

---

54 Clerke 81-2, saying explicitly that a half proof is acceptable; and contempt was also subject to special rules in the matter of competence of witnesses: Nott Prac 11.16, 17.

55 Toth 64.

56 Toth 64. The evidence of one witness appears to be accepted to support the construction of a will in *Goring v Bickerstaffe* (M1661) Pollex 31 (Grimstone MR), (H1661-2) 1 Ch Cas 4, 2 Freem 163 (Lord Clarendon, Foster CJ, Windham J, Hale CB), but this may be by consent, as the bill was by the trustees for directions.

57 Above Ch 3 n 228 and text there.

58 Nott. Proleg 8.3, 11, TT pp 217, 220; Rawlinson and Hutchins, Lords Commissioners, in *Christ's College Cambridge v Widdrington* (H1692-3) 2 Vern 283; Lord Cowper in *Ibbotson v Rhodes* (P1706) 2 Vern 554, 1 Eq Ca Ab 229.13.

59 *Langton v Tracy* (1669) 2 Ch Rep 30 (counsel arg; the court decides on another ground); *Hobbs v Norton* (H1682-3) 1 Vern 137, 2 Ch Cas 128 (counsel *arg*, apparently rejected); *Alam v Jourdan* (P1683) 1 Vern 161, 1 Eq Ca Ab 229.12 (Lord Guilford); *Kingdome v Boakes* (H1690-1) Pre Ch 19; *Christs' College Cambridge v Widdrington* (H1692-3) 2 Vern 283 (Rawlinson, Hutchins Lords Commissioners); *Lady Montague v Earl of Bath* (1692) 2 Ch Rep 421, Nels 196, 2 Freem 121, 193, 3 Ch Cas 55, 2 Eq Ca Ab 671, per Somers LK; Gilbert *Evidence* 109. See also the discussion above ch 2 § 2 *(4)* (c).

60 Proleg. 8.3, 11, cited above; *Earl of Feversham v Watson* (P1678) Nott CC No 823, 79 SS at 645. One possible antecedent is the rule prohibiting affidavit against affidavit (above ch 2 n 257 and text there). Another is the report in *Observations* that Egerton "said [th]at ag[ains]t Usurers Banckruptes periured p[er]sons Cosiners etc. Quilibet p[rae]sump[ti]o crescit in p[ro]ba[ti]onem and that some {illegible} semi plena proof w[i]th some p[re]sump[ti]on was sufficient to induce him to decree ag[ains]t such" (f 445v No 66). Since the defendant's bad character here reduces the burden of proof, this suggests that otherwise the defendant's denial on oath has some weight; but the point may be, rather, that the defendant's bad character reinforces independent presumptive evidence of fraud (below ch 9 § 2 *(4)*).

61 *Hobbs v Norton, Alam v Jourdan,* above n 59.

The forms of dilution are two. The first is that it appears from Gilbert's account of examinations to credit[64] that what is required is two *competent* witnesses, i.e. that only the common-law disqualifications will remove the witness from the arithmetic[65]. The second is the use of feigned issues to get around the rule. This is condemned by Lord Nottingham[66] as a "Mischief"; and in *Christs' College Cambridge v Widdrington* (H1692-3)[67] the Lords Commissioners refused to order a trial at law of a disputed item of an account on the ground that the plaintiff had had the benefit of the discovery on the defendant's oath; but by the early 1700s it was (allegedly) standard practice to order a trial at law where there was only one witness[68]. In *Ibbotson v Rhodes* (P1706) Lord Cowper said

> "he did not see the difference between doing it per Plura and per Pauciora; for to send it to law to be tried, where the Jury will certainly find it on the testimony of one witness, and then decreeing it on that verdict, is the same thing as decreeing on one witness, without trying it at all"[69].

If this represents a reservation about the practice, it had no effect; in two Irish appeals of 1709[70] and 1713[71] the House of Lords upheld the legality of ordering a trial at law on the evidence of a single witness.

The other aspect of the working of the two-witness rule which Wigmore saw as a dilution of the original rule[72] is the possibility of supplying the want of a witness by presumptions[73]. In reality, as is indicated above, this is wholly consistent with civilian doctrine. *Observations* reports of Egerton that

---

62 *Kingdome v Boakes, Christ's College v Widdrington,* above n 59.

63 Wigmore (§ 2047) saw this formulation of the rule as a variation from the roman-canon rule in substance as well as explanation, since the rule is applied to those matters positively denied by the defendant's answer and the answer does not, unlike a common-law pleading, confess everything which is not denied. However, the equity rules did require the defendant to answer positively and directly to everything charged in the plaintiff's bill, and an answer which failed to do this was exceptionable; and plaintiffs made full use of the machinery to extract sufficient answers. The suggested variance is therefore purely hypothetical.

64 Above Ch 6 n 119 and text there.

65 This may be too large an inference, but there is no authority later than *Earl of Suffolk v Greenvill* (and that doubtful) to suggest application to this rule of the exceptions to credit.

66 Above n 59.

67 2 Vern 283.

68 Gilbert *Evidence* 109; counsel *arg* in *Ibbotson v Rhodes* (P1706) 2 Vern 554, 1 Eq Ca Ab 229.13, at 1 Eq Ca Ab 229.13.

69 Ib. at 1 Eq Ca Ab 229.13. Trevor MR had, in fact, decreed it on the evidence of the single witness, possibly because the witness' evidence was to some extent corroborated by admissions in the defendant's answer; the defendant was seeking the trial on appeal. Lord Cowper ordered a trial and the answer to be read "as on oath but not as evidence".

70 *Plunket v Bishop of Dromore* (1709) Colles 421.

71 *Shee v Lawless* (1713) Colles 450.

72 § 2047 at p 291.

> My Lord Keeper houlds that in Case where any man conveys landes to another in considera[ti]on of bloud or other the like n[atu]rall consideration ... every p[re]sump[ti]on doth crescence p[ro]ba[ti]oni and semiproba[ti]ones are pleneproba[ti]ones in this Case for what is wanting in proofe is supplied by p[re]sump[ti]on of affec[ti]on and naturall love.[74]

This, like the case of defendants of bad character quoted earlier, is a fairly clear instance of the employment of the civilian concepts of full and half proof; it also illustrates the use of presumptions to add to a half proof to make a full proof. There are three instances of decrees on the basis of one witness and presumptions in Lord Nottingham's Reports[75], in the third of which, *Harvey v Harvey* (M1680), the decree is, in Lord Nottingham's report, clearly based on the presumption. By the nineteenth century this rule does seem to have become the basis of a real dilution, as the courts would then act on quite slight circumstantial evidence[76].

In the late seventeenth century the two-witness rule is an undoubted rule, and connected with the basis of testimony in the weight of the oath. It does not, however, have the structural centrality of the two-witness rule in the romano-canonical system, and, on the contrary, it is already being undermined by the use of feigned issues.

IV. Conflict of testimony

The starting point for civilian discussions of conflict of testimony was two texts from the *Digest.* D 22.5.3 calls for consideration of the witnesses' status, character, bias, and responses on examination, of the number of witnesses and of corroboration by common knowledge[77]. D 22.5.21.3 also refers to character and bias, but reduces the significance of the number of witnesses and places more emphasis on the extent to which the evidence fits the circumstances[78]. 'Alciatus' and the *Refor-*

---

73 This term at this date covers both some matters which would now be regarded as presumptions, and others which would now be regarded as items of circumstantial evidence. Cf below Ch 9 § 2.

74 f 457v No 170.

75 *Spencer v Hunlock* (P1674) Nott CC No 80, 73 SS 41 at 42 "though sworn but by one witness, ought to be believed because it is such a promise as ought to have been made"; *Sutton v Jewks* (H1675-6) Nott CC No 394, 73 SS 268 "one witness with acts concurrent ... is a good ground to make a decree for the plaintiff"; *Harvey v Harvey* (M1680) Nott CC No 1060, 79 SS 850 at 851, decided on presumption (acquiescence by the plaintiff) but also sworn by one witness; the same point more fully reported and the decision affirmed on a rehearing by Jeffreys C (M1686) 2 Ch Cas 180.

76 Wigmore § 2047 cites Gresley, *Evidence in Equity* (1837) 4. Cf also Maddock op cit pp 338-9

77 *consentiens fama;* "common knowledge" is Honoré's translation in Mommsen, Krueger & Watson ed. *The Digest of Justinian.*

78 "Si testes omnes eiusdem honestatis et existimationis sit et *negotii qualitas* ac iudicis motus cum his concurrit, sequenda sunt omnia testimonia; si vero ex his quidam eorum aliud

matio base their treatment of conflict of testimony primarily on the second text, Zouch and Wiseman primarily on the first, and Domat synthesises the two[79]. 'Alciatus' adds that the judge should if possible try to reconcile conflicting depositions[80] and Ayliffe that more credit is given to affirmative than negative witnesses[81]. *Forme et Certenty* cites, without quoting, a discussion in the *Policraticus* of John of Salisbury which draws on the same sources in the Digest[82].

Gilbert's account of this issue is fairly clearly drawn from these or similar sources. He says that (1) "If Men's swearing can be reconciled, such Interpretation shall be put upon it as may make them agree"[83]; (2) "one affirmative Witness countervails the Proof of several Negative"[84]; (3) If there are equal numbers of witnesses on either side, their credit is to be considered; witnesses to credit affect the credit of the primary witnesses in proportion to their own credit; "The credit of a witness is to be judged from his State and Dignity in the World, for Men of easy Circumstances are supposed more hardly induced to commit a manifest Perjury"; bad character and relationship to parties, though insufficient to disqualify, diminish credit[85]; and (4) if the witnesses are equal in number and credit, they may be judged by the amount of circumstantial detail given in their testimony[86]. No English authority is given for these propositions either in the printed text or in the MSS, and one of the people who copied the text thought it appropriate to cite Domat[87]. In place of Hale's[88] discussion of cross-examination and demeanour we find the elaboration of criteria of credibility of a civilian type.

Lord Guilford[89] offers a somewhat different approach to the question "What is truth – in case where witnesses swear directly contrary to one another". He lists as "Topicks"

"1. Credit of witnesses
2. Probability of the Matter
3. Testimonys concurrent. Temptations, inclinations, education

---

dixerint, licet impari numero, credendum est id quod *naturae negotii convenit*". "Fits the circumstances" is Honoré's translation of the second phrase emphasised.

79 'Alciatus' 219v-220r; *Reformatio* 251 c 26, 255 c 44; Zouch *EI* 89; Wiseman 18; Domat 3.6.1.12, 3.6.3.15.

80 220r.

81 544.

82 f 545r.

83 110. The sub-title "The Weighing of Evidence" is absent from both MSS, which instead sidenote the passage "Bounds of Credibility".

84 110-1.

85 111.

86 111-2.

87 Lincoln's Inn Hill MS 79, citing "Strahan's Domat p 418 pr 12", which is nothing to do with the subject; probably an error for 3.6.1 pr 12, (cited above) at Strahan ii p 441.

88 Quoted above § 2.

89 Add 32518 f 152b.

4. Testimonys without doubt
5. Arguments from consequences
6. Behaviour of persons accused
7. Farther detection of time"[90]

These criteria are intended for trials by jury or by peers[91]. Even so, "behaviour of persons accused" comes low on the list and behaviour of witnesses on the stand does not make an appearance[92].

In spite of the lack of any citation of authority in Gilbert[93], there is some evidence that judges in Chancery in this period were using at least some of these criteria to assess conflicts of witness evidence. It is rare for this sort of case to have been fully reported. Nonetheless, there are full reports of judicial reasoning about conflicts of testimony in some cases which are reported for other reasons, such as the prominence of the parties.

"Reconciling" the depositions can be seen in *Lord Grey v Lady Grey* (T1676, H1676-7)[94], where Lord Nottingham says that acquiescence by a son in acts of ownership by his father, where the father had bought land in the son's name, may be merely the courtesy due from a son to his father[95]; *Earl of Feversham v Watson* (P1678)[96], where Lord Nottingham goes to some lengths to interpret the evidence given by the one witness for the plaintiff on a particular point as in reality compatible with the evidence of the defendant's several witnesses. The number of witnesses is also relied on in *Feversham v Watson*[97]. The "credit" of witnesses is used in the sense of their social standing in *Floyer v Strachley* (1631)[98], and in *Lady*

90 The context of the rather curious final point is that this was directed as a polemic against those peers who believed themselves bound to decide *secundum allegata et probata* (Add 32518 f 153r) in the Popish Plot trials, and therefore to believe the Plot Witnesses in spite of the fact that over the course of a succession of trials their stories had changed significantly (on which cf Kenyon, *The Popish Plot* (above Ch 6 p 227 n 76) *passim*): North I 204-5.

91 Paras 3-6 following this outline concern the fact that the jury is trier of fact and the need for the judge to "hold the seals", and cf previous note. For Guilford's conduct of trials as CJCP cf Roger North's account, North I pp 144-7.

92 From Roger North's account, I 79ff, Guilford was hostile to Hale as a judge as well as politically; and the merits of jury trial were in any event a matter of political controversy. Hale's account, therefore represents a view, not necessarily the orthodox view, of the question.

93 In fact, this is not very surprising. The citation of authorities in the MSS of Gilbert is largely confined to those cases which are actually noted or discussed in the text, and even these side-notes may have been added after the original text was written.

94 (T1676) Nott CC No 526, 2 Freem 6; (H1676-7) Nott CC No 643, 1 Ch Cas 296, Rep t Finch 338, 2 Swanst 594 ((T1678) Nott CC No 833 not SP).

95 79 SS at 485.

96 (M1677) Nott CC No 773, a preliminary point; (P1678) Nott CC No 823, 2 Freem 35, Rep t Finch 445 (hearing before Finch C assisted by North CJ); rvsd HL, 79 SS 646.

97 79 Selden Soc at 645.

98 Nels 13.

Montague v Earl of Bath (1692)[99], and what Gilbert calls their "skill", the amount of detail in their depositions, in *AG v Vernon* (H1685-6)[100].

What is missing from Gilbert's account, however, but present in Guilford's, (and in those of 'Alciatus', the *Reformatio* and Domat) is the extent to which conflicts of testimony are resolved by reference to "presumptions" and circumstances. For example, in *Earl of Shrewsbury v Talbot* (1595) in Star Chamber, "probability and presumptions" are central to the argument between the two sides' counsel on the credibility of the central witnesses. In *Grey v Grey*, in the end "the parol declarations in this case are both ways", so "there being no certain proof to rest on as to parol declarations, the matter is left to construction and implication of law"[101]. The witness evidence conflicting, the conflict is settled by the presumption of advancement. Similarly in *Feversham v Watson* Lord Nottingham is helped to the conclusion that there was no waiver of a condition precedent, contrary to the evidence of one witness for the plaintiff, by the antecedent improbability of the covenantor's having agreed to waive the condition without any payment[102]; in *AG v Vernon* the defendant's witnesses' evidence that the undervalue of property was not as great as that alleged by the Crown's witnesses was countered by the evidence of the speed and secrecy with which the patent of grant was passed raising a presumption of fraud[103]; and in *Montague v Bath* the court called in aid the doctrine that fraud cannot be presumed[104] as well as a variety of points making it unlikely that the late Duke had been, as the plaintiffs alleged, in some way imposed on by the defendant and his counsel.

It is only in *Montague v Bath* that there is any suggestion that what a witness has sworn may be false, and there it is merely that the witnesses may be mistaken as to their identification of handwriting, which the judges have themselves identified by inspection and comparison[105]. Overall, then, the limited evidence there is suggests that Gilbert's account, while overschematic and lacking any reference to

99 2 Ch Rep 421, Nels 196, 2 Eq Ca Ab 671, 2 Freem 121, 193, most fully in 3 Ch Cas 55; 3 Ch Cas 55 at 81, per Treby CJ "I speak with all due respect to my lord Carmathen's evidence".

100 1 Vern 370 at 389 (2 Ch Rep 353, not SP; (M1684) 1 Vern 277, preliminary proceedings before Lord Guilford). The substance of the decision should probably be handled with some caution, as it appears from *Vernon v Benson* (1722) 9 Mod 47 at 48 that "upon the accession of King William to the Crown, it was not thought expedient to rest his right to the forest upon this decree".

101 79 Selden Soc at 484.

102 79 Selden Soc at 645.

103 1 Vern 370 at 387, 388.

104 Below Ch 9 § 2 *(4)*.

105 *Per* Powell B, 3 Ch Cas at 58. Powell B also commented sarcastically on an alleged contradiction between evidence given by Sir Thomas Stringer and the existence of a draft in his hand to the opposite effect. In fact, however, Stringer hadn't given evidence, and this comment seems to be merely a party gibe: Stringer was a Whig, and Powell one of the few Tories on the bench at this time.

presumptions[106], does identify the sorts of factors used by equity judges in deciding on conflicts of evidence.

V. Hearsay and opinion

The framework for assessing the weight of testimony discussed so far informed the treatment of oral hearsay and opinion. In civilian doctrine both the corroboration of witnesses by each other, and the assessment of the relative credibility of individual conflicting depositions, depended on the circumstantial details elicited in taking the deposition. The witnesses were therefore to be examined on the reasons for their knowledge, and failure to give reasons adversely affected the weight of the deposition[107]. In consequence of this rule it was well established that witnesses must speak to knowledge gained from their own senses[108]. This in turn carried with it the rejection of testimony to the witness' belief or judgment, and of testimony *ab alio auditu*, a formula which clearly falls to be translated as "hearsay"[109]. There were, however, a range of limits and exceptions[110]; the most frequently cited in our authorities is the case of old boundaries and other ancient facts[111]. In adition it is important to note that these rules form part of the guidelines for assessing the weight of depositions; there is no mechanism actually to strike out expressions either of hearsay, or of opinion or belief.

Gilbert says that

> "The Attestation of the Witness must be to what he knows, and not to that only which he hath heard, for a meer hearsay [MSS "Man's hearing"] is no Evidence; for it is his Knowledge that must direct the Court and Jury in the Judgement of the Fact, and not his mere Credulity, which is very uncertain and various in several persons; for Testimony being but an appeal to the Knowledge of another, if indeed he doth not know, he can be no Evidence: Besides, though a Person testify what he hath heard upon Oath, yet the Person who spake it was not upon Oath; and if a Man had been in Court and had said the same Thing and

106 Although presumptions are used in argument throughout Gilbert's text, the only substantive discussion of them he gives is simply lifted from Coke.

107 'Alciatus' 208v No 21; Maranta 562 Nos 9-14; *Principia Quaedam* 29, 75; Zouch *El* 90; Philippus Decius *De Regulis Iuris* (Lyon, 1528) 99r Nos 5, 6, cited *F&C* f 546v.

108 'Alciatus' 208v, "de auditu et visu suo"; Maranta 562.9, "ex quinque sensibus"; Cotta 880-1; Vulteius 371v-372r; Ayliffe 540.

109 For depositions *de credere* or *de credulitate* see 'Alciatus' 208v No 16; Maranta 562.15; Cotta 866-7; *Reformatio* 254-5 c 42. On the antecedents and some details on the *ab alio auditu* rule see M. Damaska, 'Hearsay in Cinquecento Italy' in *Studi in onore di Vittorio Denti* (Padova, 1994) i 59-89; and among our sources, Maranta 563.18, *Reformatio* 230 c 26 (exception), Vulteius 372r, 507v-508r, and cf Ayliffe 540, not from the senses of another.

110 Damaska 68-73.

111 Maranta 563.18; *Reformatio* 230 c 26, 254-5 c 42; Ayliffe 544. Cf Cotta 31, recitals in old documents to prove *communis opinio*.

had not sworn it, he had not been believed in a Court of Justice; for all Credit being derived from Attestation and Evidence, it can rise not higher that the Fountain from whence it flows, and if the first Speech was without Oath, an Oath that there was such a Speech makes it no more than a bare speaking, and so of no Value in a Court of Justice, where all things were determined under the Solemnities of an Oath; besides, nothing can be more uncertain than the loose and wandering Witnesses that are [MSS "Evidence that is"] taken upon the uncertain Reports of the Talk and Discourse of others."[112]

The only exception Gilbert offers to this rule is that previous statements by the witness may be used to strengthen (or, at least when they are upon oath, to weaken) the credibility of the witness[113]. The reasoning for excluding hearsay is twofold. The first aspect (somewhat confusing) is that it depends on the witness' opinion of the veracity of the out of court declarant (his "credulity"[114]). The second is that the out of court statement is not on oath, therefore worthless.

It is worth noticing two things about this rule. The first is that, like the civilian *ab alio auditu* rule and unlike the modern rule against hearsay, it is not a general rule covering both oral and documentary statements out of court and even "assertive" conduct. The second is that, at least on its second justification, it does not apply to sworn statements not made in the present proceedings. Gilbert's account shares both these features with the attitude of the equity jurisdiction to hearsay up to his time. There is no instance in the reports before 1714 of either a document, or depositions in a former cause, or even an affidavit, – or, on the common-law side, oral evidence of testimony given in a former trial – being described as "hearsay" or excluded as such; though there are instances of witness evidence being described as "hearsay" or "mere hearing". Documents, and evidence of matters previously said on oath, are governed by different rules.

How far does Gilbert's account fit the authorities in equity? The first point to be made is that there does not appear to be an exclusionary rule in the sense in which that would now be understood. There is no instance in the reports of depositions, or the answers to particular interrogatories, being suppressed on the ground that they contain hearsay. The second is that there are, in fact, only three examples of an item of evidence given by a witness being described as "*hearsay*". The first is a brief comment in *Deighton v Thorpe, Mounson et al'* (1594) in Star Chamber: "to speak of 'hearesaye' and to swear, are two [different] things"[115]. Somewhat clearer

---

112 *Evidence* pp 107-8.

113 108. The marginal citations are not in the MSS, and the rule as stated by Hawkins (Pleas of the Crown II, 431, cited in the printed editions) is not quite the same as that stated by Gilbert.

114 OED *credulity* sense (1), willingness to believe, not necessarily (as in modern times) unfounded willingness to believe.

115 (H1593/4) Hawarde 3; Baildon's translation from the Law French, except for the word 'hearesay', and his insertion of [different] to clarify the sense. In *Sir Antony Ashley's Case* (M1611) Moo KB 816.1105, Coke CJ said that suspicion based on hearsay ("sur report dun auter") was no ground for an accusation.

is *Montague v Bath*, where Treby CJ says, in order to discount evidence, that it is "but a hearing by a third hand"[116], and Somers LK (of the same evidence) "there is no proof of it: it is at most but an hearsay, testified by one witness"[117]. In *Lady Granville v Lady Beaufort* (1709)[118] Lord Cowper said that proof of what the lawyer (since dead) who drew the testator's will said in his lifetime as to his instructions from the testator was "evidence, but the slenderest sort of evidence"[119] as to the testator's intention[120]; Treby CJ's comment seems to be to the same effect, that this is a very weak sort of evidence, and Somers LK says that it is not proof not merely because it is hearsay but also because it is only proved by one witness.

On the other hand, the first half of Gilbert's explanation – that the witness must swear to his own knowledge and not to his belief – is supported by a number of precedents. Witness evidence given to rebut the presumption of satisfaction is described as "meer conjectures" in *Peacock v Glasscock* (1630)[121]; evidence that the testator said something "to that effect" is rejected (not excluded) by Wright LK in *Re Darrell, Trelawney v Molesworth* (1700) on the ground that "that makes the witness the judge"[122], and by Lord Cowper in *Granville v Beaufort*[123]; and "belief" that a post-nuptial settlement had been executed in pursuance of a bond given before marriage is described by Lord Cowper as "inability to swear" to the existence of the bond in *Willson v Pack* (1710)[124].

There is rather more discussion of "hearsay" in common law authorities. These share the characteristic that they are limited to out of court oral statements which are not on oath[125]; the earlier cases at least suggest that the issue is a matter of the weight, rather than the admissibility of the evidence[126], and a case of 1646 is explicit:

---

116 3 Ch Cas 55 at 80.

117 Ib. at 119.

118 (1709) 2 Vern 648, 1 P Wms 118; rvsd HL on other grounds, 3 Bro PC 37.

119 2 Vern 648 at 649.

120 For the admission of evidence of intention by way of exception to the parol evidence rule cf above Ch 4; in this context direct evidence of what the testator or grantor said was regularly admitted. A written note of advice by counsel was admitted as evidence of his client's intention to authorise an agent to make an absolute sale of property in *Cropley v Marquess of Newcastle* (1662-3) 1 Ch R 225.

121 1 Ch Rep 45.

122 1 Eq Ca Ab 231 (2 Vern 378, 2 Eq Ca Ab 297, and aff'd HL Colles 163, none on SP). On 'making the witness the judge' cf *Reformatio* 248 c 16.

123 2 Vern 648 at 649.

124 Pre Ch 295, 2 Eq Ca Ab 155.2; at Pre Ch 297,8.

125 There is one instance of a deposition being described as "hearsay" in debate in the House of Commons on a bill of attainder in 1696: *Fenwick's Trial* 13 St. Tr. at 600.

126 On proof of nuncupative wills, *Rolfe v Hampden* (1541) 1 Dy 53b, "the jury paid little regard", & cf *Chadron v Harris* (n.d.) Noy 12; allowed as proof to maintain the surmise of a prohibition where there was a statutory two witness rule, *Strensham v Cullington* (1590) Cro El 228, *per cur; Austen v Pigot* (1599) Cro El 736; *Webb v Petts* (n.d.; 1602 x 1607) Noy 44;

> A person that may be admitted as a Witness, at a tryal may give words in Evidence to the Jury that were spoken to him by another person, who by the Rules of the Court might not be admitted as a Witness at the tryal. For it is but matter of Evidence, and it is left to the Jury how far they will give credit to them.[127]

In the later seventeenth century, however, there was clearly some development of the law towards an exclusionary rule with distinct exceptions. The process itself is not entirely clear[128]; the conclusion drawn from it by Hawkins, discussing criminal proceedings, is:

> It seems agreed, that what a Stranger has been heard to say is in Strictness no manner of Evidence either for or against a Prisoner, not only because it is not upon Oath, but also because the other Side hath no Opportunity of a cross Examination; and therefore it seems a settled Rule, that it shall never be made use of but only by way of Inducement or Illustration of what is properly Evidence ...[129]

From the rather limited range of equity authorities, it does not seem that this development at common law found any reflection in equity at this period. It is notable, however, that the two cases from the later part of the period in which oral hearsay is offered and explicitly discussed are both cases in which the intention of a party or testator is in issue; there is no example of use of a third-party statement to prove any other sort of fact. It may be, therefore, either that the problem is one of the sources, or that the point that a witness must in general swear to his own knowledge is simply too obvious to be taken.

VI. Conclusion

The evidence discussed here suggests that, at least in equity, witness demeanour under cross-examination was not regarded as a primary test of the veracity of witnesses; and even in relation to evidence to a jury, it is not mentioned by Lord Guilford and is not the primary basis of credibility in Gilbert's account. What then was the basis of the weight of testimony?

The answer seems to be, first, and primarily, the weight of the oath. This stands out as central in Gilbert's account, and this view is corroborated by other evidence: the use of party oaths in equity, contemporary concerns about compulsion to swear,

---

Ford v Nedham (1617) Noy 28; *Bennet v Snell* (1623) Palmer 377. Both areas involve exceptions within the civilian *ab alio auditu* rule, since a nuncupative will is a dying declaration and the prohibition cases turn on prescription (*facti antiqui*).

127 *Anon* (1646) Style Prec. Reg. 114, KB.

128 Prof. Richard D. Friedman and I are currently working on the development of the hearsay rule at common law.

129 ii 431; paraphrased, Bacon 313.

the centrality of the oath in discussions of exceptions to children and infidels as witnesses[130], and the treatment of hearsay.

Secondly, the standing (credit) and freedom from bias of the witnesses are clearly important. This is shown by the development in this period of the law relating to exceptions to witnesses (above Ch 6); it is also displayed in the methods for dealing with conflicts of testimony.

Third, corroboration plays a significant role. This is evident in equity in the application of the two-witness rule, and also in discussions of conflict of testimony. Corroboration need not be by other witnesses, but can also come from presumptions; this is clear in both areas.

Fourthly: *in equity,* as was discussed in Chapter 5, the procedure for the examination of witnesses corresponds to the roman-canon system for securing the independence of testimony from the parties, requiring examinations to be (theoretically) by an officer of the court and (theoretical) court control of interrogatories, and providing for separate and secret examination of witnesses and prohibiting (in general) re-examination to the same point.

These principles conform in fundamentals to the principles for the weight of testimony in the roman-canon system. The significant variations are (a) the special weight given to the oath; and (b) the possible shift in the latter part of the period towards the use of feigned issues. This latter point will be discussed further below in Chapter 10; it may represent a shift towards the line of thought which saw jury trial and adversary cross-examination in open court as a superior test of the weight of testimony.

130 Above Ch 6 §§ 3, 4 *(2).*

Chapter Nine

The Burden and Standard of Proof and Presumptions

In the modern common law the standard of proof is generally one of subjective persuasion of the trier of fact[1]. Though in criminal cases persuasion "beyond reasonable doubt" is required, in civil cases persuasion "on the balance of probability", voices have been raised doubting the validity of the distinction[2]. The burden of proof has therefore been said to have two elements, the risk of non-persuasion of the trier of fact, and in jury trials the "evidential burden", the duty of adducing sufficient evidence to leave the issue to the jury[3]. Presumptions in the modern law appear largely as historical anomalies; their effect, where they exist, is to reverse either the legal or the evidential burden of proof[4].

Roman-canon concepts in this area contrast radically with this modern approach. The standard of proof was (at least in theory) purely objective, so that (we have as already seen) items of proof might count as a full proof, half proof, etc; and in consequence the burden of proof was in origin a unilateral concept, a threshold the party making an allegation must pass[5]. In this context presumptions were considered not merely as legal rules affecting the incidence of the burden of proof, but as *items of proof* to be added into the scale. There was therefore an elaborate learning of presumptions to go alongside the learning of instruments and that of witnesses[6].

Discussions of these questions in early modern equity tend to show a theoretical framework closer to the roman-canon system than to the modern common law of evidence. The standard of proof is objective, the burden of proof is correspondingly largely unilateral, and presumptions play an important role in the system of proof. However, this does not represent a marked difference between equity and

---

1 Cross 140.

2 Cross 142.

3 Cross 105.

4 Thayer Ch 8; Wigmore § 2490; Cross 131 ff.

5 'Alciatus' (205r) finds it necessary to comment on the fact that witnesses should be heard on both sides in *crimen falsi*; for Conset (107) it is necessary to comment that the defendant can use the same probatory term as the plaintiff; and cf the discussion of the burden of proof in Ayliffe, 444.

6 Besides the references cited below, Thayer 342 n2 cites Menocchius *De Præsumptionibus...* as having 1167 folio pages of small print; Andrewes argues that the use of presumptions is of divine law (75, citing Genesis 3, 8 and 4, 6 & 10; 81, citing Deuteronomy 22, 17.

common law thinking about proof, since common-law thought is marked with the same characteristics; and in the later part of the period, the 1690s and 1700s, there are possible signs of the beginning of the emergence of the modern concepts.

1. The burden and standard of proof

1. Burden

The civilians allocated the burden of proof by the doctrine that *ei incumbit probatio qui dicit, non qui negat* and the consequential result that while in general the burden of proof was on the plaintiff, in *exceptiones* (pleaded defences) the burden of proof was on the defendant[7]. This involved some complications in relation to negative allegations: there are diverse statements in 'Alciatus', Cotta, *Principia Quaedam*, the *Reformatio*, Gentili and Wood[8]. Gilbert reproduces the general doctrine[9]; he tries to explain the problem with averments negative in form by reference to presumptions, giving as an instance the plea *ne unques accouple in loyal matrimony*[10]. Earlier common law discussions of the burden of proof tend to be put in terms of who ought to begin to give evidence to the jury, which suggests that the concept of "burden of proof" does not fit very well with jury trial. If, however, these discussions are taken as discussions of the burden of proof, they are on the whole consistent with the doctrine that the party who is "in the affirmative" has the burden[11].

---

7 D.22.3.2; 'Alciatus' 203r, 204v-205r; *Reformatio* 226 c 6, 227 c 10, 229 c 8; Domat 3.6.1.4,5; Ayliffe 255.

8 'Alciatus' 205r No 11, D has the burden in a "negativa, habens in se implicitam affirmationem"; Cotta 8, negative exception not to be proved, 599, "negativa ... improbabilis est"; *Principia Quaedam* 30, "in negativa iuris, ei qui negat incumbit probatio; the *Reformatio* under the heading "aliquando negativa probanda est" (230 c 25) refers to allegations of disqualification by a special law; Gentili ii 146 says generally that "Regula numquam fallens, ut negativam probet, qui in ea se fundat" (citing D 42.1.4); Wood 309-310, no proof of a negative, unless attended with circumstances of time and place.

9 104-5.

10 P 105. A negative is said not to be triable in *Mullineux' Case* (M24 Eliz) Moo KB 178; in *Yelding v Fay* (T1594) Moo KB 355 it is said that for this reason you cannot plead not guilty when the essence of the tort is nonfeasance; and a negative is said not to be provable in *Dent v Reeve* (M1623) Benl 139, and Coke, 2 Inst. 662. Cf above Ch 8 nn 11-13 and text there.

11 *Dean &c of Exeter v Trewennard* (H1562/3) 1 Dy 80a, defendant beginning in *plene administravit* said by reporter to be unusual because in the negative; *Spyrtie v Rede* (H1565/6) 2 Dy 247b, *Heydon v Ibgrave* (T1586) Gould 23, (*Haydon*) 2 Dy 24b n, (*Heidon*, H1586/7) 3 Leo 162, ((*Heywood*) 1 And 148 not SP; *Heydon v Ibgrave* (H1555/6) 2 Dy 129 b *semble* not SC), *Andrews v Lord Cromwell* (T1605) Moo KB 762, tenant to begin in writ of right because in the affirmative; *Anon* (T1627) Lit 36, stated generally. "Where proof should come

In equity it seems to be axiomatic that a party has the burden of proving his assertions of fact; so much so, in fact, that the point is rarely referred to and then usually in the context of circumstances in which the burden of proof is on the defendant[12].

The burden of proof is fairly clearly a unilateral obligation, to present objectively sufficient proofs. The two witness rule is evidence for this, as it fits only with a unilateral obligation. Also, as was seen in Chapter 8, the problem of contradictory proofs on the same point (conflict of testimony)[13] is in general not discussed in terms of resort to the burden of proof. In spite of this underlying unilateral character, issues relating to conflict of proofs could be generalised in a 'bilateral' way. Thus the *Reformatio* says:

> ... si a diversis partibus contraria fortassis allegantur, et proponentibus hujusmodi probationes adhibitae fuerint, fortori probationi adherendum erit. ...[14]

A similar approach appears in *Fowler v Ayliffe* (H1707/8), where Lord Cowper said that "I must go upon the better evidence" as a reason to prefer a receipt, to show that nothing was due on a bond, to letters showing that the receipt was false[15].

2. Objective and special standards of proof

The standard of proof in equity was *prima facie*, as in civilian doctrine, the objective standard in terms of the relationship between confessions, writings, witnesses and the two-witness rule, and the various types of presumptions[16]. We have already seen the rules for confessions, writings and witnesses, and presemputions similarly call for separate discussion.

The civilians recognised special standards in a range of cases, mostly by way of exceptions allowing lesser proofs to be used[17]. In serious criminal causes, on the

---

from" is referred to in discussions of the pleading rules in connection with exemptions and provisos in criminal cases (cf Zuckerman 92 LQR 402).

12 *Colwell v Child* (P1667) 1 Ch R 195, 2 Ch Cas 86, 2 Freem 154, Harg 174 f 22, Grimstone MR; Nott. Prac. 6.7, *TT* 116, *Kyman v Rigby* (M1672) Nott Proleg 23.8, *TT* 298; *Jevon v Bush* (M1685) 1 Vern 342, Jeffreys C; *Shales v Shales* (M1701) 2 Freem 252, 1 Eq Ca Ab 382.9, Harv 1105 226, Wright LK; *Hilliard v Stapleton* (M1701) 1 Eq Ca Ab 86.3, Wright LK.

13 § 3. On conflict between witnesses and documents cf above Ch 4.

14 226-7 c 7.

15 2 Eq Ca Ab 185.4

16 For general scales of proof see 'Alciatus' 203v; Conset 108 (Lyndwood 108 v. *probationes legitimas,* cited by Conset there, gives merely a list of proofs); Ayliffe 444; and on the medieval law, Lévy, *Hierarchie.*

17 For examples see above Ch 6 § 5 *(1)*(b)(iv) (necessity), Ch 8 nn 39, 54 and text there (summary proceedings and contempts in particular; Clerke 89 (standing to call for an

other hand they required proofs *luce clariores* (clearer than daylight), an expression which obviously has to some extent a subjective character[18].

The expression *luce clariores* was certainly used in Star Chamber[19], and it is possible that there is some connection with the idea at common law that a high standard of proof is required for a felony conviction; Shapiro has made a strong case for doctrinal borrowing in other areas of standards of proof in criminal matters, though not in this one[20].

In civil equity *luce clariores* was not relevant. However, there are a number of cases in which a "full proof", "strong proof" or other similar formulae were used to state some requirement going beyond the general requirements. The clearest instance is in relation to fraud, which I will discuss separately, but similar expressions were also used in relation to trustees' liability for negligence[21], exceptions to the parol evidence rule[22] and to the documentary originals rule[23], and proof of the basic facts for or rebuttal of the presumption of resulting trust[24]. These references may represent germs of the modern vaguely expressed "subjective" standard of proof. However, it is equally possible that what is going on in these cases is the exclusion of presumptive/ circumstantial evidence and a requirement of "direct" proof by confession, instruments or witnesses.

---

account), 96 (proof of debt); Gentili 145-6 (secret matters), 148 (notice), 221 (fraud & duress); Ayliffe 446 (cases hard to prove).

18 *Reformatio* 228 c 13; Vulteius 370r; Wood 310. Cf generally Langbein, *Torture* Ch 1 and sources cited there; Brundage, *Medieval Canon Law* (Longman, 1995) 142-3. Cotta 672 says that a party seeking a penalty "debet clare et plene probare", so that the suppletory oath is not available; Zouch *SQ* cl 9 No 32 makes it a disputable question "An de praesumptionibus quis de crimine sit condemnandus".

19 *Parsons v Herne* (H1593/4) Hawarde 5, *per* Lord Buckhurst (cited above Ch 2 n 36); *Talbot v Wood* (1595) Hawarde 13 at 15-16, quoted above Ch 8 n 47 and text there.

20 *Beyond Reasonable Doubt and Probable Cause* (Berkeley, 1991).

21 *Palmer v Jones* (H1682/3) 1 Vern 144, Lord Guilford (reversing Lord Nottingham (P1678) Nott CC No 824), to charge a trustee with more than he had received "then the proof must be very strong".

22 E.g. *Vesey v Vesey* (1638) Harg 174 f 6, Coventry LK; cf at law – *v Tempest* (1638) Clayt 61, NP, Berkeley J, "shall be well proved" to avoid a bond.

23 At law, *Knight v Dauler* (P1664) Hardr 323, *Dancer* 1 Keb 7 (1 Keb 220, 282, 311 not SP), secondary evidence must be strong and cogent to prove a record, burnt; in equity cf the special precautions taken in relation to burnt depositions in *Kynaston v Countess of Derby and Earl of Bridgwater,* (H1626/7) i Sanders 155 (cited and other reports listed above Ch 3 n 175).

24 *Gascoigne v Twing* (H1685/6) 1 Vern 366, 1 Eq Ca Ab 232.7, *Petit v Smith* (P1696) 1 P Wms 7 ((M1695) 1 P Wms 7, 5 Mod 247, Comb 378, 1 Ld Raym 86, Com 3, prohibition to ecclesiastical court on same point), *Kirk v Webb* (M1698) Pre Ch 84, 2 Freem 229, 2 Eq Ca Ab 743, Harv 1105 205, at Pre Ch 88 *per* Trevor MR, *Halcott v Markant* (T1701) Pre Ch 168, 2 Eq Ca Ab 744.3, Trevor MR, *Lady Granvill v Lady Beaufort* (1709) 2 Vern 648, 1 P Wms 118, Cowper C, "plain" proof (rvsd HL (1710) 3 Bro PC 37), *Buckley v Littlebury* (1711) 1 Eq Ca Ab 244.9, "full" proof (3 Bro PC 43 not SP).

II. Presumptions

For present purposes it is unnecessary to discuss the detailed history of all the specific presumptions used in equity. Three topics are relevant to my present concerns: (a) the importance of presumptions in the system of proof; (b) the classification of presumptions; and (c) how presumptions worked. In addition (d) one specific case, the practice of presuming fraud, is of general importance in indicating the beginning of a decline of the strategic role of presumptions.

1. The importance of presumptions

The strategic role of presumptions in the system of proof in our period can be indicated in two ways. The first is the range of topics in relation to which presumptions are referred to in the authority. In equity, these include length of time, as leading to presumptions of regularity of transactions[25], payment of debts[26], and possession under a good title or lost agreement or grant[27]; the presumptions of resulting

---

25 *Byden v Loveden* (1613) Toth 54, *Blackham v Sutton Coldfield* (T1675) Nott CC No 29 (No 330, 1 Ch Cas 270, not SP), *Fowke v Green* (T1675) Nott CC No 232 (1 Ch Cas 262 not SP), *Price v Evans* (M1675) Nott CC No 308, (P1676) Nott CC No 482, 2 Ch Cas 215, *Ramon v Stacy* (M1675) Nott CC No 320, *Gartside v Ratcliff* (M1676) Nott CC No 589 (Nott CC No 529, 2 Ch Cas 292, 1 Eq Ca Ab 169.2, not SP), *Lyford v Coward* (M1683) 1 Vern 196, 2 Ch Cas 150, *Knight v Adamson* (M1689) 2 Freem 106, 2 Eq Ca Ab 226. Cf Cotta 31-2.

26 *Charnocke v Sherington* (?1596) (among cases of this year) Harl 1576 f 150, *Moyle v Lord Roberts* (1629) Nels 9, *Sibson v Fletcher* (1632) 1 Ch Rep 59, *Carpenter v Tucker* (1634) 1 Ch Rep 78, *Coles v Emerson* (1634) 1 Ch Rep 78, *Geofrey v Thorn* (1634) 1 Ch Rep 88, *Bidlake v Lord Arundel* (1635) 1 Ch Rep 93, *Baldwin v Procter & Colby* (1636) 1 Ch Rep 102, *Hales v Hales* (1636) 1 Ch Rep 105, *Dennis v Nourse* (1636) 1 Ch Rep 106, *Popham v Earl of Desmond* (1639) 1 Ch Rep 105, *Bales v Procter & Colby* (1639) 1 Ch Rep 144, *Hunton v Desmond* (1670) 2 Ch R 44, *Powell v Godscale* (H1673/4) Rep t Finch 77 (*Godsall v Powell* (M1675) Nott CC No 318 not SP), *Corey v Corey* (M1677) Rep t Finch 331, *Heupert v Benn* (P1678) Rep t Finch 344, *Parker v Ash* (M1684) 1 Vern 256, *Fotherby v Hartridge* (P1687) 2 Vern 21, *Sherman v Sherman* (M1692) 2 Vern 376, 1 Eq Ca Ab 12.12, 375.2, *Mackdowell v Halfpenny* (H1704/5) 2 Vern 484, *Crosby v Middleton* (H1709/10) 3 Ch Rep 99, Pre Ch 309, 2 Eq Ca Ab 188; rebutted, *Lady Hatton v Jay* (1637) 1 Ch Rep 117, *Winchcomb v Winchcomb* (1674) 2 Ch Rep 101, *Bright v Frampton* (M1675) Nott CC No 341 (No 303 not SP); cf Domat 3.6.4.11 citing D.22.3.26; and for other civilian presumptions of payment, 'Alciatus' 226v following D 22.3.4, Fulbecke *Parallelle* ii 28v, 31v-32.

27 *Blackwell v Simpson* (1582-3) Ch C Ch 163, Stowe 415 f 140b, *Sedgwick v Ap Evan* (1582-3) Ch C Ch 167, Stowe 415 f 142, *Grimes v Smith* (1596-7) Toth 172, *Clench v Tomley* (1603) Cary 23, as *Townley v Clench* Harg 281 f 42, *Winchcomb v Hall* (1630) 1 Ch Rep 40, *Neale v Lister* (1633) Toth 172, *Churchill v Brewer* (H1634/5) Toth 172, *Caesar v Gater* (1636) Toth 172, *Warman v Seaman* (T1675) Nott CC No 290 at 73 SS 198-9 (T1672) Nott Proleg 10.22, TT 230, (M1675) Nott CC Nos 313, 370, Pollex 112, Rep t Finch 279, 2 Ch Cas 209, not SP), *Peacock v Neale* (M1675) Nott CC No 327, Rep t Finch 266, *Wintle & al' v Carpenter & Pisburgh* (M1680) Rep t Finch 462, *Pencose v Trelawney* (T1683) cit 1 Vern 196, *Lyford v Coward* above n 19, *Knight v Adamson* above n 19, *Finch v Resbridger*

trust[28], advancement[29], and satisfaction[30]; the rule that *omnia praesumuntur contra spoliatorem*[31]; and inequality of consideration, as leading, with other circum-

---

(M1700) 2 Vern 390 as *Lord Guernsey v Rodbridges* (1708) Gilb R 3, 2 Eq Ca Ab 518, *Steward v Bridger* (M1705) 2 Vern 516, *Newburgh v Newburgh* (1712) 3 Bro PC 553. It is possible that some of the earlier cases involve *laches* rather than presumed title; but cf Ballow I.4.27, where *laches* and presumption are treated as one doctrine. Cf Lyndwood 196 v. *cum possessione*; *Reformatio* 231 tit. *De Possessione*.

28 Generally, Ballow II.5. *Purchase in the name of another, voluntary conveyance: Binion v Stone* (P1663) Nels 63, 2 Freem 169, *Cook v Fountain* (1675-6) Nott CC Nos 273, 500, 3 Swan 585, *per* Lord Nottingham only where necessary ((1674) 1 Mod 107, (1686) 1 Vent 413, not SP), *Drury v Drury* (T1675) Nott CC No 292, *Lord Grey v Lady Grey & al'* (T1676) Nott CC No 526, 2 Freem 6, (H1676/7) Nott CC No 643, 1 Ch Cas 296, Rep t Finch 338, *Riddle v Emerson* (M1682) 1 Vern 108, 1 Eq Ca Ab 381.3, *Kingdon v Bridges* (T1688) 2 Vern 68, 1 Eq Ca Ab 70.12, 242.6, *Earl of Plymouth v Hickman* (T1690) 2 Vern 167, *Rundle v Rundle* (H1691/2) 2 Vern 252, (P1692) 2 Vern 264, 2 Freem 123, 1 Eq Ca Ab 119.9, *Wilkinson v Brayfield* (M1693) 2 Vern 367, 1 Eq Ca Ab 258.1, *Kirk v Webb* (1698-9) above n 18, *Newton v Preston & al'* (M1699) Pre Ch 103, *Halcott v Markant* (T1701) above n 18, *Shales v Shales* (1701) above n 12, *Kinder v Miller, Kender v Milward* (1701-2), *Skett v Whitmore* (P1705), both above p 183 n 187. *Surplus of estate: Foster v Munt* (M1687) 1 Vern 473, *Cordell v Noden* (T1690) 2 Vern 148, Pre Ch 12, 1 Eq Ca Ab 144.5, *Cunningham v Mellish* (M1691) 2 Vern 247, Pre Ch 31, 1 Eq Ca Ab 273, *Lady Bellasis v Crompton* (T1693) 2 Vern 294, 1 Eq Ca Ab 381.5, *Petit v Smith* (P1696) 1 P Wms 7 ((M1695) 1 P Wms 7, 5 Mod 247, Comb 378, 1 Ld Raym 86, Com 3, KB, prohibition to ecclesiastical court), *Anon* (?H1695/6) Harv 1105 190, *Countess of Bristol v Hungerford* (T1697) 2 Vern 645, Pre Ch 81, 3 P Wms 194n, *Bayley v Powell & Mead* (M1698) 2 Vern 361, 2 Freem 225, Pre Ch 92, 1 Eq Ca Ab 224.1, 1 Bro CC 333, Harv 1105 202, *Dormer v Bertie* (1699) Pre Ch 94, 2 Eq Ca Ab 430, 434, Colles 128, *Pawlett v Lady Morley* (M1702) 2 Freem 263, 2 Eq Ca Ab 436, Harv 1105 237, *Griffith v Rogers* (T1704) Pre Ch 231, 1 Eq Ca Ab 245, *Cooke v Walter* (?M1704) 2 Freem 276, 1 Eq Ca Ab 44, Harv 1105 250, *City of London v Garway* (H1706/7) 2 Vern 571, 1 Eq Ca Ab 272.5, *Smith v Goodman* (P1707) 2 Vern 586, *Wingfield v Atkinson & Myres* (M1711) 2 Vern 673, *Ball v Smith* (H1711/12) 2 Vern 675, 1 Eq Ca Ab 245, *Colesworth v Brangwin* (H1711/12) Pre Ch 323, Gilb R 72, 2 Eq Ca Ab 438, *Wych v Packington* (1712) 3 Bro PC 44.

29 *Mouse v Mouse* (P1649) Harl 1576 f 235, *Scroope v Scroope* (M1663) 1 Ch Cas 27, 2 Freem 171, Harv 1105 152, *Strode v Strode* (M1672) Nott Proleg 13.13, (P1675) Nott CC No 211, *Cecill v Marky* (T1675) Nott CC No 280, *Drury v Drury* above n 22, *Lord Grey v Lady Grey* above n 22, *Elliot v Elliot* (T1677) Nott CC No 690, 2 Ch Cas 231, (M1677) Nott CC No 754, *Ebrall v Dancer* (P1680) Nott CC No 1016, 2 Ch Cas 26, *Baylis v Newton* (T1687) 2 Vern 28, *Mumma v Mumma* (P1687) 2 Vern 19, 1 Eq Ca Ab 328.8, *Jennings v Selleck* (T1687) 1 Vern 467, 1 Eq Ca Ab 381.7, *Kingdon v Bridges* (T1688) 2 Vern 68, 1 Eq Ca Ab 70.12, 242.6, *Back v Andrews* (H1689/90) 2 Vern 120, Pre Ch 1, 2 Eq Ca Ab 230.1, *Shales v Shales* (1701) above n 12, *Bateman v Bateman* (P1702) 2 Vern 436, 1 Eq Ca Ab 218.3, 382.10, *Lamplugh v Lamplugh* (M1709) 1 P Wms 111, 2 Eq Ca Ab 415.3. Possibly antecedent, though not the same rule, is *Observations* f 457v No 170, on a conveyance in consideration of blood the presumption of natural affection supports other half proofs (above Ch 8 n 74 and text there).

30 Generally Ballow IV. 1.1. 5; *Maynard v Moseley* (P1674) Nott CC No 78 at 73 SS 40, *Christ's Hospital v Gold* (H1675/6) Nott CC No 437, *Haggett v Freake* (T1676) Nott CC No 512, *Pickering v Rudings* (H1676/7) Nott CC No 628, *Pitt v Pidgeon* (M1677) Nott CC No 756, *Bloys v Bloys* (M1679) Nott CC No 979, *Duffield v Smith* (M1692) 2 Freem 185, Harv 1105 165, *Goodfellow v Burchett* (T1693) 2 Vern 298, 1 Eq Ca Ab 204.7, 239.26, *Bromley v*

stances, to a presumption of fraud[32]. Presumptions were thus potentially relevant and important in most if not all areas of equity litigation, affecting title to land, trusts and succession, and contractual liabilities[33].

At common law "substantive" presumptions tended to be statutory: the presumption of fraud in relation to voluntary conveyances under 13 Eliz c 5 and 27 Eliz c 4[34], the presumptions in relation to stabbing and infanticide introduced by legislation in the reign of James I[35], and the presumption of death under the *Cestui Que Vie* Act 1667[36]. In addition, however, Coke gives prominence to presumptions as evidence of guilt in criminal trials[37].

Secondly, "presumptions" in the loose sense of the use of the expression to describe factual generalisations, persistently appear in the period as explanations and justifications for rules of evidence/ proof. I have already shown this tendency at work in relation to the rules governing the use of documents (above Ch 3) and witness evidence (Chs 5, 6), and it is as common in common law arguments as those in equity. An analogous case is that Jenkins in several places uses presumption tags as explanations of procedural or substantive rules[38]. In other words, in spite of the

Jefferies, Fettiplace & al' (1700-1701) 2 Vern 415, 2 Freem 245, Pre Ch 138, 1 Eq Ca Ab 18, *Hassel v Knatchbull* (1703) Colles 305.

31 *R v Arundel & Howard* (T1616) Moo KB 832, Hob 109, *Earl of Holland v Garrett* (P1673) Nott Proleg 19.14, (M1674) Nott CC No 147, *Smith v Ireland* (H1673/4) Nott CC No 69 (*Ireland v Thurston & Smith* (T1675) Rep t Finch 213 not SP), *Brown v Savage & Sayer* (1674) Nott CC Nos 53, 256, Rep t Finch 184, 1 Eq Ca Ab 93.J3, *Beak v Beak* (H1674/5) Rep t Finch 190, *Holloway v Collins* (H1674/5) 1 Ch Cas 245, 1 Eq Ca Ab 300 (*Collins v Holloway* Nott CC No 184 not SP), *Gartside v Ratcliff* (1676-7) Nott CC Nos 529, 589, 1 Ch Cas 292, 1 Eq Ca Ab 169.2, *Lewis v Lewis* (H1677/8) Rep t Finch 47 (Nott CC Nos 607, 907 not SP, *Childrens v Saxby* (M1683) 1 Vern 207, 1 Eq Ca Ab 15.2, 229.11, *East India Co v Evans* (H1684/5) 1 Vern 305, *Wardour v Berisford* (P1687) 1 Vern 452, 1 Eq Ca Ab 11.2, *Hunt v Matthews* (M1686) 1 Vern 408, *Countess of Plymouth v Bladen* (H1687/8) 2 Vern 32, *Eyton v Eyton* (1700) Pre Ch 116, (1706) 4 Bro PC 149, *Haines v Haines* (M1702) 2 Vern 441, 1 Eq Ca Ab 402.3, *Sanson v Rumsey* (T1706) 2 Vern 561, 1 Eq Ca Ab 169.2, *Winne v Lloyd* (1707) 2 Vern 603, (1709) 2 Bro PC 374, *Hampden v Hampden* (1709) cit 1 P Wms 753, 13 Viner 540.1, 3 Bro PC 550.

32 Below § 2 (4).

33 It is perhaps for this reason that Harl 1576, a collection of Chancery materials, includes at f 236v a collection of un-sourced Latin extracts on the theory of presumptions.

34 Below n 60 and text there.

35 1 Jac I c 8 (stabbing) 21 Jac I c 27 (infanticide).

36 19 Car II c 6. Cf *Thorne v Rolff* (T1560) 2 Dy 185a, death presumed from 7 years absence overseas.

37 Co Lit 6b. Hale HPC II 289-90 recognises the use of presumptions but urges caution; Hawkins II 438 follows Coke. Cf Shapiro, *Beyond Reasonable Doubt* 208-216, and contrast Langbein TLP 4 & 145 n4.

38 E.g.: *stabitur præsumptioni donec probatur in contraria,* 10.18, 27.51, 31.62 at 32; *ex diuturnitate temporis omnia præsumuntur rite et solemniter esse acta,* 26.49, 47.91 at 48, 184.77 at 185, 273.93; *in odium spoliatoris,* 207.39, 320.23; *vicini vicinorum facta præsumuntur scire,* 33.65, 326.44, 327.49; *præsumptio violenta valet in lege,* 56.3.

relatively thin treatment of "substantive" presumptions by Coke and Gilbert following Coke[39], the concept of presumptions, in the sense of inductive generalisations issuing in factual conclusions and/ or legal rules, pervades seventeenth-century english thought about proof[40].

2. The classification of presumptions

In the learned laws presumptions were classified in two ways. In the first place, presumptions might be presumptions of law, which might be irrebuttable (*juris et de jure*) or rebuttable (*juris tantum*) or presumptions of fact (*hominis sive judicis*)[41]. Secondly, and far more commonly in our sources, presumptions were classified by weight into four categories: a presumption could be *necessaria (juris et de jure)* ("necessary"), which was conclusive, unless defeated by a confession; *violenta*, or *indubitata*, ("violent") which was a full proof, but rebuttable; *probabilis, universalis,* or *iudicis* ("probable"); or *levis* or *temeraria* ("light" or "rash") which was valueless[42]. Some discussions later in the period simplify the classification: Conset distinguishes between "a just presumption", which is full proof, and "a mean, or reasonable, or indifferent presumption" which is less than full proof, and Domat simply distinguishes presumption from mere conjecture[43].

Of the first classification there is no trace in the English sources of this period. As far as equity is concerned, it might be said that there was no institutional basis for the distinction. The basis in the learned laws was that presumptions of law had

39 Co Lit 6b, Gilbert *Evidence* 112-3.

40 A civilian example of this type of reasoning is Clerke 215: though subornation must be *alleged* in excepting against a witness for false testimony, only false testimony needs to be *proved*, since "probata falsitate corruptio praesumitur".

41 Wood 312-3, van Espen 3.7.5.18, but not in this form in the other sources I have used. The later eighteenth and nineteenth century English use of the distinction between presumptions of law and of fact is probably derived from Pothier *via* Evans: Shapiro, *Beyond Reasonable Doubt* 222-3. Vulteius 368r-370r dichotomises presumptions into *ex causa* (cause and effect) and *ex adjuncto* (inductive); the first class includes presumptions *iuris et de iure* and the decisory oath, and constitute full proof, while the second class includes presumptions *iuris* and *hominis* and do not on their own constitute full proof.

42 Lyndwood 108 v. *praesumi;* 'Alciatus' 206v-207r; *Reformatio* 266 c 2 (*temeraria & probabilis*), c 3 (*violenta*), 269 c 18 (*juris et de jure,* with the rule that it can be defeated by a confession which is also in Cotta 156 and van Espen 3.7.5.23-4). Cosin ii 61-4 applies the *levis/ probabilis/ violenta* classification to *indicia*, which he translates as "evidence", and has the presumption *juris et de jure* as a separate item; Ayliffe 276-7 applies the fourfold rash/ probable/ violent/ necessary classification to supicions, which he says some writers identify with presumptions (the title *presumptions* to which he cross-refers is not in fact in the book). Cotta 406 defines an *indicium* as "conjectura ex probabilis & non necessariis orta".

43 Conset 108; Domat 3.6.4.4. Zouch *EI* 88-9 admits only *violenta* and *necessaria,* possibly because he generally draws exclusively on the *Corpus Iuris;* Wiseman 16-17 refers to "strong and forcible" presumptions.

to have some basis either in the *Corpus Iuris* or in legislation[44]. When this classification came into the common law, it could be given an institutional basis in the separation of functions of judge and jury[45]. In the equity courts, however, neither of these institutional bases for distinguishing law and facts existed.

However, the second classification in terms of weight is quite well attested in contemporary sources[46]. This is important in showing both links to the doctrine of presumptions in the learned laws, and also that equity and common law shared with the learned laws the concept of presumptions as an *item of proof;* if presumptions had merely reversed the burden of proof, it would be unnecessary to refer to the classification by weight.

3. How presumptions worked

The preceding section provides a reason for supposing that presumptions were primarily treated as items of proof, rather than as legal rules reversing the burden of proof. An additional reason is that in the later seventeenth century equity authorities there does not appear to be a clear distinction between presumptions, circumstantial evidence, and rules of construction. This is not the inherently anachronistic/ teleological point made by Thayer and Wigmore that some matters which we would now regard as rules of law or items of circumstantial evidence are treated in the period as presumptions[47]. Rather, the point is that one and the same rule may be described in one case as an instance of "circumstances", in another as a "presumption", in a third as a rule of construction[48]. This ambiguity is consistent with

---

44 van Espen 3.7.5.25.

45 Though this was by no means satisfactory. Thayer 339 cites Best, *Evidence* for the proposition that "we find the same presumption spoken of by judges sometimes as a presumption of law, sometimes as a presumption of fact, sometimes as a presumption which juries should be advised to make, and sometimes as one which it was obligatory on them to make".

46 "Vehement suspicion or presumption" *Doctor & Student* 91 SS 285, "Conjectures or presumptions" *Thorne v Rolff* (T1560) 2 Dy 185a; "vehement presumption" *Dolman v Vavasor* (P1584) Moo KB 191, CP; "There is 3 kindes of presumption, *praesumptio 1. temeraria, 2. probabilis 3. violenta*" Egerton C in *Calvin's Case* (1608) as reported in Hawarde 349 at 365; "violent, probable, and light or temerary" presumptions, Co Lit 6b; "direct and manifest proof, or violent and necessary presumption", Lord Nottingham in *Cook v Fountain* (P1676) Nott CC No 500, 3 Swan 585 (other reports not SP); "some presumptions are so manifest and violent that it is impossible to resiste the evidence and conviction of them", Lord Nottingham in *Okeover v Pettus* (M1675) Nott CC No 370, 73 SS 236; "there are presumptions of several sorts, some are violent and some probable ... a probable presumption alone is no proof to rely upon; where indeed there is some proof of witnesses positive, and the presumption is probable that is added thereto, it may be a good fortifying evidence...", Holt CJ in *Montague v Bath* (1692) 3 Ch Cas 55 at 105; and cf the sources cited by Shapiro *Beyond Reasonable Doubt* loc. cit. above n 37.

47 Thayer Ch 8; Wigmore §§ 25, 38, 2491; a clear example of a presumption which later became a matter of circumstantial evidence is spoliation.

the concept of presumptions as items of proof, but does not fit the concept of rules of law affecting the burden of proof.

Another pointer in the same direction is that presumptions are combined with the evidence of a single witness to make a proof satisfying the two-witness rule[49], and may be supported as well as rebutted by evidence[50]. This *combination* of presumptions with proofs again indicates a view of presumptions as an item of proof[51].

In the 1700s there are instances of presumptions being said to cast the proof on the other side[52]. These may be regarded as germs of the modern conception, as in connection with the burden of proof *Fowler v Ayliffe*[53], and the instances of special standards of proof, may similarly be germs of modern conceptions. However, it is necessary to be fairly cautious about these indicators. This is necessary because at the same period the concept of "proof" in general still seems to remain *prima facie* the objective standard in terms of confession, writings or two witnesses, subject to the relevant special rules. If presumptions had really reversed the burden of proof one would expect that a full proof (therefore subject to the usual rules) would be needed to rebut them. In fact, it seems that presumptions could be rebutted or supported by proofs less than a full proof, in particular by parol proofs *prima facie* excluded by the parol evidence rule or the Statute of Frauds[54]. Presumptions are not, therefore, separable from the rules for the weight of proofs.

---

48 For example, the presumption of satisfaction/ rule against double provision is referred to by Lord Nottingham in *Maynard v Moseley* at 73 SS 340 in terms of presumption ("extravagant bounty shall not be presumed"), in *Bloys v Bloys* at 79 SS 771 in terms of construction ("shall never be construed"); in the context of resulting trust, Lord Nottingham refers in *Okeover v Pettus* both to "presumptions ... violent" (73 SS 236) and to "circumstances ... very pregnant" (ib. 237); purchase in the name of a child is said to be presumed an advancement in *Grey v Grey* 73 SS at 394, and said to be "a strong evidence" in *Woodman v Morren* 79 SS at 692.

49 Above Ch 8 nn 72-6 and text there.

50 E.g. *Baylis v Newton* (T1687) 2 Vern 28, *Cordell v Noden* (T1690) 2 Vern 148, Pre Ch 12, 1 Eq Ca Ab 144.5, *Cunningham v Mellish* (M1691) 2 Vern 247, Pre Ch 31, 1 Eq Ca Ab 273, *Wilkinson v Brayfield* (M1693) 2 Vern 367, 1 Eq Ca Ab 258.1, *Hassell v Knatchbull* (1703) Colles 305, *Chapman v Salt* (H1709/10) 2 Vern 646.

51 On the addition of 'imperfect' proofs to make full proof cf. Cotta 406, 707; Vulteius 373r; Wood 309.

52 *Shales v Shales* (1701), *Jones v Selby* (1710).

53 Above n 17 and text there.

54 *Rundle v Rundle* (H1691/2) 2 Vern 252, (P1692) 2 Vern 264, 2 Freem 123, to rebut presumption of resulting trust; *Bromley v Jefferies & Fettiplace* (M1700) 2 Freem 245, 2 Vern 415, Pre Ch 138, 1 Eq Ca Ab 18, excluded to rebut presumption of satisfaction; *Cuthbert v Peacock* (M1707) 2 Vern 293, 1 Eq Ca Ab 204.8, 232.6, adm to rebut satisfaction; *Lamplugh v Lamplugh* (M1709) 1 P Wms 111, 2 Eq Ca Ab 415.3, adm to rebut resulting trust on purchase. There is a good deal of authority on rebuttal of the trust of surplus estate after debts and legacies paid: *North v Crompton* (H1670/1) 1 Ch Cas 196, adm; *Cunningham v Mellish* (M1691) 2 Vern 247, Pre Ch 31, *semble* adm; *Gainsborough v Gainsborough* (H1691/2) 2

4. Presumptions of fraud

Dolum ex indiciis perspicuis probari convenit: fraud should be proved by clear *indicia*. This gnomic statement in the *Code* of Justinian[55] could be taken in two ways. If stress is placed on *perspicuis,* it could be concluded that clear evidence is required, i.e. fraud should be proved to the criminal standard and not presumed. On the other hand, if stress is placed on *indiciis,* the conclusion is that fraud is established by circumstantial evidence and hence could be presumed. Civilian authors provide support for both views. Gentili has it both ways: "dolus qui non praesumitur, conjecturis probatur (de quo late aliique) & indiciis"[56]. Domat cites the text from the Code for the proposition that fraud is not presumed[57]. Lyndwood, on the other hand, is explicit that fraud is presumed[58] and provides a catalogue of situations in which conveyances are presumed to be fraudulent as against creditors and other third parties[59].

At least before the 1690s, fraud does seem to have been presumed in several circumstances in equity. There were, of course, *statutory* presumptions of fraud in the case of voluntary conveyances under the statutes 13 Eliz c 5 and 27 Eliz c 4[60]. There also seems to have been a specific doctrine under which the Exchequer would presume fraud on the revenue[61].

However, there also seems to have been a wider doctrine in which fraud was inferred from circumstances or "badges of fraud", and this is sometimes described as "presuming" fraud[62]. Among the matters which in this period were expressed in this way are species of conduct which we would now regard as estoppel by ac-

---

Vern 252, 1 Eq Ca Ab 230.1, (M1692) 2 Freem 188, Harv 1105 168, adm; *Bellasis v Crompton* (T1693) 2 Vern 294, 1 Eq Ca Ab 381.5, adm; *Petit v Smith per cur* adm; *Bayley v Powell & Mead* (M1698) 2 Vern 361, 2 Freem 225, Harv 1105 202, Pre Ch 92, 1 Eq Ca Ab 224.1 adm; *Smith v Goodman* (P1707) 2 Vern 586, *semble* adm; *Docksey v Docksey* (1708) 2 Eq Ca Ab 429, (1710) 3 Bro PC 39, adm; *Granville v Beaufort* (1709) 2 Vern 648, 1 P Wms 118, (1710) 3 Bro PC 37, adm; *Wingfield v Atkinson* (M1711) 2 Vern 673, adm; *Buckley v Littlebury* (1711) 3 Bro PC 43, 1 Eq Ca Ab 244.9, adm in HL rvsg Recorder of London; *Gale v Crofts* (1713) Dick 23, 2 Eq Ca Ab 415, 494, exc. Ballow VI.2.5 says that later cases restricted the availability of parol evidence in this context.

55 C.2.20.6; quoted, in variant forms, by Lyndwood 20 v. *sine dolo; Principia Quaedam* 10; Domat 1.18.3.3.

56 ii 221. Cf also Cotta 307, forgery is not to be presumed; 349, fraud (on creditors) is presumed from a single large alienation of property.

57 1.18.3.3.

58 20, v. *sine dolo;* 161, v. *fraude.*

59 162, v. *Rex;* 165, v. *eo ipso.*

60 Holdsworth's view, IV 481-2, that these statutes were held in *Twyne's Case* (M1601) 3 Co 80b, Star Ch, and cases cited there, to create an *irrebuttable* presumption, seems to read back later authority; this issue in fact remained unsettled down to the nineteenth century.

61 *Waller v Topham* (M1661) Hardr 218, *AG v Horsham* (H1667/8) Hardr 477, both Ex(E).

62 For the Elizabethan period cf Jones, *Chancery* ch 12 & esp. p 483.

quiescence or encouragement[63], or as contracts involving undue influence[64]; cases of part performance and secret trusts[65]; as well as species of fraud on creditors not caught by the Elizabethan statutes[66]. Though *express* references to a *presumption* of fraud are rare[67], fraud is undoubtedly inferred from circumstances and "badges" in most of these cases, which (as is apparent from the previous discussion of the working of presumptions) would not have been seen as different in principle.

There was common law authority for the view that fraud could not be presumed[68]; and in *Montague v Bath* (M1692)[69] a strong court of Somers C assisted by the Chief Justices and Powell J used the doctrine that fraud cannot be presumed as a part of the grounds of their decision[70]; the argument was subsequently repeated by counsel[71], and Nelson cites Domat on the point[72]. It is not clear how much the immediate effect on the practice of the courts was, but at some point be-

---

63 *Deguilder v Depester* (T1675) Nott CC No 219, Rep t Finch 206, called fraud at Nott CC No 345, 73 SS 234; *Wakeham v Carter* (P1680) Nott CC No 1023; *Baxter v Strode* (T1682) Nott CC No 1158; *Fowkes v Joyce* (H1689/90) 2 Vern 19, Pre Ch 7; *Raw & Potts v Potts* (M1691) 2 Vern 229, Pre Ch 35; *Henning* (Gilb *Huning*) *v Ferrers* (1712) (Gilb 1711) Gilb R 85 1 Eq Ca Ab 356.10.

64 *Mildmay v Duckett & Mildmay* (P1678) Nott CC No 822, *Ayscough v Ayscough* (P1681) Nott CC No 1098, *Englefield v Englefield* (P1681) Nott CC No 1138, (P1686) 1 Vern 443, (P1687) 1 Vern 446.

65 Above Ch 4 § 2 *(2)* (b).

66 *Wytham & Bland's Case* (M1673) Nott CC No 5 (No 172 not SP), conveyance *pendente lite; Elam v Davis* (M1673) Nott CC No 16, preference; *Norcliffe v Worsley* (M1674) Nott CC No 130, conveyance *pendente lite; Gaythorne v Headley* (H1677/8) Nott CC No 791, sale of term on fi. fa. to party at an undervalue; *Herne v Meeres* (T1687) 1 Vern 465; *Lewkner v Freeman* (H1699/1700) 2 Freem 236, Harv 1105 212, deed not to be presumed fraudulent "unless it appears [sc. by circumstances], or is so proved" (Pre Ch 105, 1 Eq Ca Ab 149.5 not SP); *Bateman v Bateman* (P1702) 2 Vern 436, 1 Eq Ca Ab 218.3, 382.10, declaration of trust to defraud purported trustee's creditors.

67 E.g. *Ring v Hele* (1681) 2 Ch Rep 221, inequality of value as leading to a presumption the settlor would not knowingly enter the bargain; *Earl of Arglas v Muschampe* (1683) 2 Ch Rep 266, 1 Vern 237 (1 Vern 75, 135, 1 Eq Ca Ab 133 not SP), a "catching bargain" case, *per* Lord Guilford at 2 Ch Rep 269-70 "the over-value ... is not of itself sufficient ground ... whereupon this Court can presume fraud: yet it is a great evidence of fraud, where there are other circumstances concurring"; *Jones v Selby* (T1710) Pre Ch 300, argued by counsel at 302-3 that not to presume fraud, Lord Cowper's response at 303 that "he sat there to condemn frauds, therefore might presume them, unless they prove the contrary".

68 *Case of Oxford University* (T1613) 10 Co 53b at 56; *Webb & Juck v Worfield* (M1616) J. Bridg 110 at 112; *Crisp v Pratt* (T1639) Cro Car 550, March NC 34, W Jon 437, to conclude that fraud must be expressly found by verdict. This rule was cited as an argument for a feigned issue to be directed in *White v Hussey & al'* (T1690) Pre Ch 13, 2 Eq Ca Ab 478.2, but rejected.

69 3 Ch Cas 55; other references above Ch 2 n 260.

70 Treby at 3 Ch Cas 75, Somers at 3 Ch Cas 114.

71 *Jones v Selby* above n 67, rejected.

72 In a note to *Brown v Savage & Sayer* Rep t Finch at 186 citing Strahan I p 256 (= 1.18.3, above).

tween then and now the specific results achieved by the "presumption" of fraud came to be explained in other ways or to be attributed to equity having a wider concept of fraud than the common law.

The presumption of fraud therefore shows us a sharp, and important, divergence between equity and law; and the signs are that at the end of the period the first steps are being taken towards equity beginning to follow the law on this issue, though it clearly remains controversial. But it can hardly be supposed that this doctrine was developed *ad hoc* in the course of trials at *nisi prius*. The entire controversy revolves within the conceptual universe of civilian thought about proof and presumptions.

Thayer recognised the theory of presumptions as a branch of the law of evidence which was affected by borrowing from romano-canonical theory[73]. However, he saw this borrowing as a late (nineteenth century) and highly superficial appropriation of an inappropriate general theory[74]. At least as far as equity is concerned, this view does not fit. The workings of presumptions in equity in this period display a more deep-going fit with the civilians' approach, and one which is deeply integrated in concepts of proof and of the burden and standard of proof which share this fit.

---

73 Thayer 341 f.

74 Ib 343-4.

Chapter Ten

Conclusions

I have now followed early modern equity proof doctrine, and its relationship to the common law and to civilian proof concepts, through the several instruments of proof and their interrelationships. It is now time to return to the general questions posed in Chapter 1: first, the relationships between equity proof and the origins of the law governing evidence to a jury; and second, the general relationships between equity, common law and civil law in the period.

I. Equity proof, trial by jury, and the origins of the law of evidence

If one thing should be clear from the last eight chapters, it is that the view argued by Wigmore and Holdsworth that evidence rules were developed first at common law and then (inappropriately) imported into equity cannot stand. The relationship between equity proof and common law evidence at the time of the origins of the law of evidence is a good deal more complex.

It is true that there is some direct evidence of equity following the law. First, in relation to certain estoppels, particularly the rule that a fine with proclamations is a bar in equity as well as at law, equity clearly followed the law[1]. Second, from the early eighteenth century there is some direct evidence in the shape of statements by Gilbert and Lord Hardwicke that equity follows the law in relation to the competence of witnesses, or, more exactly, that the rules are the same; and this has some tenuous support for the later seventeenth century[2].

Thirdly, there are from an early date instances of equity judges bringing in the common law judges for consultation in causes involving matters of proof. The earliest reported instance of this is in the 1480s, and there are others from the 1590s, 1630s, 1670s, 1690s and 1700s[3]. This suggests at minimum a desire to avoid unnecessary conflict between the jurisdictions in this area[4].

---

1 Above Ch 4 § 1 *(1)*.

2 Above Ch 6 nn 6-7 and text there.

3 YB P 22 Ed IV 6b, pl 18; *Bulwer v Levet,* (c. 1595) above Ch 6 n 274; *Earl of Suffolk v Greenvill,* (1631) above Ch 3 n 228; *Fry v Porter,* (1670) above Ch 4 n 41; *Montague v Bath,* (1692) above Ch 2 n 260; *Litton Strode v Falkland,* (1708) above Ch 4 n 54.

However, the evidence for equity "following the law in matters of evidence" in the sense of receiving rules which had previously developed in jury trials is reducible to the early eighteenth century statements about witnesses, which is weak and late. The clearest instance of equity following the law is in the matter of the effect of records and deeds, but (i) at the time this was at law a matter of pleading, not evidence to a jury; (ii) in any case this is a special case because of the extent to which the rules of the effect of documents are inseparable from the security and transferability of titles to land; and (iii) although equity is *said* to follow the law in treating fines and recoveries as bars, the practice is not wholly consistent[5].

In other areas (confessions, other matters concerning documents, and witness evidence) the rules appear, either first in equity (self- incrimination, compulsion of witnesses, legal privilege) or contemporaneously in both jurisdictions (documentary originals, exceptions to witnesses). In relation to the use of the oaths of the parties both to compel confession and in their own favour, and to the methods of the examination of witnesses, it is patently obvious that equity cannot have followed the law since the system is radically different.

The evidence for equity being more hospitable than common law to witness as opposed to documentary evidence, *at the time of the development of the common law rules of evidence to a jury on this point,* is also unsatisfactory. Whatever the position earlier[6], from the time of Egerton the parol evidence rule developed in parallel in both jurisdictions; from the 1600s to 1677, equity was harder on parol contracts than the common law; after 1677 the application of the Statute of Frauds in equity did not display a general openness to witness evidence.

The conclusion that the relation between the two jurisdictions in relation to proof/ evidence cannot have been one of equity simply adopting rules developed at law to control the jury also has some evidence to support it in the direct evidence of interactions between equity proof and common law. Some of these matters I have already discussed; others need fuller discussion here. In the first place, parties resorted from law to equity to solve problems of proof at law. Secondly, some new rules and procedures were introduced into the common law at this period which were clearly imitations of rules and procedures which already existed in equity. These cases suggest equitable influence on the law rather than the reverse. On the other side, however, in the later part of the period there was a definite tendency to resort from equity to common law trial, through the mechanism of the feigned issue, to solve problems of proof in equity.

---

4 Compare the discussion of relations between the jurisdictions in in the Elizabethan period in Jones, Ch 13.

5 Above Ch 4 § 1 *(1)*.

6 This is not to deny the trite fact that before this period equity had a history of giving relief against common law estoppels and on parol contracts. But it is possible that the key to this fact is not a common-law suspicion of juries (and therefore witnesses) not shared by equity judges, but rather the availability in equity of compulsion to confess (above Chs 2, 4).

1. Resort from law to equity

There were four major ways in which parties resorted to equity to resolve problems of proof at law.

(1) Bills were brought to obtain the defendant's oath, sometimes with a view to further equitable relief, but also with a view to subsequent relief at law. I have discussed the use of the defendant's answer and the limits of this procedure in Chapter 2.

(2) Equity relieved against some common law estoppels. I have discussed this in Chapter 4.

(3) As is discussed in Chapter 7, compulsion of witnesses was considerably earlier in equity proof than in the case of witnesses to a jury, and equitable orders were used to compel witnesses to attend for jury trial before compulsion was made available at law.

In addition, throughout the period bills were brought to have witnesses examined by commission, either *in perpetuam memoriam* for future use at law where the witnesses were aged or infirm, or for use in current actions at law where the witnesses were unable to travel due to age or illness or were overseas. There were a number of specific rules about this procedure which are not relevant here[7]; I have discussed some problems in relation to the usability of the depositions in Chapter 5.

(4) At least in the earlier part of the period, bills were brought to change the venue of trials at law on the ground of the influence of the adverse party[8], and to obtain new trials[9]. In the mid to later seventeenth century the common law courts seem to have liberalised their own procedures for dealing with these problems, but relief was still available in equity[10].

In addition, there are a number of minor or less well-documented uses of the equity jurisdiction to solve proof problems at law. (i) Orders were made to require parties to consent to the admission of documents[11] and depositions[12] inadmissible

---

7 See Jones pp 254-263 for the Elizabethan period; Gilbert *FR* 140-1, *Evidence* 44-51.

8 Jones 476-8; Tothill p1, title ACTIONS; *Isley v Pelham* (H1590/1) Monro 621; *Observations* f 452v No 138, f 464v No 208.

9 *Mallery v Vintner* (H1639/40) Toth 25; *Pitt v Corbet* (M1673) Rep t Finch 41, Nott CC No 11; *Robinson v Bell* (T1690) 2 Vern 146.

10 Below nn 24-5 and text there; change of venue, *Percy v Atkinson* (M1677) Nott CC No 768, *Earl of Kildare v Eustace* (H1686/7) 1 Vern 437, *per cur* (other reports not SP); *contra, Ewelme Hospital v Andover Corporation* (M1684) 1 Vern 266, 1 Eq Ca Ab 79.1, bill to change venue dismissed. For discussion of bills for new trials, *Tilly v Wharton, Wharton v Tilly* (T1700) 2 Vern 378, 419, 1 Eq Ca Ab 377.4, *Tovey v Young* (P1702) 2 Vern 437, Pre Ch 193.

11 *Crockhay v Woodward & Smith* (1617) Ritchie 74, *Lady Griffith v Boynton* (P1661) Nels 82, Harg 174 f 12v, *Brisco v Banbury* (M1675) Rep t Finch 237, Nott CC No 331 (*Banbury v Brisco* (1676) 1 Ch Cas 287, 1 Freem 15, 2 Freem 8, Nott CC Nos 445, 522, 572, 602,

or possibly inadmissible at law. (ii) In the earlier part of the period there are instances of injunctions being used to stop proceedings at law on the ground that witnesses have been improperly joined as parties[13] or are unavailable[14]. (iii) Rather more important than either of these, though further from my present concerns, was the injunction to stop suits at law, either where the plaintiff in equity relied on an equitable presumption[15], or, in the later part of the period, to bar excessively repeated ejectments[16], i.e. to impose a cause of action estoppel where at law an estoppel by record would not arise[17].

The overall extent of actual or potential equitable interference with the rules of proof (i.e. estoppel and trial) at common law was therefore considerable; a fact which is inconsistent with the idea that *in general* equity followed the law in these matters.

2. Law imitates equity

"Where the *Chancery* is regular in its remedy, why is not that law?" wrote Lord Guilford in his commonplace book, giving a list of examples which include

"Pl[ain]t[iff] to give oath for discharg
Def[endan]t to give oath for charg
Execut[ors] &c to acco[unt] upon oath
Com[mission] to exam[ine] witnesses
Releev ag[ains]t penaltys
...
Plead deeds when lost or seals broke
...
To discover assets upon oath
..."[18]

(H1680/1) 2 Ch Cas 42, Nott CC No 1081, not SP), *Norwich v Sanders* (T1677) Rep t Finch 302, *Lady Holcroft v Smith* (T1702) 2 Freem 259, 261, 1 Eq Ca Ab 224, Harv 1105 233, 5.

12 *Appesley v Mutton* (H1572/3) Monro 408, *Stanley v Pegg* (M1655) Hardr 22, *Ward v Primrose* (1655) Harg 174 f 2v, *Rich v Jaques* (M1663) 1 Ch Cas 31, 2 Freem 174, 1 Eq Ca Ab 80.K1, *Bush v Risley* (M1670) 1 Ch Cas 187, *Betsworth v Clerke* (M1674) Rep t Finch 435, *Denew v Cullen & Stock* (H1677/8) 1 Ch Cas 305 (M1677) Nott CC No 728, 3 Swans 662, Rep t Finch 437, not SP), *Marsden v Bound* (T1685) 1 Vern 331, *Lady Holcroft v Smith* (T1702) above n 11, *Gilbert v Emerton* (T1705) 2 Vern 503.

13 *Angrome v Angrome* (1583/4) Ch C Ch 176, Stowe 415 f 144v.

14 *Swigo v Hanbury* (1582-3) Ch C Ch 156, plaintiff (defendant at law)'s witnesses overseas. Cf *Armsted v Parker* (M1674) Rep t Finch 471, unavailability of witnesses ground for relief against verdict, but defendant in equity's oath then conclusive.

15 For examples see cases cited above Ch 9 § 2 *(1)*.

16 *How v Tenants of Bromsgrove* (1681) 1 Vern 22, 1 Eq Ca Ab 79.1, *Ewelme v Andover* (M1684) 1 Vern 66, 1 Eq Ca Ab 79.1, *Earl of Bath v Sherwin* (1706) Pre Ch 261, Gilb R 2, 2 Eq Ca Ab 171, (1709) 4 Bro PC 373.

17 Because the true parties would not appear on the face of the record.

In fact, though some of Guilford's proposals to give the common law courts equity powers had to wait for 1875, in our period the common law courts did in a number of ways imitate equitable proof or attempt to do so. In some of these cases it is quite clear that what is going on is the creation of new rules or remedies in imitation of equity. In others the argument is essentially *post hoc propter hoc,* but the accumulation of instances makes such an argument plausible.

(1) In the 1690s – 1700s the common law courts are seen operating a procedure by which parties could obtain a rule of court requiring documents to be brought into court for inspection. Though the limits on this procedure discussed in the cases make it appear as in form at least a species of *mandamus,* it is fairly clearly devised as a means by which parties could get discovery of at least some documents without going to equity[19].

(2) Lord Nottingham says that the common law courts imitated Chancery by making it the course of the court in suits on bonds that payment of principal, interest and costs would oblige the plaintiff to accept until plea, or the defendant to have a perpetual imparlance[20]; an Act of 1697 provided for analogous relief in the case of bonds to secure performance of covenants (8 & 9 Will 3 c 11 s 8), and Somers' 1705 *Act for the Amendment of the Law...* (4 & 5 Anne c 3) provides for payment to be pleaded at common law against a single obligation (s 12), and for payment into court of principal, interest and costs to bar further action for the penalty (s 13). Both are ways in which equity relieved against common law estoppel by deed as a matter of course, and there can be no doubt that here common law is imitating equity.

(3) As was discussed in Chapter 7, after 5 Eliz c 9 gave a penalty for failure of witnesses to attend, the common law courts started to issue subpoenas *ad testificandum* under their judicial seals, a practice complained of by Egerton, who also complained that the Common Pleas had taken to issuing subpoenas *ad respondendum.*

(4) In the interregnum the Upper Bench appears, from Style, to have asserted a power to take depositions from witnesses unable to attend trial[21]. After the Restoration this practice evidently disappeared, because Guilford calls for it as a reform, and there was an attempt to give the common law courts this power, rejected in the Commons, in the Bill leading to Somers' Act (above). This is quite clearly an attempt to imitate the equity procedure[22].

---

18 Add 32518 f 4r; square brackets my expansions. The full text is printed, with further discussion, in Macnair 'Imitations'

19 Macnair, 'Imitations' at nn 46-7.

20 *Proleg* 5.10,11, *TT* 203.

21 *Anon* (M1646) Style Prac Reg 113; ib 353 probably SC.

22 This is discussed in more detail in Macnair 'Imitations' at nn 35-42.

(5) In *Howard v Tremaine* (1692-3) counsel argued for the admission of depositions at law inter alia on the ground that if they are rejected it will defeat the Chancery practice of examination *in perpetuam memoriam;* the depositions were admitted[23].

These are clear instances of the common law imitating equity proof rules and procedures. Two others are somewhat weaker, because perhaps merely *post hoc propter hoc.*

(6) I have given reasons, above Ch 4, for supposing that a large part of the Statute of Frauds was directed to bringing common law rules into line with equity.

(7) As is indicated above, after the equity courts had for some time been intervening in common law procedure to move the venue of trials, and to order new trials, the common law courts developed a procedure for change of venue[24], and liberalised the grounds of application for a new trial[25].

Even if these last two cases are less clear, to the instances of resort from law to equity to relieve against problems of proof at common law we can add a substantial body of common law or statutory rules made, as Guilford suggested, in imitation of the regular remedies in equity.

3. Resort from equity to law: the feigned issue

In the eighteenth century it was alleged to be common practice in equity to send issues of fact to be tried by jury by the mechanism of the "feigned issue" – a claim which misled Chesnin & Hazard into suggesting that the courts of equity before the nineteenth century could not determine issues of fact without directing a jury trial[26]. Though this view is obviously wrong, nonetheless the use of the feigned issue does represent a major resort from equity proof to common law trial. Henry Horwitz' statistical study of Chancery records has shown that the procedure in fact remained very rare in Chancery[27]; but it is somewhat overrepresented in the reported cases, as will be seen below, and did become prominent in debate in the early eighteenth century.

---

23 Above Ch 5 nn 44-51 and text there.

24 *Herbert & Vaughan's Case* (n.d.) Latch 12, *Anon* (n.d.) Latch 118, KB, *Bovell v Sherwood* (1639) Clayt 73, NP, *per cur, Proctor v Phillips* (M1662) Hardr 311, Ex(L).

25 Up to the sixteenth century the only ground seems to have been procedural irregularity, but during the second half of the seventeenth it expanded to a general availability where the judge certified that the verdict was against the weight of the evidence. Baker *IELH* 89, 100, Metnick "From Neighbour-Witness to Judge of Proofs", 32 *AJLH* 201 at 212f, and add *Anon* (M1646) Style Prac. Reg. 310, contra *Anon* (M1646) (!) Style Prac Reg 311.

26 "Chancery Procedure and the Seventh Amendment: Jury Trial of Issues in Equity Cases before 1791", 83 *YLJ* 999, effectively demolished by Langbein, "Fact Finding in the English Court of Chancery: A Rebuttal", 83 *YLJ* 1620.

27 *Chancery Equity Records and Proceedings 1600-1800* (London, 1995), 19-20.

The mechanism of the feigned issue is described by Ballow as "a feign'd Issue in an Action upon the Case directed by the Chancery for the better informing and guiding the Conscience of the Court". The mechanism was that the court directed the issue to be tried; the parties would then bring *assumpsit* on a fictitious wager as to the truth of the issue, and plead to issue on its truth or falsity[28].

When the device appeared and therefore who may have been responsible for it and why is not clear. It does not seem to have been in use down to the time of Francis Bacon, i.e. to the 1620s[29], but had clearly been in existence for some time when Nottingham complained of it in his *Prolegomena* (1670s)[30].

The fictitious wager mechanism appears markedly similar to the roman law mechanism of feigned wager in the interdict procedure[31]. This might suggest that it was, in fact, adopted with a view to the trial of matters of pure equity not triable at law. However, it is not clear that it was conceived at the outset as a resort from proof to trial, though this is fairly clearly what it became. In the second half of the century and in the 1700s its scope remained controversial.

It is clear from Jones' work that the practice of sending issues to be tried antedates the specific mechanism of the feigned issue[32]. The early cases, however, seem to proceed on the basis of a distinction between matters at law, *prima facie* triable, and matters of equity, which required proof[33]. If the matter was purely at law, the parties would be dismissed to law[34]; if there was some admixture of law, in some cases they would be dismissed to law with liberty to resort back on the equity reserved[35], a practice which continued at least into the later eighteenth century[36]. In some such cases, however, the court would *after proof* direct a trial to be

28 Blackstone, *Commentaries on the Laws of England* (17th edn, London, Tegg, 1830) Vol 3 pp 451-2. The earlier practice books do not describe the feigned issue, but it is possible on this to presume continuance as far back as the term "feigned issue" is found.

29 *Tigh v Tigh* (1618) Ritchie 84, cited by Chesnin & Hazard as a possible early instance, is not a feigned assumpsit but trespass with a special issue directed. In addition to the absence from Ritchie, it is not mentioned by Norburie, *The Proceedings* (1649) *The Practice ... Unfolded,* (1651), or Tothill who is rather more up to date than either of these books. An argument from silence is problematic, however, as it is also absent from books written after the practice was well established, such as Gilbert's *Forum Romanum.*

30 Proleg 8.11, *TT* 220. Yale, *TT* Introduction p 76 dates the book to 1674.

31 Lee, *Elements of Roman Law,* pp 471-2. The similarity is noticed by Blackstone, above n 28.

32 Jones 473-481.

33 It is also worth noting the existence in civilian doctrine of some matters which fell to be proved by *communis opinio,* i.e. local reputation, particularly boundaries and prescriptive titles (above Ch 8 n 111) and local custom (Ayliffe 196). In these areas trial by jury might have been seen by civilians as preferable to proof by two witnesses; though *contra* Ridley 222 on the boundaries of parishes, arguing that proof by witnesses is as good.

34 Jones 473-4.

35 Jones 474-5, 478.

36 Chesnin & Hazard 1003-5.

had. At this stage this entailed directing a specific action to be brought and how the parties were to plead in it[37].

In this context the emergence of the feigned issue may at first be merely a procedural simplification. It allows the court of equity to specify directly the issue to be tried, with stereotyped directions as to pleading, as opposed to the older methods of dismissal to law with liberty to resort (which risked the suit at law being decided on immaterial pleading errors) or detailed direction of a specific form of action and pleadings (which involved additional costs in equity).

If so, however, this procedural change opened the door to a change in the role of directed trials. The older procedural mechanisms were adapted to and pointed to the assumption that matters of pure equity were not triable, but required to be proved. The feigned issue, because it was artificial and controlled by the court of equity, could in practice be used to deal with any disputed issue of fact.

In spite of Lord Nottingham's complaint about the multiplication of feigned issues, the majority of reported cases in which trials are directed in the period seem to involve issues triable at law. The reports do not distinguish between directed actions and feigned issues, but in 100 cases where a trial of some sort is reported to be sought or directed, of the issues directed 23 concern common law title to land or goods[38], 16 questions of custom, prescription or boundaries[39], 14 contractual matters which (apart from pleading, etc, problems) might have been

---

37 Jones 479-481; cf also *Observations* f 470v No 237, on dismissal to law can obtain directions to compel the defendant to appear and plead promptly. Chesnin & Hazard 1003-5 seem to conflate dismissal with liberty to resort on the equity reserved with directed action.

38 *Chetwyne v Walker* (26 Eliz) Ch C Ch 175, Stowe 415 f144 (printed 29 Eliz but MS 26 and with cases from 26), *Wright v Okeon* (28 Eliz) Cromp J. Cts 44b, *Anon* Cary 16 prob SC, *Robsart v Turton* (1637) 1 Ch Rep 112, *AG v Straite* (T1655) Hardr 4, *Peterborough v Mordaunt* (H1674/5) Nott CC No 200 (other reports not SP), *Prestidge v Eden* (H1673/4) Rep t Finch 59, *Stutville v Rossell* (P1674) Nott CC No 86, *Devereux v Devereux* (P1676) Nott CC No 465, *Crosse v Ridley* (P1676) Nott CC No 505, *Cock v Collins* (M1676) Nott CC No 591, *Lloyd v* ——— (M1677) Nott CC No 717, *Pitt v Pidgeon* (M1677) Nott CC No 756, 1 Ch Cas 301, *Tomlinson v Smith* (H1677/8) Nott CC No 799, *Meynell v Read* (P1679) Nott CC No 937 ((T1677) No 696, (H1681/2) No 1143 not SP), *Creed v Wallis* (M1679) Nott CC No 982, *Erwyn v Denham* (M1679) Nott CC No 987, *Lord North v Lord Grey* (T1680) Nott CC No 1031, Dick 14, *Hale v Thomas* (T1681) Nott CC No 1109 ((M1685) 1 Vern 349, (M1686) 1 Ch Cas 182, 186, subs procs), *Newburgh v Bickerstaffe* (H1684/5) 1 Vern 295, *Blynman v Brown* (T1691) 2 Vern 232, *Montague v Bath* (1692) 3 Ch Cas 55, *Johnson v Northey* (H1700/1) 2 Vern 407, Pre Ch 134, *Wilson v Story* (1706) Colles 382.

39 *Anon* (?1603) Cary 24, Stowe 415 f 97b, *Hutchings v Strode* (1634) Nels 26, Harg 174 f 10, *Chichly v* ——— (T1658) Hardr 116, *Randal v Head* (P1661) Hardr 188, 1 Eq Ca Ab 35, *Waller v Farmer* (T1661) Hardr 202, *Bush v Risley* (M1670) 1 Ch Cas 187, *Smith v Sallet* (1672) 2 Ch Rep 76, *City of London v Earl of Dorset* (P1674) 1 Ch Cas 228, 1 Eq Ca Ab 232.4, *Thrill v Burdett* (M1675) Nott CC No 302, *Strode v Strode* (M1675) Nott CC No 338 (other reports between same parties not SC or SP), *Percy v Atkinson* (M1677) Nott CC No 768, *Holden v Willmot* (M1679) Nott CC No 969, *Mascall v Wallis* (T1681) Nott CC No 1116, *Edwin v Thomas* (M1687) 1 Vern 489 (2 Vern 75 not SP), *Buxton v Hutchinson* (P1688) 2 Vern 46, *Harrington v Horton* (1706) 4 Bro PC 624.

tried at law[40], 13 controverted wills, usually of land[41], 7 forgery and associated questions[42], 6 quantum of damages or value[43], and 6 miscellaneous other issues which might have been pleaded to issue at law[44] – making around 85% of the total[45].

By comparison, the direction of trials to deal with matters *prima facie* equitable seems relatively unusual. There are no cases reported before the Restoration. Thereafter, trust or no trust is directed four times, two at the end of the period[46],

---

40 *Promise, agreement or release, Sutton v Errington* (22 Eliz) Cary 97, *Carteret v Wolstenholme* (M1677) Nott CC No 776, *Fashion v Atwood* (M1679) Nott CC No 983, *Lockner v Strode* (H1680/1) 1 Ch Cas 48, *Balch v Tucker* (H1680/1) 2 Ch Cas 40, *Cookes v Mascall* (H1686/7) 2 Vern 34, ((H1690) 2 Vern 200 not SP), *Jacobsen v Hennekius* (1714) 5 Bro PC 482, *reality of alleged bond, Vanhoven v Giesque* (1706) 4 Bro PC 622, *Shee v Lawless* (1713) Colles 450 *payment, Bryan v Rent & Newton* (M1673) Rep t Finch 3, *Carteret v Wolstenholme, Vanhoven v Giesque* (1706), *breach, Norton v Searl* (P1675) Nott CC No 217 (Rep t Finch 149 not SP), *Jarvis v Middleton* (H1680/1) Nott CC No 1073, *Crosby v Middleton* (H1710) 3 Ch Rep 99, Pre Ch 309, & cf *Thomas & Porter v Bishop of Worcester* (1667) 1 Ch Cas 95, 2 Freem 137, Harv 1105 116, whether waste by a copyholder wilful so as to lead to a forfeiture, *accountable at law, Gilbert v Emerton* (T1705) 2 Vern 503.

41 *Hawtre v Lady Wallop* (1666-7) 1 Ch Rep 265, (Nels 119 not SP), *Okeover v Pettus* (M1675), *Cole v Mordant* (P1676) Nott CC No 496 (from the Delegates, by consent, the propriety doubted by Lord Nottingham), *Howell v Griffith* (T1676) Nott CC No 534, *Rogers v Bamfield* (M1677) Nott CC No 724, not of will of personalty proved in the ecclesiastical court, *Stent v Atwick* (M1677) Nott CC No 726, *Vicars v Vicars* (M1677) Nott CC No 727, *Hide v Seymor* (P1678) Nott CC No 825, *Lyford v Coward* (M1683) 1 Vern 196, 2 Ch Cas 150, *Hall v Dench* (1684) 2 Ch Rep 297, 1 Vern 329 ((1685) 1 Vern 342 not SP) *Carvill v Carvill* (1684) 2 Ch Rep 301, *Serjeant v Puntis* (T1697) Pre Ch 77, *Cook v Parsons* (M1701) Pre Ch 184.

42 *Parker v Serjeant* (M1674) Nott CC No 133, *Spavin v Drax* (T1675) Nott CC No 179, *Squibb v Sir Edmundbury Godfrey* (M1676) Nott CC No 610, *Vicars v Vicars* (M1677) above, *Hatcher v Curtis* (H1679/80) Nott CC No 991, *Blois v Man* (T1680) Rep t Finch 454, *Fitton v Earl of Macclesfield* (H1684/5) 1 Vern 264, 287 ((P1683) 1 Vern 168 not SP). In view of *R v Taverner* (P1573) 3 Dy 322b, forgery punishable in Star Chamber, and *Clench v Tomley* (1603) Cary 23, as *Townley v Clench* Stowe 415 f 97, Harg 281 f 42, the court a better judge of documents than the jury, the use of trials in this context may be an aspect of the generalisation of the feigned issue, but forgery was certainly triable at law in the earlier period even if these cases indicate a parallel jurisdiction in the english bill courts.

43 *Trist v Buckeridge* (H1673/4) Rep t Finch 47, *Inglett v Inglett* (T1675) Nott CC No 279 ((M1676) No 582 not SP), *Temple v Rouse* (M1675) Nott CC No 342, *Carteret v Wolstenholme* (M1677) above n 52, *AG v Vernon* (H1685/6) 1 Vern 370, 2 Ch Rep 353, *per* Jones CJ ((M1684) 1 Vern 277 not SP), *Lloyd v Cardy* (1701) Colles 353. This probably heavily understates the frequency of issues of this type, as *quantum damnificatus* issues must have been as common as relief against penalties.

44 *Scot v Rayner* (P1664) 1 Ch Cas 50, Nels 93, death; *St George v St George* (M1674) Nott CC No 145, infancy; *Dodsworth v Anderson* (P1679) Nott CC No 942, bankruptcy; *Earl of Kildare v Eustace* (H1686/7) 1 Vern 428, 437, 2 Ch Cas 188, identity of persons; *Bellasis v Compton* (T1693) 2 Vern 294, *non compos; Plunket v Bishop of Dromore* (1709) Colles 421, assets.

45 As is apparent from the footnotes, there is some double counting due to cases where multiple issues of distinct kinds are directed.

notice or no notice twice[47]; fraud is directed to be tried four times[48], and refused to be tried three times[49]; matters arising on accounts are twice refused to be tried[50].

Nonetheless, in the 1700s it could be said in absolutely general terms that it was normal practice to direct a trial where there were conflicting proofs[51] or on the testimony of a single witness[52], and that directing a trial had "never before been objected to"[53]. This period may have been a high-water mark in the use of trials: Ballow says that a trial should not be directed on trust or no trust (though he then adds, "especially where a trust appears by implication from the nature of the case", which suggests that trust or no trust *can* be directed to be tried in some circumstances)[54].

Why did this transition take place? The cases and contemporary comments suggest three motivations. In the first place is the desire of plaintiffs to evade the two-witness rule (discussed above Ch 8 § 3). Second is the problem of resolving conflicts of testimony[55]. Both these motives imply the beginnings of a transition from an objective to a subjective standard of proof, for which there is also some direct evidence in the cases[56]. This transition was not unique to English law; Langbein has found evidence for a similar transition in continental criminal procedure beginning in the same period[57].

Third, and predominant in later accounts of the rise of the feigned issue, is perceived defects in the system of examination of witnesses on commission as com-

---

46 *Temple v Rouse* (M1675) above n 43, with other issues, *Bevan v Dike* (M1679) 2 Ch Cas 3, trust proved but not alleged on the pleadings, *Allibon v AG* (1707) Colles 393 (resulting trust /fraudulent conveyance), *Dawson v Franklyn* (1713) 4 Bro PC 626, 2 Eq Ca Ab 631.

47 *Temple v Rouse* (M1675) above n 43, *Framlingham v Harly* (M1681) Nott CC No 1136.

48 *Needler v Wright* (P1661) Nels 57, Harg 174 f8, *Jason v Jervis* (H1684/5) 1 Vern 284, whether deed fraudulent under 27 Eliz c 4; *Davy v Davy* (M1669) 1 Ch Rep 144, 1 Eq Ca Ab 32, whether fraudulent intent in keeping owner of rent out of distress; *Ibbotson v Rhodes* (P1706) 2 Vern 554, 1 Eq Ca Ab 229.13, concealment of title from subsequent mortgagee.

49 *Brisco v Banbury* (M1676) 1 Ch Cas 287 at 291 "for fraud or not is proper for this court", *Colston v Gardiner* (H1680/1) Nott CC No 1090, 3 Swans 279n, 2 Ch Cas 43, not where fraud apparent, *White v Hussey* (T1690) Pre Ch 13, trial not necessary to decide whether conveyance fraudulent.

50 *Holland v Garrett* (M1674) Nott CC No 147, *Christ's College Cambridge v Widdrington* (H1692/3) 2 Vern 283.

51 *CJ* xv 198, *Harrington v Horton, Vanhoven v Giesque, Wilson v Story, Allibon v AG, Jacobsen v Hennekius.*

52 Above Ch 8 nn 66-71 and text there.

53 *Allibon v AG,* above n 46, *per* counsel for the Crown *arg.* The statement is obviously false, but must have had some plausibility.

54 Bk VI c 3 § 7, p 132; this statement is reproduced without comment by Fonblanque II 495.

55 Cf Ch 8 § 4, and above n 51.

56 Above Ch 9 § 1 *(2).*

57 *Torture* Ch 3.

pared to the common law system of adversary cross-examination in open court. This was referred to as a motive of feigned issues in the opposition to the proposal to extend the power to take depositions to the common law courts (above). The general point that adversary cross-examination in open court is better was made by Gilbert, writing at about the same time, and by Atkyns in the 1690s[58]. However, this argument was not new, having been made by Hale in the Restoration, Popham in the 1600s, Smith in the 1560s and Fortescue in the 1460s[59]. The antiquity of this argument in favour of common law trial suggests that its mere intellectual force, on its own, is not sufficient to account for the change. Moreover, there were countervailing arguments which might have been advanced as to the deficiencies of jury trial[60]. I would suggest that two other changes are involved.

Firstly, I have suggested in Chapter 5 that there may have been during the mid-seventeenth century, or possibly earlier, a shift from the use of Justices of the Peace and county notables as commissioners to the use of country attorneys, and a corresponding decline in the status of commissioners from judicial to ministerial officers, leading to a more restrictive approach to their duties. If this suggestion is correct, this "dejudicialisation" of examination on commission would inevitably have lead to a decline in the value, or perceived value, of the depositions; a point made by Gilbert in contrasting equity examination with the original civilian form[61].

Secondly, the question of trial by jury was in the seventeenth century (as, indeed, later) a politically contested issue. Jury trial was, in fact, an aspect of the "ancient constitution" ideology[62]. In this context the events of 1640-60 and 1689 gave a substantial boost to the Fortescue/ Hale line of argument for the superiority of jury trial. The Chancery escaped abolition in the Civil War and Interregnum, but the other major english bill courts were destroyed and not restored[63]. In this context an ideological shift towards "juryism" may have been an element feeding in, together with the decline of examination on commission and the general shift towards a subjective standard of proof, to the expansion of the feigned issue procedure.

---

58 Gilbert, *Evidence* 44-5; Atkyns, *An Enquiry into the Jurisdiction of the Court of Chancery* (London, 1695), 31.

59 Above Ch 8 n 22 and text there.

60 Cf Holdsworth *HEL* vi 388-390.

61 *Evidence* 44-5.

62 See Veall, *The Popular Movement for Law Reform* (Oxford, Clarendon, 1970) 156-9; and the debate in the early 1680s triggered by *ignoramus* juries, for which see Burnet, *History of My Own Time* (ed Airy, Oxford, Clarendon, 1900) Part I Vol II pp 301-3, North, *Examen* (London, 1740) 89, 90, 94, 108, 110-4, 115 after 120 (double pagination), Hawles (attr) *The Englishman's Right* (1680) and *The Grand Juryman's Oath & office explained* (1681), Somers (attr) *The Security of Englishmen's Lives, or the trust, power & duty of the grand juries of England* (1682).

63 Holdsworth *HEL* VI 112.

This point brings me to the last element of the relationship between equity proof and common law trial: which is conflict between proof and procedural concepts, intimately limked in some aspects to conflict between common law and civil law. Some common lawyers criticised equity, and the civilian courts, for general citation[64] and the requirement to answer on oath[65]; they criticised equity courts for relieving parties on lost documents[66], and for relieving them against the conclusive effect of documents[67]; for examining witnesses in the civilian secret mode[68]; and for presuming fraud[69]. In these conflicts, the relationship of forces shifted over the period; which side was in the ascendant cannot be said to have been fully settled even at its end.

The relation between equity proof and common law trial over the period is, therefore, not a straightforward one either of equity following rules developed at law to control the jury, or of complete independence, or of the common law simply following existing developments in equity. Equity operated *in relation to* law; law, conversely, could not ignore equity. There was no area of equity – even trusts – on which rules at law did not bear; and, conversely, no area of law was unaffected by the equity jurisdiction (until the abolition of Star Chamber and the provincial Councils). Equity was not merely a specialist juridiction. Equity and law were not parallel legal orders, like secular and ecclesastical law, but terms of a contradiction within a single legal order.

When we locate the origins of the law of evidence to a jury within this relationship, the starting point has to be the late medieval common lawyers' idea that jurors were witnesses sworn to tell the truth and as such were not subject to proof rules which all conceded were binding on judges, and the persistence of this idea as an effective line of argument at common law down to the time of *Bushell's Case* in 1670 if not later[70]. In More's response to St German in the early 1530s we find an early instance of the claim that jurors are judges[71]; and thereafter the idea that the jurors are in some sense judges of fact gradually gains ground, and over the same period rules governing the evidence which can be led to a jury and its effect appear and become increasingly prominent, as we have seen in passing in this book.

Why did the judges change their mind about interference with jury fact-finding, from 'casting off all quarrels' onto the jury in the 1530s, to ruling on evidence and punishing recalcitrant juries in the 1630s? It seems probable that one element was

---

64 Above Ch 2 n 7.

65 Above Ch 2 n 70 (and the materials discussed by Levy, *Origins of the Fifth Amendment*).

66 Above Ch 3 n 190 and text there.

67 Above Ch 4 nn 3-9.

68 Above Ch 8 n 22 and text there, and this Chapter n 58.

69 Above ch 9 § 2 *(4)*.

70 Above ch 1 n 32.

71 Above ch 1 n 114.

the intervention of equity in common law procedure, the resort of parties from law into equity which we have seen above; just as the competition of general citation and liberality in pleading in equity had motivated the King's Bench to invent its own summary procedure in the Bill of Middlesex[72]. *Post hoc* is not necessarily *propter hoc*, and the general increase in the strength of the state, the revival from the 1560s of the english civilian profession[73], and the general cultural context of the Renaissance, are obviously also relevant; but the intervention of the courts of equity in common law procedure was a very direct pressure.

The intervention of courts of equity may, therefore, have furnished an important pressure driving the development of rules of evidence to a jury at common law. However, the shape those rules took need not have been a simple matter of the common lawyers copying rules from the equity courts. In the first place, the sources for equity proof doctrine largely begin at the same period as the first steps in common law evidence doctrine. Secondly, both common lawyers and equity lawyers relied in some areas on the proof rules of the medieval law to shape the rules they developed: particularly in relation to the classification of usable documents (above, Ch 3) and their effect (above, Ch 4), and the disqualification of witnesses by infamy (above, Ch 6 § 4 *(1)*). Thirdly, in a number of areas there is direct or near-direct evidence of common lawyers referring directly to civilian sources on proof matters – *not* to these sources as being in use in equity – which falls to be discussed in the next section.

Finally, as we have already seen, some common lawyers explicitly differentiated their own proof practice from that of equity and the civil laws. Here the question of proof rules became intimately connected with more general debates about the 'ancient constitution' and the role of the jury[74]. Connecting the question of proof/evidence in this way with the political-ideological debate over the jury helps, as has I have already suggested in relation to feigned issues, with the chronology of relations between equity and law; it is at the same period, the later seventeenth and early eighteenth century, at which a connection to political history would lead one to expect an ascendancy of "common law" ideology, that we also find the first assertions that equity follows the law in relation to witnesses, and some slight evidence of re-theorisation of some rules in equity, for instance in relation to self-incrimination[75], exceptions to witnesses[76], the two witness rule[77], and the burden and standard of proof[78].

---

72 M. Blatcher, *The Court of King's Bench 1450-1550* (London, 1978); Baker, *IELH* 47-53, 121.

73 Helmholz, *Roman Canon Law* Ch 2.

74 Above n 62.

75 Above Ch 2 § 2 *(1)*.

76 Above Ch 6 § 5 *(1)* (b).

77 Above Ch 8 § 3.

78 Above Ch 9 § 1.

Do common law systems vary from civil law systems by having a system of rules of evidence because of the historical role of trial by jury, as Thayer and Wigmore argued? The answer is both yes and no. It is 'yes' because it is reasonably clear that the introduction of rules of evidence subjected the jury to a judicial control which had been absent in the later fourteenth, fifteenth and early sixteenth centuries; and if, as I have suggested here, this change was partly driven by the pressure of equity intervention, that pressure in turn was in part a response to the perceived problems of jury trial in the late middle ages.

It is 'no', however, at a more fundamental level. This is that *judicial* factfinding in equity (and, indeed, at common law) was thought to be subject to rules governing the nature and *quantum* of proof *before* rules of evidence were applied to jury trial; and, indeed, many of the rules of evidence applied at law by 1700 appeared in equity sources before they appeared at common law. Moreover, the idea that judicial fact-finding was subject to proof rules, and many of the specific rules which came to be used, were shared with or drawn from the civil law tradition. The creation of the law governing evidence to a jury was therefore in its own time a *convergence* (albeit not a complete one) between the common and the civil laws. The explanation of the difference which exists today is to be sought only partly in this period; partly, and perhaps more significantly, it should be sought later in the history of the two traditions, in the period of the abolition of the old law of proof in continental europe.

II. Equity, common law, and civil law

This book has provided three sorts of reasons for supposing that equity proof was a system which applied the general principles of the roman-canon law of proof. The first is parallelism of content; the second linguistic echoes; and the third instances of direct citation. In the first place is evidence that equity proof principles were strikingly parallel to the principles of proof in the learned laws.

In spite of certain survivals of older views and exceptions, in the later sixteenth and the seventeeenth century the equity courts applied the roman-canon principle that the judge was to decide *secundum allegata et probata,* with the result that facts relied on by the plaintiff had to be both alleged and proved. Similarly, the mechanism of compulsion to answer on oath itself was characteristically civilian/ canonist and so perceived by contemporaries; though the precise place of this mechanism in the english bill procedure was significantly different from the canonist answer to positions, this variance could be explained by the supplementary role of the jurisdiction; and the canonist rule that positions should not be incriminating or defamatory had a close analogue in the rules applied in Chancery and Exchequer from the reign of Elizabeth. As in the roman-canon systems, a confession in court was capable of forming a full and conclusive proof against the party confessing; confessions out of court had less weight and were regarded, if oral, with suspicion. And as in the roman-canon systems, a confession was *in general* only proof against the party confessing.

Contemporary English lawyers, like the civilians and canonists, organised discussions of proof/ evidence by separating documents and witnesses as instruments of proof. On the basis of a brief general survey of the roman-canon and medieval common law rules relating to proof by documents, it seems that these were to a considerable extent parallel, though the common law rules varied from those of the learned laws in giving particular weight to records and deeds.

In relation to the rules governing the use of documents as proof in equity, and as evidence to a jury, the fundamental distinction in the learned laws between public and private documents was present both in equity and at common law; but it was shaped by the medieval common law distinction between records and deeds. Unlike the medieval common law pleading rules, but like the learned laws, public documents other than records, and private documents other than deeds, were usable. It was not clear whether private documents were used primarily as admissions, or also as testimonial or circumstantial evidence; I suggest that their primary use was as admissions, though these other uses were available and use of private documents as testimony increased in prominence towards the end of the period.

Documents which were to be used themselves required to be proved. The rule requiring the production of the original document and its exceptions corresponded fairly closely to the equivalent rules in the learned laws and more so than to the medieval common law *profert* rules; the rule requiring proof of execution of private documents was present in both systems. These rules were therefore on the whole closer to the roman-canon system than the medieval common law rules had been.

The procedure for the examination of witnesses and the principles expressed in this procedure were substantially the same in equity as in the roman-canon system. Dawson's argument to the contrary, based on the use in equity of party interrogatories and commissioners to examine witnesses, missed the facts that (a) both these practices were in use in the canon law, and (b) in theory in equity interrogatories were subject to judicial control and commissioners officers of the court.

The body of rules governing exceptions to witnesses as a whole was a good deal closer to roman-canon concepts than has previously been admitted, and there was some direct evidence of reference to the learned laws in relation to particular rules. Wigmore's specific arguments against roman-canon influence in this area cannot be sustained on the evidence. There were, however, significant variations from the learned laws in relation to affinity and dependence.

Compulsion to testify was well established in the learned laws by our period; it is found in equity well before it appears in relation to witnesses to a jury at law. The rule against self-incrimination as a reason not to answer specific interrogatories was present both in the *jus commune* and in equity. Legal professional privilege had some antecedents in the learned laws, and could also be explained in self-incrimination terms.

The fundamental guarantee of the credibility of testimony was the weight of the oath. This was a variation from the learned laws, in which, though testimony was required to be on oath, the greater emphasis tended to be put on the absence of exceptions to the witness, corroboration and the procedural mechanisms guaranteeing independence of testimony from the parties. However, the equity procedure did not use cross-examination as a test of the credibility of the witness (as Hale suggested was the case in jury trial). As in the learned laws, two witnesses were required to make a proof in equity, though there may have been a tendency in the latter part of the period to evade this requirement by resort to trial at law. And discussions of conflicting testimony both in equity and common law tend to refer to questions of the number and social standing of the witnesses and to corroboration by presumptions/ circumstantial evidence, not to witness demeanour; in this respect there was again a marked similarity to the learned laws.

The standard of proof in equity, as in the learned laws, was primarily an objective one, and the burden of proof was in consequence a unilateral obligation to present sufficient proofs, and was generally governed by the principle that *ei incumbit probatio qui dicit, non qui negat.* Presumptions had a central strategic role in proof; they were classified, as in the roman-canon systems, into "violent" and other presumptions, i.e. by weight; and as in the learned laws, they were conceived of as *items of proof* to be weighed in the scale of the objective standard, rather than as rules regulating the burden of proof. In the later part of the period, however, there were indications of the beginning of a shift towards a subjective standard of proof and of a decline in the role of presumptions, illustrated by the question of presumptions of fraud.

The minimum possible conclusion to be drawn from this survey is that the concepts of proof in equity in this period were strikingly similar to the leading principles of the law of proof in the learned laws. Striking similarity may, of course, be merely coincidental. It is, however, reinforced by linguistic echoes and direct citations. Linguistic echoes suggest, though they obviously cannot prove, borrowing. Examples are Egerton's references to *plena* and *semiplena probatio*[79] and to "*juramentum supplementorum*"[80]; Lord Nottingham's use of the tags that confession is above a thousand witnesses[81] and *in testem testes et in hos, sed non datur ultra*[82]; and, more generally, references to *secundum allegata et probata*[83]; the terminology of "exceptions" to witnesses, as opposed to the medieval common law "chal-

79 Above Ch 8 n 74.

80 Above Ch 6 n 259.

81 Above Ch 2 n 176.

82 Above Ch 5 n 30.

83 Above Ch 2 nn 35, 36, 45.

lenges"[84]; and the terminology of the classification of presumptions[85], the last two of which were shared with common law authorities.

Among instances of direct citation of civilian sources the clearest and most general is *Forme et Certenty*'s chapter on proof. Other direct references in equity can be found in *Bulwer v Levet* (1590s) on spouse witnesses[86]; Egerton's comment on restored good character[87]; Master Carew's rulings in *Wyley v Vincent* (1607) and *Whyte v Oxenbridge* (1608) on disinterested party witnesses[88]; and, towards the end of the period, Gilbert's use of civilian materials to construct his *Forum Romanum,* and Nelson's citation to Domat on presumptions of fraud in *Rep. t. Finch*[89].

Common law evidence is considerably less strikingly similar to civilian proof concepts, and in some areas, as we have seen, it is consciously divergent. However, parallelism can be found in some aspects of the law of documentary evidence, of the rules governing exceptions to witnesses, witness compulsion and privilege (one area which was fairly clearly developed in Chancery), and some burden and standard of proof matters. Moreover, here, too, we can find linguistic echoes: *nemo tenetur seipsum prodere;* Coke's reference to 'slippery memory' in *The Countess of Rutland's Case*[90], and his formulation of the documentary originals rule in *Dr Leyfield's Case*[91]; the latin tags for the necessity principle[92]; in the later seventeenth century, the concept of 'public' documents, as distinct from the medieval common law formula 'records'[93], and references to *crimen falsi* in connection with infamous witnesses[94]; and, shared with equity, 'exceptions' rather than 'challenges' to witnesses, and the language and classification of presumptions.

Here, too, there is some direct evidence of reference to the learned laws: *Trial of Treasons* (1556)[95] on parties and witnesses; Hale's citation of Covarruvias in relation to infidels[96]; Duncombe's approving reference to Farinaccius and Mascardus in his 1682 preface to *Trialls per Pais*[97]; and, towards the end of the period, Gilbert's use of civilian sources in his *Evidence.*

---

84 Above Ch 6 nn 15-19.

85 Above Ch 9 § 2 *(2).*

86 Above Ch 6 n 274 and text there.

87 Above Ch 6 n 63 and text there.

88 Above Ch 6 n 190 and text there. This, of course, assumes that I have correctly interpreted these cases.

89 Above Ch 9 n 46.

90 Above Ch 4 nn 45-7 and text there.

91 Above Ch 3 n 160 and text there.

92 Above Ch 6 nn 240-5 and text there.

93 Above Ch 3 § 2 *(1).*

94 Above Ch 6 nn 81-3 and text there.

95 Above Ch 6 n 159 and text there.

96 Above Ch 6 n 102 and text there.

97 Above Ch 1 n 29.

This is a small number of direct citations; as I indicated in Chapter 1, we are not talking about a full-scale "Reception" allowing proof arguments like those used by Gentili in the Admiralty. However, in the context of the degree of parallelism found, the presence of even a few direct citations is a substantial support for the view that borrowing of elementary ideas is the simplest explanation of the appearance of the rules, at least in the earlier part of the period and to some extent in the later. In sum, both equity proof (very strongly) and common law evidence rules (rather less strongly) were influenced by civilian proof concepts. This conclusion tells us something important about the relationship of the common law, equity and civil law in the early modern period.

In the first place, it corroborates the contemporary view of both common lawyers and civilians that equity procedure was broadly civilian in character; though, as I indicated in Chapter 1, the judicial bench in these courts was mixed, the bar composed of common lawyers, and the degree of sophistication of the use of civilian sources involved relatively low. Given the nature of the interactions between common law and equity discussed in the previous section, this means that the idea that there was a threat to the common law in the early seventeenth century[98] was neither paranoia, nor the result of the inability of the common lawyers to think outside the frame of their own law. Given the degree of conformity to roman-canon proof concepts in the english bill jurisdictions that this survey reveals, we *don't know* what would have happened if the Star Chamber and other english bill jurisdictions had not been abolished, leaving the Chancery almost in splendid isolation. Given the evidence for influence of the learned laws on the common law, the shortage of university-trained civilians need not have been an obstacle to a substantial romanisation of proof procedure at law.

On the contrary, this evidence reinforces Pawlisch's argument that lawyers trained in the common law tradition were eclectic, not exclusive in their reasoning[99]. The medieval common law materials did not provide a sufficient basis in themselves for the solution of the problem of proof; and even Coke, the great apostle of the autonomy and supremacy of the common law, used civil law materials as supplementary sources to address this problem. This practice continued down to the end of the period studied here. The relative rarity of direct citation suggests that it may have been more acceptable to borrow civilians' arguments than actually to cite them directly; a view which would be consistent with common lawyers' objections to the civil law as a "Sea full of waves" in which the vast and contradictory range of citable authority rendered the law uncertain[100].

---

98 Baker, 4 Ir Jur 368 at 368; Levack, *The Civil Lawyers in England 1603-41* (Oxford, Clarendon, 1973) Ch 4; Prest, *The Rise of the Barristers* (Oxford, Clarendon, 1986) 260, 262-7, 271-2.

99 Above Ch 1 n 59.

100 Coke, *Second Institute*, Proem, cited Helmholz, *Roman Canon Law* 14; W. Clerk, *An Epitome of Certain Late Aspersions cast at Civilians* (Dublin, 1631) sigs A2r, Br-Cv.

At the same time, the point is not simply that (some) English lawyers knew (some) basic civil or canon law. The rules appear from the outset not as an accumulation of exercises of judicial discretion but as *binding rules:* the judge in equity is *bound by* the general principles of the law of proof, and so, arguably, is the trial jury. It seems, therefore, that the assumption both of equity interference with common law procedure, and of the invention of the common law of evidence, is that the existing custom and practice of the courts is *subject to rules of natural (or divine) law;* and a substantial part of these rules were derived from the civil law tradition.

If these inferences are correct, they place the mental universe of the common lawyers at considerably less distance from that of their european contemporaries than does, for instance, Pocock's conception. It follows that we have to read the disputes of the period over common *versus* civil law not as the product of the peculiar mind-set of the common lawyers, but as disputes about certain concrete issues, such as trial by jury, the self-incriminatory oath, the secret examination of witnesses, the enforceability of securities, finality in judicial proceedings – which were driven, partly because of the role of the civilians in the courts of equity, to become disputes about the role of the civil law, the ultimate basis of the authority of law, and the nature of the King's sovereignty. The ideas of the immemoriality and supremacy of the common law then have to be seen, as Brooks and Sharpe[101] argued, as political gambits in these concrete disputes.

Secondly, however, the story of what did happen cannot be a simple one of "the common law procedure developed in the middle ages (country) *versus* Romanising importations (court)". Oppositionists were perfectly capable of using romanising proof arguments when it suited their book, and *vice versa* Court supporters were perfectly capable of arguing that the jury should be able to act of its own knowledge[102]. These arguments were, therefore, probably legal-political gambits rather than the expression of genuine beliefs. This again supports the inference that the ideas of immemoriality and supremacy of the common law were legal-political gambits. It also offers some reinforcement to the view that the conservative and consensus-oriented terms of overt political discussion in the period should not be taken at face value; given that there is little reason to suppose that even Coke 'really' believed in the entire autonomy of the common law, as opposed to vigorously defending this doctrine as a tactic in legal and political argument, there is

101 72 *P&P* 133.

102 Thus, in the 1606 debates the roles are reversed in the course of the debate (above Ch 6 nn 170-176 and text there); in 1679-81 Whigs are found arguing in relation to the Plot trials that they are bound to decide according to the evidence (above Ch 8 n Ch 8 n 89) and then in relation to *ignoramus* juries that the jury is free to act of its own knowledge (Somers, cited above n 62).

103 Cf Hirst 92 Past & Present 79 at 81-3, Hill "Political discourse in Early Stuart England" in *A Nation of Change and Novelty* (London, Routledge, 1990).

little more reason to suppose that other public utterances about constitutional matters should not be read as tactical[103].

To uncover civilian influence in the rather technical area of proof and procedure therefore casts a new light on important questions about the place of the common and civil laws in the politics of the early modern period. There is a political devil lurking in the technical detail.

Bibliography

I. Works cited by abbreviation

1. Printed primary sources (including modern editions)

'Alciatus'	Andreas Alciato [attr.] *D. Andreae Alciati Iuriscon. Claris Iudiciarii Processus Compendium* (Lyon, 1573)
Andrewes	Lancelot Andrewes, Disputation on *ex officio* procedure (1590s), printed in E. Lake, *Memoranda Touching the Oath Ex Officio* (London, 1662)
Ayliffe	John Ayliffe, *Parergon Iuris Canonici Anglicani* (London, 1727)
Bacon	Matthew Bacon (attr) *The New Abridgement* Vol I (London, 1736)
Ballow	Henry Ballow (attr) *A Treatise of Equity* (London, 1737)
Blackstone	Sir William Blackstone, *Commentaries on the Laws of England* (17th edition, London, Tegg, 1830)
Bowyer	*The Parliamentary Diary of Robert Bowyer 1606-7*, ed D.H. Willson (Minneapolis, University of Minnesota Press, 1931)
Bracton	*Bracton De Legibus et Consuetudinibus Angliae,* ed G.E. Woodbine & S. E. Thorne, Cambridge, Mass, 1968-77.
CJ	*Journals of the House of Commons* (London, 1760-)
Clayt.	John Clayton, *Reports and Pleas of Assizes at Yorke...* (London, 1651)
Clerke	Francis Clerke, *Praxis in Curiis Ecclesiasticis* (London, 1684)
Clerke Prax Adm	Francis Clerke, *Praxis Curiae Admiralitatis Angliae* (3rd Edition, Latin with english translation, London, 1722)
Co Lit	Sir Edward Coke, *The First Part of the Institutes of the Laws of England, or, a Commentary upon Littleton* (11th edition, London, 1719)
Coke Fourth Inst	Sir Edward Coke, *The Fourth Part of the Institutes of the Laws of England* (6th edition, London, 1681)
Conset	H[enry] C[onset], *The Practice of the Spiritual or Ecclesiastical Courts* (London, 1685)
Cosin	Richard Cosin, *An Apologie of Certaine Proceedings Ecclesiasticall* (second edition, London, 1593)
Cotta	*Catellanii Cottae Memoralia ex Variis Utriusque Iuris Doctoribus Collata* (Lyon, 1573)

Covarruvias *QP*	*Practicarum Quaestionum Liber*, in Covarruvias, *Omnia Opera*
Covarruvias *VR*	*Variarum Resolutionum* in id.
Crompton	Crompton, *Laucthoritie & jurisdiction des courts de la Maiestie de la Roigne* (London, 1594)
Domat	Jean Domat, *Les Lois Civiles en leur ordre naturel* (Paris, 1705; & trans. J. Strahan, London, 1722). I have used Strahan's translation but checked it against the 1705 French edition which is in the British Library; citations are therefore to (Book). (Title). (Section). (subsection).
Fortescue	Sir John Fortescue, *De Laudibus Legum Angliae,* ed & trans S.B. Chrimes, Cambridge, CUP, 1949
Fulbecke	W. Fulbecke, *A Parallele or Conference...* (London, 1618)
Gaill	Andreas Gaill, *Practicarum Observationum, tam ad Processum Judiciarum, Praesertim Imperialis Camerae, Quam Causarum Decisiones Pertinentium, Libri Duo* (Amsterdam, 1663)
Gentili	Alberico Gentili, *Hispanicae Advocationes Libri Duo* (reprint, Classics of International Law Series, NY, OUP, 1921)
Gilbert	Sir Jeffrey Gilbert, *The Law of Evidence* (Dublin, 1754; reprint, NY, Garland, 1979)
Gilbert *FR*	Sir Jeffrey Gilbert, *Forum Romanum* (London, 1758)
Glanvill	*The treatise on the laws and customs of the realm of England commonly called Glanvill,* ed. G.D.G. Hall, (London, Nelson, 1965)
Hale HPC	Sir Matthew Hale, *The History of the Pleas of the Crown* (London, 1736; reprint, London, Professional Books, 1971)
Hawarde	J. Hawarde, *Les Reportes del Cases in Camera Stellata* ed. & trans. W.P. Baildon (privately printed, 1894)
Hawkins	William Hawkins, *A Treatise of the Pleas of the Crown* (London, 1721; reprint, London, Professional Books,
Hudson	William Hudson, *A Treatise of the Star Chamber,* in Francis Hargrave ed, *Collectanea Juridica* Vol II p 1
Knafla	L.A. Knafla (ed) *Law and Politics in Jacobean England, the Tracts of Lord Chancellor Ellesmere* (Cambridge, CUP, 1977)
LJ	Journals of the House of Lords (London, 1769-)
Lyndwood	W. Lyndwood, *Provinciale* (Oxford, 1679)
Maranta	*Dn. Rob. Marantae Venusini Speculum Aureum et Lumen Advocatorum Praxis Civilis, Novisssime Recognitum ... per ... Petrum Polleriumas ...* (Lyon, 1573)
Monro	C. Monro (ed) *Acta Cancellariae; or, Selections from the Records of the Court of Chancery...* (London, Benning, 1847)
Norburie	George Norburie, *The Abuses and Remedies of the Chancery,* in Francis Hargrave ed, *Collectanea Juridica* p 423

North	Roger North, *Lives of the Norths* (ed. Jessop, London, Bohn, 1890)
Nott. CC	*Lord Nottingham's Chancery Cases* ed. D.E.C. Yale, Selden Society Vols 73 and 79. Citations are to case number.
Nott. Prac. Nott. TT Nott. Proleg.	*Lord Nottingham's "Manual of Chancery Practice" and "Prolegomena of Chancery and Equity"*, ed. D.E.C. Yale (Cambridge, CUP, 1965). Citations are to Prac[tice]. (Title). (Number) or Proleg[omena]. (Chapter).(Number), TT (page).
PQ	*Principia Quaedam et Axiomata ex Iure Civili Sparsim Collecta* (London, 1581)
Pufendorf	Samuel Pufendorf, *De Jure Naturae et Gentium* (1688, reprint, *Classics of International Law* series, Oxford, Clarendon, 1934)
Reformatio	*Reformatio Legum Ecclesiasticarum* ed. E. Cardwell, (Oxford, OUP, 1850)
Ridley	Sir T. Ridley, *A View of the Civile and Ecclesiastical Law* (London, 1607)
Ritchie	J. Ritchie ed, *Reports of Cases decided by Francis Bacon* (London, Sweet & Maxwell, 1932)
Rolle Ab.	Henry Rolle, *Un Abridgement des plusieurs cases et resolutions del Common Ley* (London, 1669, 2 vv)
Rot. Parl	*Rotuli Parliamentorum; ut et petitiones, et placita in Parliamento* (London, 1765, 6 vv)
St German D&S	Christopher St German, *Doctor & Student*, ed. Plucknett & Barton, Selden Soc Vol 91
St German SGCS	JA Guy (ed), *Christopher St German on Chancery & Statute*, Selden Soc Supp. Series No 6 (London, 1985)
Sanders	G. W. Sanders, *Orders of the High Court of Chancery* (London, Maxwell, 1845)
SR	*The Statutes of the Realm. Printed by command...* (London, 1810-22)
St. Tr.	*A Complete Collection of State Trials...* compiled by T.B. Howell, and... T.J. Howell... (London, 1816-1826, 33 vv)
Style Prac Reg	William Style, *Regestum Practicale, or the Practical Register* (London, 1657)
Swinburne	Henry Swinburne, *A Brief Treatise of Testaments & Last Wills* (London, J. Windet, 1590; reprint, New York, Garland, 1978)
Tothill *Proceedings*	William Tothill [attr], *The Proceedings of the High Court of Chancery* (London, 1649, bound with Tothill's Reports)
TPP	*Tryalls per Pais* (First edition, London, 1665; second, by G.D. [attr. Giles Duncombe] London, 1682; third, London, 1695; fifth, London, 1718). Citations indicate which edition is referred to.

van Espen — Z.B. van Espen, *Jus Ecclesiasticum Universum* (1700; edition ed. JP Gilbert, Venice, Graziosi, 1769). Citations are to (Pars). (Tit). (Cap). (Qu)

Viner — Charles Viner, *A General Abridgement of Law and Equity* (Aldershot, 1742-56, 23vv)

Vulteius — Hermannus Vulteius, *Jurisprudentiae Romanae a Justiniano Compositae Libri Duo* (Marpurgi, 1590)

West — William West, *Symboleography Part II, Chancery* (London, 1594)

Wiseman — R. Wiseman, *Law of Laws: or, the Excellency of the Civil Law above all Humane Laws whatsoever* (London, 1657)

Wood — Thomas Wood, *A New Institute of the Imperial or Civil Law* (London, 1704)

Zouch *EI* — Richard Zouch, *Elementa Iurisprudentiae* (London, 1636)

Zouch *DIE* — id., *Descriptio Iuris Ecclesiastici* (London, 1636)

Zouch *SQ* — id., *Specimen Quaestionum Iuris Civilis* (London, 1653)

2. Manuscript sources

Add — British Library Additional Manuscript (Number)

CUL — Cambridge University Library Manuscript (Class, Number)

F&C — Anonymous Chancery treatise, beginning "Forme et Certenty de Bills", Cambridge University Library MS Gg 2.31 ff 520r - 551v

Harg — British Library Hargrave Manuscript (Number)

Harl — British Library Harleian Manuscript (Number)

Hill 79 — Lincoln's Inn Hill MS 79

HLS — Harvard Law School Manuscript (Number)

Lansd — British Library Lansdowne Manuscript (Number)

Observations — Anonymous Chancery collection, titled "Observa[ti]ons in Course of Chancery Practice", Cambridge University Library MS Gg 2.31 ff 437r - 480v

Sloane — British Library Sloane Manuscript (Number)

Stowe — British Library Stowe Manuscript (Number)

3. Secondary works

Baker IELH — J. H. Baker, *An Introduction to English Legal History* (3rd edition, London, Butterworths, 1990

Bryson	W. H. Bryson, *The Equity Side of the Exchequer* (Cambridge, CUP, 1975)
Cross	*Cross on Evidence*, (6th edition by Sir Rupert Cross and Colin Tapper, London, Butterworths, 1985)
Dawson	John P. Dawson, *A History of Lay Judges* (Cambridge, Harvard UP, 1960)
Engelmann	Arthur Engelmann and others, *A History of Continental Civil Procedure* (London, John Murray, 1928)
Esmein	A. Esmein, *A History of Continental Criminal Procedure* (London, John Murray, 1914)
Holdsworth *HEL*	Sir William Holdsworth, *A History of English Law* (London, Methuen & Sweet & Maxwell, 3rd edition, 1944)
Jones	W. J. Jones, *The Elizabethan Court of Chancery* (Oxford, Clarendon, 1967)
Langdell	C.C. Langdell, "The Development of Equity Pleading from the canon law of procedure" in Association of American Law Schools ed, *Essays in Anglo-American Legal History* Vol II (Boston, Little, Brown, 1908)
Lévy	J. P. Lévy, *La Hiérarchie des Preuves dans le Droit Savant du Moyen-Age* (Paris, Sirey, 1939)
P&M HEL	Sir Frederick Pollock and F.W. Maitland, *The History of English Law before the time of Edward I* (reissue, Cambridge, CUP, 1968)
Simpson	*Contract* A.W.B. Simpson, *A History of the Common Law of Contract* (Oxford, Clarendon paperback, 1987)
Spence	G. Spence, *The Equitable Jurisdiction of the Court of Chancery* (London, Stevens, 1846-9)
Thayer	J. B. Thayer, *A Preliminary treatise on evidence at the common law* (Boston, Little, Brown, 1898; reprint, Rothman, Kelley, 1969)
Wigmore	J. H. Wigmore, *Treatise on Evidence at Common Law* (New York, Little Brown, 3rd Edition, 1940). (citations are generally to section number).

II. Other works

1. Printed primary sources

Angelus, de Clavasio, Summa Angelica de Casibus Conscientiae (Argentine, 1489; Caën, 1517)

Atkyns, Sir Robert, An Enquiry into the Jurisdiction of the Court of Chancery (London, 1695)

Bathurst, C. [attr.], The Theory of Evidence (London, 1751)

Biblia Sacra Iuxta Vulgatam Versionem ed. R. Weber & al. (Stuttgart, 1994)

Brown, W. [attr], Praxis Almae Curiae Cancellariae (London, 1694)

Burnet, Bishop G., The History of My Own Time (ed Airy, Oxford, Clarendon, 1900)

Caesar, Sir Julius, The Ancient State, Authority and Proceedings of the Court of Requests, ed. L.M. Hill (Cambridge, CUP, 1975)

Calendars of Assize Records (London, HMSO, 1975-)

Calendars of Proceedings in Chancery in the Reign of Elizabeth (London, Record Commissioners, 1827)

Camden, W., The History of the most renowned and victorious Princess Elizabeth late Queen of England (selected chapters, ed. McCaffrey, London, University of Chicago Press, 1970)

Clerk, W., An Epitome of Certaine late Aspersions cast at Civilians ... (Dublin, 1631)

Comyns, Sir J., A Digest of the Laws of England (London, 1762-7)

Corvinus, A., Arnoldi Ioh. F. Corvini Digesta per Aphorismos Strictim Explicata (Amsterdam, 1642)

Covarruvias, D., Didaci Covarruvias a Leyva Toletani ... Omnia Opera (Frankfurt am Main, 1592)

– In Constitutionis Secundae ex rubrica de Pactis, in id.

Decius, P., Philippus Decius De Regulis Iuris (Lyon, 1528)

D'Ewes, S., Journals of the Parliaments of Elizabeth I (1693; reprint, London, Scholarly Resources, undated)

Diversity de Courtz et lour Jurisdictions (London, 1526)

Duck, A., De Usu et Auctoritate Iuris Civilis (London, 1679)

Elyot, Sir T., The Book Named the Governor (ed. S.E. Lehmberg, London, Everyman's Library, 1962)

An Essay on the Nature of Oaths, and Judicial Evidence (London, 1715)

Fortescue, Sir J., De Natura Legibus Naturae in Works, ed. Lord Clermont

Fusco, P., Singularia in Iure Caesario et Pontifico (Frankfurt, 1600)

Groot, W., De Principiis Juris Naturalis Enchiridion (Cambridge, 1673)

Hacket, J., Scrinia Reserata (London, 1693)

Hake, E., Epieikeia (c. 1600) ed. D.E.C. Yale (New Haven, 1953)

Hale, Sir M., History of the Common Law, (ed. C.M. Gray, London, University of Chicago Press, 1971)

Hughes, W., The Grand Abridgement of the Law continued (London, 1660- 1663)

John, of Salisbury, Ioannis Saresberiensis Policraticus sive de nugis curialum, & vestigiis Philosophorum libri octo (Lugduni Batavorum, 1595)

Lake, E., Memoranda Touching the Oath Ex Officio (London, 1662)

– Notes Touching Alteration of Some Laws (London, 1662; appended to the above)

Lambarde, W., Archeion (1591; ed. C.H. McIlwain & P.L. Ward, Cambridge, Mass., Ames Foundation / Harvard UP, 1957)

Leges Visigothorum ed. Zeumer, MGH Leges (fol) vol. v

Lipenius, M., Bibliotheca Realis Juridica (Leipzig, 1757)

Locke, J., An Essay Concerning Human Understanding (ed P.H. Nidditch, Oxford, Clarendon paperback, 1979)

– ib Version A (ed Aaron & Gibb, Oxford, OUP, 1936)

– ib Version B (ed Nidditch, Sheffield University, 1982)

Ludolph, of Saxony, Expositio ad Psalterium (Venice, 1521)

– Vita Iesu Christi (Lyon, 1517)

– ib. ed. L.M. Rigollot (Paris, 1878)

Maddock, H., A Treatise on the Principles and Practics of the High Court of Chancery (London, 1815)

Marlowe, C., The Jew of Malta (ed N.W. Bawcutt, Manchester, MUP, 1978)

More, Sir Thomas, The Complete Works of Saint Thomas More vols ix (ed. J.B. Trapp, New Haven, 1979) and x (ed. J.A. Guy & al., New Haven, 1987)

Nelson, W. [attr] The Law of Evidence (London, 1717)

– An Abridgement of the Common Law (London, 1725-6)

North, R., Examen (London, 1740)

Oughton, T., Ordo Judiciorum (London, 1738)

Peake, T., A Compendium of the Law of Evidence (London, 1801; reprint, NY, Garland, 1979)

The Practice of the High Court of Chancery Unfolded (London, 1651)

Proceedings in Parliament 1626 Vol I: Lords Proceedings (ed Keeler, Cole &Bidwell, New Haven, Yale UP, 1991)

St German, C., Salem & Bizance, in More, Complete Works x

Shepherd, W., An Epitome of all the Common and Statute Laws of this Nation (London, 1656)

– The Faithfull Counsellor (London, 1651)

– A Grand Abridgement of the Common and Statute Law of England (London, 1675)

Singularia Doctorum in Utroque Iure (Frankfurt, 1596)

Smith, Sir T., De Republica Anglorum (ed. M. Dewar, Cambridge, CUP, 1982)

Somers, John Lord, (attr) The Security of Englishmen's Lives, or the Trust, Power and Duty of the Grand Juries of England (1682)

Syntagma Communium Opinionum (Lyon, 1608)

Tractatuum ex Variis Iuris Interpretibus Collectorum (Lyon, 1549)

Vinnius, A., Justiniani Institutionum (Amsterdam, 1669)

– In quattuor libros Institutionum imperialium commentarius (Amsterdam, 1692)

West, W., Symboleographia (London, 1590)

Wood, A., Athenae Oxonienses (ed Bliss, Oxford, 1848)

2. Secondary works

Arnold, M. S., Introduction to Selden Soc Vol 100

Avery, M. E., "The History of the Equitable Jurisdiction of Chancery before 1460" 42 BIHR 129

Baker, J. H., "The Common Lawyers and the Chancery" (1969) 4 Irish Jurist 368

– "Criminal Justice at Newgate 1616-27" (1973) 8 Irish Jurist 368

– "English Law and the Renaissance" [1985] CLJ 46

– English Legal Manuscripts in the USA (London, Selden Society, 1990)

– Introduction to id. ed., The Reports of Sir John Spelman, Selden Soc Vol 94

– ed., Judicial Records, Law Reports, and the Growth of Case-Law (Berlin, Dunker & Humblot, 1989)

Baker, R. W., The Hearsay Rule (London, Pitman, 1950)

Barnes, T. G., "Mr Hudson's Star Chamber" in Guth & McKenna (eds) Tudor Rule and Revolution (Cambridge, CUP, 1982)

Bartlett, R., Trial by Fire and Water (Oxford, Clarendon, 1986)

Baxter, S. B., William III (London, Longman, 1966)

Beattie, J. M., Crime and the Courts 1660-1800 (Oxford, Clarendon, 1986)

Bell, H. E., An Introduction to the History and records of the Court of Wards and Liveries (Cambridge, CUP, 1553)

Bellamy, J. G., Criminal Law and Society in Late Medieval and Tudor England (Gloucester, 1984)

Besnier, R., "La Dégénérescence des caractères Normands des preuves dans la procédure civile après la Rédaction du Grand Coutumier" (1959) 37 Rev. hist. de droit francais et étranger 48-61

Birks, P., ed., The Life of the Law (London, Hambledon, 1993)

Bosch, J. W., "La preuve dans l'ancien droit néerlandais" in Receuils de la Société Jean Bodin Vol XVII (1965) 453

Brooks, C. W., and Sharpe, K. "History, English Law and the Renaissance" 72 Past & Present 137

Brooks, C. W., Helmholz, R. H. and Stein, P.G Notaries Public in England since the Reformation (Norwich, Erskine, 1991)

Bryan, I., Interrogation and Confession: A Study of Progress, Process and Practice (Aldershot, Ashgatz / Dartmouth, 1997)

Burgess, G., The Politics of the Ancient Constitution (London, 1992)

– Absolute Monarchy in Early Stuart England (New Haven, 1996)

Campbell, John Lord, Lives of the Lord Chancellors and Keepers of the Great Seal of England, from the earliest times till the reign of King George the Fourth (4th edition, London, Murray, 1856-7)

Carter, P. B., Cases and Statutes on Evidence (2nd ed., London, 1990)

Chaytor, M., "Household and Kinship: Ryton in the late sixteenth and early seventeenth centuries" 10 History Workshop 25

Cheney, C. R., Notaries Public in England in the Thirteenth and Fourteenth Centuries (Oxford, Clarendon, 1972)

Chesnin, H. / C. G. *Hazard,* Jr., "Chancery Procedure and the Seventh Amendment: Jury Trial of Issues in Equity Cases Before 1791" (1974) 83 YLJ 998

Childs, J., The British Army of William III 1689-1702 (Manchester, Manchester UP, 1987)

Clanchy, M. T., From Memory to Written Record (London, Edward Arnold, 1979)

Clark, J. C. D., The Language of Liberty (Cambridge, 1994)

Cobbett, W. / J. *Wright,* The Parliamentary History of England from the earliest period to the year 1803 (London, 1805-1813, 15vv)

Cockburn, J. S. (ed), Crime in England 1550-1800 (London, Methuen, 1977)

– Introduction to Calendars of Assize Proceedings (London, HMSO, 1985)

Cockburn, J. S. / T. A. *Green,* ed., Twelve Good Men and True (Princeton, 1988)

Coing, H., "English Equity and the Denunciatio Evangelica of the Canon Law" (1955) 71 LQR 223-241

Collinson, P., The Birthpangs of Protestant England (Basingstoke, Macmillan, 1988)

Cowley, J. D., A Bibliography of Abridgements (London, 1932)

Cromartie, A., Sir Matthew Hale 1609-1676 (Cambridge, 1995)

Dahm, G., "On the Reception of Roman and Italian Law in Germany" in G Strauss ed, Pre-Reformation Germany (London, Macmillan, 1972)

Damaska, M., "Hearsay in Cinquecento Italy" in Studi in onore di Vittorio Denti (Padua, 1994) 59-89

Dizionario Biographico Degli Italiani vols ii (Rome, 1960), xxx (Rome, 1984)

Doe, N., Fundamental Authority in Late Medieval English Law (Cambridge, 1990)

Donahue, C., "Proof by Witnesses in the Church Courts of Medieval England: An Imperfect Reception of the Learned Law" in Arnold et al ed, On the Laws and Customs of England, Essays in Honor of S. E. Thorne (Chapel Hill, University of North Carolina Press, 1981)

Elton, G. R., F. W. Maitland (London, 1985)

Foss, E., The Judges of England (London, 1857)

Gilissen, J., "La Preuve en Europe du XVIè au debut du XIXè Siecle" in Receuils de la Société Jean Bodin Vol XVII (1965) 757

Gray, C. M., "The Boundaries of the Equitable Function" 20 AJLH 192

Guy, J. A., The Cardinal's Court (Hassocks, Harvester, 1977)

– The Court of Star Chamber and its Records to the Reign of Elizabeth I (London, HMSO, 1985)

– "The Development of Equitable Jurisdictions, 1450-1550" in in EW Ives and AH Manchester (ed) Law, Litigants and the Legal Profession (London, RHS, 1983)

– The Public Career of Sir Thomas More (Brighton, Harvester, 1980)

Haley, K. H. D., The First Earl of Shaftesbury (Oxford, Clarendon, 1968)

Hamburger, P., "The Conveyancing Purposes of the statute of Frauds" (1983) 27 AJLH 354

Harris, J. W., Law and Legal Science (Oxford, Clarendon, 1979)

Hayes, J., Le Statute of Frauds en droit Anglais (Thèse, Paris 1929)

Helmholz, R. H., Marriage Litigation in Mediaeval England (Cambridge, CUP, 1974)

– Introduction to id. ed., Select Cases of Defamation Selden Soc Vol 101

– Roman Canon Law in Reformation England (Cambridge, CUP, 1990)

Heward, E., The Masters in Ordinary (Chichester, Barry Rose, 1990)

Heydon, J. D. / C. M. G. *Ockelton,* Evidence Cases and Materials (3rd ed., London, 1991)

Hill, C., Society and Puritanism in Pre-Revolutionary England (London, Mercury, 1966)

– Some Intellectual Consequences of the English Revolution (London, Weidenfeld & Nicolson, 1980)

– "A Bourgeois Revolution?" in Collected Essays Vol III (Brighton, Harvester, 1986)

– "Political discourse in Early Stuart England" in A Nation of Change and Novelty (London, Routledge, 1990)

Hill, L. M., "The Two Witness Rule in English Treason Trials: Some Comments on the emergence of Procedural Law" (1968) 12 AJLH 95

Hirst, D., "Revisionism Revised: the place of principle" 92 Past & Present 79

Horwitz, H., Parliament, Policy and Politics (Manchester, MUP, 1979)

– Chancery Equity Records and Proceedings (London, HMSO, 1995)

Howard, M. N. / P. *Crane / D. A. Hochberg,* Phipson on Evidence (14th ed., London, 1990)

Hyams, P. R., "Trial by Ordeal: The Key to Proof in the Early Common Law" in Arnold et al ed, On the Laws and Customs of England, Essays in Honor of S.E. Thorne (Chapel Hill, University of North Carolina Press, 1981)

Ibbetson, D. J., "Sixteenth Century Contract Law: Slade's Case in context" (1984) 4 OJLS 295

– "Words and Deeds: the Action of Covenant in the Reign of Edward I" (1986) 4 Law & History Review 71

Jenkins, D., "Eighty Years On: In Defence of Maitland" (1981) 2 JLH 107-142

Kaye, J. M., "A Note on the Statute of Enrolments 1536" (1988) 104 LQR 617

Kelley, D. R., "History, English Law and the Renaissance" (1974) 65 Past & Present 24-51

– Rejoinder to Brooks and Sharpe, (1981) 72 Past & Present 143

– The Human Measure (Cambridge, Mass., 1990)

Kenyon, J. P., The Popish Plot (London, Penguin, 1974)

Kunkel, W., "The Reception of Roman Law in Germany: An Interpretation" in G Strauss ed, Pre-Reformation Germany (London, Macmillan, 1972)

Landsmann, S., "The Rise of the Contentious Spirit" 75 Cornell LR 497

Langbein, J. H., "The Criminal trial Before the Lawyers" (1978) 45 U Chic LR 263

– "Fact Finding in the English Court of Chancery: A Rebuttal" (1974) 83 YLJ 1620

– "Historical foundations of the Law of Evidence: a View from the Ryder Sources" (1996) 96 Col. LR 1167

– "The Historical Origins of the Privilege Against Self-Incrimination at Common Law" (1994) 42 Mich. LR 1047

– Prosecuting Crime in the Renaissance (Chicago, 1974)

– "Shaping the Eighteenth Century Criminal Trial" (1983) 50 U. Chic LR 1

– Torture and the Law of Proof (Chicago, 1977)

Leadam, I. S., Introduction to id. ed., Select Cases in the Court of Requests, Selden Soc. Vol 12

Lee, R. W., The Elements of Roman Law (London, Sweet & Maxwell, 1956)

Levack, B. P., The Civil Lawyers in England 1603-1640 (Oxford, Clarendon, 1973)

Levy, L. W., The Origins of the Fifth Amendment (New York, OUP, 1968)

Lockyer, R., The Early Stuarts (London, Longman, 1989)

Macfarlane, A. ,The Origins of English Individualism (Oxford, Blackwell, 1978)

– Marriage and Love in England, 1300-1840 (Oxford, Blackwell, 1986)

– The Culture of Capitalism (Oxford, Blackwell, 1987)

Macnair, M. R. T. "The Early development of the Privilege against self- incrimination" (1990) 10 OJLS 66

– "Equity and Volunteers" (1988) 8 Legal Studies 172

– "A Fragment on Proof by Francis North, Lord Guilford" (1993) 7 The Seventeenth Century 143

– "Sir Jeffrey Gilbert and his Treatises" (1994) 15 JLH 252

– "Juge et Jugement dans les juridictions anglaises d'equity au début des temps modernes" in R. Jacob ed., Le juge et le jugement dans les traditions juridiques européennes (Paris, 1996)

– "Common Law and statutory imitations of equitable relief under the later Stuarts", in C. W. Brooks and M. Lobban ed., Communities and Courts (London 1997)

Maitland, F. W., English Law and the Renaissance (Cambridge, 1901)

Metnick, J. M., "From Neighbour-Witness to Judge of Proofs: the transformation of the English Civil Juror" (1988) 32 AJLH 201

Metzger, F., "The Last Phase of the Medieval Chancery" in A. Harding (ed) Law Making and Law Makers in British History (London, RHS, 1980)

– Das Englische Kanzleigericht unter Kardinal Wolsey (Ph.D. dissertation, Erlangen, 1977)

Murphy, P., Murphy on Evidence (5th ed., London, 1995)

Nörr, K. W., Zur Stellung des Richters im Gelehrten Prozess der Frühzeit: Iudex secundum allegata non secundum conscientiam iudicat (Munich, 1967)

Oldham, J., The Mansfield Manuscripts (Chapel Hill, 1992)

Pawlisch, H., "Sir John Davies, the Ancient Constitution, and the Civil Law" (1980) 20 Hist. J. 689

Pennington, K., The Prince and the Law 1200-1600 (Berkeley, 1993)

Plucknett, T. F. T., A Concise history of the Common Law (5th ed., London, 1956)

Pocock, J. G. A., The Ancient Constitution and the Feudal Law (second edition, Cambridge, CUP, 1986)

Pollard, A. F., Wolsey (London, 1929)

Post, J. B., "Equitable Resorts before 1450" in EW Ives and AH Manchester (ed) Law, Litigants and the Legal Profession (London, RHS, 1983)

Prest, W., The Rise of the Barristers (Oxford, Clarendon, 1986)

Pronay, N., "The Chancellor, the Chancery, and the Council at the end of the Fifteenth Century" in H. Hearder & H.R. Loyn ed., British Government and Administration (London, 1974)

Rabel, E., "The Statute of Frauds and Comparative Legal History" (1947) 63 LQR 174

Razi, Z., "Family, Land and the Village Community in Later Medieval England" 93 Past & Present 3

Reid, R. R., The King's Council in the North (London, 1921)

Sainty, J. C., The Judges of England (London, 1993)

Shapiro, B., Probability and Certainty in Seventeenth Century England (Princeton, Princeton UP, 1983)

– Beyond Reasonable Doubt and Probable Cause (Berkeley, University of California Press, 1991)

Sharpe, K., Crime in Seventeenth Century England (Cambridge, CUP, 1983)

Silving, H., "The Oath: I" 68 YLJ 1329

Simpson, A. W. B., "The Rise of the Treatise" (1981) 48 U Chic LR 632

Staves, S. M., Players' Scepters: Fictions of Authority in the Restoration (London, University of Nebraska Press, 1979)

Stebbings, C., ed. Law Reporting in Britain (London, 1995)

Sutherland, D. W., The Assize of Novel Disseisin (Oxford, Clarendon, 1973)

Veall, D., The Popular Movement for Law Reform 1640-1660 (Oxford, Clarendon, 1970)

Watson, A., Legal Transplants (Edinburgh, Scottish Academic Press, 1974)

– The Making of the Civil Law (Cambridge, Harvard UP, 1981)

– Sources of Law, Legal Change, and Ambiguity (Edinburgh, Clark, 1984)

– The Evolution of Law (Oxford, Blackwell, 1985)

Wijffels, A., "Law Books at Cambridge 1500-1640" in P. Birks ed., The Life of the Law

Williams, P., The Council in the Marches under Elizabeth I (Cardiff, 1958)

Yamey, B. S. / H. C. *Edey*, / H. W. *Thompson*, Accounting in England and Scotland: 1543-1800 (London, Sweet & Maxwell, 1963)

Youdan, T. G., "Formalities for Trusts of Land, and the doctrine in Rochefoucauld v Boustead" [1984] CLJ 306

Zuckerman, A., "The Third Exception to the Woolmington Rule" 92 LQR 401

Table of Statutes

References in this Table and that of Cases, below, are (with one exception) to [Chapter No.].[footnote number]; different footnotes within Chapters are separated by commas, and different Chapters by semicolons. These references indicate either a citation in the footnote, or discussion in the text at that footnote.

Table of Cases

MIX
Papier aus verantwortungsvollen Quellen
Paper from responsible sources
FSC® C105338

Printed by Libri Plureos GmbH
in Hamburg, Germany